RADIO PRIEST

Charles Coughlin, the Father of Hate Radio

DONALD WARREN

THE FREE PRESS

NEW YORK   LONDON   TORONTO   SYDNEY   SINGAPORE

THE FREE PRESS
A Division of Simon & Schuster Inc.
1230 Avenue of the Americas
New York, N.Y. 10020

Designed by MM Design 2000, Inc.

Manufactured in the United States of America

printing number
10 9 8 7 6 5 4 3 2

Library of Congress Cataloging-in-Publication Data

Warren, Donald I.
    Radio priest: Charles Coughlin, the father of hate radio / Donald
Warren.
    p.   cm.
    Includes bibliographical references and index.
    ISBN 0-684-82403-5
    1. Coughlin, Charles E. (Charles Edward), 1891–1979.   2. Catholic
Church—United States—Clergy—Biography.   3. Right-wing extremists—
United States—Biography.   4. Radio in politics—United States.
5. Radio in religion—United States.   6. United States—Politics and
government—1919–1933.   7. United States—Politics and
government—1933–1945.   I. Title.
BX4705.C7795W35   1996
282′.092—dc20
[B]   96-15519
                                                        CIP

To My Wife, Kristine

Contents

Preface

I SAW AND HEARD Father Coughlin in person only once. He had already passed into obscurity at the time, following years of national notoriety. It was in 1958, at the New Year's mass at his famous Shrine of the Little Flower in Royal Oak, Michigan, where the priest had begun his career in media more than thirty years earlier. Garbed in a rich purple vestment, he moved his hands in sweeping gestures to augment the deep and forceful intonation of his words. His homily prophesied for the year to come: "Blood will run in the streets of Moscow before the new year is out!" This was, of course, vintage Charles Coughlin. His prediction was less than accurate, of course; nevertheless that voice, with its evocative timbre and Shakespearian resonance, was riveting. I was hearing that same galvanizing force that moved millions to follow him throughout a career that is now largely forgotten.

For me, growing up in Detroit, Coughlin was a fascinating figure of local lore: both loved and hated, he was clearly someone whose career cannot be reduced to a single dimension. It may well be argued that the conventional standards of biography should not be applied to media figures, for theirs is a life of fused private and public selves. In the case of Charles Coughlin, to know the real man behind the microphone is certainly beyond the ken of the author. Here lies the particular dilemma of this study: how to discern whether the subject is the mirror of his audience or its manipulator. And this remains the problem regardless of how one feels about his message. Moreover, the temptation to obliterate this duality—inner versus other-directed self—must be set aside. For as a media personality Charles Coughlin was both the creator and the captive of his enthusiastic public.

Introduction:
Vox Populi

IN THE WAKE OF the April 19, 1995, Oklahoma City bombing, the existence of a powerful hate movement—primed by paranoid fears of government control, fed and fostered by talk radio—was suddenly and frighteningly catapulted to national consciousness. Underground groups within a larger paramilitary network of organizations—the so-called Patriotic Militias—offered a dark and deeply troubling view of American life. Yet at least once before in our nation's history, an organized domestic terror group had been exposed in blazing headlines. Ironically, its roots are in the same state: Michigan. The story of the earlier events unfolded just two weeks after New Year's Day in 1940: "18 Seized in Plot to Overthrow U.S.," declared the *New York Times;* the *Detroit Free Press* front-page headline was, "Plot for U.S. Revolt and Assassinations of Congressmen."[1]

The eighteen men indicted on January 14, 1940, were members of the Brooklyn unit of a national paramilitary organization known as the Christian Front. Two years earlier, their inspirational leader, a Catholic priest, had told his followers to form "neighborhood platoons" to protect themselves against a powerful enemy force, composed largely of Jewish communists, that was threatening the nation's survival. The group's plan to embark on a campaign to bomb public buildings and to murder key government officials, however, never came to fruition.

This book relates the story of hate radio, and its inventor, Charles Edward Coughlin (pronounced "cawglin"). He was described as "silver tongued" and "golden voiced" and referred to as both the "mad monk of Royal Oak" and the "Radio Messiah." For over a decade and a half, from 1926 to 1942, this Catholic priest, certainly one of America's most persuasive mass media orators, held significant political power. In his ascendancy he commanded an army of the disaffected that numbered within its ranks elderly pensioners, farmers, rural and small-town merchants, and disillu-

1

sioned urban middle-class men and women of many religious denominations whose allegiance to the "Good Father" was most often expressed by mailing in one- or two-dollar contributions to his radio program, "The Golden Hour of the Shrine of the Little Flower," broadcast from Royal Oak, Michigan.

In the generation before *charisma* was a code word for leadership, Father Coughlin exuded it. His vibrant, magnetic personality riveted the attention of tens of millions across America and beyond. Glimpsed now only in blurred snatches of depression-era newsreel footage, Coughlin seems almost demonic. In angry tones of condemnation, he attacked Franklin Roosevelt for being "anti-God." His radio addresses were replete with phrases describing American society as controlled by powerful "banksters," "plutocrats," "atheistic Marxists," and "international [a code word for Jewish] financiers," all denounced in the body language of his clenched fist or menacingly pointed finger. His image was that of the right-wing extremist, a denizen of the lunatic fringe.

During the Great Depression of the 1930s radical-right conspiracy theories appealed to many average, middle-class citizens. These victims of economic catastrophe needed to blame someone—some group or malevolent cabal—for destroying their chance to achieve the American dream. Millions of bewildered and angry men and women turned to this radio priest for solace and solutions. In his weekly newspaper, *Social Justice,* and in his radio broadcasts, the priest became the voice of the people against a political elite and against alien minorities whom they thought were intent on betraying the nation. The thousands of letters that poured into his Shrine of the Little Flower each week offered proof that the radio priest was an authentic voice of the American majority.

Coughlin invented a new kind of preaching, one that depended on modern technology: the microphone and transmitter. He ushered in a revolution in American mass media by his dramatic ability to blend religion, politics, and entertainment in a powerful brew whose impact is still being felt decades after his demise as a public figure. Two significant media phenomena, televangelism and political talk radio, stem back to him. In both his broadcasts and his incendiary tabloid newspaper, Coughlin sustained a national presence and created a citadel to his world fame. He frequently delivered his broadcasts from a specially equipped office in his church, with its startlingly modern 150-foot "Crucifixion Tower" and its unique, octagon-shaped shrine, built during America's worst depression.

From this stage he sent thunderbolts of dramatic oratory across America and onto the world stage.

In 1939, sociologists Alfred and Elizabeth Lee edited a detailed critique of Coughlin's major radio addresses, *The Fine Art of Propaganda.* Treated as a primer on "the chief devices used . . . in popular argument and by professional propagandists," the authors gave the radio priest credit not for inventing them so much as perfecting their application.[2] He had sold his political, economic, and even religious ideas by means of modern merchandising techniques that rely on psychological identification and subliminal advertising approaches that are now basic to American consumer culture. His weekly newspaper, *Social Justice,* had as its most popular feature prize contests and quizzes, the latter usually based on key themes he developed in his radio broadcasts. Thus, Charles Coughlin understood the concept of and devised the means to create "infotainment."

Father Coughlin also became the first of America's media-created personalities to move from talk to direct political organization by creating a grassroots lobbying force composed of millions of loyal listeners, the National Union for Social Justice (NUSJ), and then converting it into a third political party. He thereby established a precedent for future religious figures who would build political movements based on media audiences: the Moral Majority, under the direction of Reverend Jerry Falwell, and the 700 Club, whose creator, Reverend Pat Robertson, launched a presidential bid.

In the 1930s, Coughlin rose to a position of prominence shared by no other religious figure before him and few since. Among those who claimed him as their confidant—but later disavowed his support—were leading public figures such as Franklin Roosevelt and Joe Kennedy. Still others paid homage to him even after he was shunted to the fringe of American society, among them Clare Booth Luce, Douglas MacArthur, Bing Crosby, and Eddie Rickenbacker. He drew to his political and messianic cause talented and dedicated individuals such as the world-renowned architect Philip Johnson and literary lights such as Ezra Pound, Hilaire Belloc, and Hugh Walpole. His desire to step onto the world stage even brought him to the attention of Benito Mussolini, Adolf Hitler, and Joseph Goebbels. He traveled in elite circles funded by members of the Fisher family of General Motors, Henry Ford, and wealthy Wall Street speculators.

That ethnic, religious, or racial dissension and conflict might be bred by users of the electronic pulpit and election platform was first noted by the distinguished journalist and author Walter Lippmann in his classic study, *Public Opinion,* published in 1922. Lippmann argued that modern mass communication created "pseudo environments" that thwarted the ability of the average citizen to make political judgments based on facts. His solution was to rely on trained experts to help the public understand the world around them. In 1927, philosopher John Dewey's influential volume *The Public and Its Problems* saw emerging electronic media as serving to divide and atomize society, with a mass audience eventually replacing any common purpose or genuine sense of community. The disparate but cogent insights of both Lippmann and Dewey regarding the social impact of electronic mass communication serve as the critical base for explaining the power of Charles Coughlin and all those who have become his broadcast heirs: angry media personalities who practice an electronic demagoguery by projecting qualities of populist sincerity and trustworthiness while providing a forum for violence-provoking political expressions.

By the 1960s, America's airways began crackling with the aggressive, and sometimes offensively acerbic, tones of radio talk show hosts whose rapid-fire style has become a standard component of radio broadcasting, first for local stations and eventually for the national networks.

The growth of political talk radio depended at first on the novelty of the broadcasting. By the 1980s, this format emerged as an electronic form of gladiatorial combat in which competition and rating wars drove individual personalities and station managers to ever more daring methods for stimulating audience interest. Low in cost and technically simple to direct, talk radio and television offers a forum for the alienated members of society and, in fact, seems to treat the provocation of and parading of the lunatic fringe as a conventional element of programming.

There is little doubt that expressions of ethnic and racial bigotry fuel the marketing value of political talk shows. The theatrical value of hosts who air such views is high for local stations. The entertainment value of bigotry became institutionalized by the late 1980s, with the result that hatemongers no longer need to press to have their case presented but are now being sought out to stimulate program ratings. Increasingly, talk radio hosts of prominence in major market areas compete as purveyors of ethnic slurs. For example, in New York, a caller over station WABC once asked whether it was possible "that the lower intelligence of blacks, as documented by William Shockley, is responsible for the complete lack of morality in the blacks, especially toward children."[3]

The disturbing event that brought public attention to the danger of talk media as a means of arousing vigilante violence was the 1984 murder of Denver talk show host Alan Berg by a coterie of individuals who were members of an organization, The Order, with direct ties to the large neo-Nazi Aryan Nations organization. Berg was liberal and Jewish. His often taunting and abusive exchanges with callers were hallmarks of his nightly program.

In his widely discussed 1986 Broadway play and subsequent 1988 film, *Talk Radio,* Eric Bogosian illuminated the drama and intense dynamic engendered by a character based on the murdered Berg. Interviewed about his play, Bogosian explained, "If the callers don't provide the drama, the host will. He is a skilled professional, sculpting each show from the raw material available. He adroitly cuts off callers as it suits him, while egging on others, knowing just what the audience wants. He is an actor as well, playing the part of a sincere, concerned, and sometimes angered observer."[4]

By the end of the 1980s, talk radio was undergoing an evolution that paralleled the developments in Charles Coughlin's career more than a half-century earlier. Radio has offered a sounding board for political discontent and an outlet for individual psychological distress. According to political scientist Murray Levin, it is "a particularly sensitive barometer of alienation because hosts promote controversy and urge their constituents to reveal the petty and grand humiliations dealt [them] by the state, big business, and authority." This function of talk radio as a conduit for populist protest both mirrors and shapes a mood of middle-class political disaffection. Even more disturbing is Levin's suggestion that "lurking behind the fears of the callers [to talk radio] . . . are dark pathological areas that need only the prodding of a forceful individual to burst into destructive flame."[5]

In fact, the formula for talk radio was perfected seven decades ago. Within two years of going on the air from one Detroit station in 1926, Charles Coughlin's radio addresses were being carried on more than a dozen others, with his sermons using tough, almost profane language to address the enemies of the common people. In one broadcast in the early 1930s, Coughlin assailed both capitalism and communism as twin evils, asserting, "Modern statecraft, modern finance, and modern industry seem to have forgotten that a carcass of decayed meat cannot help but breed maggots!"[6] During his bid for political power in the 1936 presidential campaign, he described Franklin Roosevelt as a "liar," words that shocked his church but delighted his millions of followers.

From the start of his national fame, Charles Coughlin seemed driven by a need to use his extraordinary gift for radio oratory to change America. Friends and enemies alike saw in him a candidate for high political office, perhaps even the presidency itself (though as a naturalized citizen, this was impossible). He did not run for public office, and ultimately he failed to achieve the goals to which he had aspired in his adopted land. Yet there was a moment when he had the power to rattle both major political parties. As a lightning rod of controversy, the priest seemed to enjoy playing the defender of principle in a world of compromise. He saw himself entering the political arena not as a priest cum politician but as a martyr sacrificed on the altar of religious principle. While preaching moral absolutism in his role as religious tutor to millions of radio listeners, he seldom practiced it in his personal life. His bishop described him as "not balanced" and "out of control," and it was these basic character flaws that inexorably led to his undoing as a public figure.

To sum up Charles Coughlin as simply a charlatan and liar—or as one journalistic critic called him, "the P. T. Barnum" of radio—is to ignore how much the audience creates the media celebrity. It is not simply the issue of pleasing and maintaining the loyalty of listeners or viewers but of giving something of one's self. And the sense of special intimacy that the radio priest projected and understood—a lesson FDR came to grasp and apply as well—was that the new electronic medium could allow the distant speaker to share daily life with the unseen audience. Millions listened to the radio priest out of a comfortable habit rather than with a full ingestion of his often strident and vitriolic attacks against evil conspirators.

Charles Coughlin's emergence as a national media celebrity defined a critical turning point in American public life and popular culture. He was the first public figure to obliterate the distinction between politics, religion, and mass media entertainment. No longer could the skills of the theater be subordinated to the talents of the policymaker. Both increasingly would be merged in the merchandising of ideas through the electronically projected sound in the ear and image on the screen. The radio priest stood at the dawn of an age in which radio and later television could create media celebrities who could rival in their power those public figures who held elective office or claimed a political following.

Keeping in mind the lessons of the meteoric rise and ignoble fall of Charles Coughlin as a mass media icon, we now turn to a full examination of the life he led and the career he fashioned.

1

A Child of Circumstance

Once more I delve into the future, and with anxious heart I wait, to see what wonders still are there in store for me; I behold a parish church, with the pastor at the gate, and my heart grows glad when I recognize Charlie of [St. Michael's College].

1911 high school class prophecy for Charles Coughlin

The American people are peculiar people. They're guilty of adulation. They make heroes out of sinners and they make saints out of criminals sometimes. And any person who gains prominence, as a football player or as an actor or as a person in the public eye—they're idolized. . . . I wasn't a big person. See, most people who gain all this type of prominence I had are accidental. They're children of circumstance.

Charles E. Coughlin, interview

CHARLES EDWARD COUGHLIN, the only child of a staunchly religious Catholic family, was of Irish ancestry and Canadian by birth. The boy's great-grandfather Patrick had come to America in the 1820s to work among his fellow Irish immigrants in the construction of the Erie Canal. Charles's grandfather Daniel had apparently spent part of his life as a lumberman in Canadian forests, then later moved to Buffalo, New York, and eventually settled in Hamilton, Ontario.[1] Thomas Coughlin, Charles's father, was born in Ladoga, Indiana, in 1862, the eldest son in a family of fifteen. Beginning at age sixteen, he spent seven years stoking coal on Great Lakes steamers, a job that nearly killed him

8

when he contracted typhoid fever in 1885. There is more than a little confusion about Tom's occupational history after that. One early biography of his famous son indicates he did find work in Hamilton, at twelve dollars a week as foreman in a local bakery; a second version elevates his status to that of manager. Late in his life, Charles Coughlin recalled his father as having come to Canada as a steel salesman and later working as a railroad land agent.[2]

It was Tom Coughlin's role as sexton of St. Mary's Cathedral in Hamilton, Ontario, that provided the opportunity to court a woman ten years his junior and to marry her in November 1890. One year later, on October 25, 1891, Amelia gave birth to a seven-pound, blue-eyed boy.[3] While clearly working-class in their roots, Charles's parents raised him in a modest but comfortable middle-class setting. The house, a two-story brick home, was virtually in the backyard of St. Mary's Cathedral, so close that "sitting at table, the [Coughlin] family could hear the sound of the Cathedral organ."[4] In later years, Charles recalled the constant presence of nuns from nearby St. Mary's coming and going between his home and the church. With the tragic death of his younger sister, Agnes, at the age of eighteen months, Charles became the center of attention for a mother who had one clear ambition for her son: the priesthood.

In Charles Coughlin's childhood there was something more than mere doting overprotectiveness by his mother. It was obvious to many that Amelia Coughlin not only wanted her son to become a priest; she wanted to control the most mundane details of his life. At five years of age, Charles was sent off to St. Mary's school dressed in a white middy blouse and a pleated blue skirt, his brown hair in long ringlets. At the boys' entrance of the school, he was turned back by a priest who sent the child home to ask his mother whether he was a girl or a boy. That night the ringlets were cut off, and the next morning he went to school wearing pants.[5]

In both his boyhood neighborhood and at his boarding school in Toronto, Charles was known as an outgoing, rough-and-tumble lover of sports and mischief. One story relates an incident that occurred when he was ten years old. He and his friends encountered a particularly tall house, and one of the older boys suggested seeing if anyone could throw a stone over it. Everyone but young Coughlin had a try, and finally the group accused Charles of being "yellow" for not even attempting the feat. According to a boyhood friend, he then "calmly reached down, picked up a stone, flinging it clear over the roof, as he'd known he could do right from the start."[6]

When it came time for young Charles to enter high school, his parents, at the urging of priests at St. Mary's, enrolled him at St. Michael's prep school, attached to St. Michael's College of the University of Toronto. According to one biography, the trauma of being separated from her twelve-year-old son left his mother "heartbroken." Each week over the next four years, his parents made the forty-mile drive to bring Charles the cakes and pastries that his mother had baked for him. On one visit, Amelia Coughlin also brought her son a valise containing several velvet suits. The priest's cousin recalled that "Charles couldn't play with his classmates because of the way he was dressed. And so the priest down there wrote to her and told her to buy some boy's clothing for him."[7]

Charles entered the University of Toronto in 1907 and completed his studies in 1911. His transcripts from the university reveal a far from impressive overall academic record. Up to his final year in college, his performance was mediocre: one A, seven B's, and 17 C's. When he transferred within the university to St. Michael's College in his senior year, he did manage a straight-A record.[8]

Drama mixed with bluff would become a hallmark of Charles's public life. This fondness for gestures was evidenced by one incident that occurred during his college days. In a theology class one afternoon, he was assigned to deliver a twenty-minute talk without notes. Charles took pains to let everyone know beforehand that he had not taken time to prepare anything in writing. For nearly an hour and a half, he held forth on the assigned topic; "there were a great many quotations in his talk, but they were mostly from the Apocrypha which Coughlin knew the others weren't very familiar with. And although he ended with a text that contradicted the whole point of what he'd been saying, they were so caught up in the torrent of his rhetoric that only a couple of them realized it."[9] A classmate recalled the recitation: "He was letter perfect, and if he was not, I was in no condition to find fault, nor was anyone else. We sat hypnotized." With regard to the bluffing tactic, it was not clear whether the teacher took note, "but if he did . . . he certainly gave no sign. Like the rest of us, he appeared overcome by Charlie's oratory." The result "was a signal triumph for Mister Charles Coughlin. Word was spread around of 'Chuck's agile mind,' and how he 'put it over.' "[10]

In his senior year Charles had toyed with pursuing a career in the law or sociology, but after graduation, in 1911, he seemed to flounder, uncertain what to pursue.[11] The summer he graduated, he made a three-month tour of the Continent using funds provided by a generous uncle.[12] Upon his return home, Coughlin determined to begin studies for the priesthood and entered St. Basil's Seminary in Toronto. As a novice, Coughlin was required to spend a full year in prayer and meditation. One biographer reports that the seminary student was forced to interrupt his studies when Amelia Coughlin fell gravely ill. As the mother lay in a coma, "her son knelt in prayer at her bedside," and she made a "miraculous" recovery.[13]

Coughlin's career as a priest was shaped by Catholic teachings of the latter part of the nineteenth century that emphasized a new direction of clerical activism in an industrial society. The Basilian Order, founded in France early in the nineteenth century, however, emphasized the study of medieval church doctrine, which opposed modern economic developments and the role of money, banking, and, particularly, usury. In the Basilians' view, the church had turned away from its roots of strongly condemning the loaning of money with interest. According to the Basilians, that condemnation had unaccountably eased. Restoring this prohibition, Basilians hoped, would end the social ills of the contemporary world. Taken from the teachings of St. Thomas Aquinas, the papal encyclicals *Summa Theologica* and *Rerum Novarum* (On the Condition of the Working Class), promulgated by Pope Leo XIII, reflected this same critique of capitalism and nostalgic longing for the socially integrated (organic) community.[14]

On June 29, 1916, at the age of twenty-five, Charles Coughlin was ordained a Catholic priest.[15] He was promptly invited to join the teaching faculty of a boys' college located in Sandwich (now Windsor), Ontario, just across the river from the burgeoning industrial center of Detroit. The school, Assumption College, was administered by the Basilian fathers, who took the traditional vows of chastity and obedience but not that of poverty. Only two years later, under the 1918 code of Canon Law promulgated by Pope Benedict XV, the so-called sodalities (unattached religious communities of priests) were abolished. Priests could become either full members of religious orders or members of a particular congregation. Those who wished to remain members of the Basilian order were instructed to choose which of the two communities they would join: the order or the congregation. In effect, the newly ordained would have to add the third vow of poverty to remain in the community. The alternative was to resign from the order and become a diocesan priest. Charles Coughlin was one of five who left the order. He joined the diocese of Detroit. Ironically, the radio priest would build first a local and then a national following by claiming he was the champion of the poor.

As a diocesan priest, Coughlin taught on the faculty of Assumption College from 1916 to 1923. In these seven years he taught a variety of subjects, including history, Greek, English literature, and drama. He focused much of his creative energy on drama, specifically the staging of Shakespearean dramas, and it was here that he made his contacts and reputation across the river, in Detroit. Coughlin befriended the family whose generosity had provided Detroit with its new Bonistelle Theatre, and consequently a number of Assumption College student productions were presented there.

Coughlin's flair for theatrical excellence caught the attention of a church official of even higher rank than the dean of his college. For the annual school play in 1921, the talented priest decided to stage *Hamlet*. As a number of the players were boys from his community, Bishop Michael Francis Fallon, bishop of London, Ontario, had been invited to attend the event, which made a strong impression on Coughlin. Afterward, Bishop Fallon told his priests, "I think I'm going to have to readjust my estimate of Charlie Coughlin. I thought he was a bullshooter, a windjammer. I have seen that play several times on the legitimate stage, produced by professionals, and there were parts in it that Coughlin caught that I never saw handled right before!"[16] The bishop would not be the last to revise his estimate of Charles Coughlin.

Yet despite his successes and the acclaim they brought to his school, it was becoming clear to his peers and superiors that Charles Coughlin was not a team player. Coughlin had special talents and extraordinary energy but also a disregard for the rules and a strong push to make an iconoclastic mark. Fellow faculty told the dean that students were spending more time preparing for Coughlin's plays than on their other studies: "[Dean] Moylan very quietly would admonish him, 'These other teachers have a right to a fair shake on time. . . . You must remember you're not a Shakespearean company, you're at a small college!' "[17]

Coughlin commuted to Detroit often while teaching at Assumption and soon had gained a reputation as one of the most impressive religious orators in the Detroit area. In addition to his teaching duties at Assumption, Coughlin served as assistant pastor to two Detroit churches. He was as well a sought-after luncheon speaker at Rotary and Lions clubs, and he displayed a special talent at winning the interest, and eventually the financial support, of local businessmen, merchants, and professionals. His reputation rapidly extended beyond the Catholic community, to Protestants and Jews as well. Coughlin gained the allegiance and financial support of non-Catholics by projecting a zeal for his own church in a uniquely contemporary fashion. He would pepper his sermons with colloquial and even near-profane language, couched in a speaking style more akin to modern advertising, with simple and direct messages, than conventional. Coughlin sounded more like a superconfident salesman than a traditional preacher.

Eventually Coughlin left Assumption, to become a diocesan priest across the river in Detroit. And in the words of a brother Basilian, it was not a "happy finish."[18] His leave-taking was awkward, and it left more than a taste of bitterness in the mouths of his former associates. Coughlin's reputation for monopolizing his students' time had already alienated him from his fellow faculty members, and his personal exploitation of them compounded the ill will. In 1923, his last year at the college, he had used his own pupils to build a new house for himself. He did not pay them, pointing out that this work would give them construction skills. Even more galling to his colleagues than the financial benefit he derived from this arrangement was his subsequent neglect of the home, which he used infrequently, since he was on campus only to teach his classes. Finally, the growing fame he experienced in Detroit, visiting parishes for talks and leading retreats and novenas, engendered more than a small amount of jealousy among his colleagues at Assumption.

Yet there was more to the friction between Coughlin and his brother Basilians. A former colleague decades afterward bluntly described the problem: "Charlie was informing on his fellow priests." The Basilian told of an incident in which what appeared to be a casual conversation with a colleague led to Coughlin's asking: "Do you remember one time you came to me to say that the priest in the flat with you was showing some signs of being too friendly with the maid that did the rooms?" When the other priest realized what Coughlin was getting at, he said, "You must have dreamt it! I never in my life would dare say a thing like that." "What he was trying to do was to smear the other guy's name [and] this fella lied like a trooper." In another case, "Charlie was going around making charges of homosexuality against L. [who] was from a wealthy family and could have got the best lawyers. . . . Moylan [the rector] told him, 'You're doing just exactly what he wants you to do . . . the very fact that he raised the issue, names a man, he smeared Assumption College.'"[19]

In the spring of 1924, when Coughlin severed all ties with Assumption College, construction bonds were floated for a giant bridge to span the thriving commercial waterway that divides Canada from the United

States. Nine-thousand two-hundred feet in depth, it was and remains the longest international suspension bridge in the world. Officially opened for traffic on Armistice Day 1929, three weeks after the crushing stock market crash, the bridge served as a prophetic symbol of the path to public fame along which a Canadian priest would swiftly travel in his adopted land. Coughlin's destiny was to become, in the words of Ruth Mugglebee, "one of the small number of men of religion in the United States who are as universally known as the stars of public life."[20]

One of Charles Coughlin's first students at Assumption, in reaching for a metaphor to assess the personality and remarkable career of his former teacher, alluded to Ivanhoe, the knight who had lost his direction: "You have to allow for the wind. Genius is always that way. They create a wind. Coughlin was that way."[21]

Charles Coughlin recalled that he met Michael Gallagher, the aging bishop of the Detroit diocese, when they both were train passengers returning to Detroit from a small Michigan farming community, West Branch, where the priest frequently conducted services and ministered to that rural population. According to Coughlin, they became instant friends. It was clear that the older bishop took a strong and fatherly liking to the brash Canadian, not only because of his soaring oratory but also for his fund-raising abilities. Although Coughlin was never "private secretary to the Bishop," as he told one of his last biographers in 1973, he nevertheless did become a kind of favorite son to the older cleric.

For his part, the resourceful Bishop Gallagher had something in mind for the super-salesman drive of his young protégé. The bishop had traveled to Europe, and his visit had included a stop at the shrine newly dedicated to Saint Therese of Lisieux, the Little Flower, a blessed young nun whose devotion to Christ earned her canonization as the youngest Catholic saint in May 1925. Gallagher saw a divine purpose in naming a church in her honor in the burgeoning community of Royal Oak, a few miles north of Detroit. Served for a half century by only one Catholic church, Royal Oak, with its several hundred new families drawn to the area by the auto industry, seemed a perfect site.

Just after New Year's Day 1926, Bishop Gallagher authorized Father Coughlin to establish the Shrine of the Little Flower.[22] Public notice was served on April 12, 1926, in the local newspaper, the *Royal Oak Tribune,* which heralded the event as more ambitious than the mere constructing of a new church. Calling Coughlin "an honors graduate of Toronto University," the front-page story told not only of the establishment of a new parish but of the "founding of a national magazine, 'The Shower of Roses,' to deal particularly with the devotion to the Little Flower of Jesus and related subjects." Announcing that Coughlin would edit the new publication, the priest was quoted as saying that "it will make its appeal to men and women in all parts of the country who have shared in the devotion to Ste. Therese." He added, "The magazine plan has the approbation of Bishop Gallagher, and other bishops have shown interest in the project."

Funds were loaned to the priest for acquiring the land, and a brown-shingled wooden church building was completed in May 1926. There is some question as to the exact size of the diocesan loan with which Coughlin was encumbered; the figure varied from $79,000 to $100,000 in the priest's reminiscences.[23] As with all of Coughlin's career initiatives, this one was boldly sketched and theatrical to the core. With only a modest parish of approximately two dozen or so families, the priest built a church with a seating capacity of 600. The pews of the new church had once been theater seats.[24]

Coughlin recalled the celebration of his first mass at the Shrine of the Little Flower in June 1926:

> At that time the Grand Truck freight trains thundered not more than a hundred feet distant from the front of the church. . . . Surrounding the church was an acre of mud. . . . Much to my chagrin . . . I discovered that there were less than twenty-eight families who planned to attend the Shrine regularly. . . . It was rather dreary to stand facing the small congregation and what appeared to be an endless multitude of empty chairs.[25]

While celebrating his own boldness—"I believe I possessed that pioneering spirit which was crowned with the determination of youth"—he admitted to "a sprinkling of ignorant optimism" and also expressed personal anguish about the "middle-class families struggling to pay for their own homes and to educate their children" and "found it impossible to bear the financial burden which ruthlessly I had acquired [the diocesan loan]."[26] In a 1970 interview, Coughlin offered a more specific assessment: "I discovered I had only twenty-eight families, thirteen of which were mixed marriages. It wasn't too bad when the husband was Catholic, but when the wife was the Catholic, I couldn't expect much money."[27]

Although he had faith in his protégé's promotional talents, Bishop

Gallagher knew that repaying the diocesan loan would necessitate the use of all the fund-raising creativity Charles Coughlin could muster. One of Coughlin's ideas was to ask his friend Wish Egan, a scout for the Detroit Tigers, to invite ballplayers out to the Shrine. Egan not only obliged "but arranged for Babe Ruth and a number of other members of the New York Yankees to make an appearance." Years later, Coughlin recalled what this brainstorm had yielded: "As news spread, the streets outside the church were mobbed." Ruth was quoted by the priest as quipping, "Listen, Father, you say Mass and do the preaching and leave the collection to us."[28] Yet another innovative funding strategy Coughlin created was the establishment of the League (later, the Radio League) of the Little Flower, whose members contributed a "nominal sum each year as a fee for the purpose of making the story of the Little Flower better known among men."[29]

The animosities that had plagued Coughlin's ties to his Basilian brothers now resurfaced among fellow priests in the Detroit diocese. Coughlin's brash style, the perception of the favoritism afforded him by Bishop Gallagher, and his tendency to exploit others for his own ends all caused tension. In one instance, while called in to a rural Michigan parish that needed to raise funds by holding a fair, the priest was accused of skimming off a large share of the proceeds for his own diocese rather than for the local church.[30] And according to his former student and brother Basilian, Father James Dwyer, Coughlin earned a reputation as an informant:

> There was a priest with some sort of temptation toward boys. It's one of those things that turns up periodically. . . . Well, Charlie and another young priest . . . they observed that H was having these boys go to his room. Then the complaints came from the parents, and so [Coughlin] just gathered his information and went to Bishop Gallagher. Gallagher . . . announced a court trial. And H knew he was caught. And he never appeared at the trial, but by the fact that he was refusing to come to the trial, he was condemned for this in absentia.[31]

When the moment arrived for the formal dedication of the Shrine of the Little Flower, Charles Coughlin was treated to a virtual boycott of the event by his priestly peers:

When they went to have the dinner, there was only Gallagher, his
secretary, Charlie, and his assistants. . . . Now, that did not mean
they approved of Father H, but what they did not approve of was
the way he [Coughlin] did it. That he suddenly became a spy in
their midst . . . he had gone from a Community [the Basilians] to
there [Detroit]. . . . The point was that he was still sort of a guest
in their house.[32]

What drove Coughlin? What explains his incessant striving? Mere financial hardship hardly explains a career of messianic dimensions. His personality was both compulsive and flawed. Indeed, his self-explanation is
highly revealing. Coughlin invented a fable of his motivations that became the basis for an enduring myth recited in all biographies and writing, by critics and friends alike. It concerned opposition to bigotry and
especially the Ku Klux Klan. In a pamphlet he published in 1930, *Stations of the Cross,* Coughlin claimed to have encountered and opposed
anti-Catholic cross burnings early in his career:

Fiery crosses flashed their crimson light upon a peaceful starlit
night. . . . It occurred to me that surely no Christian would dare
to use the emblem of love and sacrifice and charity to express hatred. Surely, there must be some mistake! The whole ghastly affair—the red battalion of fiery crosses which blazed from the
Gulf of the Great Lakes and from Golden Gate to the Statue of
Liberty—must have been lighted not by the torch of faith but
rather by a brand snatched from the hell of ignorance. . . .
    Then, out of a clear sky was born the idea of the Radio
League of the Little Flower. . . . Let the radio pulpit . . . with its
charity and tolerance be the logical answer to the prejudice and
bigotry of those who had been misinformed![33]

A Hollywood version of the priest's life, pilot-filmed in 1933, depicted Coughlin's being roused from his bed and summoned to the newly
constructed Shrine of the Little Flower. Close beside the small wooden
structure stood a fiery cross while a narrator described "the angry flames
not twenty yards distant from its walls." In this melodramatic re-creation
of the alleged cross burning, Coughlin's portrayer shouts: "Bigots! Bigots! I'll construct a church that will stand as a monument in defiance of

hatred!"[34] In his 1982 analysis of the careers of Charles Coughlin and Huey Long, historian Alan Brinkley alludes to the tale of Coughlin's decision to answer the challenge posed by the Ku Klux Klan "when, only two weeks after the completion [of his church] the Klan planted its flaming cross on the front lawn, Coughlin rushed to the scene and helped beat out the fire."[35]

Over several decades, Charles Coughlin described other encounters with the Klan. In 1972, as part of an extensive interview, one of the few he provided after the 1930s, the priest recounted,

> Soon after we started building I learned that the Ku Klux Klan was about to get a court injunction [because of a deed flaw] to stop construction. Michigan had one of those odd laws to the effect that no injunction could be issued once the roof was on. It was the start of a three-day holiday, so I rounded up a good bunch of carpenters, and we worked around the clock, by torchlight at night, and when the court opened Tuesday morning the church was topped off.[36]

In another incident Coughlin told author Sheldon Marcus in 1970 of coming in contact with the Klan's presence in his community by joining a funeral procession passing by his shrine, and "he succeeded in winning them to his side."[37]

In fact, documentary evidence for Coughlin's early opposition to bigotry is lacking. Contemporary newspapers do not take note of any Klan activity with regard to the Shrine of the Little Flower. In his classic study of Klan membership and its Detroit area manifestations, historian Kenneth Jackson records Klan meetings near Royal Oak and offers a detailed review of its publications and a description of its activities in the mainstream press. Had such confrontations of the kind alluded to by Coughlin taken place, it is likely the Klan itself would have taken note of it.[38] Grant Howell, a veteran reporter for the *Royal Oak Tribune*, when asked about the Klan incident, expressed great skepticism. He pointed out that the community of Berkley, Michigan, adjacent to Royal Oak, was a Klan stronghold with little history of anti-Catholicism: "for nearly half a century there was already a Catholic church in the community of Royal Oak, St. Mary's."[39]

During the time of the construction and opening of Coughlin's church—the spring and summer of 1926—the *Royal Oak Tribune* recorded no activities by the KKK. The paper did note incidents of fires (including one at the Berkley fire station) as well as automobile accidents, which were becoming a serious problem on Woodward Avenue, the main street where Father Coughlin's Shrine was located. On October 8, 1926, the *Tribune* reported the application of the Klan for a parade permit. The next month it carried two front-page stories regarding the KKK. In one, the prosecuting attorney of Oakland County was investigating the organization's violation of a 1923 ordinance forbidding marching with masks. The second briefly noted that "nearly 150 members of the Ku Klux Klan in uniform and masks paraded through the village of Berkley early Saturday night," with a motorcycle police officer leading the parade.[40]

Bill Rasmussen, a retired Royal Oak police officer, told me in a telephone interview in 1994 that, as a collector of Father Coughlin memorabilia, he possessed the cross that allegedly had been burned on the lawn of the Shrine of the Little Flower in 1926. When I visited his home, he directed me to the location of this cross, and I found attached to it a 1968 receipt for the purchase of the object from the "Troy Historical Exhibit." It was signed by a woman who had told Rasmussen that her mother "took it home after it went out." Wrapped in straw and newspaper, the cross stood less than five feet high. It showed no signs of having been singed by fire.[41]

The episode of the burning cross underscores one of the most basic rules of the successful bigot: to claim the credentials of the antibigot. The public relations myth that grew up around the origin of Charles Coughlin's media career went unchallenged. It was not simply that the priest himself and his closest associates believed it but that those who witnessed his soaring career equated success with virtue. This suspension of disbelief would shield Coughlin from early attacks on his integrity and buy him a longer time as a credible exponent for the underdog, since it appeared that he himself had suffered their same fate.

2

Inventing the Political Soap Opera

When one thinks of the hundreds of miles travelled by Saint Paul along the coastal cities of Greece, when one visualizes historically the hundreds of converts which he drew to Christ . . . he cannot but know the potential good which can be accomplished by his successors who are making use of God's latest gift to man—the radio.

Detroit Free Press, January 17, 1927

COUGHLIN CULTIVATED THE IMAGE of a solitary fighter for justice in a complacent world, yet his career depended on a cadre of intimates: talented publicists and politicians, key financial backers and advisers, and fellow priests who offered their devoted services. All shared a fear of communism, and most enjoyed the common ethnic and religious bond of Irish Catholicism. Each was, like Coughlin, obsessed with the political and economic power of Jews. All came under the spell of Charles Coughlin and at the same time sought to use his charismatic gift for their own purposes.

A number of those who hitched their wagons to the volatile priest ultimately suffered public attack and even ignominy. Several had their professional lives destroyed by their association with Coughlin. As long as the priest was a force in American society, they labored on his behalf and gloried in being his intimate, even if they themselves frequently remained outside the public limelight, but many turned away from Charles Coughlin once he was relegated to the fringes of American politics.

Detroit in the 1920s was a boom town flourishing on automobiles and bootleg liquor smuggled across the Detroit River from Canada. Amid this excitement, the exuberant promotional skills of Charles Coughlin, while not applied to quite so tangible a product, nevertheless drew him into the inner circles of the brash entrepreneurs who were transforming America's landscape and lifestyle. As a pioneer in broadcasting, the priest offered a new product that was similarly altering the social milieu of his adopted country.

It was at the posh and exclusive Detroit Athletic Club that Coughlin was first introduced to those who became his intimate cadre, whom the priest labeled the "evil four": a flying ace, the owner of a radio station, and two brothers, Fred and Lawrence Fisher, who were among the leading auto magnates of the era. (In the 1920s, the emblem "Body by Fisher" on General Motors cars had become a mark of high-quality auto construction and a symbol of prestige.)[1] For Coughlin, the fact that the prestigious Fisher family became parishioners of the Shrine of the Little Flower was a source of more than just pride. Paul Weber, a longtime parish member and leading figure in the Catholic labor movement, remembers an annual donation by Fred Fisher of $10,000 as a personal Christmas gift to the Shrine's founder. In the earliest years of his career, recalls a GM engineer, Coughlin would receive the latest-model Fisher Body–designed Cadillac sedan, adorned with a handcrafted and uniquely designed silverplated hood ornament.[2]

The Fisher Brothers designed and built a magnificent marble-decorated edifice that was soon nicknamed "The Golden Tower," because of its gleaming copper roof. Located directly across from the massive neoclassical General Motors headquarters, the two impressive structures formed a virtual new downtown—"The New Center" of the auto capital of America. When the Fisher Building was completed, it became (and has remained) the tallest skyscraper in the Motor City. Radio station WJR, located on the Fisher Building's top floor, expressed the new era leadership the Fisher family offered in the growing auto industry.

A key investor in the new station, WJR, was World War I flying ace Eddie Rickenbacker. Shortly after his military career ended, he had tried his hand at automobile manufacturing and produced a car bearing his own name. His subsequent business career included a long tenure as president of Eastern Airlines. Throughout his lifetime, Rickenbacker held to a far-right political philosophy that included a deep fear of the New Deal and concern for the fate of the white race.[3]

But among the "evil four" it was George A. "Dick" Richards, owner of station WJR, who was the pivotal figure in launching Coughlin's media career and sustaining it by serving as the priest's chief financial backer and confidant for many years. According to various published accounts of how WJR first carried the priest's broadcasts, it was the Catholic station manager, Leo Fitzpatrick, who spoke to his boss about the idea. Although Richards was an Episcopalian, he decided, he told me, that he would like "to hear Coughlin preach a sermon." According to Coughlin, "He came over to the church two or three Sundays and he kept coming after that."[4]

Within four years of its founding in 1922, radio station WJR was on the brink of failure; it was owned by Jewett Radio, whose sales of phonograph and radio equipment had dipped sharply. Leo Fitzpatrick, its manager, steered it through this rocky passage largely with the advertising provided by one sponsor: George A. Richards's Buick dealership. By the early 1920s, this dealership was one of the most lucrative outlets for GM cars in the nation. Deeply impressed by the new selling tool for automobiles, the sponsor now became the station owner. "Dick" Richards took out an option to buy the failing radio outlet and turned it into one of the most envied and commercially successful radio stations in the nation.

Richards was a ruddy-faced entrepreneur with an imperious style of management. James A. Quello, who became station manager in the mid-1930s (and decades later became chairman of the Federal Communications Commission), described Richards as a "promotional genius." But for those who worked closely with him, he was a tyrannical and terrifying personality—"a cross between P. T. Barnum and Louis XIV." An anecdote that made the rounds of old hands at his Detroit station related to Richards's habit of making unannounced visits to his staff. On one occasion when he dropped in at the music studio of his station on the twenty-eighth floor of the Fisher Building, it happened that two of the rehearsing musicians had left their homburgs atop a piano. Richards, obsessive about tidiness, had come to show new advertising clients around. At the sight of the hats, "he pitched them out the window. And when the sales manager asked, 'What are you doing Mr. Richards?' he said, 'Those damn hats have no business on a baby grand!' "[5]

Coughlin and Richards were both impulsively mischievous, and both loved sports and horse racing. They were frequent visitors to the local racetracks, where, to avoid being noticed, the priest wore civilian clothes. When Coughlin appeared as a guest in the private box Richards held as owner of the Detroit Lions professional football team, he and the priest, according to the station owner's daughter, "were a bawdy and fun-loving pair." They both relished the shock value of spewing forth a stream of locker-room-style expletives. The close friendship between the Catholic priest and the Anglican business promoter was to last through more than two decades of Coughlin's controversial career. Richards himself later became embroiled in the most protracted and complex FCC case of licensing regulation in the agency's history; the station owner enforced a policy of slanting news to fit his far-right and anti-Semitic views.[6]

In the late 1920s, WJR was the keystone in the broadcasting arch of the fledgling CBS network. According to the longtime CBS executive Frank Stanton, the Detroit station "was as strong and effective in terms of physical performance as any station in the network" and was "the center-hold of our whole middle-western operation. . . . JR was a clear channel and you could sit [and hear it] almost any place in the midwest." This status gave Richards, as the most important advertising client, "one helluva hold on the attention and the affection of the people who ran CBS. . . . So when he came in the front door and said, 'I want something,' everybody saluted and said, 'Yes, Mr. Richards'. . . . He could release a thunderbolt from Detroit and it was felt on Madison Avenue."[7]

Coughlin's spending a parish loan on launching a series of religious broadcasts can be viewed as either foolish or a marvelous stroke of genius. Certainly the church needed funds badly, and radio broadcasts were a creative means to extend far beyond its two dozen parish families. And in short order, Coughlin's finances would take an exponential leap as a result of radio donations. Less than three years since Coughlin's withdrawal from the Basilian order, he had become the pastor of his own church. Now he stood on the brink of a new career, one for which there were no precedents and no rules of conduct.

At 2:00 P.M. Detroit time, October 17, 1926, less than four months after he began offering masses at the Shrine of the Little Flower, Charles Coughlin made his first broadcast. Wearing vestments and a black biretta on his head, he stood at the altar of his brown frame church structure built with a loan of $79,000 or more and costing $101,000. The microphone was suspended near his round, smiling face. He was one week shy of his thirty-fifth birthday.

Commercial broadcasting in the United States was only six years old when Coughlin's "Golden Hour" programs began in the fall of 1926. NBC, the first network, had been formed that very year. Charles Coughlin was not the first priest to use the radio; beginning in the early 1920s, the Paulist Fathers had been giving talks on religious subjects. Yet Coughlin was the first to be aired regularly. His earliest broadcasts were actually catechism classes directed at children; hence, the radio program was first known as "The Children's Hour." In January 1927, Coughlin took another pioneering step in religious broadcasting: he offered the first Catholic religious services over the radio. As with every other step in his career, it was marked with controversy: some thought it sacrilegious; others found it crass. When queried by the press, Coughlin himself expressed the view that his innovation was a link with the spiritual roots of his faith.[8]

The response to his program was impressive. An enormous amount of mail poured in from twenty-three states. Word of mouth soon increased the success of Coughlin's radio broadcasts, as he invited listeners to join his new "radio congregation," soon christened "The Radio League of the Little Flower."

Over the years, both friends and foes of Coughlin have credited him with being a master of mass psychology. Later, when he was reviled as a seditious traitor, Coughlin's techniques of broadcasting were used to exemplify the key elements of propaganda.[9] With the hindsight afforded by an age of sophisticated market research, we can readily grasp the causes of Father Coughlin's media impact. There was, for example, a unique design and content to the priest's radio talks—a formula that relied on the social psychology of identification. In Coughlin's words, the influence process was called "translation": "First I write in my own language, the language of a cleric," and then, "using metaphors the public can grasp, toning the phrases down to the language of the man in the street. . . . Radio . . . must not be high hat. It must be human, intensely human. It must be simple."[10] A prime example of the method was an event that riveted the nation's attention: the kidnapping of Charles Lindbergh's infant in 1932.

Kidnapper, remember when you were a little boy. For a moment remember your mother whose breast suckled you and whose arms encircled you. . . . But there is another mother, too, Anne Lindbergh!

Do you realize you have her first baby? Do you realize that you are holding away from her arms flesh of her flesh, blood of

her blood; that you are not injuring the baby half so much as you are crushing her heart as in a great press, making her bleed the wine of sorrow?[11]

The priest's official biographer and key adviser, Louis Ward (creator of "Ward's Automotive Reports"), a successful public relations practitioner in Detroit's auto industry, credited the radio priest with "knowing the mind of the American public" and being "conscious of its limitations and cognizant of his reactions. . . . His was the mastery of those hundreds of keys and stops which, when touched, played either melody of hope or a requiem of sorrow, upon that great organ, the human heart."[12]

Yet ultimately Coughlin's oratorical technique was less important than his remarkable voice. In 1935, writer Wallace Stegner called it "a voice of such mellow richness, such manly, heart-warming confidential intimacy, such emotional and ingratiating charm, that anyone tuning past it almost automatically returned to hear it again. . . . Warmed by the touch of Irish brogue, it lingered over words and enriched their emotional content. It was a voice made for promises."[13] Stegner elaborates on his description of Coughlin's voice:

A beautiful baritone . . . his range was spectacular. He always began in a low rich pitch, speaking slowly, gradually increasing in tempo and vehemence, then soaring into high and passionate tones. . . . His diction was musical, the effect authoritative. . . .

His Irish ancestry betrayed itself in the way he trilled his r's, making the word "church" sound like "charrch." He held his e's unduly long—as in "unpreeecedented." Sometimes he mispronounced words. . . . He made "the Treaty of Versailles" sound like "the Treaty of Ver-sales."[14]

But there was far more than an intriguing voice capable of moving an audience to deep emotional response. Behind the dimensions of the voice lay a person who soon became known to his listeners through magazine articles and newspaper profiles. In one instance, *Boston Globe* reporter Ruth Mugglebee began with an interview on the women's emancipation movement and found herself writing a full-length, effusive biography of the radio priest. Mugglebee traveled to Royal Oak early in 1933 in order to spend weeks in the company of the famous priest. "What listeners could only imagine in their minds' eye," she wrote, "was confirmed by the presence of the man himself." As enthralled as many in Coughlin's radio audience, Mugglebee described the priest as the country's "most daring apostle of truth," a man "of broad shoulders and broad mentality . . . a man of scholarly intellect and death-defying conviction . . . a man of deep humility, of captivating charm, of winning sincerity, of seething, burning, boiling emotions for the right, of bitter snarling contempt for the wrong." The "momentum of a country's applause pushed him onward. . . . He asked for no glory," she wrote, "though he was helpless to refuse recognition."[15]

What occurred was a special reciprocity between speaker and listener. To an uncanny degree, Charles Coughlin constructed a personal bond between himself and each listener. The result was the transcendence of physical, social, and denominational distance: Coughlin had built an electronic neighborhood. Reflecting on Coughlin's broadcasts from the perspective of half a century, network radio pioneer Frank Stanton assessed the priest as the "greatest voice of the twentieth century," adding, "Coughlin was ahead of the industry and had a better grasp of what the medium could do in the area of ideas than the industry did. The industry . . . looked upon radio as an advertising medium and didn't make the connection between the use of the medium for selling merchandise and the use of the medium for moving ideas." Stanton recalled that his family "listened avidly and contributed more to the Golden Hour than to their local church." He described the remarkably ecumenical appeal of the Coughlin broadcasts:

We were in a neighborhood that was . . . probably anti-Catholic. Very white, Anglo-Saxon Protestant. But no one that I knew at that period in Dayton . . . [brought] up the Church issue at all with Coughlin. . . . He seemed to reach out and break that barrier down. Radio broke it down. I think if people had seen him in his habit . . . it might have turned some people off.

I knew a family quite well and their three children. The father . . . he swore by Coughlin. What Coughlin said was "it." This was a family with limited reading exposure. Local papers and maybe the *Literary Digest*. They were religious, Methodists. . . . But what Coughlin said, by God, the old man of the house, he swore by it.[16]

Membership in the Radio League of the Little Flower in 1930, at a contribution of one dollar per person per broadcast, assured the enrollee of "remembrance in the daily Mass offered at Calvary Hill Jerusalem." Deceased persons could also be enrolled (and would receive membership cards at the address of their living relatives) for one dollar. A longtime member of the shrine congregation recalled that "the dollars flooded in and were carried in gunnysacks over to the bank."[17] In one day in the early 1930s, Coughlin himself made a deposit to a local bank of over $21,000 in one- and five-dollar bills.[18]

In 1930, two out of five American families had a radio, and in the urban Northeast and the Midwest, where Charles Coughlin's voice was heard weekly, more than half had a receiver. The priest had discovered a key principle of mass media influence: linking his individual audience by means of personal networks of friends and neighbors who relayed what was said in a broadcast, thus widening and intensifying the scope of its impact. When Coughlin's listeners gathered in small groups around the radio set, they were preparing the way for being more than a passive and atomized mass. They were forming a cohesive electronic community.

The fame the radio priest enjoyed evolved more rapidly than that of any political figure and matched most closely the adoration afforded the stars of the silver screen. Coughlin excited and involved his followers, shattering the indifference bred by a society that was growing large and bureaucratic. He personalized politics and abstract ideas in a way that reestablished a connection with, even a sense of control by, grassroots America, both urban and rural, over the machinations of big business and big government.

Like Walter Winchell a decade later, Coughlin broke down the barriers between political opinion molding and celebrity. By fusing his talent and training in the thespian arts with an entirely new medium of communication, Coughlin transformed radio broadcasting, and thereby public discourse, in American society. From his time on, no one could ignore the fact that this new medium required a technique that projected a sincerity, warmth, and power based solely on the human voice. One of Coughlin's former associates summed up what the radio priest achieved: "He had the power to use radio in a way that it had never been used before, which was to really sell a political viewpoint. Before he ever got into the political sphere he had the children's hour . . . this is the stuff I remember as a kid. . . . And that's how he built his audience. He just car-

ried those people along . . . and gradually swung them over to his . . . political viewpoint."[19]

In later decades, radio would give rise to evangelical preachers, and
television would expand their base. Coughlin is their founding father.
The phenomenon, too, of talk radio—with its politically oriented hosts—
must also trace its existence to the radio priest. Coughlin did not have an
individual call-in line, but he lacked little else that they would have.

In Coughlin's broadcasts, politics and religion began to meld. Slowly
at first, then dramatically, he focused on current political issues. Virtually
everyone who has ever written about the radio priest alludes to this shift.
Louis Ward described the political focus as a rather self-conscious and
automatic progression: "His ultimate end . . . the salvation of human
souls. But it is clear his proximate object was . . . the renaissance of dis-
tributive justice. . . . That a counter-revolution must be organized was
plain and evident to this historic-minded Priest of the radio."[20]

Ruth Mugglebee described Coughlin's target thus: "Insidious forces
were in a malignant stage. Their cancerous seizure was just poisonously
beginning to permeate a nation's body."[21] But this is too general a statement of Coughlin's enemy. In his earliest radio broadcasts, the priest had
spoken on such controversial subjects as birth control and prohibition.
These were just the opening salvo in a war against modernism and radicalism. Coughlin's restless energy called for using iconoclastic means to
defend tradition. What was to be the immediate target of the assault?

Early in 1928, Coughlin delivered a series of sermons that directly
and personally attacked Norman Thomas, Socialist party candidate for
president. In a poetically phrased yet biting fashion, Coughlin launched
his radio war: "This sentimentalist can daub the canvas of romance with
the tears of his lamentations, but it is a truism that in our scheme of things
we cannot get along without capitalists. Only the soft-brained radical . . .
attempts to have the laboring man declare a war of sabotage against the
millionaire."[22]

Thomas wasted no time in striking back. In these early years of radio,
there was no equal time doctrine that could be invoked, so the socialist
leader wrote to the Michigan senator, James Couzens, who sat on the
Federal Radio Commission, accusing Coughlin of "serious misrepresentation of the nature of socialism and the Socialist Party and hopeless confusion of it with Communism."[23] In response, WJR announced some
restrictions on future broadcasts by the radio priest, specifically requiring
him to avoid any direct mention of the Socialist party "that would give

rise to controversy." Mugglebee recognized the broader importance of what had occurred: "It was the first time that Father Coughlin's veracity and accuracy of facts and statements made over the air had been challenged." But the incident was also significant for revealing how readily Coughlin could be placed in the role of victimized and martyred voice of truth.[24]

Time and again over the next decade the radio priest would give his audience suspense and excitement, using the behind-the-scenes exposé format of the gossip columnist. He had brought scoop journalism to the radio, a technique employed later by Winchell. With a mixture of biting political attack, soothing organ music, and spiritual discourse, Coughlin "tried each season to give his audience something new, something that would 'hold' them, yet enlighten them."[25] Anticipation, week after week, was the secret of his success.

One of President Herbert Hoover's first official acts in the spring of 1929 was to ask leading social scientists to examine the state of the economy. The economists proclaimed it to be sound and wrote in their 950-page report, "Acceleration rather than structural change is the key to an understanding of our recent economic trends . . . prudence on the part of management . . . skill on the part of bankers . . . our momentum is remarkable." Written in April 1929, the report was not published until after the October crash.[26]

According to the widely read columnist and political analyst Walter Lippmann, the 1929 stock market debacle was the beginning of an epoch of social disintegration: "A demoralized people is one in which the individual has become isolated. He trusts nobody and nothing, not even himself. He believes nothing, except the worst of everybody and everything. He sees only confusion in himself and conspiracies in other men."[27]

Such was the social climate in which Charles Coughlin emerged as a grassroots leader: spokesman for those who had grown distrustful of the establishment's explanations of the overwhelming economic disaster. Even those unaccustomed to relying on the authoritative words of a priest—Protestants and Jews—found themselves turning to Father Coughlin. He was creating an ecumenism of discontent. In their search for a restored confidence in the American dream, Americans of all religions were responding to a person who seemed to embody its essence. Coughlin was showing that America was still a place where a lone entrepreneur could make it, and if the priest was expressing anger over the current economic debacle, he was speaking on behalf of all Americans who had suffered its severe consequences.

Yet despite his enormous success, Coughlin had not overcome a sense of frustration and a lack of clear focus to his fame. As his closet associates sensed, and his early biographers documented, he needed to find a cause célèbre to galvanize the public and fulfill the great and divine purpose to which he aspired. He identified it shortly after New Year's Day 1930: he would become the champion of Christ against communism, the "red serpent." It began with a seemingly innocuous news story regarding Soviet Russia. On January 12, 1930, the radio priest delivered a Sunday sermon, "Christ or the Red Serpent," recounting "the news from Russia" that "by government decree the mistletoe and holly of Christmas have been abolished." He warned that the United States was being corrupted from within by this same "purple poison of Bolshevism," which was undermining, even destroying, family life:

> There are in America this afternoon approximately 2,000,000 men and women, who, during the last ten years, have scorned the basic family and national doctrine of Jesus Christ. These have sought divorces with the right to remarry despite the sanctity of the contract by which they joined hands and hearts for better or for worse. There are the two million whose happy dreams of youthful romance have been dissipated. . . .
>
> Because of their own poor judgment and their lack of foresight they have joined the rabble in this modern Pilate's Hall as they shout: "Give us Barabbas—Crucify Christ." Give us the political economy of Lust, of Russia, of Bolshevism, of Christlessness.[28]

The structure of the address was a prototype of what was to be a decade of radio lectures providing a dramatic link between world political events and their immediate impact on individual lives. Its ingredients included a dazzling array of statistics and startling revelations, overwhelming by their sheer force. The address drew a powerful response from listeners, and the priest received a large volume of positive mail.[29]

One week later, on January 19, 1930, Coughlin again focused on the red menace: "America is seriously tainted with the purple poison of Bolshevism. Between it and the Catholic church there is war unto death. . . . International socialism not only strives to break down the permanency of the American family; it aims at the Nation itself." In this address he employed another favorite technique of his: repeating a previous address followed by a discussion of reactions by his listeners. Quoting a letter from a person identified with the initials O.W.C., Coughlin alluded to that letter's "Communistic-minded" contents, which had criticized the priest's talk as "theological rather than scientific." Coughlin mockingly noted, "I am glad that I received your letter and the hundreds of others in protest from Communists and free lovers," and he proclaimed in his climax: "Christian parents—American parents . . . Choose today! It is either Christ or the Red Fog of Communism. It is either the marriage feast of Cana or the brothel of Lenin!" This second address was greeted with even more mail than the first, including a large number of letters from "priests, from Catholic laymen, from patriotic Americans, and from industrialists and financiers condemning him for fighting imaginary windmills."[30]

Another key element was added to the next week's broadcast, on January 26, foreshadowing Senator Joseph McCarthy by two decades—the naming of names:

> The honorable Bertrand Russell . . . obtruded himself before thousands of students in America, openly taught complete sexual freedom and all its indulgences without marriage. . . . In 1926, at "The Play House" in Washington there appeared Scott Nearing, formerly a teacher of economics at the University of Pennsylvania. He spoke to a packed house on the stability of the Russian Soviet Government. His audience, at 50 cents a head, applauded his every word. . . . This took place within a stone's throw of the Capitol.[31]

As the depression deepened, Coughlin argued, so would the potential for a communist-inspired social revolution in America, with the funding coming directly from Moscow to the head of the American Communist party, William Z. Foster: "He received $1,250,000 to spend in America for the purpose of stirring up discontent in our industrial centers. The first disturbance occurred . . . at Pontiac, Michigan, not 20 miles distant from the shrine where I am speaking."[32]

In 1930, there were many in the nation concerned about the danger of the extreme left's seizing a moment of near chaos in America and taking power. A number of them were to be found in Washington. Within a few weeks of his sermons warning about the twin dangers of socialism and communism, Coughlin was offering testimony to a committee of the House of Representatives. Officially entitled the Special Committee to Investigate Communist Activities in the United States, it was commonly referred to as the Fish Committee, in honor of its chairman, Hamilton Fish, Jr., a New York congressman who had served in World War I and had become one of the key members of Congress to sound the alarm regarding communist subversion.

Hamilton Fish's committee was the forerunner of the House Un-American Activities Committee, which operated from the mid-1930s until the late 1950s. In these later reincarnations, it would rivet public attention on both communist and Nazi domestic infiltration but concentrated on the danger from the extreme left. Under chairman Fish, the Special Committee to Investigate Communist Activities in the United States convened a series of hearings in the spring of 1930 focused on the causes for labor unrest around the nation, particularly its urban centers. Witnesses were called to testify regarding the organization of the Communist Party in the United States and other groups deemed to be promoting "Communist propaganda."

On a searingly hot day in July 1930, Father Coughlin served as the star witness for the Fish Committee when it held hearings in Detroit. After explaining that the philosophical roots of bolshevism derived from "the Hebrew, Karl Marx," the radio priest was cross-examined by members of Congress.

> QUESTIONER: Have you had occasion to come into contact with some communistic activities?
>
> FR. COUGHLIN: Yes, sir, to this extent: I have a chain of broadcasting stations, and I have received 300,000 letters from my work in this field.
>
> QUESTIONER: Isn't it that the communists seek to socialize by direct force?
>
> FR. COUGHLIN: I will give you a little information. . . . Any American who professes to have dabbled into this subject of socialism has heard of the name of Adam Weishaupt. . . . The German professor in the year 1776 organized his sympathetic associates into the "Order of the Illuminati." . . . Said he, "Destroy Christianity and civilization will be happy." Such is the though[t] of the Old

Testament, if I may call it such, of socialism. Such is the religion of its author.

QUESTIONER: And do you think there is any danger of the communists making great strides?

FR. COUGHLIN: Yes, sir. In the French Revolution there were only 22,000 interested in it. The Russian Revolution of 1917 had less than 500,000 communists in it that were interested in it. We have approximately 500,000 communistically minded people in this country at least. . . . Unrest is on the increase. . . .

QUESTIONER: Do you think there is any danger of communism in this country?

FR. COUGHLIN: I think by 1933, unless something is done, you will see a revolution in this country.[33]

Harry A. Jung, declaring himself a specialist in the danger of foreign influences on American society, followed Coughlin as a witness. Established as an authority on communism in the labor movement in Chicago, Jung was asked, "What do you think is the race furnishing most communists in Chicago?" He replied: "I could not say as to the exact number each race might furnish"; when told to give his "conception" of the proportions, he answered, "I must say it is Jewish." Explaining that the question was a difficult one, since there are "Polish Jews and German Jews and Russian Jews," Jung replied, "I think it would be a safe estimate to say 66⅔ percent." When discussing the same topic, Coughlin proffered, "It does happen that 90 percent of the Soviet government is Jewish." He added that "in this country the communists are not the Jews. I think it is a libel on the Jewish race to say that only Jews are communists."[34]

What Jung and Coughlin said about Jews, as well as what the radio priest's contemporary biographer Ruth Mugglebee described as his "abstract discourse" on the origins of bolshevism, held little interest for the horde of reporters from around the country who were crammed into the sweltering hearing room in Detroit's federal building. Their labors were rewarded when Charles Coughlin dropped a bombshell: "There is a movement . . . to take down our Stars and Stripes and put up an international flag . . . and that movement is headed by Mr. Henry Ford."[35] Coughlin explained that by Henry Ford's contracting to build tractors for the Soviet Union, "he was abetting the spread of communism." Mention of the popular industrialist ensured headline coverage of the hearings:

"Blames Ford for Red Flare! Accuses Ford of Spreading Communism; Priest Cites One Case Where Thousands Failed to Get Jobs in Auto Plant. Says Ford Is Helping Communism."[36]

In the fall 1930 broadcast season, Charles Coughlin was heard for the first time over a national radio network, CBS. A shortwave hookup even carried his voice around the world on station WCAU in Philadelphia. Within three weeks, so many more letters to the radio priest arrived that fifty-five clerks were needed to process the mail. A year later that number would be nearly doubled, to ninety-six. A new post office was constructed in Royal Oak solely for coping with the bags of mail arriving almost daily for the Shrine of the Little Flower. In an average week, eighty thousand letters were delivered to Coughlin's church. This frenetic activity and the soaring popularity of the priest coincided with the growing economic disaster. By the close of 1930, the depression and a particularly bitter winter had settled over the land. As the new year dawned, bread lines lengthened and Coughlin's voice grew ever louder.

Coughlin chose an ironic title, "Prosperity," for his first sermon of 1931. According to Ruth Mugglebee, it would be a talk of "spicier content and unprecedented license." But the radio priest did not give the planned address. Instead, his office in Royal Oak issued this press release:

> Father Coughlin was informed by the Columbia Broadcasting System that a considerable number of protests had come to its attention regarding his sermons. . . . Father Coughlin made mention over the Columbia Broadcasting System tonight that these letters of protest had been lodged against him from sources which were altogether unknown, and appealed to his radio audience to express their pleasure whether or not these sermons would be continued.[37]

The next day, as CBS was flooded with an estimated 350,000 letters, Coughlin penned an "open letter," addressed to "my friends," in which he compared the state of American society to the eve of the French Revolution and referred to "a cowardly behind-the-back attack [being] made against the 'Golden Hour' with the hope of throttling free speech."[38]

On January 11, the Sunday following the original scheduling, Charles Coughlin did deliver "Prosperity," one of his most significant radio addresses and an event that signaled his emergence as an orator without peer in America's national public life. Moreover, in it he enunciated a thesis that became virtually a signature theme of his radio sermons: that "international financiers" had caused the 1929 stock market collapse. On this occasion, the priest linked the event to the ideas of "Karl Marx, a Hebrew."

This line of argument was not one that the radio priest himself had developed, although he did give it his own special articulation. Rather, major portions of the address were drawn, virtually word for word, from a speech by the chairman of the Committee on Banking and Currency of the Congress, Louis T. McFadden, Republican of Pennsylvania. Long a maverick in his own party, McFadden had once called from the floor of the House of Representatives for Hoover's impeachment.[39]

In the nearly suppressed radio address of January 11, Coughlin discussed the harsh terms of the Versailles Treaty and how it had required "blood bond" reparations payments, which he asserted were permitting low interest rates to be charged by Federal Reserve banks during the 1920s. He linked this to the financial exploitation of Germany, in effect asserting that this subsidized the "purchase of millions of stocks purchased on margin" and made "playing the stock market . . . as popular as playing bridge." Now, Coughlin claimed, "The Depression [is] with us, but the banks for the most part were saved." In sum, declared the priest, "The unrest of Europe and the industrial distress of the world are traceable, in great part, to the illegitimate cradle of the Treaty of Versailles, which has only made a mockery of peace. . . . It has wrecked corporation after corporation; has emptied thousands of purses and bank accounts; has weakened many capitalists and has paralyzed millions in the middle class." Coughlin then linked these developments with the campaign for getting involved in the League of Nations: "Perhaps . . . these facts offer you some explanation why there is so much anxiety . . . for us to join the World Court of the League of Nations with France and England against Germany and Italy with the hope to save some of the billions invested by our international financiers in the blood bonds of an unjust Treaty." In a blistering attack on this "program of deception," the priest acknowledged his reliance on Congressman McFadden, citing the "clear and uncontrovertible proofs which he had relayed in a two-minute telephone conversation on New Year's day, 1931, followed by a Saturday morning call on January 3."[40]

The radio priest had strongly hinted, and his supporters were encour-

aged to suspect, that the effort to censor the Versailles address were the
result of White House pressure on CBS. Ruth Mugglebee states that
Hoover administration aides met secretly with CBS officials, who "were
subservient to the idea of clamping down the lid on the priest's revelations."[41] According to Louis Ward, the opportunity for a suppression attempt came from eavesdropping on the telephone conversations between
McFadden and the radio priest:

> Just a little before midday [on January 2, 1931], Father's secre-
> tary long-distanced Washington at National 3120 where she was
> accustomed to contact Mr. McFadden. . . . After an unusual de-
> lay, the telephone connections were completed, the number was
> confirmed and Congressman Louis McFadden was requested to
> come to the phone. Then came the question: "Who wishes to
> speak to Mr. McFadden?" The reply: "Father Coughlin." After
> another delay, a voice came over the wire from Washington say-
> ing: "This is the White House speaking." . . . The secretary from
> the Radio League of the Little Flower read certain excerpts from
> Father's prepared discourse and asked if the figures and facts as
> read were correct. The answer from the gentleman, whom the
> secretary presumed to be Mr. McFadden, was in the affirmative.
> "Until that moment, no one but Father Coughlin and his four per-
> sonal secretaries could have known the content of the Sunday
> discourse."[42]

As Coughlin was rehearsing his Sunday talk, Ward reports, he received a long-distance call from CBS vice president Edward Klauber at
midnight Saturday. Klauber reported "that many complaints had been received by his broadcasting system because of the 'inflammatory' remarks
that had been made in previous discourses." Klauber then "added the request that Father Coughlin . . . should delete those things which anyone
might regard as objectionable." In reply, "Father Coughlin assured Mr.
Klauber that, not preferring to omit any portion of the discourse, he
would speak on a topic totally foreign to the [one] which he had prepared." Coughlin "immediately contacted Representative McFadden,
who denied that any call from his office to the priest had ever taken
place."[43]

Ward strongly hints that it was President Hoover himself who tried to
suppress the Coughlin address and that it was he who had authorized the

tapping of the priest's telephone. No one from CBS has ever confirmed such a scenario, although William Paley, in his autobiography, published the same year of the radio priest's death, 1979, indicated that because Father Coughlin "strayed far beyond his theological talks to messages of hate and extreme political views . . . we soon insisted upon seeing his scripts in advance." Paley noted that in regard to the infamous "Versailles" talk, "We then refused him air time for one especially inflammatory advance script and strongly suggested he confine himself to a religious theme."[44] When interviewed on the subject in 1972, Coughlin claimed,

> I was stepping on the toes of money, money, money, and I was getting too close. . . . There was a tremendous amount of pressure being put on my friend Bill Paley. . . . He had graciously arranged for me to go on CBS, and I owed him a debt of gratitude, and I couldn't see why he should be made to suffer because of the controversy around me. So when the network began demanding changes in my scripts I was glad to get out. Besides, Bill taught me how to organize my own network.[45]

This last statement is undoubtedly exaggerated. What did happen is that by the end of the 1930–1931 season, CBS had washed its hands of Coughlin. In 1984, when I asked William Paley about the events surrounding the 1930–1931 contract with Coughlin, he refused to discuss the topic except to deny vehemently his association with Coughlin: "There is no truth to my helping him set up his own network or having any relationship with him once he left CBS. There is simply no truth to that."[46]

It is impossible to determine whether there was a White House attempt to censor Coughlin's "Versailles" sermon, particularly if one relies on Coughlin or CBS sources for information. Did Hoover engage in some skulduggery here? While conducting research for a book on U.S. Naval intelligence, Jeffrey Dorwart discovered the secret diaries of a Hoover aide that fueled discussion of a 1930 "Hoovergate." Dorwart claimed that the president used a naval intelligence officer, Glenn Howell, to steal files from the office of a Democratic party official who had copies of a book manuscript highly critical of the chief executive. Secret tape recordings made by Hoover have also come to light.[47] Herbert Hoover's presidential papers contain an anecdote told by Edna Ferber to journalist William

White in which the well-known writer recounts her discovery of a White House wiretap in a hotel room she was occupying early in 1931.[48]

Even before the CBS controversy, the remarkable impact of Coughlin's addresses had made him an opponent to the sitting president. He had tapped the enormous bitterness of a growing number of Americans directed toward the nation's chief executive. Any official effort to muzzle his radio sermons would have seemed only to augment his credibility in the eyes of his adoring public.

Beginning with the fall 1931 broadcast season, Coughlin assembled his own independent chain of stations covering an area from St. Louis, Missouri, to Portland, Maine. Early in 1932, the network was expanded from eleven stations to twenty-seven, and covered an area from Kansas City to Bangor. The radio priest now engaged in a campaign of direct attacks on Hoover. The sermon broadcast on February 12, 1932, "The Secret Is Out!" was a savage assault on the personal integrity of the president. The priest quoted from an article he had found in the public library in a mining magazine published in 1912, "The Economics of a Boom." Coughlin implied that Hoover had advocated a formula by which insiders parlay their initial limited investment by offering shares to the public based on a highly inflated figure representing the capitalized value of a worthless mine.

> In 1912, Mr. Herbert Hoover termed as "idiots" those people who would listen to the suave, salesman talk of promoters who by deceit and subterfuge coaxed money from widows as was done here in Royal Oak and elsewhere to invest with many mining ventures which were failures before they were started. . . .
>
> Idiots who parted with it! Idiots! I hang on that word "idiots." It is a word to conjure with, I-D-I-O-T-S—idiots! My friends we are deeply indebted for this shocking piece of information. . . . We are taught that it is quite moral and just to filch money from innocent "outsiders" and pass it into the soft hands of the guilty "insiders." . . . The world around us is facing the sordid, burning facts of unemployment, of starvation, of unjust taxation. . . . No longer can the people who love their homes and love their country be lulled into inaction by the idle optimism of the sleek parasites who exist on the crumbs dropped from the advertising table of calloused conscienced exploiters.[49]

Louis Ward claimed that this particular discourse sounded "the death-knell of Herbert Hoover's political career." More than a million favorable letters reputedly flowed to the Royal Oak Shrine following this Valentine's Day broadcast. A letter of concern written by a Hoover campaign worker to the president's secretary, Theodore Joslin, noted that the explanation of the 1912 article on mining investments offered by President Hoover—that it had been written tongue in cheek—did not come across as effective, and that the term *idiots* that had been used in the mining article was properly explained as an insult to the average person. Joslin's reply dismissed the problem, saying that "it must be borne in mind that the moronic mind has a vote and alas too many voters are in this class."[50]

In his next address, Coughlin reviled the president as "the banker's friend, the Holy Ghost of the rich, the protective angel of Wall Street." After that single broadcast in late February 1932, 1.2 million letters flooded the post office in Royal Oak. Week after week, as the depression deepened, Father Coughlin hurled invectives at the White House.

Some four decades later, Father Coughlin would blithely offer this explanation of his relationship with Herbert Hoover:

> There never was a finer, more stalwart American gentleman than he was. . . . President Hoover was probably the most harassed Executive we've had at a time when we needed one with more elasticity in his actions. . . . Years later, when he was living in New York at the Waldorf-Astoria, I went over to offer my heartfelt sympathies and apologies for anything I might have said while he was President, and he said, "Young man, I don't blame you. I was the symbol of our nation, and the nation needed castigation. As you know now, it wasn't my fault but I would have been a 'cad'—that is the word he used—if I had said, 'Don't blame me, blame Congress.'" That was quite a heroic statement![51]

At the time, however, their mutual dislike could not have been stronger.

3

A Player on the New Deal Team

"My Friend and future savior of the United States. It was either Roosevelt or Ruin." It was the first time I used it [the phrase]. I would say that my . . . speech at the [1932 Democratic] convention . . . swung a lot of votes to his [FDR's] candidacy.

Charles Coughlin interview, 1970

NEAR THE END OF HIS LIFE, Charles Coughlin boasted, "I was instrumental in removing Herbert Hoover from the White House."[1] While certainly an exaggeration, there is little doubt that Charles Coughlin helped destroy one public figure's career while helping to pave the way for another. Destiny linked the careers of Coughlin and Franklin Roosevelt in what would later turn into a struggle between the two men for power and influence. As the 1930s opened, they were close allies, and Coughlin was FDR's champion.

The name Roosevelt first came up in a radio sermon given by Father Coughlin in the fall of 1930:

Fellow countrymen, in this hour of sadness and depression we dare lift up our eyes to the better things to come. The glorious sunrise of yesterday shall return once night has gone. Pay no heed, therefore . . . to those men who intimate that our system of economy is basically wrong. Spurn them when they advocate the doctrines that smack of communism, of Russian Sovietism. Another Roosevelt shall have the courage to uncloak the hypocriti-

40

cal human factors who have debased our system. . . . Another Roosevelt shall labor for the development of our own country![2]

Nearly two years would pass before the two men met each other. In this interim, a kind of mutual fascination developed, a slow waltz of political necessity that eventually took on the character of a major political alliance, albeit short-lived. In January 1931, during the "censorship" episode with CBS, Coughlin had written to Franklin Roosevelt, then governor of New York, requesting his intervention. FDR responded with a polite but noncommittal letter expressing his sympathy.[3] Roosevelt had already been in contact with and sought the help of a close friend of the radio priest: Frank Murphy, mayor of Detroit and later a U.S. Supreme Court justice. Murphy had known Coughlin for some time prior to FDR's 1932 presidential campaign. In fact, Murphy had relied heavily on Coughlin in his own 1930 mayoral campaign.

In later years, Coughlin could not recall who first introduced him to Franklin Roosevelt. It is likely to have been either Frank Murphy or Hall Roosevelt, brother-in-law to FDR. As controller for the city of Detroit, Hall Roosevelt wrote FDR in the spring of 1931, telling him that the priest "would like to tender his services: [Coughlin] has a following just about equal to that of Mr. Ghandi [*sic*]." Hall advised that Coughlin "would be difficult to handle and might be full of dynamite, but I think you had better prepare to say 'yes' or 'no.' "[4] Without doubt, Frank Murphy was one of those who pushed strongly for a "yes."[5]

There is some difficulty as well in establishing when and where Coughlin and FDR had their first private meeting. In a 1970 interview, Coughlin placed it "in the spring of 1932 at a New York hotel." Sheldon Marcus quotes the radio priest as placing the initial face-to-face contact at FDR's Poughkeepsie estate. Marcus wrote that Roosevelt "seemed very impressed with his [Coughlin's] knowledge of social problems," and "Roosevelt promised Coughlin that he would be his close confidant on economic and social issues. Coughlin [for his part] promised he would throw his support behind Roosevelt's presidential candidacy."[6]

But the main topic of conversation in that meeting appears to have been the Walker affair. The flamboyant Democratic mayor of New York City, James J. Walker, was being investigated by a state commissioner regarding serious charges of personal corruption. Coughlin told biographer Marcus that Roosevelt "made it clear to me that he had to get rid of James [Walker], one way or another."[7] Yet as governor, Roosevelt was facing a delicate political dilemma, since he owed much to New York City's Tammany Hall and felt he had to avoid alienating those still committed to its mayor.

The Walker investigation posed a dilemma for the radio priest as well. Months before his meeting with FDR, Coughlin had attended the annual Fireman's Communion Breakfast of the Holy Name Society in New York City and had charged that Rabbi Stephen Wise and others who attacked Mayor Walker "were Communists and Socialists."[8] When asked about this in 1972, Coughlin said that he had at first thought the accusations against Walker "were too preposterous to believe. When they turned out to be true, I was shocked to death."[9]

Coughlin recalls that FDR invited him to attend a session of the Walker investigation being convened in Albany and that "it was a masterful performance by the governor. . . . After it was over I came out and Mr. Roosevelt was gesticulating to me, and I was smiling back, but the reporters could see that I was on his side."[10] But following the visit, Coughlin mulled over the Walker situation and wrote a letter to FDR in which he warned that the case "was a perilous one" and that America's "twenty-odd million Catholics could easily be offended by how it was handled." The priest mentioned rumors that Roosevelt was considered anti-Catholic because the judge in the Walker case, Samuel Seabury, "was a member of the Klan."[11] When Jimmy Walker resigned shortly after the Albany hearings, FDR's and Coughlin's conundrum was resolved. Later, with some bitterness, Coughlin would accuse FDR of using him to avoid the charge of anti-Catholic bias.[12]

According to historian Alan Brinkley, Roosevelt "was suspicious of Coughlin from the first day they met." Furthermore, once FDR was elected, "Coughlin rapidly became something of a pest."[13] When another historical researcher, Charles Tull, sought to clarify FDR's attitude toward the priest, he received a curt response from Eleanor Roosevelt. When he asked, "Do you recall your late husband's opinion of Father Coughlin?" she replied, "He disliked and distrusted him." "What was your own opinion?" "I never liked or trusted him."[14] Nonetheless, FDR was willing to make use of Coughlin, however he may have felt about him.

For Coughlin, a highlight of the 1932 presidential campaign was his address before the Democratic National Convention in Chicago. While he had been sprinkling his radio addresses with pro-Roosevelt hints, being invited to address the assembled delegates was the first acknowledgment of his importance in FDR's campaign. Decades after, the priest recalled that his speech was meant to sound extemporaneous, "but it was all carefully staged. 'Hi, there, Father: Why don't you come on up to the microphone and say a few words?'" Coughlin's opening words drew raucous laughter: "Of course I am not a Republican and most people know that. And perhaps I am not going to say I am a Democrat, because this thing of religion should not be identified with any political party." This time, he was met with sustained applause.[15]

The priest returned to Royal Oak and wired the future president, saying: "I am with you to the end. Say the word and I will follow." A few days later Coughlin wrote again, telling FDR that "your personal welfare and the success of the Democratic Party in the forthcoming election are both close to my heart." In a letter written a month later, the priest offered Roosevelt his fealty in even more explicit terms and called for a partnership: "I am willing to adopt your views which I know will be just and charitable. But the main point is that we work in harmony."[16] As the Roosevelt campaign drew to a close, it was clear that support from Michigan's Frank Murphy and Charles Coughlin would be essential for winning that critical industrial state.

FDR adopted some of Coughlin's main themes and even co-opted some of his rhetoric. In an important speech given in Detroit on October 2, 1932, entitled "The Philosophy of Social Justice Through Social Action," the presidential candidate declared:

> I am going to refer to some of the fundamentals that antedate parties and antedate republics and empires, fundamentals that are as old as mankind itself. . . . One of these old philosophies is the philosophy of those who would "let things alone." The other is the philosophy that strives for something new—something which I believe the human race can and will attain—social justice through social action.[17]

Roosevelt was quoting Pius XI's encyclical of 1931, *Quadragesimo Anno* (Forty Years After), which had built on the foundation of Pope Leo XIII's *Rerum Novarum*. The essential point was to steer a course between laissez-faire capitalism and revolutionary socialism. Such advocacy of state intervention on behalf of the working class implied that Catholicism would no longer be committed to the sanctity of private property above any other. From his earliest radio days, Charles Coughlin acknowledged a deep indebtedness for his economic philosophy to these two church

documents. While candidate Roosevelt was careful to include statements
from Protestant and Jewish religious sources and did not mention Coughlin's name, FDR was unmistakably identifying himself with the Royal
Oak radio messiah.

With Roosevelt's decisive victory in November 1932, a barrage of
flattering compliments, advice, and suggestions for how to run the country now issued forth from the radio priest.[18] Perhaps Coughlin sincerely
believed—or was himself swayed by his own radio oratory, as he sought
to convince his millions of radio listeners—that he was an important
member of the New Deal team. Years later in a private interview, the
priest, with characteristic exaggeration, described his early relationship
with FDR:

> I was with him I'd say every two weeks at least. If not at his of-
> fice at least at his home. And even before he went to Washington
> in February [1933]. I went to his office in New York . . . it was
> down in the eighties or seventies, some street down there. And he
> was having his portrait painted. I spent the day with him there
> where he was making out his Cabinet. And that was the day
> when I said: "Well, now listen you promised me some things and
> I have only one friend that I have in mind and his name is Frank
> Murphy. . . . We need a good man over in the Philippines, how
> about it?" He says, "Frank is the governor of the Philippines." So
> that's how close I was to Mr. Roosevelt.[19]

For Coughlin's radio audience, it was indeed a triumph that FDR was
in the White House and that the radio priest had helped to put him there.
The Catholic community took special pride in this partnership. Coughlin's and FDR's exuberance and optimism about the future of the country
seemed to make the two soulmates. Four decades after meeting FDR, the
priest painted their early relationship in warm and friendly coloration:
"Whether up in his home in Poughkeepsie or down at his home in Manhattan he was always affable and charming. . . . I would come armed
with a few stories and he would tell some to me. We never talked too
seriously you know. But I think when you got to know the man you
couldn't help but love the man."[20]

Coughlin frequently boasted to his close associates about his having
helped write FDR's first and second inaugural addresses, including, from
the latter, the phrase, "Let us drive the money changers from the temple."
Father Peter Wiethe, a close confidant of the priest, recalled Coughlin's

telling a story about staying at the Mayflower Hotel in Washington with FDR: "Ray Moley [one of Roosevelt's top aides] came to Father Coughlin and said: 'The "boss" had another inaugural speech. He may not use ours.' And they sat up all night, they were so disgusted with the situation, you see. So he claims . . . the next day, the day of the inauguration, he took both speeches along. And hadn't made up his mind which he was going to give. At the last moment he took Father Coughlin and Ray Moley's speech out of his pocket and gave that one."[21]

In his mailings to listeners, Coughlin praised the new president and suggested that people write to FDR about the problems of the day. He preached hopeful patience: "Meanwhile let us pray and be not discouraged with any little reverses which may occur. Eventually we will win out under Mr. Roosevelt's generalship."[22] Coughlin's influence at the White House was carefully noted. Theodore Joslin, Herbert Hoover's former private secretary, wrote to Hoover that "business . . . is disturbed by some of his [FDR's] intimates." Joslin cites as an example that "the Catholic priest in Detroit is received all too cordially." He noted that FDR's private secretary, Marvin McIntyre, called the priest by his first name and that Eleanor Roosevelt greeted him cordially: " 'Why, Father, I am so glad to see you, come right in.' And taking him by the arm she went into the President's office with him and they were there for an hour." Joslin added, tersely, "This is informal to say the least."[23]

In retrospect, those close to FDR tended to play down Coughlin's role in the early days of the New Deal. Certainly Coughlin took every opportunity to exaggerate it. One thing was clear: Father Coughlin's star was rising with Franklin Roosevelt's. Al Smith, who in 1928 was the first Catholic to run for the presidency, now lost influence in New England and among average Catholic citizens. Coughlin was the new Catholic spokesman.

From the earliest days of his fame, Charles Coughlin's business acumen was both praised and condemned: no one was neutral on the subject. News about the enterprising priest made fascinating copy:

Priest Crusade Cost Thousands a Week

What becomes of the hundreds of thousands of dollars that pour into Father Charles Edward Coughlin's charge in two out of three of the 200,000 letters he receives every week?

It goes out in several channels. It costs $8000 for instance, for line charges and station facilities for the weekly broadcast. Father Coughlin's bills for clerks and secretaries and stamps and printing amount to many thousands a week. . . .

Father Coughlin is recognized in Detroit as one of the ablest money raisers that town of fantastic riches and promotions ever has had.[24]

The broadcasts of the "Children's Hour" were highly popular attractions at the Shrine; the annual ice cream picnic attracted as many as 50,000 people. One of the earliest church parishioners recalled, "A lot of people smelled graft and corruption. Where did the money go?"[25]

As early as 1928, despite problems of paying the mortgage on his wooden church, Charles Coughlin was already hard at work on plans for an ambitious replacement for the original structure. With the enormous success of his broadcasts, he was soon able to build a "colossal monument to Christian Charity, a defiant challenge to bigotry."[26] So successful were his fund drives that by May 1929 the skeleton of a massive marble edifice thrusted itself boldly skyward amid the modest middle-class suburb that was rapidly gaining national and even international fame. When it was completed, Coughlin held a dedication ceremony in 1931, speaking from a special balcony built on the face of what became known as the Charity Tower.

Well before the completion of the tower project, Coughlin was making plans for an equally impressive and entirely new Shrine of the Little Flower. Granite and limestone were brought from quarries in Vermont and Massachusetts, and the outer walls were carved with the official flower of each state. The most radical feature of the Shrine was its main altar, located in the center of the church in a departure from tradition (but later consonant with the precepts of Vatican II). A poetic description notes: "It is the main altar to which all eyes are drawn. . . . Set on its steps in polished emerald pearl granite . . . it is the largest monolithic altar in this country, a solid block of faultless white Carraran marble weighing eighteen tons. Designed so that Mass may be celebrated on either side."[27] Inside the adjacent Charity Tower, Coughlin built a private office and broadcasting facility. Reached by a narrow, winding staircase, the exterior was crowned with a head of Christ, above which was carved a dove "of huge proportions and exquisite design . . . expanding its wings over the entire universe represented by the spheres and the stars."[28]

The newly erected Shrine, with a "theme park" character, became a tourist mecca shortly after it opened in fall 1936 and remained so for decades. Father Coughlin arranged special boat and train excursions, which reached their peak during the summer months. Busloads of thirty thousand or more tourists came each Sunday and could be seen milling about the grounds. "There was a pond there . . . and the people used to throw hundreds of dollars in change."[29] A gas station, a motel, and other amenities were operated by the Shrine during the height of Father Coughlin's fame. In the basement of the church, a staff of over one hundred handled the huge daily volume of mail.

The profitability of the Shrine was evident even during Word War II, when, despite gasoline shortages, two hundred or three hundred cars at a time parked around the church. During this time there were eight masses held each Sunday, with attendance at each averaging 3,000.[30] Near the end of his life, Coughlin told interviewers that he had raised more than a million and a half dollars to fund the completion of a complex, which eventually included a grammar school, a high school, and a convent.

During the height of Coughlin's fame, an adjoining souvenir store was often crowded with purchasers eager to snap up gold crosses, sterling silver rosaries, and autographed photos of Coughlin. (A favorite item for sale, though not of a strictly religious nature, was a silver-plated automobile gearshift level.) Father Coughlin's parents ran the shop, whose reputation for lucrative sales was unflatteringly described by one former parishioner as "the highest in the holy trinket retail field." Such brash commercialism did not sit well with all of the Shrine's visitors. "One day a woman came into the gift shop. She came in with a shopping bag, and in the bag was a chain. She went nuts! She smashed every case in the souvenir shop. As she broke the cases, she shouted that she was 'casting the money changers from the temple!' Father closed it [the shop] down. It wasn't opened again after that."[31]

Ruth Mugglebee concluded that Father Coughlin "wasn't in the priesthood for fame or material gains," but he did offer financial advice to friends, newlyweds, and pastoral colleagues, and he did relish having a hand in the game of finance. Despite fashioning a political career around the theme of evil bankers and Wall Street manipulators, the priest was an obsessive follower of the stock market throughout his life. This was not merely a way to track the doings of the enemy, but a fun-loving flair for investment.

In the last decade of his life, when Coughlin was no longer in the limelight, a newly appointed deacon remembered being invited out for dinner with Coughlin. During the course of the evening, the deacon began to feel that the elderly priest "had really liked me." After a stimulating conversation, the young cleric remembered that his host drew a slip of paper and a pencil from his pocket and scribbled a brief note, jotting it down on the roof of his Thunderbird sports car. Coughlin explained that he was offering an insider's stock tip. As the deacon recalled, Coughlin said, "This is the company, just buy this, it's going to be a good company. . . . I think you should invest in!" He got into his car and drove off. The newly appointed deacon glanced at the missive: "The name of the stock was a company called Wendy's. This was 1970! I don't even remember a Wendy's until 1976! I didn't know anything about it, so I just looked at the slip of paper and threw it away."[32]

With Coughlin's fame, fortune, and influence came enemies. In 1933, he was strongly attacked by the *Free Press*. This so-called newspaper war was instigated early in February when one of the two largest banks in Detroit, the Guardian Trust, reported privately to the Reconstruction Finance Corporation (RFC) that it could not meet its demands for withdrawals unless it obtained a loan of $50 million. Only one strategy to save this large popular bank seemed possible under existing rules: the bank's largest depositor, and one of its stockholders, the Ford Motor Company, would have to guarantee its deposits with collateral assets to the extent of $7.5 million. But Henry Ford was unwilling to support this plan. Emissaries from the Hoover White House, the Treasury Department, and the RFC hastened to Detroit to reason with him. The undersecretary of the treasury feared that if Guardian fell, the other major Detroit bank chain, the First National, might also break.

When the Roosevelt administration took office, President Hoover's plea to solve the Detroit banking crisis fell on deaf ears. Instead, FDR declared a national bank holiday. The 576,000 bank customers in Detroit affected by the extended holidays waited for the new administration to resolve the matter.[33] Confidence in financial institutions was at an all-time low, and Detroit had become a flashpoint of national panic and anger. Who was responsible? What could be done? Into this turbulent cauldron stepped the Reverend Charles Edward Coughlin.

The newspaper war began when, in a special broadcast of March 26, 1933, Coughlin focused on the Detroit banking crisis. He called the local banking community "the den of forty thieves, the hide-out, the blind pig financial institutions where shady transactions are prepared and where are printed the depositors' passports to doom." The priest then accused one individual, a director of one of the major banking groups, of using his role as a newspaper publisher to "spread their [Detroit bankers'] propaganda . . . in the columns of *Detroit Free Press* . . . a paper published by the president of the Detroit Bankers Company . . . Mr. E. D. Stair." Coughlin, referring to a series of what he called "scurrilous articles," accused Stair and other key local bankers of "attempting to prevent the Government-controlled bank from opening its doors and serving the people of Detroit!"

The priest described the *Free Press* as "a rabid, partisan paper . . . a paper that was wedded to the past with its exploitation; a paper religiously opposed to the 'New Deal,'" engaged in "misrepresentations" and "professional obstructionism." Coughlin declared that "the Stairs fight the battle for those with unsecured loans, officer's loans, wholly out of proportion to any credit they are entitled to. Every penny of this is the people's money, the small depositor's money, the small businessman's money, swept away in this banking debacle." In contrast, the radio priest placed himself on the side of "the biggest interest in this Democracy, the interest of the people."[34]

A counterattack was swift in coming. The day following the radio address, the *Free Press* penned an editorial, "Coughlin: The Demagog," that charged the priest with "slandering the directors of the two outstanding banking groups of Detroit" and accusing banks of having done "much to bring about the present [crisis] situation. He robbed the people of confidence in these directors and their banks and was one of the chief causes of withdrawals of funds." The paper then asked: "How long will this ecclesiastical Huey Long be allowed to slander decent citizens of this city in the name of God?"[35]

Over the next week, the *Free Press* waged a three-pronged media campaign against the "political radio haranguer." First, it hinted that political animus and "sinister newspaper influences" were guiding the priest. The rival Hearst paper, the *Detroit Times,* was charged with putting the radio priest up to the attack on E. D. Stair as part of an FDR plot. Next, it charged him with hiding behind his priestly garb, "using the strength of the Church to give him prestige."[36] Finally, the *Free Press* interviewed Coughlin's bishop and mentor, Michael Gallagher, who did not know about the sensational broadcast. "I did not have an opportunity to review it. When I called Father Coughlin he told me it [the radio talk] was not finished and he probably would be working on it all night."[37]

On the third day of the war, the paper dropped the bombshell: "Fr. Coughlin's Gambling in Stocks with Charity Donations Is Revealed." The story claimed to have uncovered a series of withdrawals from bank accounts held in the name of the Shrine of the Little Flower and used to buy stocks on margin, including local automotive company securities. The newspaper wrote:

> There is gold in the radio racket. That is proven by the bank balances maintained by the Reverend Charles E. Coughlin. . . . Contributions have also permitted Father Coughlin to plunge into the stock market. . . . On February 27, 1929, the account of the priest shows the bank bought him five hundred shares of stock of the Kelsey-Hayes Wheel Corporation. . . . On that day Father Coughlin transferred from the League of the Little Flower account $9,216.28; drew $4,233.72 from his personal account; cashed a check on another local bank for $6,000, and borrowed $10,587.50 on a note.[38]

Malcolm Bingay, editorial director of the *Free Press,* years later wrote of the fortuitous circumstances under which the information about Coughlin's transactions was revealed:

> One of the rare nights that I was able to get home for dinner and a change of clothes I had just sat down to eat when a reporter called me on the phone. "There is a young fellow here in the office who insists on seeing you and you alone. . . . He hints that he has some evidence in the bank case. He has something under his arm that looks like a wrapped-up stovepipe. . . . I'm afraid he may be just one of those nuts. . . ." I left my half-finished dinner and raced down to the office: "I worked as a clerk in the branch bank in the Fisher Building where Father Coughlin did his banking. When the banks closed I still had my passkey. Tonight I went to the bank and took out the whole record of Father Coughlin's dealings in the stock market. Here it is." . . . I rushed them down to the photographic department and had photostatic copies made of all of them as quickly as possible. This done I returned the

originals to the frightened youth, who hurried out into the night to return them whence they came.[39]

Now Coughlin struck back. He referred to *Free Press* publisher E. D. Stair as "Edward 'Deficit' Stair" and charged that the paper had erased the real name of the stock purchased. He proclaimed: "This newspaper is entirely responsible for the [banking crisis] . . . [readers] are being daily poisoned with ink from this advocate of libel." But on Monday, using the same purple prose style of the radio priest, the *Free Press* responded through writer Malcolm Bingay's "Good Morning" column by offering a pessimistic prophecy:

> One of the great problems before our Civilization today is the sinister insidiousness of the radio. . . . Long after Coughlin has passed out of the picture . . . the insidious radio will still be before the people. . . . It steals into the home with its whispered words, coming from no man knows where. It is a voice and it is gone. There is no record. There is no permanent printed word. The poison of the demagog, of the atheist, the communist, and the lecherous fills the air of the home and is gone, leaving its stain. Vile and suggestive song, words of double meanings, pour forth to be subconsciously accepted. And there is no written record to prove the injury, no way of combatting the evil that is done.[40]

As the time neared for Coughlin's next weekly radio address, rumors were rampant that the forthcoming broadcast would be jammed. Coughlin warned that "several intimations have come to us that the broadcast of this afternoon will be disturbed by malicious persons. Keep tuned to your announcer for two or three minutes after the disturbance."[41] It sounded like a replay of CBS's concerns with the "Versailles" broadcast. The radio priest's warning followed a midweek bombing at his home. Coughlin described how "glass in every basement window was broken" and damage to pipes and canned food had occurred. According to Louis Ward's account, "Hundreds of pounds of foodstuffs . . . stored in the basement of Father's home for God's Poor Society—food . . . for the poor—broke the force of the explosion and saved life and limb . . . the novena [which required Father Coughlin to be away] saved Father's life."[42]

Detroit's public now eagerly awaited the Sunday address. Would he be contrite or defiant? In a masterful exercise of oratory and evasion, Coughlin repeated his charges against Stair and then sought to wrap himself in the mantle of Christ:

> My friends, as we approach the end of this broadcast season, it is apposite that I restate the position of the Catholic Church and of its clergy relative to their discussing economic questions officially—a question that was forced upon me by the *Detroit Free Press*. . . . I have dared to defend the poor and the exploited; dared to do my duty, cost what it may! . . . If, occasionally then, I have used the scourge of rhetoric to help drive out of public leadership those who have controlled the policies of poverty . . . I have done less by far than the patient, loving Master Who scourged the money-changers from the temple. . . . Whom they crucified because the high priests of compromise framed Him with fake witness.[43]

Within a few months of the newspaper war, Louis Ward, close aide to the radio priest, published his full-length biography of Coughlin. The timing was not coincidental. A full chapter was devoted to a refutation of the *Free Press* attack on Coughlin's financial dealings. The Detroit paper had, according to Ward, run "a libelous creation of an original invoice doctored to suit the malice and taste of the author of the libel . . . with the intent of deceiving the public." Ward charged that by printing the "doctored" photostatic copy of the various buy and sell orders, the *Free Press* had painted a false picture of the radio priest as "generally not averse to stock gambling." Ward sought to depict the speculating priest as a frugal shepherd, concluding that Coughlin had *saved* $97,000 of the original $110,000 investment by not placing it "in the failed banks" and not following "bankers' advice." He went on to claim that "had Coughlin bought Detroit Bankers stock, the $110,000 would have vanished, and a theoretical liability of $17,060 would have remained as a souvenir."[44]

Neither side won the media war. The *Free Press,* in its haste to reveal the stock purchase, had added Coughlin's name to forms copied from bank records, thus blemishing its own case. Yet the battle with the *Free Press* left permanent scars on Coughlin's personal reputation and made one powerful media institution, a major Detroit newspaper, an enduring foe.

There were broader implications as well to the newspaper war. One of these was the ease with which Coughlin could take on the role of a martyr—a lesson not lost on Franklin Roosevelt. Angered, suspicious, and distrustful as he was of the less-than-humble radio priest, FDR would not risk a direct confrontation despite numerous provocations over the ensuing years.

Within weeks of the conclusion of the newspaper war, Charles Coughlin was asked to testify before a one-man grand jury investigation of Detroit's banking crisis. During his three days of highly publicized remarks, headlines appeared in both the *Detroit News* and the *Detroit Times.* Yet readers of the Motor City's third major daily, the *Free Press,* faced a total news blackout of Coughlin's testimony.

In fact, Coughlin had tried to initiate the hearings. Early in June, he wrote to Jesse Jones, the newly appointed RFC chairman, requesting a federal investigation of the Detroit banking collapse. That same month, the radio priest pressed Marvin McIntyre, FDR's appointment secretary, to bring the matter to the attention of the president, "as a sincere favor." Coughlin stressed that "one word from him [FDR] will set Homer Cummings [the new attorney general] in action." Roosevelt took no action.[45]

Finally, on June 14, 1933, the state of Michigan established a special grand jury to investigate the Detroit banking crisis. Popular *Detroit Free Press* journalist Malcolm Bingay described the event as "the strangest grand-jury session ever held in the history of American law. The hysteria in the old town was such that nobody trusted anybody."[46] As the work of the Michigan grand jury dragged on into late summer, public attention became focused on the event when Charles Coughlin was called to testify. The sessions were opened to the public, and the niceties of legal procedure were soon overcome by the noises of popular outrage.

As a throng of reporters and the curious public overflowed the federal building courtroom, spilling into the hallway and onto the sidewalk, the ebullient radio priest was sworn in and questioned by prosecuting attorney Harry S. Toy:

Q: When did you first become interested in banking?
A: Banking in general during my university course, and in the local situation about two and one-half years ago.
Q: Have you studied banking practices?
A: I have.
Q: What caused your interest in banking here?

A: My first motive was the perennial gossip . . . concerning conduct of the banks, the organization of the holding companies and especially some of the opinions expressed in Washington by [Senator] Carter Glass and [Cong.] Lewis [*sic*] T. McFadden.[47]

In other testimony, Coughlin implied that he possessed inside information on banking practices, information that he claimed was given to him during meetings with Frank Murphy and B. F. Stephenson, a business associate. When asked to name the banking officials who provided inside information, the priest demurred, saying, "They might be accused of treason to the banks they represented." When pressed, he stated, "I knew from reliable sources in Washington and from the directors of the Detroit banks that the situation was serious two weeks before the holiday. . . . I heard from Directors their banks were 'about to break.'" Coughlin ended his testimony dramatically with a blast directed at the officers and directors of the two Detroit banking groups, whom he had attacked for insider loans and falsifying records. He now coined a new word for the lexicon of depression-era America: "Why are the depositors to suffer while the banksters . . . continue with their show? I'll tell you why: because . . . the banksters don't want to have the whole banking mess disclosed, with the possibility of some of them going to jail."[48]

Coughlin's words catapulted the banking issue to the front page of local newspapers. The *Detroit Times* headline screamed, "Bankers Looted Trusts, Wrecked Banks—Coughlin," while the *Detroit News* wrote: "Throng Held Spellbound by Magic of Priest's Voice."[49] Clearly, the radio priest had been the star witness.

Like his vilification of the "banksters," Coughlin's defense of the Roosevelt administration in his testimony was also widely publicized. Only the mention of former President Hoover might have upstaged the spirited performance of the priest. In one especially controversial segment of testimony, Coughlin referred to Hoover as a "voter in England who had promoted more than 100 mines not one of which ever paid dividends." Foster Bain, a close associate of Hoover, promptly sent a telegram to the presiding judge, Harry B. Keidan, pointing out that Coughlin's reference pertained to a mining article in a book whose author was a self-proclaimed fraud. (This same discredited article had been used previously by the radio priest in attacks on Hoover during the 1932 presidential campaign.)[50]

Herbert Hoover was bitterly angry that his name had been raised in the Detroit hearing. He told a journalist acquaintance privately by letter what he would not tell Coughlin publicly:

You perhaps saw the volume of material vomited through the Associated Press from Detroit about myself. . . . This morning I received a telegram from a friend which he sent to the judge and which he gave to the associated press. This gentleman, an eminent man in the mining profession, was the editor of the Journal from which Father Coughlin quoted and on which he based his volcano of mud. . . . If the associated press is going to run columns of the mouthings of a communist like Coughlin, it at least ought to run the equivalent dispatch to their exposure.[51]

Hoover also complained to his friends that the U.S. senator from Michigan, James Couzens, a Democrat, had "staged" Coughlin's attack in an attempt to embarrass the former chief executive. He received conflicting advice on the wisdom of coming to Detroit to testify in his own behalf. One of Hoover's friends declared Coughlin to be "mentally irresponsible . . . his rantings will serve to discredit him." Another thought that "right-thinking Americans" would not be influenced. A former cabinet member under Hoover, Patrick Hurley, told the ex-president he was certain both "Couzens and Coughlin have lied [but] you would be drawing intense national attention to the muckrakers if you would go to Detroit."[52] After the hearings had ended, Roy Chapin, Hoover's former aide, who had been tempted to go to Hoover's defense and even testify on Hoover's behalf, offered his own assessment: "One or two strong Republicans thought that Coughlin made such a spectacle of himself that any refutation of his charges was needless."[53]

No sooner had news of Coughlin's "bankster" testimony reached the national media than speculation arose that President Roosevelt had put the priest up to his attack in an effort to test the waters for bank reform policies. According to this theory, FDR could back away from the controversial radio priest if the attack on Detroit bankers did not sit well with the public. It is far more likely, however, that Coughlin acted on his own and sought to impress the new administration with his personal influence. By staging a dramatic show, the priest may have hoped to convince FDR that he had a potent ally in the Motor City. Roosevelt's private papers suggest that the president and his staff were appalled by Coughlin's testimony. Jim Farley, FDR's key campaign adviser, recalled that "Roosevelt was as angry as hell at Coughlin for getting the administration involved in that mess."[54]

But there was a lesson to be learned: Roosevelt and his aides were reluctant to call the radio priest's bluff in public. Privately, Marvin McIntyre, FDR's secretary, complained to key Roosevelt political adviser Louis Howe, "I think Reverend Father took considerable liberties with the facts and most certainly misquoted me [in stating that he was speaking at the request of the administration]." The White House staff was momentarily tempted "to take some action" but in the end elected to "just pass this up."[55] In one of his last interviews late in his life, Coughlin acknowledged the lesson he had learned from the affair: "Listen. I was never stupid. I realized the President now considered me burdensome. But he owed me things. After all I helped make him President. Besides it wasn't him who was against me. It was the people around him. I was determined that I would win him back."[56]

The Detroit bank hearings degenerated into an inquiry about the solvency of the two major banking units as of the day the governor of Michigan declared the bank holiday. On September 18, 1933, the inquiry ended. The next day, Judge Keidan pronounced the two major Detroit banks to have been solvent after all. Moreover, the indictments against several Detroit bankers were eventually dropped despite a complex set of Senate investigations under Senator Ferdinand Pecora.[57]

Without doubt, Charles Coughlin had carried off a remarkable coup in his testimony. His role in the Detroit banking crisis demonstrated that he could be an effective performer off the air as well as on the radio. In one sentimental moment of local glory, he had toyed with his connections to the Roosevelt administration while requiring it to take some nominal action against the bankers he had attacked. Amid the depression, the targets against whom Coughlin directed his hostility were indeed vulnerable. Regardless of the merits of their case, his victims were unable to rebut his charges openly. He had become a master practitioner of the classic art of the political demagogue, wearing the collar of a servant of God.

The priest's image was that of the outsider with insider's knowledge. When attacked, his role as defender of the people only grew.

4

Off the FDR Bandwagon

Now he [Coughlin] considers himself as a newly installed
protector of our country's destiny. . . . He imagines himself
as the only man of authority in these United States. . . . It
will soon come to a point that you will become the object of
attack . . . should your governmental policies and actions in
any way conflict with the militant ideals and preaching of
Father Coughlin.

A local Democratic party official to Franklin Roosevelt, 1935

THE POPULAR *Literary Digest* noted in 1933 that "perhaps no man has
stirred the country and cut as deep between the old order and the
new as Father Coughlin."[1] That same year, the Royal Oak priest was said
to be receiving more mail than the president. When in February 1934 a
New York radio station, WOR, asked its audience who, other than the
president, was the "most useful citizen of the United States politically in
1933," almost 55 percent named the radio priest. When WCAU in Philadelphia asked its listeners to choose between the radio priest and the New
York Philharmonic on Sunday afternoons, 112,000 favored the radio priest
and only 7,000 the Philharmonic. A first edition of Coughlin's complete
radio discourses sold nearly 1 million copies. One food company asked to
sponsor his radio program at $7,500 a week (half its total cost), and Hol-
lywood offered half a million dollars to produce *The Fighting Priest,* a film
in which Coughlin would play himself.[2] Coughlin refused both offers.

Charles Coughlin became a magnet for those who realized that their
economic and political ideas could be transmitted through his enthralling
voice. Shortly after reaching national prominence as a silver-tongued orator, the priest pressed the interests of currency reformers, especially

with regard to the establishment of a silver rather than a gold standard. As early as the broadcast season of 1931–1932, Coughlin attacked the gold standard, which he alleged was maintained solely at the behest of British bankers.

George Le Blanc was a staunch inflationist who soon convinced Coughlin that he possessed an insider's knowledge of the operation of the international currency, and, according to Louis Ward, "was conversant with it from every angle of capitalistic philosophy and of racial psychology."[3] Le Blanc certainly possessed impressive business credentials. This tall, gray-haired, and distinguished native of Montreal had been the New York manager of American Express in 1912 and was appointed vice president of the Equitable Trust in 1914. In 1929, he had resigned to open his own investment counseling office. One contemporary account describes him as a mysterious figure who had "pursued a checkered career as an executive in various Wall Street financial institutions." His acquaintances labeled him something of a loudmouth. And *Fortune* magazine wrote that "hardened Wall Streeters thought [Le Blanc] was a visionary and blowhard."[4] His ideas of revaluation of the dollar based on a silver standard, however, had drawn the attention of Senator Elmer Thomas of Oklahoma, head of the Senate Banking Committee, and Professor Irving Fisher of Yale University, a monetary expert to whom President Roosevelt turned for advice. Fisher reputedly called Le Blanc "one of the eighteen Americans who understood money."[5] (For several years during the depression, Le Blanc, at the suggestion of Father Coughlin, gave Bishop Gallagher, Coughlin's superior, advice on the finances of the Detroit diocese.)

The other member of Coughlin's dynamic duo of monetary advisers was Robert M. Harriss, a "plump, bit-jowled commodity broker who had been active in New York politics in the Borough of Queens." *Fortune* called him a "man of means interested in the fate of the dollar."[6] A priest confidant of Coughlin recalled that Harriss had enormous wealth and at one time he was president of the Texas Ranchers' Association. As late as the 1980s, Harriss's investment partner for many years, Edward Voss, was listed among the Forbes 400.[7] In 1936, Harriss was a key figure in the financing of a number of Charles Coughlin's enterprises, including those directly linked to political action. Near the end of his life, Harriss was pivotal in the campaign to have Douglas MacArthur run for president in 1948.[8]

Under the tutelage of Le Blanc and Harriss, the radio priest was propelled into a gold revaluation campaign during his broadcast season of 1932–1933. Using the words of William Jennings Bryan, Charles Coughlin denounced "those modern pagans who have crucified us on a cross of gold" and advocated eliminating the "filthy gold standard" and replacing it with a silver standard. In response, congressional offices were swamped with letters supporting the radio priest. Free and unlimited coinage of silver, also the cry of William Jennings Bryan's silver populists at the end of the nineteenth century, now became the battle cry of a Catholic priest of the mid-1930s.

Robert Harriss was the liaison between Charles Coughlin and Senator Elmer Thomas of Oklahoma, a powerful silver advocate who introduced an amendment to the Silver Purchase Act of 1933 that greatly increased the amount of silver the federal government would be required to purchase to 95 percent of the annual output of American silver mines.[9] (A good proportion of this was mined in the senator's home state.) This legislation was a coup for many western congressmen and was, according to one historian, "the most remarkable special interest triumph of the period."[10] This large subsidy to the silver mines of the country cost the government nearly $1.5 billion over the fifteen years following its adoption.

The Roosevelt administration was reluctant to shift the nation's currency base to a silver standard and instead supported retaining a bimetal (gold and silver) monetary system. As legislative action loomed in the spring of 1934, FDR's secretary of the treasury, Henry T. Morgenthau, Jr., authorized release of a list of names of the major silver speculators. On April 28, 1934, the House Committee on Coinage, Weights and Measures cited the names of major silver hoarders. Included was an "A. Collins" of 331 Dewey Avenue, Royal Oak, Michigan, who had purchased in January, on 10 percent margin, twenty futures contracts, for March delivery. Each contract equaled 25,000 ounces, for a total of 500,000 ounces. This investment of $20,000 was made through the brokerage firm of Harriss and Voss of New York. It also listed Robert Harriss as a major holder of silver futures purchased on low margins.

When the so-called silver list was made public, reporters flocked to Amy Collins, who indicated that she had invested the funds as the treasurer of the Radio League of the Little Flower on her own volition, without informing Father Coughlin. She claimed she made the investment based on the "President's word that he would raise prices to 1926 levels." She added defiantly that "while I raise my voice against gambling and speculation, I shall continue to be its [the Radio League] financial agent and invest this surplus league money in American commodities and securities."[11]

In his next Sunday broadcast, the radio priest angrily denounced the secretary of the treasury for authorizing the release of the silver investors' names:

> Mr. Henry Morgenthau Jr. has completed his clumsy effort to protect the gold advocates, the Federal Reserve bankers and the international bankers of ill repute. . . . It was expected of Mr. Morgenthau . . . to prevent any silver legislation for the ultimate benefit of the one billion Orientals who from time immemorial have identified their trade and commerce with Gentile silver.[12]

FDR, angered by Coughlin's statement, told the head of the Catholic Welfare Conference that he "resented the statement that Father Coughlin . . . had invested funds of the Radio and the Little Flower Shrine, trusting in the word of the President. . . . The President said it was not even an investment of funds but a speculation."[13]

A slow waltz of political wariness had been in progress almost from the moment that FDR had met with Charles Coughlin. Since FDR's election in November 1932, the radio priest had tied his own identity to that of the president. This association was so firmly established in the public mind that well-known journalist Marquis Childs facetiously call Coughlin's Royal Oak office a "second White House."[14] When the priest suggested that his listeners write to President Roosevelt to express their gratitude for his leadership, "the White House mail room was inundated with hundreds of rapturous letters, so many that the normally swift replies were delayed up to several weeks."[15] Meanwhile, letters by the thousands flooded the newly created post office in Coughlin's community, Royal Oak.[16]

From the beginning of their relationship, it was apparent that FDR wanted the radio priest's backing but sought to keep him at arm's length. As he grew increasingly disenchanted with Coughlin's actions, he and his aides tried not to alienate the powerful cleric. Now this early partnership between FDR and Coughlin turned into an awkward and increasingly bitter rivalry. Flattering remarks and small favors were still exchanged between the White House and Royal Oak, but the radio priest's advice on policy issues was being ignored.[17] Then, in November

1933, an incident occurred that closely paralleled that of the Detroit "bankster" episode. Speaking to a large audience at the Hippodrome in New York, Coughlin attacked those who were critical of Roosevelt's monetary policy, singling out former governor Al Smith as an example, and he hinted that his remarks had been sanctioned by the administration. By sending a telegram to the White House staff saying he was "going the limit" in support of FDR, the priest had sought, but not obtained, official endorsement for his remarks.[18]

Although the New York City speech impressed the enemies of the administration with Coughlin's media skill, it failed to elicit any positive response from FDR.[19] By this time, Roosevelt and his staff viewed the relationship with Royal Oak as an awkward, imbalanced, and even seriously unsettling threat. Perhaps most important, this uneasy alliance was creating in the minds of the public exactly the kind of image Roosevelt did not want: that he was being guided by radical demagogues bent on undermining the economic and political structure of the nation. The mistake in dealing with Coughlin had become evident to the White House: nothing should be left open-ended. Coughlin's ambiguous role had allowed the perception to grow that the priest was part of FDR's inner circle. For his part, the priest continued to cultivate the perception that he was at the center of national power, but behind the scenes. FDR fumed to his key aide, Jim Farley, "He should run for the Presidency himself. Who the hell does he think he is!"[20]

After the Hippodrome speech, Coughlin began to realize that the president was putting him off and in private, but not yet in public, expressed anger and wounded pride. Still, he had no intention of being relegated to the status of a Jim Farley—FDR's campaign manager in the elections of 1928 and 1932—who, though intensely loyal, had been discarded when he was no longer useful. When interviewed in 1970, Coughlin told author Sheldon Marcus, "Listen. I was never stupid. I realized that the President now considered me burdensome. . . . We were supposed to be partners. He said he would rely on me. That I would be an important adviser. But he was a liar."[21]

Coughlin's ambivalence toward authority—the dependency he felt on it and his testing of its limits—is a vital key to understanding the priest's personality. It surfaced when he left the Basilian order to become a diocesan priest, freeing himself of a lifestyle of communal constraint. There were clearly marked stages in all the pivotal relationships of Coughlin's public career: an intense and almost uxorious subservience to an authority figure, followed by daring action designed to get attention, followed by a failure to gain sustained favor, followed by a sense of betrayal, and finally an embittered turning against the adored figure.

By late 1934, Coughlin had become even more frenetic, as if he were competing with the man in the White House whom he sought to impress, to counsel, and perhaps, in his most arrogant moods, to control. Failing all of this, he struck out on his own and formed his own organization in November 1934, the National Union for Social Justice (NUSJ). It was not a party, but it certainly looked like the beginning of one.

As political pundits attempted to size up what Coughlin was aiming for and how to interpret this new lobbying organization, the priest pushed ahead with its development. A critical first step was the formulation of a set of sixteen principles. Most were not detailed enough to serve as planks for a political party, but a few seemed to suggest vaguely populist political and legislative goals:

1. Liberty of conscience and education
2. A just, living annual wage for all labor
3. Nationalization of resources too important to be held by individuals
4. Private ownership of all other property
5. The use of private property to be controlled for the public good
6. The abolition of the privately owned Federal Reserve Board and the institution of a central government-owned bank
7. The return to Congress of the right to coin and regulate money
8. Control of the cost of living and the value of money by the central bank
9. Cost of production plus a fair profit for the farmer
10. The right of the laboring man to organize unions and the duty of the government to protect these organizations against the vested interests of wealth and of intellect
11. Recall of all non-productive bonds
12. Abolition of tax-exempt bonds
13. Broadening the base of taxation on the principle of ownership and ability to pay
14. Simplification of government and lightening taxation on the laboring class
15. In time of war, conscription of wealth as well as of men

16. Human rights to be held above property rights; government's chief
     concern should be with the poor; the rich can take care of them-
     selves.[22]

Coughlin sought to dissociate his new organization from conventional lobbying groups and to avoid the perception that it was merely a
vehicle for political ambition: "It is our intention to drive out of public
life the men who promised us redress . . . and have broken their promises. . . . No, the National Union is not a third political party. . . . It is political in that it proposes to support legislation favorable to the common
good of the majority of the people."[23]

Within a few weeks of its creation, the NUSJ was a potent weapon.
Shockingly, it was used against the president himself in his effort to have
the United States join the World Court. This political battle was the opening skirmish in a decade-long struggle between isolationism and internationalism, whose outcome would determine American participation in
World War II. Charles Coughlin played an important part in that drama—
and in the process jeopardized his future as a public figure.

During his incumbency as president, Herbert Hoover had delayed
submitting a proposal to the Senate that the United States join the World
Court. Now, after the proposal had languished on Capitol Hill for four
years, FDR sent it to the Senate on January 16, 1935. Straw polls predicted a White House victory, and the administration seemed confident of
winning a two-thirds majority in a Senate top-heavy with Democrats.
Had a vote been taken on January 25, a Friday, it is likely that FDR would
have achieved his goal.

In the eyes of contemporary analysts and participants, both favorable
and unfavorable to the World Court resolution, Charles Coughlin turned
the tide against the president with a radio sermon delivered on January
27, less than forty-eight hours before the vote:

> My Friends: If I am properly informed—Tuesday of this week—
> Tuesday January 29—will be remembered by our offspring as
> the day which overshadowed July 4. The one date with our inde-
> pendence. The other with our stupid betrayal! . . . Today—to-
> morrow may be too late—today, whether you can afford it or not,
> send your Senators telegrams telling them to vote "NO" on our
> entrance into the World Court. . . . Keep America safe for Amer-
> icans and not the hunting ground of international plutocrats![24]

Coughlin accused Roosevelt of subverting the national interest and of "selling out the American people to the international bankers." He charged that both the League of Nations and the World Court had been created "for the purpose of preserving by force of arms . . . [their] plutocratic system." American involvement in the international judicial body would "lead to the pilfering of Europe's $12 billion war debt to the United States, participation in another war, and the destruction of the American way of life."[25]

A flood of telegrams poured forth after the Coughlin attack. By the time of the vote, over 40,000 had been delivered to the Senate opposing U.S. participation in the World Court.[26] The messages had to be carted in wheelbarrows to the Senate Office Building. Along with the help of Huey Long, the Hearst chain of newspapers, and even Will Rogers, the radio priest had spearheaded a stunning defeat for Roosevelt. Senator Borah, a leading opponent of the court, wired Coughlin his congratulations: "How deeply indebted we are to you for the great victory. Thank you again and again."[27]

In his next radio address, on February 3, the radio priest exulted in his victory, praising the Hearst newspapers and the group of senators who had opposed the court, calling them "second only to the . . . stalwart patriots who signed the Declaration of Independence." Coughlin explained to his listeners that "through the medium of the radio and the telegram you possess the power to override the invisible government; to direct your representatives on individual matters of legislation."[28]

Coughlin's outcry against the World Court resolution had struck several responsive chords in the American consciousness, among them anger at Europe's default on World War I debts and fears that European intrigue would lead to U.S. involvement in another war. One key effect of the resolution's rejection was to make isolationist legislation and attitudes more legitimate and to label those who opposed withdrawal from international cooperation as un-American. The victory engineered by the radio priest and his allies aroused a dormant but growing opposition that would act as a brake on many efforts by the Roosevelt administration to engage in preventive actions against the rising dictators in Europe— Hitler and Mussolini.

In explaining the reasons for his defeat in the World Court fight, FDR acknowledged "the deluge of letters, telegrams, Resolutions of Legislatures, and the radio talks of people like Coughlin." FDR suggested to his future secretary of war, Henry L. Stimson, that "in normal times the radio and other appeals by them [Coughlin and other demagogues] would not have been effective. However, these are not normal times; people are jumpy and very ready to run after strange gods."[29] A letter sent to FDR's key adviser, Louis Howe, from a local party official made this assessment of the radio priest's influence:

> Say what you please, suppress it as the press had done, the fact is that the credit or discredit for the defeat of the World Court resolution . . . belongs exclusively to Father Coughlin. . . . Now that he has achieved such a personal triumph in one of the most important international matters of this generation, and in a most spectacular way, having set up the killing job only a few days ago, he now becomes a bigger menace to the President and to our government than ever.[30]

Flushed with victory over the World Court controversy, Coughlin now pushed forward in his efforts to restructure the Federal Reserve banking system, calling for a full takeover of state banks and the creation of an all-powerful national bank. In early 1935 his drift away from the Roosevelt administration became more evident. Was he aiming to form a new political party?

On the evening of May 22, 1935, Coughlin set forth his ideas for the National Union to an audience at Madison Square Garden. This throng of enthusiastic listeners was described by the sedate *New York Times* as a "reincarnation of the multitude that stormed the old Garden to hear William Jennings Bryan in his arraignment of the gold standard in 1896."[31] Reportedly, 1,160 police were required to keep it in order. The response was surpassed only by the greeting for Charles Lindbergh after his historic 1927 flight across the Atlantic. By 9:15 in the evening, 23,000 persons had paid 50 cents admission, including 6,500 people who heard the speech from the basement. The crowd was described as "young" and hailing their "new emancipator," who set forth his populist manifesto:

> One hundred years ago Samuel Morse perfected the telegraph. This invention plays an important part in the restoration of democracy of the American people. Real democracy is not only satisfied to elect suitable representatives to Congress. It is likewise interested in the passage of specific legislation. The National Union, employing not only the radio, but also utilizing the

telegraph, or when time permits, the nationally owned post office, proposes to revive the meaning of democracy as it was con-
ceived by the fathers of this country.[32]

Coughlin sent a warning specifically to "the persuasive lobbies of the
United States Steel Corporation, of the motor industry, the United States
Chamber of Commerce, of the American Association of Bankers [who
have] kept their professional advocates at Washington." In a stirring climax, he declared: "Behold those whose feet cluttered the steps of the
White House and of the Capitol. Representatives of wealth, representa-
tion of class legislation! . . . The National Union openly professes that it
is an articulate, organized lobby of the people!"[33]

The formation of the NUSJ was a significant event, both for the politics of the day and with regard to the growing importance of mass media
as a social force. It represented not only the fusing of politics with
celebrity but marked the beginning of audience participation, in which
the passive mass became an action group. It would be repeated in the televangelism of the 1970s and 1980s, in the Moral Majority, and in the political candidacies of other religious and celebrity figures, such as the
Rev. Pat Robertson.

In February 1935 Frank Murphy, whom FDR had appointed as governor
general of the Philippines, was recalled from his post for a consultation
with the president. Over the next several months, he played a central role
in assessing Charles Coughlin's ambitions and loyalty to the New Deal.
In his first political fence-mending mission, Murphy met with the priest
at dawn in Detroit, following a meeting of the Michigan Democrats the
evening before. The two met for several hours, including a lunch, and
both tried to put a purely social face on the exchange.

During the next few months, Coughlin seemed to drift further from
the New Deal and more frequently and more openly hinted at a political
break with FDR. On the second anniversary of Roosevelt's inauguration,
he praised the good intentions of the New Deal while describing it as
"two years of surrender, two years of matching the puerile, puny brains
of idealists against the virile viciousness of business and finance, two
years of economic failure."[34] Yet only a week later, the priest declared, "I
still proclaim to you that it is either 'Roosevelt or Ruin.' I support him today and will support him tomorrow." Just a month later, Coughlin warned
his radio listeners of the dictatorial tendencies of the New Deal.[35]

When Murphy was hospitalized with a serious illness in the late spring of 1935, Coughlin visited him several times. Murphy then wrote to FDR's secretary, Missy Le Hand, that "discordant elements" would, "beginning about next January get on the Roosevelt bandwagon" and Coughlin would "not be aligned with disaffected elements."[36]

After he returned to the Philippines in the summer of 1935, Murphy received a stream of pessimistic political assessments from Charles Coughlin: "I feel that I should tell you of a few observations. . . . Not one New England State will go for President Roosevelt. His cause is definitely lost there. . . . New York is quite hostile, of course. Pennsylvania is dubious and is swinging away from him. Huey Long can control at least three States, directing them away from Mr. Roosevelt. . . . Michigan and Illinois are practically lost to the cause of the Democrats."[37]

He also suggested deep antipathy toward FDR: "The President's policies are un-American. Norman Thomas is a piker compared to Roosevelt. After all, Thomas stands for a poor brand of Russian communism." By the end of the summer of 1935, prospects for a reconciliation with FDR on Coughlin's part appeared to grow remote. Coughlin charged that FDR had "broken every promise that he has made . . . he seeks means and methods closely allied with socialism and communism. . . . For the most part I shall remain silent until Mr. Roosevelt will commit himself either to retain or reject the present advisers."[38]

Roosevelt had another key channel to the political intentions of Charles Coughlin: Joseph P. Kennedy. Evidence of a growing friendship between the two Irish Catholic public figures had been growing since the first Roosevelt campaign.[39] Now, three years later, Kennedy was heading up a major New Deal agency, the Securities and Exchange Commission, and was to be one of Roosevelt's biggest reelection campaigners. He was also "fascinated by Coughlin's talent on the radio. He revelled in what the priest could accomplish. He was intrigued by Coughlin's use of power."[40]

As Coughlin's political intentions grew more difficult to assess, FDR may well have speculated that his two emissaries to Royal Oak were not achieving their goal. In fact, the more contact each seemed to have with the priest, the more they were being used to send a message of despair, and even divisiveness. In one letter, Coughlin alluded to the leftward trend of the New Deal as a reason that he might not support Roosevelt in 1936, inserting the comment, "Joseph Kennedy agrees with me." One day earlier, Kennedy had written to bolster confidence in the president's ability to overcome the climate of criticism emerging in the press around the country. He added a handwritten note on Coughlin, saying, "I heard from the Rev. Father this morning and he is more disgusted than ever."[41] In turn, in his letter mailed a day later to Frank Murphy, Coughlin mentioned an invitation he had received from FDR: " 'P.S': Will go to Hyde Park this coming Tuesday to see R. Will let you know results."[42]

When Coughlin arrived at about 3:00 A.M. on the morning of September 10, Joe Kennedy met him at the train station. After joining Kennedy and Coughlin for breakfast, the president came directly to the point of the meeting: "Cards on the table, Padre. Cards on the table. Why are you cooling off to me? Why are you criticizing the things I'm doing?"[43]

Roosevelt had tried to keep Coughlin's visit a secret, but reporters got wind of it and in a press conference two days later questioned FDR about the meeting. "It was a social visit," declared the president. When asked about whether there would be a follow-up talk, Roosevelt replied, "Not that I know of." When queried about Joe Kennedy's role in the meeting, FDR answered, "I have no idea, except to act as chauffeur, I guess."[44]

When asked to stay for dinner by the president on the evening of the marathon Hyde Park meeting, Coughlin and Kennedy had demurred, claiming that "they already had made plans to dine with a friend in the Berkshires."[45] What Roosevelt did not know was that the friend, in Great Barrington, Massachusetts, was a key to bankrolling a potentially powerful political challenge to Roosevelt. Coughlin was preparing a third-party bid.

What transpired at the Hyde Park meeting remains a subject of speculation. No documentation exists that sheds light on this last effort to make peace between FDR and Charles Coughlin, who were to become, in a few months' time, full-fledged political adversaries.[46]

Over the years, Coughlin offered a number of versions of the meeting. In one variation, he said that he had been eager to meet with Roosevelt but had been admonished to stay away by his bishop: "I therefore went immediately to see Gallagher, who gave his consent to the visit." Coughlin indicated that Bishop Gallagher gave him a photostatic copy of a check written to the Mexican Communist party signed by Secretary of Treasury Henry Morgenthau and was told to ask Roosevelt for an explanation. In the same interview the priest recalled:

I told him [FDR] that I wasn't criticizing anything that he was doing, but only some of the administrators. He said, "Come on, Padre, the truth." I said, "We have bad news from Mexico. This is it." I took the photostat of the check from my pocket and showed it to him. As he was looking at it I told him that Michael Gallagher's afraid we are going soft on communism.[47]

Two years later, Coughlin was interviewed again and asked: "Was there one thing in particular, one issue or one incident, that caused you to break with the Roosevelt administration?" He replied:

There was, but I can't talk about the specific details because there are some people living that can't stand this thing. But the fact was that some evidence had come to the attention of my Bishop which indicated that certain officials in the Roosevelt administration were helping the Communist cause overseas. Well, Bishop Gallagher called me to his home one day, it was in the summer of 1935, and he said, "Now Charles, you're through supporting the New Deal and Mr. Roosevelt," and he showed me the evidence. [When] we [he and Joe Kennedy] went down to [see] the President . . . and . . . he asked why I hadn't been around much, I sort of hemmed and hawed a bit, so finally he told Joe to "go look at the pigs"—he didn't have any pigs, of course; it was just a little joke he used to make. Joe laughed and went out, and then I showed the President the evidence that Michael Gallagher had received.[48]

A third interview, conducted in 1970, was not meant for publication. When asked about his break with Roosevelt, he responded:

Well, it happened over this entrance into war. . . . I knew we were going into it. And I was pledged as all those around him to keep my mouth shut. It was a state secret. . . .

For eight hours that day I sat in with Mr. Roosevelt telling my version of why we shouldn't get into this, telling him that Marxism, no matter what faith it was, would have to explode against both Christians and Jews. . . .

I also tried to persuade him that if we got in it that it was go-

ing to be the downfall of the United States and the persecution of
the Jews. . . . I says, "Don't go into this thing because the poor
Jews will be the ones to suffer from this thing and they have suffered enough. You can't depend on this Marxist thing in Russia
and, as a matter of fact, Nazism is only another breed of Marxism, one's the left wing and the other's the right wing of the same
bird of prey. Let them fight it out between them. And I hope they
destroy one another!"[49]

There is no way to validate any of the different accounts Coughlin offered his interviewers, although each contains a grain of truth as to
the issues that divided the priest and FDR. No documentation for the
"Mexican check" exists; the matter may at best be attributed to Roosevelt's friendly relations with the Mexican government, whose anticlerical policies at the time rankled many Catholics. And certainly the issue
of avoiding U.S. involvement in Europe's problems was a major focus of
the radio priest's politics, already evident in the World Court fight. In his
comments to interviewer Eric Thuma in 1970, Coughlin does reveal one
of his most frequently asserted rationales for his obsession with the role
of Jews in world affairs and his alleged desire to protect them from unjust
persecution.

Two months after his meeting with Roosevelt, Coughlin expressed
anger over the direction FDR was taking. Writing to Frank Murphy in the
Philippines, he recounted, "I was down to see Mr. Roosevelt and spent
eight hours with him during which time I did most of the talking." Before
his meeting with FDR, Coughlin's criticism to Murphy had carried a note
of overconfidence that suggested the New Deal was about to collapse.
Now added to the drumbeat of attack was a note of cynical, almost paranoid resignation that the New Deal would be taken over by subversive
forces: "I sincerely fear that Mr. Roosevelt . . . will be re-elected unless
an unforeseen miracle occurs." Coughlin went on to warn Murphy "of a
plot [to] insure an FDR victory for the purpose of ruining him entirely . . . and the rest of the Jews who surround him."[50]

Coughlin and FDR met once again, and for the last time, early in
1936. It was obvious, however, that their final break had occurred at that
Hyde Park meeting the previous fall. On November 17, 1935, the *New
York Times* had carried the headline story: "Coughlin Breaks with Roosevelt."

5

"I Know the Pulse of the People"

After reading and hearing many of his [Coughlin's] speeches, I am struck by their technical similarity to those of Hitler. . . . Like Hitler's the priest's speeches tap the underlying prejudices of listeners.

Raymond Gram Swing, *Forerunners of American Fascism*

IF THERE WAS GOING to be a serious third-party challenge to FDR in the 1936 presidential campaign, the radio priest would need to call on his Wall Street crowd contacts in order to provide at least the initial funding for such a grandiose undertaking.

Following the daylong meeting between FDR and Charles Coughlin, the president suggested that his two visitors stay overnight. The priest demurred, indicating that he and Joe Kennedy had an appointment "with a friend in Great Barrington." This friend, an obscure figure, would be mentioned only once in the national media, at the very close of the radio priest's political career. In April 1942, the mysterious backer was called to testify before a federal grand jury investigating charges of sedition against Coughlin. Until then, Francis Keelon had managed to keep his media profile restricted to the local papers or to obscure references in the national press.

Keelon not only bankrolled Coughlin in his 1936 political campaign but was at the very center of the priest's career from the moment they first became acquainted, on an ocean voyage in 1932. In those early days, Keelon's home was often discussed in the New England media. The *Berkshire Courier* wrote in September 1935:

71

Father Coughlin arrived Tuesday evening after spending the day in conference with President Roosevelt. . . . About 9:00 . . . a movie camera sound truck established what appeared to be a movie studio in the Keelon living room. A battery of strong lights were set up, a movie camera, ponderous in size, mounted on a tripod, and extensive sound apparatus was hauled in, so that Father Coughlin could tell the world by means of newsreel of his tribute to [Huey] Long.[1]

Calling Coughlin "one of the most distinguished visitors to the Berkshires in recent years," the local newspaper made the most of its story, yet over the next several days, local reporters frustratingly failed to discover the details of the continuing conference inside Keelon's estate, Hilltop.

Tracking Coughlin from Boston to Great Barrington, reporters from national syndicates converged on the Keelon estate but learned that no one had been at the house for days. On another occasion they found two visitors present—Thomas O'Brien of Massachusetts and Congressman William Lemke of North Dakota—and conjectured that these individuals would "figure prominently in the political news of the country during the coming year."[2] In fact, both would head the national presidential ticket for a Coughlin-inspired political party.

Francis Keelon was one of a number of self-made entrepreneurs whom Coughlin was drawn to in his public career but whose background and business dealings were often less than sterling. He was at one time a vice president of Irving Trust and had a seat on the stock exchange at a very young age. His financial career was mercurial.[3] Joanna Keelon described her half-brother as a "person who didn't talk very much" and "who always looked sort of angry. . . . Frank was not affectionate or warm. . . . He had . . . a superiority complex. . . . I couldn't talk to him. . . . I was afraid of him."[4]

Joanna was a houseguest at the several estates owned by her brother, including Hilltop, overlooking Lake Mansfield. Sold to Keelon in April 1935, the seventy-five acre estate had a large colonial home, stables, and servants' quarters. The builder and first owner had been one of the designers of the Chicago World's Fair in 1933. Joanna referred to the home as "Coughlin's House." She described her brother as signing the mortgage and deed of ownership, with the radio priest being a silent partner.[5]

There was a special feature in the study, beyond the fireplace against which Coughlin casually leaned as he hosted the impromptu press conference in the first days that his Union party was born. On one occasion, according to Joanna, her brother Dale "told me after we had come back from a swim at the lake, 'I want to show you something, but don't tell anybody that I did it.' So he took me into the library. Then he goes over to the fireplace and presses something. And all of a sudden all the books [across the wall] open up, and what's there? An altar. A Catholic altar with candles, everything! And then Dale says to me: 'This is where Charles says Mass when we're too drunk to go down to the church!' . . . He [Francis Keelon] and Charlie said Mass many times when he was stinking drunk!"[6]

Joanna remembers one particular weekend at Hilltop that shocked her and raises a key question about Coughlin and fascism in America. She recalls a guest who said, "'What a shame, Jews are walking around, free to enjoy this country!' . . . They said Hitler was the greatest man that every lived. . . . So I'm the only one around that didn't like Hitler. . . . They had a German flag there, draped over a table, the German flag!"[7]

As the key 1936 campaign decisions were formulated in both major political parties, a Republican party supporter wrote to a top aide of former president Hoover that "the day of machine politics is over. Mussolini, Stalin or Hitler did not arrive by way of an organization, and in this country Father Coughlin has shown the futility of the so-called organized parties."[8] In such a pessimistic climate, Coughlin thrived as a borrower, improvisor, and spontaneous promoter. He sensed the country's malaise and walked a careful line between openly embracing any foreign ideology and attacking others for having done so. The restless emotionalism of his career was a logic that defied conventional political categorization.

Despite the New Deal, a powerful wind blew from Europe across the national political landscape—a rumor that democracy had failed, that it was outmoded, that new "isms" must be the basis for solving the economic and social problems of the country. There was what bordered on hysteria about the fragile future of the American way of life. One of the best-selling books that year, *It Can't Happen Here*, written by Sinclair Lewis, was a fictionalized account describing how America might become a fascist dictatorship in the wake of the 1936 presidential election.[9] Popular journalist and radio commentator Raymond Gram Swing's *Forerunners of American Fascism* was a nonfiction book with a similar message.

Swing cited Coughlin and Huey Long as two of the most dangerous antidemocratic figures on the contemporary political stage.[10]

Could America be an exception, or would it succumb to the viruses
infecting Europe? The alienation emerging in American society toward
established parties and politicians—what historian Arthur Schlesinger,
Jr., called "rumblings in the night"—spoke of American fascism. Often
the argument was presented in terms of inevitable choice: communism or
fascism. Harvard-educated Lawrence Dennis first wrote of the defects of
America's economic system in 1932 in *Is Capitalism Doomed?* followed
four years later by *The Coming American Fascism*, which argued "that
only under a disciplined central state could the evils of finance be curtailed and the folly of a collectivist economy avoided." He saw 1936 as
the year in which a "substantial number of the in-elite, adopting a clear-
cut fascist ideology, could easily unite under a common political banner . . . the out-elite and the masses in a movement along orderly and
nonviolent lines of procedure to effect the most desirable sort of fascist
revolution conceivable."[11] In describing fascism as superior to both
communism and liberalism, Dennis cited "Coughlin and his League for
Social Justice . . . [as] both humane and helpful [in demanding the correction of] the injustices of the present social situation."[12]

Critics of the New Deal and of FDR saw the large-scale efforts to
bring government into the economic sphere as sure signs of socialism.
Regulation of business through production quotas and price setting
smacked of Italian fascism, with its integration of business, labor, and
centralized governmental coordination. For FDR and the country as a
whole, 1935 and 1936 would bring a welter of new movements and new
challenges, and the era would give birth to the term "lunatic fringe."[13]

Father Coughlin's unconventional mass support raised fears about
his political goals. Many on the political left viewed him as representing
the threat of fascism. In a March 1935 national radio address, New Deal
official General Hugh Johnson told Coughlin: "Someone sent me a par-
allel of what both you and Adolf Hitler proposed and preached and they
are as alike as peas in a pod. As a foreign-born you could not be president
but you could be a Reichsführer—just as the Austrian Adolf became dictator of Germany. . . . You have not chosen the swastika. You have a more
sacred device. . . . No swastikas for Nazis—but a cross!"[14]

Because of an equal-time agreement at NBC, the vituperative verbal
sparring match between Johnson and Coughlin lasted for several weeks.
Whether FDR had officially sanctioned the attacks on Coughlin is not

known, but the exchange certainly seemed like a trial balloon. Johnson's mudslinging provided an opportunity for Coughlin to paint himself as a victim of an establishment smear: "The moneychangers have . . . marshalled their forces behind the leadership of a chocolate soldier for the purpose of driving a priest out of public affairs."[15]

Even some of Coughlin's followers found his pronouncements menacing. One disillusioned backer wrote to him in March 1935, "I fail to see . . . more than sheer destructive criticism in your utterances. . . . The mask is becoming dangerously apparent. The tone, as well as the substance of your speeches is . . . more fascistic than truly democratic."[16] And Ruth Mugglebee, in a second edition of her biography, expressed the fear that Coughlin had become "a highly dangerous leader of the mob."[17] Among the public as a whole too, criticism spread from the left to others. New Deal critic Westbrook Pegler called the National Union for Social Justice a "one-man organization subject to the same personal dictation as Hitler's Nazis and Mussolini's Fascists."[18]

The vagueness of goals and Coughlin's tightly held power suggested to many that the NUSJ was an authoritarian enterprise strongly reminiscent of European fascism. In June 1935, the priest declared, while testifying in Congress, that "if Congress fails to carry through the President's suggestions, I foresee a revolution far greater than the French Revolution." Was he suggesting an end to democratic government? In an extensive interview defending the NUSJ as democratic, Coughlin denied such accusations: "Is it fascist in form? Absolutely not! . . . Just how the National Union will function is being developed according to the multitude of circumstances determining conditions in each district. . . . But we reject atheistic communism! We disavow racial Hitlerism! We do not accept fascism!"[19]

Coughlin freely acknowledged his one-man rule over he NUSJ. He appointed the executive board, wrote the constitution, drafted resolutions, proposed legislation, established committees, dictated the rules and regulations, and appointed the national officers.[20] Initially, he stated, "I am the Union for Social Justice."[21] To maintain tight control over local units of NUSJ, he empowered himself and his appointed trustees with incontestable authority to expel anyone from the organization, a position he justified by saying that he wanted only "those who will support our principles *at all times*."[22] But he described his position as only temporary, until the NUSJ could hold a national convention, which it did in the summer of 1936.

*   *   *

Coughlin drew to his side a number of talented political publicists and organizers. One of them was Philip Cortelyan Johnson, who saw in the radio priest a focus for his own emotional and intellectual drive. In later
decades, Johnson would achieve success as one of the world's most
renowned architects. When in league with Coughlin, he acted as both political organizer and strategist: seeking the advancement of the leader he
thought could solve America's economic problems.

Born into wealth—his family's business was the White Sewing
Machine Company of Cleveland—Johnson graduated from Harvard in
1930 with a degree in fine arts. In searching for meaning and focus in
his life at a time of social upheaval, Johnson was still unsure of his future
profession. During several summers in the 1930s, the young student
took time away from his graduate studies to travel across Europe, where
he heard Hitler speak. He became so enamored of European right-
wing trends that in December 1934, he, along with his friend Alan
Blackburn, formed the National party. The *New York Herald Tribune*
noted, "Gray shirts are worn at meetings, but Mr. Johnson sternly denies any Fascist leanings. The party has about 100 members. . . . The
aims of the party seem to be to provide an entirely new form of government."[23]

The National party proved unable to attract any significant interest,
though, so Johnson went south to Louisiana, where he worked on behalf
of Huey Long. When the maverick political figure was assassinated in
September 1935, Johnson and Blackburn traveled to Royal Oak "because
he [Coughlin] seemed the most dynamic populist at the time."[24]

Coughlin began publishing a nationally circulated weekly newspaper, *Social Justice*, in March 1936 and asked to do some writing and
serve as a National Union campaign organizer. Johnson recalls preparing
"his big rallies. . . . The largest he ever had was in Chicago. . . . The great
[Soldier's] field was so crowded you couldn't move. . . . Of course the
police were all pro-Coughlin, especially the Irish. We said, 'We want the
sirens and all the trimmings,' so we went into Chicago with sirens blasting! We had a photograph of Father Coughlin sixty feet high. That was
our high point."[25]

"When he spoke it was a thrill like Hitler. And, the magnetism was
uncanny. . . . The excitement was . . . it was like getting drunk. I try to
think what it was like then. It was so intoxicating, there's no use saying
what he talked about. . . . The yelling and screaming drowned out any

rock concert you ever heard of. . . . The days were so heady that . . . that's the part I cannot transfer to my friends of the public today. That feeling of tension that we all felt, and the great relief that a great orator could impart to us."[26]

With an audience in the tens of millions, several million of whom the radio priest claimed were enrolled in the NUSJ, speculation about Coughlin's role in the 1936 presidential election became an almost daily obsession of news journalists. Rumors that the priest might make a bid for the presidency surfaced but were quickly scotched by the recognition that his Canadian birth prevented any direct line to the White House. Yet with the backing of a cadre of wealthy individuals such as Francis Keelon, the nickname for Coughlin's weekly broadcast, "The Hour of Power," took on a menacing aura. To his opponents, the radio priest was Rasputinesque. FDR even conducted a secret survey of Coughlin's financial sources and toyed with the idea of challenging the priest's naturalization as a U.S. citizen.[27]

As the 1936 presidential election campaign began to heat up, two major questions were on the minds of American political observers and, in particular, leaders of both major parties: Would Coughlin act on rumored plans for a third political party? (signs pointed clearly to yes), and, Who would his allies be? As befit his "both ends against the middle" role, Father Coughlin sought out and, in turn, was wooed by groups across the entire political spectrum, Republicans and conservatives included.

Coughlin painted a picture of a titanic struggle between himself and Roosevelt, and he sought allies among the president's political enemies, all now united in bitter opposition to FDR's bid for a second term. He rallied his followers—1.2 million of them NUSJ members—and steered them between Democrats and Republicans, attacking both parties as servants of the "money changers."[28]

Although the NUSJ was organized on the basis of congressional districts, Coughlin steadfastly denied any desire to form the organization into a political party:

If we planned to be a political party we would plan to place candidates in the field for congressional office. This is foreign to the concept of the National Union. . . . As a matter of fact we seek no candidate for political office. Candidates must seek us. We believe in perfecting the two main political parties in this nation. We believe in rescuing them from the ward heelers and the un-

seen rulers of the financial world. We do not believe in establishing a third or fourth party which would only succeed in adding
confusion to confusion.[29]

Coughlin was now close to playing the role he had most relished four
years earlier: arbiter of the fortunes of both major political parties. This
did not in fact occur, but he was able to fashion an amazing piece of theater in 1936. The plot unfolded as a play in three acts. First was an en-
nobling effort to escape tawdry political parties. The middle act was a
virtual one-man show that seemed, even to many previous admirers, a
selfish exercise in megalomania. Act 3 featured a Hamlet-like detach-
ment from a political creation that, when failing to achieve its promise,
caused its star protagonist to retreat into a martyred state of despair.

As his public identification with the New Deal waned, Coughlin
sought common ground with one of the most reactionary organizations in
the nation, the Liberty League. Funded and organized by bankers, industrialists, and the wealthy, this group had been lambasted by the radio
priest in October 1934 for "seeking the destruction of the New Deal."
Coughlin had said that the Liberty League was "the mouthpiece of
bankers, one of whose officers profiteered on shells and munitions as his
agent went about the world stirring up war in the name of peace."[30] Yet
by the spring of 1936, rumors of a Liberty League–Coughlin alliance had
reached the press:

> Although no responsible leader dignifies the [Liberty] League
> candidacy . . . it has sent the high command into a state of jitters.
> They shudder at the thought that an [Al] Smith-[William] Coha-
> lan, [Richard] Colby revolt may swing millions of Democratic
> conservatives against the New Deal. . . . But plans are under
> way to nail the protest of the Liberty Leaguers against FDR's
> renomination. According to talk in hotel lobbies, ex-justice Co-
> halan . . . is Father Coughlin's legal adviser in New York. Key
> Democrats say they have legal and political evidence that Mr.
> Cohalan is closely associated with the Detroit priest.[31]

One of the most fascinating and least publicized political machinations of the 1936 election season was Coughlin's flirtation with a potential Republican candidate whom the priest had four years earlier labeled
the Archangel of Wall Street: Herbert Hoover. Despite the obvious ideo-

logical and personality differences between the two men—taciturn Hoover had muttered his deep antipathy to the priest to his closest intimates, who had attributed to Coughlin a major role in defeating their candidate—a courting process took place between Coughlin and the backers of the ex-president. In presenting himself to the Hoover forces, Coughlin sought to remake his image from one of leftist radical to "Mr. Republican."

In mid-May 1936, Coughlin told reporters he foresaw no third political party and had no personal interest in one: "Such an organization would be merely a gathering of malcontents with personal grudges to bear." Yet interviewed on May 27, he hinted at a political conversion, indicating that "the only hope for saving America lay in a 'renovated Republican Party.'" He added that "only if the GOP frontrunner, [Alf] Landon, won the nomination even that hope would be lost and that the NUSJ would be forced to concentrate activities in Congress and wait until 1940 for any effort to influence the presidential election." On the same day, he told the *New York Sun* that "a renovated Republican Party possessing a contrite heart for its former misdeeds and an honest standard-bearer in whom I could repose complete confidence are all that are necessary to convert this nation from ruinous Rooseveltism." A week later, he reiterated the key theme of his political respectability: "Christ would advocate what I am advocating; if I am a radical Christ is a radical!"[32]

A number of Republican stalwarts wanted to co-opt Coughlin, a strategy with an advantage to their party—either as a way to capture his constituency or to take the limelight away from him. Yet there were dangers inherent in adopting Coughlin, as FDR and his advisers had discovered following the 1932 election. One Hoover backer wrote in 1935, "It would certainly seem that Huey Long and Father Coughlin have become a real menace to the Administration; but it would also seem like playing with nitroglycerin to lend them any encouragement in the hope that as a result of their opposition a conservative will come to power."[33] Still, some of Hoover's advisers pressed on. Wrote one of them:

> It was a great mistake to ignore Father Coughlin. Believe it or not, it is my firm conviction that any candidate that Father Coughlin puts his thumbs down on will have one hell of a time electing himself, and to that end I have always wished that Mr. Hoover would say some little thing in approbation. . . . [He]

might well say that if . . . Coughlin is doing anything, he is
teaching the American people to think for themselves. . . . I
would not care in what manner he endorses . . . but I am sure that
some slight endorsement of that kind would change the opinion
of Mr. Hoover among ten or twelve million voters and certainly
that portion that was Catholic.[34]

As the Republican strategy for the upcoming party convention crys-
tallized, backdoor negotiations began in earnest between Herbert Hoover
and Charles Coughlin. Through mutual friends, the former president's
aides began to approach the radio priest directly. One intermediary, in a
memo to Hoover, summarized Coughlin's position as he understood it:
"Roosevelt is positively communistic and must be removed. Our troubles
are not from the capitalistic system but from errors made which can be
rectified, and Republicans are best to do it." The priest was said to be "ir-
revocably against Roosevelt and Landon . . . if Landon is nominated
[FDR's campaign manager Jim Farley's] dream will be realized, as they
know they can blow him out of the water and lick him easily." Coughlin
was also quoted as saying, "Mr. Hoover . . . is absolutely sincere," but acknowledging that Mr. Hoover "will have a job getting action at the convention."[35] Indeed that was the case.
    Without any opposition, the Republicans nominated Alf Landon as
their 1936 presidential standard-bearer. Only after did even a suggestion
of the Coughlin-Hoover alliance leak out. Under the heading "Strange
Bedfellows," Drew Pearson reported that "Coughlin told his friends that
moments before Hoover's speech at the Republican Convention . . . the
priest had received two long-distance telephone calls from the ex-President." According to Pearson, Coughlin was told that Hoover "was going
to blast the Federal Reserve System as revised by the New Deal Banking
Act of 1935. At the last minute, however, Hoover changed his mind . . .
and deleted all references to the radio priest's pet hate."[36]
    It is difficult to judge how serious Coughlin was about his overtures
to Hoover or, for that matter, whether campaign strategists for the former
president felt capable of effectively co-opting the radio priest. There is
also the exaggeration always present in Coughlin's recounting of events
to both friends and foes. Coughlin, in the last years of his life, offered effusive praise of Hoover, and even claimed that they had met in a face-to-
face discussion during his presidency, much as the priest had done with
FDR.[37]

How can we explain the strange bedfellows of 1936? The flirtation that Coughlin engaged in might have seemed inconsistent to many, just plain expedient to others, an ideological sellout to his followers. Such views fail to consider that from the earliest days of his fame, Coughlin declared himself to be above conventions of ordinary politics and to have entered that arena not as simply another competing figure but as someone who had higher goals. Fighting against the World Court, for example, he worked closely with the right-wing William Randolph Hearst. Coughlin was a bit ahead of his time in splitting his ticket—that is, supporting issues identified with the traditional left (cheap currency and controls on the economic elite) while also favoring ideas of the traditional right ("America First" foreign policy and a kind of ultranationalism focused on white Christian ethnicity). Given his unorthodox attacking of both left and right while borrowing from each, the radio priest was a free pragmatist, and as one who held no elective office and was responsible only to himself, his church, and his army of supporters, he was doubly free.

In his search for an alliance with his former political foe in the months preceding the 1936 presidential campaign, Coughlin assured Herbert Hoover's representatives that his NUSJ would remain "independent of [the followers of the deceased] Huey Long and other radical groups." Moreover, he had "already rejected bids from them." With regard to a third-party move if the Republicans failed to nominate an acceptable candidate, Coughlin equivocated, saying that "he hoped it would not be necessary."[38] In fact, he was already well along the road to forming an alliance with two individuals and their attendant supporters that would give the election of 1936 the flavor of a battle over the American political system.

6

"Two and a Half Rival Messiahs"

According to advices [*sic*] received today from persons close to Father Coughlin, I learn that his primary purpose . . . is to test the strength of his movement. He has no hope of winning but is willing to sacrifice some of his followers in order to prove his political power.

A party official to FDR, June 22, 1936

WITH THE ASSASSINATION of Huey Long in September 1935, the most serious threat of a fringe political movement challenging the Roosevelt administration had been removed. Like Coughlin, Long had been a close ally of FDR but had broken with him over a range of issues, mainly the Louisiana "Kingfish's" plan for the redistribution of private wealth.

Long's grandiose plan called for a drastic form of graduated income tax. After a taxpayer earned $1 million, strict limits would be placed on his or her individual wealth and inheritance—what was called a "capital levy tax." At the $8 million level, the levy would be 100 percent. "No one would have much more than three or four million dollars to the person."[1] In February 1934, Huey Long had announced the formation of Share Our Wealth clubs. This new grassroots political organization would develop on a national scale what Long had created within Louisiana: "a widespread network of supporters with whom he could retain constant communication" and which formed the basis of a new political party. The local clubs would serve as the vehicle for lobbying on behalf of the new system of tax codes—"the Long Plan."[2]

While several former aides to the slain leader fought over control of the spoils and influence systems that Long had built up, one individual declared himself heir to perhaps the most valuable property in the legacy: the national network of Share Our Wealth clubs, which he had established from California to the Deep South in the last two years of his life. The man in question had been one of his bodyguards and was an ordained Protestant preacher with a reputation for rabble-rousing oratory that was without rival anywhere else in the country. His name was Gerald L. [Lyman] K. [Kenneth] Smith.[3]

Despite Smith's claims to inheriting Huey Long's legacy, he found himself in a power struggle with other associates of the late political wizard. By the spring of 1936 most of the Share Our Wealth clubs had disbanded.[4]

Before Huey Long's assassination, fears that he and Coughlin might forge a political alliance were of serious concern to FDR and his entourage. The two, though not close friends, had met several times, and since both had defected from the New Deal, it seemed likely that they would find common cause.[5] With Long's death, the threat of a powerful rural southern and urban Catholic populist revolt diminished.[6] Would Smith and Coughlin revive that possibility? When asked in 1970 by Coughlin biographer Sheldon Marcus how they first met, Smith recalled it had been arranged by Robert Harriss, who knew Huey Long and was a key adviser to Coughlin.[7] The priest later told one interviewer that Smith "frightened" him, and to another interviewer he characterized Smith as a "viper . . . a leech . . . who was anti-Christian, anti-semitic and anti-God."[8] Mutually suspicious from the beginning of their association in 1936, Charles Coughlin and Gerald Smith were soon competing for honors as the best crowd-arousing orators in the nation.

Both men were joined in the "lunatic fringe" protest politics of the moment by a third, and incongruent, personality, Dr. Francis E. Townsend. Tall, gaunt, and white haired, Townsend was a physician in his sixties whose mild demeanor contrasted sharply with the flamboyance of his two partners. The three would form a brief and uneasy alliance.

Townsend had developed a rapidly growing national movement centered on the needs of the elderly. As he recounted it later, he was shaving one day in 1933 when he saw three elderly women sifting through garbage bags in his alley for food: "A torrent of invectives tore at me . . . the big blast of all the bitterness that had been building in me for years. . . . I want all the neighbors to hear me. . . . I want God Almighty to hear me! I'm going to shout until the whole country hears!"[9] Thus was born, or so the self-proclaimed leader alleged, what was to be the Townsend Old Age Revolving Pension Fund.

Townsend proposed that the crisis of the depression and the problems of the elderly could be alleviated in one bold stroke: everyone over age sixty would be provided with a monthly federal pension of $150 (later changed to $200), on the condition that the money was spent right away and thereby used to pump up the economy. A nationwide transactions tax on retail and wholesale purchases would finance the system. Although the idea was not new, local Townsend Clubs quickly spread the concept across the country, and the *Townsend National Weekly* began publication in 1935 to further the aims of the movement.

Townsend began mobilizing his supporters for an assault on the U.S. Congress, since the Roosevelt administration strongly opposed the plan. But when the proposal was introduced in the House, backers failed to win a roll-call vote. Fearful of being identified as blockers of the plan, two hundred representatives had absented themselves when the issue came up. Despite this early 1935 defeat, the Townsend Clubs continued to grow and remain strong.

In public, Townsend professed ignorance about Father Coughlin and his movement. In fact, Townsend had written to the priest early in 1935 and, after receiving an invitation in the fall of the year, traveled to Royal Oak.[10]

Smith, Townsend, and Coughlin all espoused common themes and drew their support from segments of American society that felt their interests were being ignored in Washington. Each man built his platform on the shared thread of the populist credo: economic elites in finance and banking were exploiting the average citizen. All three were united in their opposition to the Roosevelt administration, and for that reason alone, an alliance seemed inevitable.

Between the fall of 1935 and mid-1936, the NUSJ, with the help of Townsend and Smith and many financial backers, became the Union party—perhaps more accurately described as the "Stop Roosevelt" party. Smith contended that "FDR's campaign manager, Jim Farley, had driven him, Townsend, and Coughlin to 'congeal under a leadership with guts.'"[11]

As the name implied, the Union party was an amalgam of the social movements of all three demagogues, each of whose power rested on the intense loyalty of his supporters (though the Townsend Clubs continued as a separate set of local units). Other dissident organizations participated as well: the Farm-Labor party in Minnesota and the remnants of the Progressive party of Robert La Follette of Wisconsin. These were virtually all of the outsiders in 1936, except for the more traditional leftist socialist groups and the Communist party, which had no interest in joining the new radicals. Norman Thomas, perennial candidate of the Socialist party, characterized the Union party as "two and a half rival messiahs plus one ambitious politician plus some neopopulists plus a platform which reminds me of the early efforts of Hitler."[12]

From the outset, however, competing egos made practical coordination within the party a difficult, if not impossible, obstacle to overcome. Apart from mass rallies at which the face of unity prevailed, dark shadows of distrust and lack of mutual support plagued the Union party enterprise.[13]

At the beginning of 1936, before the party was formed, both the Townsendites and the Coughlinites had political strength. A Gallup survey, the first of its kind, in the spring of 1936 indicated a support level of over 7 percent for both. Candidates endorsed by the NUSJ won primaries for congressional races in Michigan, Ohio, Pennsylvania, and New York. Townsend supporters endorsed representatives who won across the nation, including in Michigan. But one race above all others stood out. In Michigan, there was one individual whose bid for the U.S. Senate caused both major political parties to take serious note of the potential of the newly forming Union party. His name was Louis Ward.

Ward played the part of a faithful Macduff to Charles Coughlin's Macbeth. He was a diminutive man whose barrel-waisted form was punctuated by a ubiquitous cigar planted in the corner of his mouth. A business consultant by trade, he wrote the first and only official biography of the radio priest and labored tirelessly to advance the political fortunes of the Royal Oak cleric. He personally entered several election campaigns as a candidate for public office and in 1936 came within a few thousand votes of becoming the Republican nominee for U.S. senator in Michigan.

Ward was widely recognized as the Washington lobbyist for the radio priest. He was also among the small circle of intermediaries between Henry Ford and Charles Coughlin. One of his publicity contracts included writing and editing a publication aimed at undermining the UAW-CIO, entitled the *Independent Ford Worker*. Ward was well paid, and always in cash.[14] For a short time in 1940, the publicist-writer was editor of Coughlin's newspaper, *Social Justice.*[15] Among his public-relations clients was the powerful Michigan Milk Producers Association.[16] Ward is probably best known, however, for a report on automobile production that still bears his name, *Ward's Automotive Report.*

We can only guess at what motivated Ward to serve the career of Charles Coughlin so loyally. Most likely, Ward hitched his wagon to a rising media star because he admired this fellow supersalesman and because he saw an extraordinary opportunity to shape a talent that needed guidance. Religious devotion may also have played a role. Perhaps only in America could a talented public relations man serve his professional goals well and at the same time respond to a deeply felt spiritual obedience.[17]

Ward was a college graduate who had taught high school history and government for four years in Albany, New York. After serving in World War I, he joined the Theodore A. McMannis advertising firm, one of the most successful and prestigious in the nation, and in 1933 he struck out on his own, establishing himself as a business consultant.

Ward, whom Coughlin described in a 1970 interview as having been one of the best statistical research men in the country, provided data utilized in many of the radio priest's broadcasts. Even during the Hoover administration there is evidence that Ward was a key idea man for Coughlin, informing his discussions of international trade and debt issues. This meant serving as a direct link to members of Congress and the White House staff. During his first hundred days, Roosevelt told Coughlin that he would welcome a comprehensive piece of labor legislation. The priest told Louis Ward, who recruited a team of lawyers to draft a bill.[18]

Between 1933 and 1936, Ward developed a variety of legislative proposals and testified before several congressional committees as the chief lobbyist for the NUSJ. His methods were not always aboveboard. In the case of the Frazier-Lemke farm mortgage bill of 1936, an irate Secretary McIntyre wrote:

> Mr. Ward, Father Coughlin's right-hand man, came in to see me. . . . Mr. Ward stated, "Look me in the eye—you know I have never resorted to blackmail." Then he added that he was able to keep "him" in line last Sunday night but would not answer for him next Sunday. . . . I told him that I agreed he had not resorted

to blackmail before, but having reached the mature age of fifty-seven years, I do not react to even suggestions of it. I was not a damn bit interested in a thing he had to say.[19]

Ward left the capital in late July 1936 while Congress was still in session, replaced by another, former advertising man, Fred Collins, so that Ward could prepare a run for the U.S. Senate. Filing in the Democratic primary meant challenging a prominent incumbent, James Couzens, and a popular member of Congress, Prentiss M. Brown. Yet contrary to the prediction of political pundits, Ward made the nomination race a close one. When the results were tabulated, Ward trailed by only 3,799 votes. (Ward reentered the race in the fall as the standard-bearer of Coughlin's new third party. He lost by an enormous margin, polling only 50,000 votes out of a total of 1 million cast.)

In the spring of 1936, following Ward's strong showing in the primary, the Union party had to make its most critical decision: Whom would it run at the head of its ticket? For Coughlin and Ward, such a decision would follow weeks of uncertainty as to whether there would be any national campaign. Then on June 19, two weeks after denying he had any intention of doing so, Coughlin announced the formation of the party and named the presidential candidate: William Lemke. During the first week of June, the radio priest had written to the North Dakota congressman and boastfully announced the birth of the new organization; it took short work to convince Lemke to join.

Among reporters, the joke was that the new third party had held its nominating convention in a telephone booth. There had been a flurry of calls between the radio priest and Lemke. On June 8, the priest wrote to Lemke saying: "In due time I will send you the name of our new presidential candidates."[20] When it turned out to be Lemke himself, the congressman was pleased but at first demurred, suggesting Coughlin himself should be the new presidential candidate.

William Lemke finally announced his candidacy on June 20: "I have accepted the challenge of the reactionary elements of both old parties. I will run for the presidency of the United States as the candidate of the Union Party, which I am instrumental in establishing officially." Lemke indicated that a national convention would be held in Cleveland "sometime in August" and that it would be a "mass convention similar to the one at which Lincoln launched his party."[21] Despite his optimism, Gallup polls were already showing a waning of support for the new third party. January's rating of 4.6 percent for Coughlin and Townsend had declined to 2.5 percent for the Union party by May, but rose again 5.0 percent in late August.

Said one biographer of Lemke, "He seemed to be the personification of middle-class America." Born in Minnesota, he grew up in a small farming town in North Dakota. He overcame the loss of an eye and eventually graduated from Yale Law School. Early in his political career, Lemke was removed from office during a banking scandal in 1921. The following year, he ran for governor and lost, but a decade later, he had rebuilt his political career and was elected to the House of Representatives as an ardent New Dealer. He cosponsored several bills to ameliorate agrarian problems, one of which bore his name.[22]

One historian has described the Union candidate as "amiable, fond of chihuahuas and gladioli, his face freckled by the Dakota sun and pitted by smallpox."[23] Gerald L.K. Smith recalled his party's candidate as "a complete composite of unattractiveness. He looked like a hayseed. He wore a cap. He was not eloquent and all he could talk about was money and agriculture."[24] Lemke took pride in acting and looking the part of a farmer. "Often he wore unpressed suits in Congress, and his twangy voice emerged through a day or two's growth of beard. A devout Lutheran, [he] neither drank nor smoked."[25]

The decision to run was Lemke's, but both the platform and the choice of vice-presidential running mate—Congress Thomas O'Brien of Massachusetts—were dictated by Coughlin. Candidate Lemke contributed $5,000 of his own funds toward the campaign.

Lemke clearly lacked charisma and speaking prowess and instead appeared the very epitome of a shy farm boy. (A popular joke explained Lemke's campaign slogan of "Liberty Bell Bill" by noting that both were cracked.) When the Townsend movement held its convention during August 1936 in Cleveland, Lemke was vastly overshadowed in the display put on by Gerald Smith and Charles Coughlin. The two clergymen-in-politics engaged in an oratorical duel, with the judgment being that Smith won. In his famous evaluation of the proceedings, H. L. Mencken wrote: "[Smith is] the greatest rabble-rouser since Peter the Hermit . . . the gustiest and goriest, the loudest and the lustiest, the deadliest and damndest ever heard on this or any other earth."[26]

Smith, clutching a Bible in his left hand, stood "coatless, broadshouldered, sweat plastering his shirt to his barrel chest . . . [and] roared words of hate about Wall Street bankers, millionaire steel magnates, Chicago wheat speculators, and New Deal social engineers." "Too long" he shouted, "have the plain people of the U.S. let Wall Street and Tammany rule them. We must make our choice in the presence of atheistic-communistic influences. . . . It is the Russian primer or the Holy Bible! It is the Red Flag or the Stars and Stripes! It is Lenin and Stalin or Jefferson!"[27]

As the crowd gave Smith a standing, screaming ovation, Mencken observed that Coughlin fidgeted nervously while awaiting his turn. The priest "sulked at the back of the auditorium through most of Smith's address. Coughlin now strode to the rostrum, not from the rear, but down the center aisle of the convention hall." The journalist opined that "Coughlin's long training at the microphone had given him a velvet voice and a flair for the spoken word, but he was totally lacking in that dramatic gesturing which made Smith so compelling face to face." Coughlin seemed "jealous of his supposed ally's platform delivery . . . he now looked upon Smith as a rival." The priest began speaking slowly and calmly, but midway through the forty-minute speech he began to step up the speed and volume . . . sweating as freely as had Smith, he stopped for a shocking pause. Stepping back from the microphone, Father Coughlin peeled off his black coat and Roman collar, literally defrocking himself before the audience of 10,000. Striding back to the rostrum, he roared, "As far as the National Union is concerned, no candidate who is endorsed for Congress can campaign, go electioneering for, or support the great betrayer and liar, Franklin D. Roosevelt. . . . I ask you to purge the man who claims to be a democrat from the Democratic Party—I mean Franklin Double-Crossing Roosevelt."[28] After a moment of stunned silence, the delegates stamped and shouted their approval.

FDR and his aides downplayed third parties and, in particular, the radio priest. Even privately, Roosevelt talked of the transience of figures such as Huey Long and Charles Coughlin. To a close confidant, Josephus Daniels, his ambassador to Mexico, Roosevelt described the coalition of Union party as unstable—"These fellows cannot lie in the same bed"[29]— yet the outward calm of the White House belied a concerted behind-the-scenes effort to counter Democratic defections to Coughlin.

In June 1936, a Gallup poll indicated that only 4 percent of voters were supportive of the Union party, though Coughlin boasted that he could command 9 million votes. Perhaps this was a wild boast; still, the NUSJ had some support in twenty-six states and 302 of the 435 congressional districts. The task facing Jim Farley, FDR's campaign manager for the second and last time, was to take action within each state party organization to prevent losses to Coughlin.

The affable but shrewd Farley kept close track of the Coughlin organization and its activities by means of a massive network of party workers, friends, and post office employees and worked quietly but assiduously to undermine Coughlin's power.[30] Early in 1936, Farley undertook a major investigation of the financial network that supported Father Coughlin. Postal receipts to the Shrine in Royal Oak were monitored. Louis Howe, FDR's intimate adviser, received regular reports on Coughlin from G. Hall Roosevelt in Detroit.[31]

Roosevelt's backers devised an ingenious set of strategies to weaken the impact of the Union party. In California, Democratic party operatives infiltrated the Townsend Clubs and helped prevent official endorsement of the Lemke candidacy. In Pennsylvania, Democratic party chairman David Lawrence changed the name of the state organization to "Union party" and suggested to other Democratic state parties to emulate this tactic. In the key states of New York, California, and Maryland, the Coughlin-led Union party was unable to get on the ballot because of late or incomplete qualifying petitions. The due date for nominating petitions in Kansas was noon on June 20—a scant eighteen hours after the party had been publicly announced. In Oklahoma, the filing date was May 2, and in West Virginia, May 12—weeks before the Union alliance had even been consummated. In Ohio, voters had to choose candidates under the "Royal Oak party" label.

For several strategic states, the Union party nevertheless was a genuine threat to the administration. In Massachusetts, Congressman John McCormack voiced alarm about primary results in which "forty thousand Coughlin followers placed stickers on the ballots for his candidate for Senate."[32] James Roosevelt, working in a key role in his father's reelection effort, concluded that "Coughlin is probably stronger in Massachusetts than in any other state."[33] National chairman Farley recognized Massachusetts as a Coughlin stronghold but disagreed with the president's son; he found Coughlin's influence "greater in Ohio than in any other state."[34]

Considerable Union party sentiment was also reported in Michigan, where Frank Murphy's private political poll revealed that Lemke, with almost 10 percent of the presidential vote, held the balance of power.

Congressman John Lesinski of Polish-Catholic Hamtramck, Michigan, warned Jim Farley that "Coughlin has quite an urban following here."[35]

Impressive as it was, the Union party's strength was diluted by Coughlin's former support of FDR. Now that Roosevelt was the central enemy, some followers felt the party was working against itself. A letter sent to the radio priest warned of the conflict that was emerging:

> I object strenuously to Representative Lemke as a candidate in opposition to President Roosevelt. This move has been a mistake as time will tell, unless correction is made before it is too late. . . . Probably no other force has influenced him [FDR] more than yourself and your thoughts on social justice. To turn on him now appears to me to be only base ingratitude, but also political suicide. It will gain nothing and will lose everything.
>
> . . . Already there are rumblings that rank and file Democratic voters mean to take some action in retaliation against NUSJ Congressional candidates. . . . The NUSJ will lose the favor of the President they have had, will lose many Congressional seats. . . . I implore you to reconsider and support Roosevelt. . . . Your support is necessary to Roosevelt. He can be persuaded, but he cannot be coerced.[36]

But Coughlin persisted, focusing on a broad set of issues, some purely economic, others grounded in issues of personality and patriotism. To the former, FDR would respond that social security legislation was passed and banking reforms were introduced. But to the latter, especially concerns about subversive influences within the White House, Coughlin's voice grew even more shrill and personally accusatory than it had ever been. If Roosevelt himself was not a dangerous leftist radical, Coughlin charged, then his advisers were. Even the president was a direct target in many of Coughlin's campaign speeches, in which he called FDR the "anti-God." In Bedford, Massachusetts, the priest declared, "As I was instrumental in removing Herbert Hoover from the White House, so help me God, I will be instrumental in taking a Communist foe from the chair once occupied by Washington."[37]

Neither Farley nor FDR treated these assaults lightly. Of particular concern was the Catholic constituency. Steve Early, White House press secretary, sent Jim Farley a copy of a telegram, addressed to FDR (from the captain of Harvard's Rose Bowl victors of 1920), which called for prominent Catholic laymen to organize the "intelligent thinking Catholics" to offset "the horrible statements Coughlin has made against you and the United States."[38] In response, FDR tapped Joseph P. Kennedy for this task. Kennedy, who agreed to be called out of private business after having earlier resigned as head of the Securities and Exchange Commission, first spoke on a CBS coast-to-coast hookup on the evening of October 5, 1936. He opened with a phrase with which he would be identified for several years—"I'm for Roosevelt"—then delivered a direct message in response to the issues Coughlin raised: "Tonight I have chosen to speak to you on the subject of communism which has been made an issue in this campaign in a desperate attempt to defeat the President by appeals to our patriotism. As an American citizen I resent the efforts which are now being made for low, political purposes to confuse a Christian program of social justice with a Godless program of communism."[39]

A short time later, Jim Farley wrote to his close friend Claude Bowers, ambassador to Spain, that "the campaign is about all over, and we expect a tremendous landslide. . . . Father Coughlin's influence has dropped off tremendously." In reviewing state-by-state patterns, Farley mentioned in particular that a court of appeals ruling had kept the Union party off the New York ballot, so "there is no place for his [Coughlin's] support to go except the Democrats."[40] Indeed, as the campaign wound down to its final weeks, the news coming to Jim Farley was decidedly optimistic. Sequential Gallup polls showed the Union party steadily losing ground, with Roosevelt increasing his already comfortable lead over Republican challenger Alf Landon.

Coughlin nevertheless continued to attack FDR in a highly personal way, including asserting that the president was "a liar and a betrayer." Then midway through the fall, he seemed to soften his direct attacks on Roosevelt's character and instead focused on the evil influence of his advisers: "Roosevelt has not done the things he has done maliciously, but has been a great victim of those who have surrounded him. . . . The New Deal is surrounded by atheists. . . . Surrounded by red and pink Communists and by 'frankfurters of destruction.'"[41]

The reluctance of both Coughlin and Townsend to utilize their local chapters and club structures fully on behalf of William Lemke contributed to the Union party's weakening position. Coughlin spent a majority of the $700,000 raised in the presidential campaign on his own activities, including the NUSJ convention in Cleveland, and on numerous travel bills for himself and his entourage. Little was left for supporting the Union party national headquarters and its candidate, Lemke.[42]

As the campaign wound down to its final weeks, Smith virtually absented himself from any campaigning. Coughlin also retracted his prediction of 9 million votes, saying this was based on returns in all forty-eight states and stating that "the National Union for Social Justice might have to be a martyr in this fall's election."[43]

A little over a month before the election, Coughlin spoke at a Union party rally in Philadelphia, to a crowd of only 20,000, not the 100,000 expected. Floodlights, which had bathed the thirty-foot-high white structure at the center of the field, were turned off as the lone figure mounted the booth. Reading lights were switched on, and all was darkness as Charles Coughlin addressed his audience. Declaring that a vote for either Roosevelt or Landon was a vote for "Wall Street," the priest advised his audience, "You might better stay at home and not vote at all." He then declared: "And if you should do this the election would be thrown into Congress and Mr. O'Brien would be the next Vice President and I'll be the next President!"[44]

When the final vote tally was completed, the Union party was erased from history. There were a few close local elections, but not one of the party's several dozen candidates was elected to Congress. Nationwide, the Lemke ticket drew 892,000 votes—about one-tenth of the 9 million the radio priest had boasted of in the spring and summer months. When at last the futile campaign was over, William "Liberty Bell" Lemke would only pathetically claim, "We've scared the two old parties to death."[45]

Charles Coughlin had lost much in the presidential campaign. Alienated by his direct and personal attacks on the president, many disillusioned Catholic Democrats chose FDR over the radio priest. Moreover, the tone of the politics frightened many who might have been drawn to one or another of the policy issues the Union party espoused. Years later, Coughlin himself would describe the 1936 campaign as a "horrible mistake."[46] On the day after the election he declared bitterly: "The minority is now purely theoretical. We have a one-party system now. Franklin D. Roosevelt has more power than any man ever had in history. If the people want these things, as their votes indicate they do, let them have them."[47] No doubt Coughlin felt betrayed by many in his radio audience, and it may have deepened a streak of paranoia that had heretofore been kept out of public view.

Even more than the content, the tone of Coughlin's campaign addresses struck many as revealing a deep personal vindictiveness toward
Franklin Roosevelt. Several stump speeches seemed almost to incite violence: "When an upstart dictator in the United States succeeds in making
this a one-party form of government, when the ballot is useless, I shall
have the courage to stand up and advocate the use of bullets." In a speech
in Providence, Rhode Island, Coughlin told a stunned audience of 25,000
that if Roosevelt were elected, there would be "more bullet holes in the
White House than you could count with an adding machine."[48]

Within days of the landslide victory of FDR, Charles Coughlin offered his radio listeners what could only be termed a farewell address: "I
hereby withdraw from all radio activity in the best interests of the people. . . . A few hearts will be saddened, many others elated, a vast majority totally indifferent to my departure. . . . It was high time for the
National Union to retire, to sleep. . . . It is better, both for you and for me,
for the country I serve and the Church I love, for me to be forgotten for
the moment."[49] Earlier—in May of the previous year—when Coughlin
was just launching himself directly into national politics, H. L. Mencken
opined to his friend Theodore Dreiser that the radio priest was "already
in collapse, though he doesn't know it himself."[50]

Both men were wrong. The Union party defeat was a great blow, but
Coughlin had the gifts needed to recover and Capitol Hill connections.
He would not go away.

The network of members of Congress who were on close terms with
the radio priest was extensive, and they included several who were to become famous: Senators "Pat" McCarran of Nevada and Elmer Thomas of
Oklahoma, and Representative Everett Dirksen of Illinois. One of Coughlin's close clerical associates recalled that "whenever Charlie visited
Washington, he would stay at Vice President John Nance Garner's home."[51]

Coughlin began broadcasting again in January 1937, but it would not
be until 1938 that he truly was able to recover from defeat. The occasion
was a set of proposals to restructure the federal government—the so-
called Reorganization Act—debated by Congress over an extended period in 1938.

By early 1938 the New Deal was in a great deal of difficulty. In the
famous Court-packing controversy, FDR had tried to expand the size of
the Supreme Court in order to overcome a majority hostile to important
pieces of New Deal legislation. Even Roosevelt's supporters viewed this
effort as high-handed and possibly dangerous to constitutional govern-

ment. Furthermore, despite clear signs of economic recovery during FDR's first term in office, midway through his second, signs were evident of the return of the depression at its worst. Unemployment over the winter of 1937–1938 soared to 19 percent, just a bit below the level at the time FDR first took office as president.

Improvement in the efficiency of the federal bureaucracy had been proposed for a number of years. President Herbert Hoover too had been identified with such efforts. FDR's proposals involved expanding the White House staff, extending the civil service system, putting a number of independent agencies under one or another of the cabinet-level departments, and creating two cabinet departments: Social Welfare and Public Works.

In February 1938, when Congress at last began to consider the reorganization bill, introduced the previous year, Coughlin played a key role in its defeat for that year, and in the process generated a highly creative strategy of protest.

It was a Thursday afternoon, March 24, 1938, when the Senate closed debate on the proposed legislation. Senator Edward Burke of Nebraska, one of the opponents, counted 43 votes favoring and 43 votes against the reorganization bill. When a second vote was scheduled after the weekend, Coughlin stepped onto center stage. Father Peter Wiethe, who was assigned to the Shrine of the Little Flower at the time, remembered that week's events vividly: "About five or ten to six on Wednesday [March 23] the phone rang, and Father Coughlin had . . . wonderful information from Washington. His informant told him Roosevelt gave orders to put through the Reorganization Bill by Friday night—this was Wednesday night—so that Coughlin won't even talk about it on Sunday. Yes, in 48 hours!" Wiethe recalls the radio priest got up from his table, saying, "By damn, I'm going to go on the air tomorrow night.' And he went to the phone . . . and with a long-distance phone from about six to seven-thirty . . . we could hear him."[52] Coughlin's telephone-radio broadcast blasted the "Dictator Bill" for granting Roosevelt far too much power.

The result was staggering. At eight o'clock Sunday night, Western Union had a backlog of 4,000 telegrams in New York, 2,000 in Detroit, 1,000 in Chicago, 2,500 in Philadelphia. By Monday morning an avalanche of nearly 100,000 telegrams hit Washington, and wire services had to set aside all commercial business.[53] According to Father Wiethe, Coughlin composed his powerful address by taking some newspaper clippings and the *Congressional Record* and going up to his pulpit: "Fifteen to twenty minutes before his evening address. . . . It was so dramatic, that his mother fainted."[54] The *New York Times* saw the radio priest's ability to evoke the telegraphic response as "one of the greatest victories of his career" and speculated about how he might regain his eminence.[55]

In his speech, Coughlin spoke about the need to have "modern Paul Reveres" send delegations to Washington. The Hearst newspaper chain, veterans' groups, business organizations, and others joined in the effort. At the Hippodrome in New York, the scene of previous Coughlin triumphs, a massive rally was held. When the "Reveres" arrived at the Capitol for breakfast on Thursday morning, they were greeted by smaller delegations from Philadelphia, Boston, and Baltimore. The marchers were described by one reporter as members of the "inarticulate middle classes" (certainly one of the first references to what in the 1970s and 1980s would be called the silent majority). Half of the demonstrators were women, and leading the Boston contingent was Paul Revere's great-great-granddaughter. One man wore the garb of the midnight rider and bore a sign reading: "Kill the Bill." Another read: "I see no reason why Congress should give the president powers of Julius Caesar."[56]

The reorganization bill passed the Senate by one vote but lost on a roll-call vote on April 8 in the House. "History will probably mark the crisis of President Roosevelt's political career by yesterday's defeat," opined the *New York World Telegram.* Observers of every type agreed that the defeat dealt a shattering blow to FDR's prestige and his plans for government reform. Harold Ickes, secretary of the interior and a close adviser to FDR, remarked in his diary, "It looks to me as if the courage has oozed out of the President." "Demagoguery and stupidity," Roosevelt observed philosophically in a letter to a New Deal aide, "are the natural enemies of democracy."[57]

During a major White House press conference at the end of April, FDR reviewed the reorganization defeat and broke a long-standing precedent of not acknowledging Coughlin's influence:

> All of a sudden, there broke out—I don't know who started it, but I do know who carried it on and was the gentleman from near Detroit who talks on the air and who claimed that this was an attack on the educational system of the Nation whereupon, immediately, Members of Congress, the House and Senate, were

flooded with telegrams that this bill would give the President a chance to grab all the church schools of the Nation, the Protestant church schools and the Parochial schools, although I don't know what the President of the United States was going to do with them when he did grab them.[58]

7

All the World's a Stage

"One thing for sure," Coughlin said in a soft, matter-of-fact voice, "democracy is doomed. This is our last election."

"What will happen?" I asked. "It is Fascism or Communism. We are at the crossroads." "What road do you take?" "I take the road to Fascism."

Impromptu press conference, 1936

T HERE HAS LONG BEEN a debate about Coughlin and fascism. Was he merely a populist who passed through a dangerous phase? Or did he have deeper fascistic tendencies? An examination of Coughlin's contacts suggests more the latter than the former.

In the early 1930s, a parade of visitors from around the world gave to Coughlin's Royal Oak church the aura of a Delphic shrine. German Chancellor Heinrich Bruening visited in 1932, and Randolph Churchill did so a year later. It was becoming fashionable, and even obligatory, for world travelers to stop there. As the radio priest's fame grew, an opportunity for international travel and a role in world politics seemed near at hand for him.[1]

Coughlin was becoming a key figure in an international network of monetary reformers who made effective use of the new mass medium of radio. In September 1935, for example, he had a visit from the Very Reverend Hewlett Johnson, archbishop of Canterbury, who was a strong advocate of credit reform. Just a week earlier, William Aberhart, the newly designated premier of Alberta, Canada, had paid his respects to the radio priest. Aberhart's platform included a proposal to pay each adult man and woman twenty-five dollars a month. Coughlin told the press that "both he and Alberta are to be congratulated on having made this forward step,

98

which the forefathers of the United States attempted to make, but in which they were frustrated by the Alexander Hamiltons and their successors." In turn, the premier told the press that he had come to Royal Oak seeking "the most expert advice on the continent."[2]

The Alberta experiment was part of the social credit movement, which had roots in both North America and Europe. According to social credit theory, contemporary democracy had created economic slaves: money had become the master rather than the servant. The sovereign authority of the people to control their money supply had been usurped by bankers who had set up what amounted to financial dictatorship. Individuals were faced with poverty in the midst of plenty. The social credit movement called for a national dividend to be given to each adult based on a survey of the wealth of a nation and to prevent inflation, for a "just price" for all goods. The evils of the money supply would no longer erode the "cultural heritage" to which each individual was entitled.

Social credit had originated with the charismatic Major C. H. Douglas, a retired army officer of the Royal Air Force in World War I. His writings, which first appeared in the early 1920s, linked the economic system to an ethical system. Douglas claimed that the world's financial structure was under the control of bankers who were largely "Jews and Freemasons." In 1934 he wrote:

It is my conviction that centralisation is being fostered everywhere and from the same source and with the same object—world domination. . . . The swift progress toward State capitalism everywhere [has] Jewish Finance at the apex of the pyramid. . . . Jewry as a whole has a permanent policy which is establishing the individual Jew as a member of the "chosen" superior and dominant ruling class in every country and over the whole world.[3]

Douglas saw this "Jewish power" as a sphere "in which the Jewish race operates so largely as very nearly to control . . . [what] was regarded in the Middle Ages as the sphere of 'black magic,' but which was termed 'suggestion' or the 'psychology of the unconscious.' "[4]

Douglas drew his ideas from the European intellectual tradition that identified the rise of modern capitalism with the demise of traditional religion—in particular, medieval Catholicism. Capitalism also threatened to invoke a kind of supranationalism—the race and ethnic homogeneity

that were considered essential elements of Western European civilization. The cultural superiority of Western Europe was self-evident to
Douglas, and it is called for putting local community over state authority
and for a guildlike organization of society's economy.[5]

Douglas garnered little support in England, but in Canada his ideas
were disseminated by Aberhart, whose political party gained temporary
power in two of Canada's provinces—Alberta and Quebec—in the mid-
1930s. Aberhart invited Douglas to lecture in Canada, and the two of
them had contact with Coughlin.

Aberhart was a clergyman-turned-political-leader cut from the same
cloth as Coughlin. A secondary school teacher and lay preacher, he had
been a key figure in an evangelical movement that swept across Canada's
western prairie in the 1920s. His publications and sermons generated so
much interest that a series of study clubs were formed under his leadership and led to the opening of the Bible Institute, where he served as
dean. His use of radio (he began broadcasting in November 1926, nearly
a year before Coughlin) was a major innovation; he was credited with
having a mass audience of 350,000 among the 1.2 million inhabitants of
Canada's three western provinces.

In April 1934, Aberhart first journeyed to meet with Coughlin, and
they held several more meetings over the next few months, including one
occasion when they conferred with Major Douglas in Washington, D.C.,
during his lecture tour of North America. It was during this period that
the Alberta social credit movement shifted from advocacy to direct elec-
toral politics. The previous year Aberhart had established his own daily
newspaper and a weekly radio program, "Man from Mars."

On Canada's election night, August 22, 1935, less than a month before Coughlin and FDR had their fateful Hyde Park meeting, Aberhart
announced that his Social Credit party had won a stunning victory: he
was elected premier with 54 percent of the vote, and his supporters
formed 89 percent of the provincial legislature. He proposed three essential reforms: that control over the monetary system be retired to the
masses, that a "national dividend" based on a nation's real wealth be paid
to each citizen, and that a "just price" for all goods be established. Sov-
ereignty to citizens was to be restored by organizing a Union of Electors
that would directly advise elected parliamentary officials regarding policy actions that were needed.[6] Aberhart's success may have inspired
Charles Coughlin's decision to enter politics.

For a time, Aberhart and Coughlin stayed in close touch, with the radio priest contributing three articles to *Chronicle,* the social credit news-paper. But in just a few months, in early 1936, Coughlin rejected the Alberta experiment in monetary reform and began to urge social credit enthusiasts to take his own economic advice and to read the publication that he himself was about to launch. Despite his zeal for radical change, once in office, Aberhart introduced little, if any, change in the existing provincial economic and social policies. The major outcome of five years of rule was the establishment of a social credit board, where disciples of Major Douglas sought to draw up legislation whose overall impact, according to one historian, "was to obliterate the democratic and radical aspects of the early Social Credit movement in favour of creating an authoritarian party and government."[7]

Social credit and the ideas of Major Douglas had also swayed a prominent expatriate American, Ezra Pound, who became a confirmed Douglasite. Usurers, as Douglas defined them, make money by manipulating money; these landlords, bankers, stockholders, and others, he charged, were at the core of economic evil. In a 1920 issue of Douglas's journal, the *Little Review,* Pound warmly praised the retired major's work, and returned again and again to the theme of usury in his poetry.[8]

By the beginning of the 1930s, Pound had left New York to reside in Mussolini's Italy. In 1933, Pound disparaged the American "so-called two-party system" and asserted that "Jefferson governed for twenty-four years in a *de facto* one-party condition." As for the fascism of "the Duce . . . [it] will stand not with despots and the lovers of power but the lovers of ORDER."[9]

During this same period, Pound began a lively correspondence with Charles Coughlin. When the NUSJ was formed in late 1934, the poet offered his "hearty congratulations" and expounded on his view that "the church has always been right about usury," but added, "I daresay it can't be eliminated all at once." Placing great faith in the radio priest as an exponent of "sound money programs" and a man who knew the way "to defeat the machinations of international bankers," Pound enclosed with his letter a financial contribution to Coughlin's new organization.[10]

Writing in 1936, Pound declared, "Father Coughlin speaks regularly to millions of Americans, and that means that he speaks also *for* them: I mean the fact that they listen regularly means that they share to a great extent the hopes of the speaker. . . . Coughlin has the great gift of simplifying vital issues to a point where the populace can understand their main factor if not the technical detail."[11] Throughout the Union party's 1936 election campaign, Pound offered his moral support to the cause, though he predicted a Roosevelt victory, offering that it was preferable to a Landon victory—since Landon was "ignorant and such a fool . . . Frankie is the clerver [*sic*] man."[12] In turn, Coughlin asked for a reaction to his recently launched newspaper, *Social Justice.* The reply from Rapallo, Italy, to Royal Oak, Michigan, was positive, including the advice that "Soc. Justice ought to run a review column for essential books." Pound suggested that "in the slack season after election . . . an attack on something else wd., I believe be good psychology."[13]

FDR embarked on economic policies that were anathema to the poet-economist-ideologue. To Pound this was proof positive that the president was a tool of the "USURA," an amorphous concept the poet used to describe a kind of primordial international system of Jewish financial control.[14]

In 1939, Pound made his first visit to the United States since 1911. He expressed concern about his native land in a letter he wrote to a close friend, the prominent writer and artist Wyndham Lewis: "America is damn well to keep out of war/BAD enough to have european arayans murduring each other fer the sake of . . . a few buggerin' kikes."[15]

Pound's cultural elitism and disdain for modern urban society tie him to a European tradition of desire for an aristocracy of the mind. He had a dual allegiance: to the abstract "will of the people" and to the role of the authoritarian leader as the vehicle for directing that power. Pound found in Charles Coughlin the means to carry his ideological framework out in practical ways. Not only did he offer moral, financial, and advisory support to the radio priest, but he offered the highest compliment of all: imitation. When war came to Europe in the fall of 1939, Pound offered his services to the Axis Powers, in particular, to the Mussolini government. He contracted to make regular radio propaganda broadcasts offering his views on world events. "Undoubtedly," Pound biographer Humphrey Carpenter asserts, "Ezra took Coughlin as a model when he began to broadcast regularly in 1941."[16] Both before and after the United States entered the conflict, the poet's shortwave programs were beamed to American listeners with unseemly bile—for example: "[It is outrageous] that any Jew in the White House should send American kids to die for the private interests of the scum of the English earth . . . and the still lower dregs of the Levantine."[17] When the Allies captured Pound in 1945, he was charged with treason against his country of birth. Returned to the United States, he was confined for a number of years in a psychiatric

ward and was never placed on trial for his wartime activities. Released in
1958, he returned immediately to Italy. Upon landing at Naples, his first
act was to give the fascist salute.

Ezra Pound was but one link in a chain of prominent men of letters who
paid homage to the radio priest, encouraged him, and in some instances,
lent their talents to his publications. Occasionally public figures sought
religious conversion through the Royal Oak priest. Among them was
the well-known literary scion, Sir Hugh Walpole. Following a visit to
the Shrine, he and Coughlin met again in London. Walpole included
a description of the priest in his diaries: "A quiet, stocky, gentle and
beautiful-eyed man with whom I felt instantly a strong bond. I think he
felt it for me. Our eyes constantly met during lunch."[18] Coughlin later
told a fellow priest that "he had almost brought Walpole to Catholicism"
and that "if they met again Sir Hugh would probably be baptized."[19]

There were two English literary figures who already shared Coughlin's Catholic faith as well as a number of his controversial views. One of
these, Hilaire Belloc, was best known in the first decades of the century
as a polemicist and debater (he even served two terms in Parliament). In
subsequent years, he attained recognition as a leading novelist, poet,
journalist, and travel writer. He also became a defender of the Catholic
faith against the attacks of such major literary personalities as George
Bernard Shaw and H. G. Wells.

Belloc was a prolific writer whose works on literary themes included
a series of biographies of French Revolution figures, but increasingly he
turned from writing about history to defending his church against the on-
slaughts of modern society, in particular, the political and economic system of modern capitalism and the ideology that arose to oppose its
defects: socialism. His basic view was that Europe reached its epitome of
glory first under the unifying control of Julius Caesar and then under the
Catholic church in the medieval period. When Mussolini took power in
Italy in 1922, "Belloc longed . . . for a great inspiring personal hero who
would purge society of its corruptions and would inspire the masses to return to the strong, the Roman ideal. . . . He had little doubt that the Italian *Duce* was the new Caesar."[20]

In the 1920s and 1930s, Belloc edited a series of weeklies in which
the ideas of Major Douglas and other advocates of "distributionism"
were disseminated. Belloc yearned for a return to a form of feudalism in
which the family was the primary economic unit, disciplined under the

value system of Catholicism. Like many others in his circle, he saw parliamentary democracy as unworkable and disorderly. Increasingly, despite his earlier reputation as a radical critic of the evils of capitalism, Belloc saw bolshevism and any other form of "modern revolution" as undermining the pillars of European civilization: Christianity, in particular the Catholic church.

Belloc had always peppered his writings with fictional characters who fit Semitic stereotypes, and seemed to enjoy making jibes at Jews. In rhyme he offered this description of the Rothschild residence in London: "a place of habitation for the Jewish race," and, a few lines after, "Here Rothschild lives, chief of the tribe abhorr'd./Who tried to put to death Our Blessed Lord."[21]

In 1922, Belloc penned his most controversial work, *The Jews,* which sought to review the history and source of current tensions between Jews and Christians. Identifying Jews as a distinct racial group that could never be assimilated into European societies, Belloc prophesied that if the Jews continued to behave as they did—being secretive, plotting international leftist coups, feeling superior to others—something terrible was likely to happen to them.[22] For Belloc, the "Jewish question" was an urgent one and at the very heart of world problems.

Belloc made one journey to the United States, invited for a series of academic lectures, "The Crisis of Our Civilization," as a visiting professor of history at New York's Fordham University. On the boat trip across the Atlantic he wrote:

> Talking of yids the swarm of Yids on board this sparsely populated craft is extraordinary: there are hardly 100 people on board and at least 81 are incredible: monsters of the deep. . . . There are two Americans on board. . . . Now Americans are vocally and loudly and simply and in a child-like fashion Jew-haters. So I live in hopes of an explosion before we reach the beatitudes of New York. Wouldn't it be amusing if this next outburst of blind rage against the poor old Jews were to blow up in New York? . . . If or when the New Yorkites rise against the Jews there will be a pogrom: for the Americans yield to none in promiscuous violence and bloodletting.[23]

In the fall of 1937, after corresponding with and apparently meeting him during his American stay, Coughlin began quoting Belloc in his weekly editorials for *Social Justice* and linking his own ideas regarding economic reform to that of the English literary figure. By February 1938, Coughlin announced with much fanfare that "in a series of fifty-two brilliant articles written exclusively for *Social Justice* one of the world's greatest thinkers proposes an urgent program for ending the social and economic evils that are rapidly destroying civilization."[24]

Belloc did not in fact complete his year-long commitment to *Social Justice,* although he did pen a number of brief articles during the first eight months of 1938. They were decidedly philosophical in character and did not delve into contemporary political disputations. Entitled "The Way Out," the series expounded a societal organization that focused on a return to the ideal of medieval Europe. Capitalism as the source of human exploitation was called a half-truth, with "general destitution" of the working class the real evil. The remedy was increasing property ownership. Under large-scale capital enterprises, a "proletarian mind" develops in which "work is an evil, a burden wrongly imposed on another." The "disease of monopoly" was attacked as destroying freedom and a sense of community. The answer lay, Belloc wrote, with a restoration of the guild system, which restricted competition and stabilized the value of labor.[25]

Apparently Belloc's somewhat turgid pieces did not appeal to the priest's readers, and so Coughlin sent Belloc a polite letter of thanks for the articles he had contributed. Belloc's series ended with the August 8, 1938, issue. Returning to England exhausted and in ill health, Belloc summarized his impression of the United States and mused that if England had to turn again to America for help in the event of a war, it would be "dependent upon an idiot innocent giant child."[26]

The other star of the English literary firmament with whom the radio priest corresponded, and whom he even hosted, was novelist and essayist G. K. Chesterton. A close colleague of Belloc, Chesterton had edited a weekly in which Belloc had written extensively, along with Ezra Pound and T. S. Eliot. With his brother Cecil, Gilbert Chesterton had been active as a polemicist against political corruption in England. G. K. was editor of the publication *New Witness,* which he had started in 1913 as a response to the so-called Marconi scandal, a case that turned into a British equivalent of the Dreyfus case.

Marconi had established a company in England that entered into a contract with the British government for the creation of radio stations throughout the country. In the context of war fears and political turmoil, the fact that three of the key executives in the company were Jews gave rise to a series of articles edited by Hilaire Belloc, along with Cecil and Gilbert Chesterton, which led to an official investigation of the contract.[27]

Chesterton's widely read book of the 1920s, *The New Jerusalem,* saw the Jews as a separate racial-religious group that posed a potential threat to "the essential philosophy and organic Christian structure of British society."[28] Jews were described as the agents of a "regrettable modernism," a view held widely throughout the Belloc-Chesterton circles of British intellectual life. In his autobiography Chesterton linked all societal evils of his day to a departure from the ideal of the Middle Ages. His writings are strewn with stock images of Jews as manipulators and with physically repulsive features, and although he praised Jews for their strong family bonds, he warned: "It is often the very loyalty of the Jewish family which appears as disloyalty to the Christian state."[29]

Because his books were best-sellers in the United States, Chesterton's visits were quite newsworthy. On one occasion in the early 1920s, he met with Henry Ford and offered praise for the industrialist's *Dearborn Independent* newspaper series, which detailed the alleged dangers of Jewish and black influence in America's cultural and economic life. In his last trip to the United States in 1938, Chesterton did some lecturing at Catholic University, praising the role of Francisco Franco of Spain as a savior of Western civilization.

As fascist regimes in Italy, Austria, and then Spain emerged in the 1920s and 1930s, the line between Catholic traditionalism, clerical-fascism, anti-Semitism, and anticommunism disintegrated for some intellectuals. When Mussolini invaded Ethiopia in 1935, both Belloc and Chesterton expressed their strong support. What seemed evident was the need to take a stand, and for many rightists, that meant supporting regimes whose leaders appeared to form a bulwark against the enemies of the Catholic church.

For Charles Coughlin, words alone would not be sufficient to address the perils he perceived.

In a radio sermon delivered in November 1931, Coughlin addressed the lack of leadership in America, bemoaning the absence of a head of government whose strength matched that of Kemal Pasha of Turkey, Pierre Laval of France, and Benito Mussolini of Italy. He cited them all for their "remarkable leadership, the crown of modern civilization," but singled out for particular praise the "energetic leadership" of Il Duce.[30]

That Coughlin, Belloc, and Chesterton were Catholic voices raised in support of Mussolini was not particularly surprising. The Concordat signed between the Vatican and Mussolini in 1929, granting formal recognition of and autonomy to the Vatican state and to Catholic institutions in Italy, pointed to a coexistence between the church and fascism. Nor was Coughlin's lauding of Mussolini unusual, since a majority of American intellectuals, government officials (including FDR and Herbert Hoover), and a number of leading U.S. businessmen supported the Italian dictator at first. In fact, favorable assessments of Mussolini were spearheaded by journalists at leading newspapers, including those of the Hearst and Luce chains. Glowing accounts of the Italian fascist regime gave Mussolini a reputation for vigorous and effective leadership around the world. During 1934, a Cole Porter hit tune featured the line, "You're the top—you're Musso-li-ni." By the following year, when this song was played across the country, all references to Mussolini had been deleted. By 1935, with Mussolini's invasion of Ethiopia, American public opinion had shifted decisively against the Italian leader. The Italian army's brutality and use of poison gas engendered a strong revulsion.[31]

Many of Mussolini's advisers saw the United States as fertile ground for the exportation of fascism. A Jesuit publication, *America,* offered strong praise for the Italian leader, and even the more liberal *Commonweal* defended many of his policies. President Hoover was not hesitant to work diplomatically with Mussolini, and even FDR felt some initial sense of brotherly sympathy for the economic problems faced by the Italian dictator.

Coughlin praised fascist Italy in numerous radio talks and articles in *Social Justice.* Beginning in 1933, he tried to contact Mussolini directly. He hoped to gain a useful ally and offer the Italian government a supportive voice in America. Coughlin's first overture was made just prior to FDR's inauguration in a letter to Mussolini:

> I hope that by this time you will have received the booklet on the eight discourses and the subsequent lectures which were delivered from the Shrine of the Little Flower. . . . Of course, I feel very happy in having played a part . . . in helping to accomplish the defeat of Herbert Hoover and the repeal of the Eighteenth Amendment which is related to prohibition.

Now of all the reforms in which I have engaged, I am beginning what I mean to be the most important crusade of all. The
other accomplishments in which I have been a part were national. This one must be international or else be of no value. I am
asking that if you see eye to eye with me, that you will help en-
list the services of the Italian, the English, the French, the German and the Austrian press.

This is a tremendous favor.[32]

In explaining this crusade, he wrote, "As you know, the commercial
world today possesses approximately eleven billion dollars in gold. As
most men fail to realize, the major portion of this commercial gold is
controlled not by governments, not by nations, but by international
bankers. Of course the international banker has manipulated this gold for
his selfish purposes to the detriment of civilization. . . . I am sending you
the two most recent national broadcasts on this subject. . . . Will you
please read these two lectures and form your own conclusion?" Coughlin's proposal was for a restructuring of the world economic order. In
closing his missive, the radio priest warned, "There will be no advantage
whatsoever in reducing this proposal to practice in America unless Italy
and major European nations cooperate."[33]

Mussolini's officials in the Ministry of Foreign Affairs were sufficiently interested to send a wire to their embassy in Washington: "The
noted rev. Charles E. Coughlin, Shrine of the Little Flower, Detroit,
Michigan, has sent His Excellency the head of government the letter attached here in translation. Your Excellency is kindly requested to furnish
any information regarding the question, and to present your official views
as to whether it is opportune to consider the request of said prelate."[34]
The ambassador's reply was a cautious one, however, and advised
against accepting Coughlin's offer:

The recent monetary events in this country have made a past case
of the Rev. Charles E. Coughlin's proposals. In all events I must
advise this Ministry that said reverend, an intelligent type but enamored of the idea of reconstructing the financial world, has
been frequently the subject of serious criticism, even among his
immediate associates [in the church]. Therefore, it is not advis-
able for His Excellency the head of government to enter into direct relations with him.[35]

Despite this initial rejection of an open link, Italian officials kept a close watch on the activities of the radio priest. Mussolini's government had invested large sums of money in the United States (including the hiring of an American public relations firm) in order to promote a positive image of Italy and was very sensitive about establishing direct ties to such a controversial figure as Charles Coughlin.[36]

The Italo-Ethiopian war, which had started in the fall of 1935, provided an opportunity for Coughlin to offer his services once again to Mussolini. Noting with dismay how American attitudes were rising against the Italian leader, Mussolini's Washington embassy developed a variety of strategies aimed at restoring positive, or at least neutral, perceptions. Meanwhile, the radio priest attacked the British, "whose history is crimson with the blood of Ireland and small minorities," for striking a pious attitude about the Italian attack on Ethiopia.[37] The Italian embassy in Washington then suggested mobilizing Irish-American opinion "to make use of the traditional and natural hostility of the Irish element in America against England."[38]

When FDR called for an embargo against Italy, Coughlin bitterly attacked him. The consulate in Chicago took due notice in its wire to Rome:

> The head of the "National Union for Social Justice" dedicated his radio broadcast to commenting on the message of President Roosevelt to Congress. . . . Father Coughlin . . . assumed an attitude of marked hostility to his [FDR's] foreign policies. . . . That last phrase of the speech . . . illustrates ever more clear Father Coughlin's program to influence a group of congressmen who can make their voices heard in Congress.[39]

Consular officials sent Rome numerous copies of and reports on Coughlin's radio addresses, Coughlin kept in close touch with the Italian consul in Detroit, and a mutual supporter of Coughlin and Mussolini, a Professor Robert Prusso, sent reports to Italy on Coughlin's activities.

By 1938, Italy launched a campaign to follow the German racial laws. When these actions were strongly criticized in the United States, Coughlin wrote to Mussolini, offering him access to *Social Justice*:

> So much misunderstanding has been created by the unfriendly press in America relative to your statements that I inclined to in-

vite Your Excellency to write an article for our national magazine in which you can clarify your attitude toward the Jews, toward the national question and toward any other point that you wish to make clear for the American readers.

Social Justice magazine has a million readers and will be happy not only to publicize your article but to support it editorially.[40]

Coughlin's efforts to establish an official alliance with Mussolini, however, came to nothing. For Coughlin, Mussolini was an ideological soulmate from whom he sought recognition and with whom he hoped to play a role in world events. At one point, Coughlin told Italian officials that he wanted to set up a field office for his newspaper, *Social Justice,* in Rome. (This never occurred.)

By keeping the attempt at a "Rome–Royal Oak Axis" a secret, Coughlin and his supporters were able to deny that the radio priest was a serious supporter of European fascism, but in identifying himself privately with its founder, he revealed what can only be called empathy with authoritarian rule.

When Spain's civil war broke out in 1936, Hilaire Belloc likened Francisco Franco to "Charlemagne, Roland, and Godfrey the First Crusader" and described him as the "salvation of Europe."[41] Belloc's close friend, Douglas Jerrold, provided the plane that flew Franco from the Canary Islands to Morocco to launch his revolt.

The Spanish Civil War was the dress rehearsal for World War II. In this savage contest, which lasted from 1936 to 1939, Italy, Germany, and the Soviet Union intervened to sway the outcome of the hostilities. In revolt against the leftist coalition government, General Franco became an object of both hate and veneration.

Perhaps no other conflict until the Vietnam War caused as much intellectual, moral, and political anguish in the United States. Strident protest organizations sprang up to support the Loyalist cause. Public opinion, even among Catholic Americans, was against Franco, but the issue was divisive and bitterly debated in Congress, where there was little support for direct intervention to the Loyalists. Instead, a sharp dispute erupted over the question of easing neutrality restrictions on shipping arms abroad. Such intervention was expressly forbidden by legislation passed in 1935, a year before the Spanish conflict began.

The Spanish struggle was marked by brutality on both sides. Initially evidence that the legitimate Spanish government was responsible for a reign of terror against Catholic clergy painted a picture of Franco's rebels as victims. Only with the intervention of Mussolini's and Hitler's forces on Franco's side did a different perception emerge. The bombing of the village of Guernica, later immortalized in Picasso's masterpiece, rallied Loyalist sympathizers. FDR was pressured by even formerly isolationist senators to repeal the embargo, but in the end, he stayed with neutrality and upheld a view that U.S. intervention on behalf of the Spanish government would be politically divisive. By May 1938, the tide of battle turned in favor of the rightist insurgents, and the Franco regime was recognized by the Vatican.

For Coughlin's followers, Spain was the model for the showdown between communism and fascism, and *Social Justice* offered praise and consistent support for Franco and the rebel cause. The priest was a key force in building pressure within the Catholic community, and his efforts helped forestall U.S. involvement. A headline in *Social Justice* read: "Pope Calls General Franco Savior of Civilization."[42] It was a battle cry that the radio priest might have applied to himself.

For many Catholics, Spain's Republic was a stronghold of atheistic communism and an abomination. A number of American church leaders were active in the effort to thwart Loyalist aid. Though American Catholics were divided in their personal opinions of Franco, even the liberals among them, like Paul Weber of the Catholic trade union movement (who fought Coughlin's attacks on labor unions), agreed with the radio priest on the "Spanish question":

> Coughlin made a lot of strong talks about it. . . . He really believed that . . . the Church was going to be saved if Franco would triumph. . . . Just between us girls, so did I. That's the funny part, the chummy part of all this. . . . Imagine being president of the Newspaper Guild led by Commies at that time and agreeing with Father Coughlin. Of course, I didn't agree with him publicly.[43]

By early 1939, pressure had mounted again for a repeal of the arms embargo against Spain. The Loyalist government was losing the battle against Franco's forces. Around this time, Coughlin delivered a particularly stirring radio address, which generated an outpouring of mail to Congress:

My friends, I ask you: "Shall we Americans engage in foreign entanglements?" "Shall we consider ourselves the policemen of the world?" We will not be deceived by the spurious lie that Italy and Germany are assisting the Spanish Rebels. The whole truth is that Russia assisted the Spanish Loyalists a year before an Italian soldier set foot upon the soil of Spain . . . Soon you poor or middle-class Christians will be the refugee Americans unless, like your ancestors, you will learn to stand up and fight. . . .

I have arranged with the telegraph companies to stand by these few hours to receive your telegrams. Whether you can afford it or not, send a night telegram to your Congressman today or tomorrow. Telephone to your friends—persuade them to do likewise and let the United States Government know that we refuse to be regimented into another World War through the back door of the Spanish embargo.[44]

Social Justice claimed that within thirty-six hours of the speech, 150,000 telegrams had arrived on Capitol Hill. The response elicited by that broadcast echoed up and down the aisles of Congress. Petitions holding an estimated 1.75 million signatures opposed relaxing the embargo. The radio priest celebrated the defeat of such intervention as "our greatest victory."[45]

Articles appearing in Social Justice spoke of a "resurrected Spain." Coughlin compared Franco with George Washington and Abraham Lincoln as a "rebel for Christ" and hailed the fact that "General Francisco Franco has put an end to 'democracy' in Spain. . . . No longer will Spanish 'democrats' burn churches, tie nuns together in kerosene-soaked pits, massacre bishops, priests, and ministers, mow down hundreds of thousands of innocent men, women, and children just because they were Christians."[46]

There was one idea that Coughlin stressed throughout his rhetoric:

The principle of the Corporate State may well be applied to our country with a view to perfecting democracy. Contrary to the view of many, a Corporate State is not necessarily a dictatorial one. It can flourish in an empire, in a kingdom, in a dictatorship or in a democracy. . . .

A Corporate State is predicated on the principle that society is not composed so much of individuals as it is composed of group units with the family being considered as the atom of the state.

These ideals should be adopted in America as we organize to institute a system of democratic government which will permit class to co-operate with class.

We must abandon the inefficient system of parties. . . . Instead of having American voters divided artificially into Democrats, Republicans, etc., I propose to have them divided naturally into groups according to vocations and professions.

That system should be replaced by the Corporate State election. . . . Each class of citizens grouped according to its present calling in life will have a representative in Congress whose business it will be really to represent that class.[47]

A few weeks after Franco's triumph, *Social Justice* featured the article "The Insult of Fascism," written by Coughlin himself under one of his pseudonyms:

Almost everyone will tell you that Fascism is dictatorship. . . . The so-called democratic countries, England, France, and the United States have for so long a time been the leaders and heralders of prosperity and a stable economic existence that we are aghast at the thought of that leadership passing from their hands. . . . *Always, the answer to our supposed superiority comes back in our incapacity for ten long years to solve problems that the Fascist countries are at least on the road to solving.*[48]

In Coughlin's mind, however, such theory mixed constantly with conspiracism. In a private conversation late in 1940, he was asked whether Franco had executed two Spanish bishops because they were in the hands of the Masons." "Not executed," he replied. "But Franco's real ambassadors in this country tell me six bishops have been extruded from their Sees because they were Masons. . . . Masonry and Marixism rule the world today."[49]

Beyond offering his praise for Mussolini and Franco, Coughlin never crossed to the shores of Europe to aid their cause. But he did so for another fascist movement. This one was located in England.

Major James Strachey Barnes was an Englishman from a prominent family that was one of the founding members of the International Center of Fascist Studies, located in Lausanne, Switzerland, and he served as the organization's secretary general. This organization had ties with the British Fascisti, a group created by a wealthy admirer of Mussolini and formed in May 1923, one year after the Italian leader came to power. The organization's goals were to "revive the spirit of sane and intelligent patriotism, uphold the established constitution and prevent the spread of Bolshevism and Communism."[50]

The marginal and disunited fascist groupings in Britain would have vanished from the political landscape had it not been for one man, Sir Oswald Mosley. Tall, handsome, and a member of the country gentry, he had entered Parliament in 1918 as a Conservative for Harrow. A graduate of Sandhurst (Britain's equivalent of West Point), he distinguished himself as a boxer and fencer in college more than as a scholar. In World War I he joined a flying squadron and was wounded twice. His father not only had the distinction of being a titled member of Britain's aristocracy but was the person whose visage was used in Victorian-era depictions of John Bull, the symbol of England.

This future leader of British fascism devoted his legislative energies to problems of war veterans and to criticizing the British government's policies toward Ireland. A strong supporter of the League of Nations, Sir Oswald left the Conservative party in 1922 and joined the Labour party in 1924. He began advocating a number of sweeping economic reforms aimed at credit and currency nationalization and the issuing of consumer credit to the unemployed. In a 1931 pamphlet, *Revolution by Reason,* Mosley called for the establishment of an economic council as a planning and control mechanism. His plan included regulating wages and taking over the more prosperous industries as "national corporations."[51] In March 1931, he formed his supporters into the New party, a group with frightening elements: a youth corps emphasizing gymnastics, along with a readiness to use violence. "The only method we shall employ will be English methods. We shall rely on the good old English fist."[52]

The general election of October 27, 1931, spelled disaster for the party. Of twenty-four candidates standing for office, twenty-two finished at the bottom of the voting list. The party's total vote was only 2 percent. One year later, those still loyal to Mosley formed the core of a newly announced party, the British Union of Fascists (BUF). Meetings were planned, funds solicited, and the new movement emerged in the spring of 1933 with all the trappings of a Mussolini-style blackshirt uniform and a fascist flag and emblem. The BUF was provocative, and often its public rallies became violent. This time, the organization grew rapidly. By early 1934 meetings and demonstrations were being held throughout England, Scotland, Wales, and even Ireland.

The BUF blackshirts held an inaugural rally in London's Albert Hall on April 22, 1934, attended by thousands of supporters. Spotlights focused on Mosley as he strode into the hall with a fascist-style honor guard in raised-arm salute, onlookers chanting, "Hail, Mosley" and singing fascist songs, including the "Horst Wessel Lied" of the Nazi party. In his address, Mosley declared that Jews would be expected to place the interests of Britain before the interests of Jewry, comments that were greeted with "tumultuous applause."[53] In another address shortly after, Mosley spoke of the "foreign Yiddish faces . . . behind which was . . . foreign Yiddish gold . . . from the sweepings of Continental ghettos financed by Jewish financiers."[54]

On a return visit to the Albert Hall in October, Mosley focused heavily on charges of malevolent Jewish power: "For the first time I openly and publicly challenge the Jewish interest in this country commanding commerce, commanding the press, commanding the cinema, dominating the City of London, killing industry with the sweatshops. These great interests are not intimidating, and will not intimidate the Fascist movement of the modern age." In parts of the speech he went so far as to mimic a Jewish accent. In closing he exclaimed: "They have dared in their great folly to challenge the conquering force of the modern age, and tonight they will begin to have their answer! We take up that challenge. They will it! They shall have it!"[55]

Unlike the German Nazi party, Mosley's BUF never made much headway. When members engaged in and stimulated street violence, the result was legislation banning the use of the blackshirt and other uniforms by organized political groups. Police blotters, particularly in East London neighborhoods where a large concentration of Jews resided, recorded numerous incidents of brawls, injuries, and property damage. Vote tallies recorded little support for Mosley.

Evidence of Mosley's reliance on financing from foreign fascist gov-

ernments was rumored but not made public by British government officials until the postwar period, when it was disclosed that he received
large-scale subsidies from Mussolini between 1932 and 1935.[56] When
Sir Oswald began to have an interest in Adolf Hitler, partly as a result of
his second wife's ties to the regime (her sister, Unity Mitford, had become a constant visitor to Germany, with frequent invitations to the personal company of the führer), the Italian leader terminated his financial
aid.

In April 1935, Mosley himself traveled to Germany and met Hitler
for the first time.[57] The following summer, Sir Oswald and Diana Mitford
were joined in matrimony. Adolf Hitler was a guest at the private wedding reception, and the wife of Joseph Goebbels was the hostess.[58] Over
the next three years, according to Mosley's autobiography, "It was the
habit of Hitler to convey to me his view of events through Diana."[59]

When I interviewed her in 1991, Lady Mosley recalled that Father
Coughlin had met with her husband twice in England. She remembers
that Coughlin instructed him in the most effective techniques of radio oratory: "He did this by means of a walking stick, in which he demonstrated that by staying back from the microphone and shouting and then
moving close for conveying an intimate voice, the dramatic effects de-
sired could be attained."[60]

Secretly, in order to raise funds, Oswald Mosley sought the development of a profitable commercial radio chain, Air Time Limited. He had in
mind a large audience, using stations in Britain, France, and Germany.
The idea of a broadcasting chain may have been discussed when Coughlin visited England in the fall of 1937. Lady Mosley used her influence
and secured permission to establish a station in Germany, with Hitler's
approval obtained just as World War II commenced.[61]

Early in 1938, Sir Oswald Mosley encouraged Coughlin to hire as a
writer for *Social Justice* an old friend, Major J. S. Barnes, who "had been
awarded a medal by Mussolini." His "being a member of the Pope's
household" and "having many interests in common" encouraged the radio priest to accept the suggestion. In his invitation to Barnes, Coughlin
added, "I ask you to kindly convey my regards to M., as I do not wish to
write him through the mails."[62] (By this time, members of BUF were
watched, and their correspondence was being read by British intelligence.)

Barnes wrote a large number of articles for *Social Justice* between
1938 and 1940, including a series dealing with "The Jewish Question"

and "The Jewish Problem."[63] In analyzing conditions in Europe on the verge of World War II, he expressed optimism that conflict could be avoided. His February 1939 article, "No War in Europe," claimed that "the process of breaking up Europe into National states based on race and language ... has now ... reached its logical conclusion and extreme limits."[64]

Declaring that Mussolini's "most cherished dream is a United States of Europe," Barnes argued that this new entity must be built on Christianity and that "Italy and Germany ... must be given adequate 'places in the sun' and scope for further expansion." He decried "attempts in the American press to depict the European situation as dangerous" and called on "sensible Americans" to be warned about such false propaganda. He added "Those who are contemplating a visit to Europe this year, can afford to make their plans with perfect equanimity and confidence."[65] World War II started seven months later.

8

Foreign Intrigues

I am, first of all a sinner who, at times succumbed not only to
petty vanity but to many types of worldliness. My priestly
life has found me battling the world, the flesh and the devil
in a manner which Satan has reserved for priests. . . . My
only regret is that I did not accomplish more; that I wasted
time on frivolous projects.

Charles Coughlin, 1936

THROUGHOUT HIS CAREER, Charles Coughlin exaggerated and even
fabricated his links to world leaders. In the 1930s, his priestly confreres and close associates were treated to tales that they, in turn, brag-
gingly gossiped about to others. There was the story of a secret visit to
see Hitler. The way Coughlin's business agent put it, the priest had gone
"to see the big man of Germany."[1] No such event ever took place.

Given his fertile imagination and penchant for conspiratorial plotting, separating truth from fiction in the life of Charles Coughlin is a difficult task at best. Among the more lurid instances of his desire to dabble
in foreign nations is his preoccupation with Mexico's church-state politics during the mid-1930s. Coughlin frequently engaged in rabble-
rousing oratory, on some occasions calling for a revolution to overthrow
what he considered Mexico's "Marxist regime," the leftist and anticlerical regime then in power. The question is, Did Coughlin do more than offer inflammatory rhetoric?

Beginning with the 1911 Revolution, a series of reform governments
had taken control of the Mexican nation and sought to restrict the role of
the Catholic church in national life. Provisions of Mexico's 1917 Constitution called for the secularization of public education, limitations on the

number of clergy, and restrictions on the political activities of the church. When the government actions were condemned by Mexican bishops in a pastoral letter directed to the nation's president, Plutarco Elías Calles, he responded by closing Catholic schools and deporting all foreign-born clergy. The suspension of public worship by church authorities provoked a civil war. Late in 1926, the army crushed the initial rebellions, but two and one-half years of guerrilla war followed, with looting, rape, and massacre on the part of government forces and the populist insurgents.

Early in 1927, Father Miguel Pro Juarez, a devout and determined young cleric, returned from Europe to Mexico City just as a set of more stringent government restrictions on clergy took effect. He threw himself wholeheartedly into underground activities, hearing confessions and performing other religious ministrations. Shortly after Pro's return, General Miguel Obregón, brother of Mexico's former president, and two friends were being driven to a bullfight event when several bombs suddenly exploded nearby. Though Obregón's bodyguards pursued the terrorists, they escaped, leaving a vehicle behind owned by the brother of Father Pro. Within a few days, both of the Pro brothers and another associate were executed by a firing squad before a large crowd, which included government officials. The last words of the martyred priest, "Viva Cristo Rey! [Long live Christ the King!]," became a battle cry of the persecuted Catholics, who formed the so-called Cristero rebellion. The Cristeros put down their arms in 1929 and a settlement was reached between church and state.

In the popular press of America, Mexico was portrayed as a chaotic country, led by bloodthirsty and corrupt enemies of private property, men who had no respect for religion. Catholic leaders and newspapers raised the specter of a red radicalism on America's border, an image reinforced with the election in 1934 of Lázaro Cárdenas as Mexico's president. He was described by historian E. David Cronon as "an unlettered soldier, a man of impatient action rather than a brooding intellectual. . . . His uncomplicated ideas derived more from the Mexican Revolution than from contemporary experiments in Washington or Moscow or Berlin."[2] In his zealous drive for land reform, critics saw in Cárdenas's actions, at worst, the hand of a dangerous communist or, at best, a naive tool of communists.

When Charles Coughlin built his new Shrine of the Little Flower, a bas relief of the execution of Father Pro was carved especially for the marble edifice. A month after announcing the formation of the NUSJ,

Coughlin decried the Mexican government and the support he saw it was receiving from American government and business.

> Never in the heart of Africa could be found the savagery of Mex-
> ico's present government. Never in the history of the world, not
> excepting Russia, has there been a Christian land so despoiled.
> Word comes to me from France, from England, from every State
> in our Union that Masonry—Free Masonry—From Presidents
> Polk and Buchanan down to Presidents Wilson and Roosevelt, is
> behind the scenes playing its hand to tear down the Catholic
> Church and destroy the Christian religion. . . .
>   The government of the United States . . . has aided and abet-
> ted the rape of Mexico. . . . Russia is operating at this hour . . .
> south of the Rio Grande, teaching and preaching that Beth-
> lehem's story is myth. . . . Moscow is here! The league of the
> godless is encroaching while we sit idly by with a wicked com-
> placency fearing to offend the dictator [and former Mexican
> president] Calles lest the American oil operators lose a conces-
> sion or that the doctrine of neighborliness suffer a setback![3]

The priest was responding to the news that the Mexican Senate, with the urging of President Cárdenas (along with Calles, his political mentor), had begun a debate on several amendments to the constitution that would place further restrictions on Catholic schools and called for "socialist" teaching to be included in the public school curriculum. Coughlin's was not the only voice raised in protest; several other American bishops denounced what the radio priest called "The Rape of Mexico."

As Catholic constituents lobbied Washington, the U.S. Senate and Congress were feeling increasingly strong pressure to take bold action, and candidates began to worry that the Mexican situation could have an impact on the 1936 elections. Senator Robert Wagner of New York warned of the deteriorating situation and even urged tourists to stop visiting Mexico. He accused the ruling National Revolutionary party of being responsible for "murder, robbery, imprisonment and exile of priests and thousands of innocent men and women."[4]

Immediately upon assuming the duties of his office in April 1933, Ambassador Josephus Daniels faced three major problems: deteriorating church-state relations, land reform that impinged on U.S. agriculture, and the proposed nationalization of Mexico's oil industry. As to the first, two months before he took office, he conferred with his close friend, Father John Burke, secretary of the National Conference of Catholic Bishops, and to his relief learned that the Vatican opposed armed rebellion and the clergy's involvement in partisan Mexican politics.[5]

Father Coughlin took a different view, however. As early as January 1934, in one of his Tuesday evening talks at the Royal Oak Shrine, he predicted a Mexican revolt: "The only way the Christians in Mexico can put their prayers across . . . is at the point of a gun. And that's what they're going to do in the spring. There'll be some fat, greasy scalps hanging on the wall!"[6]

Given the leftist and anticlerical bent of the Mexican government, marginalized right-wing groups and leaders inevitably sought to overturn the regime. Among the more radical of these was a small but militant organization headed by a colorful figure straight out of the tradition of Pancho Villa. General Nicholas Rodríguez was a tall, mustachioed figure whose organization, the Gold Shirts, was a typical fascist-style group of the 1930s. In 1927, Rodríguez had been jailed in Los Angeles for attempting to buy arms and smuggle them into Mexico in violation of the U.S. embargo laws. Investigative journalist John Spivak described the general as a "sixteenth-century pirate operating in the twentieth, arrogant and oozing with the charm of a confidence man."[7]

In opposing the "Red Shirt" Marxists, Rodríguez led his Gold Shirts on a raid in March 1935, attacking the offices of the Communist party. He and several of his compatriots were jailed, albeit briefly. As strikes multiplied in the strife-torn nation, the Gold Shirts became identified as enemies of organized labor and as Nazi sympathizers. People spoke of Rodríguez as wanting to be the führer of Mexico. By the summer of 1935, as the political situation became even more precarious, it seemed that the Gold Shirts would soon have the opportunity to make a bid for power. On November 20, accompanied by a band of his most loyal followers, Rodríguez arrived on horseback at the presidential palace in Mexico City:

> When members of some labor groups arranged to have automobiles block the path of the horsemen, the gold-shirted riders prepared to advance on their adversaries, whirling cowboy ropes. . . . In the struggle that followed, automobiles zig-zagged around the Plaza with the object of running into the horsemen, and the great square became a battle field. When the police ar-

rived half an hour later and brought an end to the hostilities, there were three dead and forty-six wounded. Nicholas Rodríguez was twice wounded with a knife.[8]

When, eight months later, General Rodríguez was discharged from the hospital after finally recovering, he was placed on a waiting plane bound for El Paso, Texas.

Despite being a strident voice in support of overthrowing the far-left regime of Mexico, only the most indirect hints of any connection between Coughlin and the Gold Shirts has come to light. Left-oriented investigative journalists, including John Spivak and A. B. Magil, suggest that Coughlin was somehow involved with the fascistic Gold Shirt movement through associations with two individuals, Henry D. Allen and Hermann Schwinn, who helped to send funds and provide a safe haven in Texas for Gold Shirt leader Nicholas Rodríguez, and to raise funds to keep him going across the border in Texas.[9]

Yet another bizarre incident concerned Coughlin's attempt to organize a private army from the United States in an effort to topple Mexico's government. Although possibly only a hoax, it frightened FBI director Hoover and set off alarm bells at the White House. This tale of intrigue centers on a flamboyant military figure: former Marine Corps Commander General Smedley Darlington Butler.[10]

What Butler described to Hoover bore a striking resemblance to an episode two years earlier in which he had been involved in one of the most bizarre and disturbing hearings ever held in the U.S. Congress. The so-called plot to overthrow the White House had allegedly been engineered by key figures in the newly formed American Legion. In the summer of 1934, Gerald McGuire, a wealthy Wall Street attorney, visited Butler at his home in Newton Square, Pennsylvania, and allegedly told him that "America was faced with a great danger from communism" and needed a complete change of government. He proposed developing a militantly patriotic veterans' organization resembling France's Croix de Feu, a foreign-style group that would preserve the nation. According to Butler, McGuire told him, "You should lead such an organization in a march on Washington." McGuire was quoted as saying, "We have three million dollars to start with on the line and we can get three million more if we need it."[11]

When the alleged plot was revealed, a congressional investigation was held, and Butler's sensational testimony received front-page head-lines around the nation.[12] No charges were ever leveled against the American Legion officials or the others—many of whom were wealthy individuals who had also been active in the far-right Liberty League—who had contacted Butler. McGuire testified evasively and suggested that Butler had simply misunderstood his patriotic intentions; he had no de-sire to encourage any kind of treason or conspiracy against the federal government.[13]

While the alleged plot as greeted with derision by much of the press, Butler never backed down from his story of a "bankers' gold group" that had tried to topple Roosevelt and establish a dictatorship. When the con-gressional investigating committee released its report, excluding names and much of its secret testimony, it actually substantiated Butler's charges: "There is no question that these [coup] attempts were discussed, were planned, and might have been placed in execution when and if the financial backers deemed it expedient." "To be perfectly fair to Mr. McGuire," Butler testified several months later, "he didn't seem blood-thirsty. He felt a show of force in Washington would probably result in a peaceful overthrow of the government. He suggested that 'we might even go along with Roosevelt and do with him what Mussolini did with the King of Italy.' "[14] In May 1935, the *New York Times* carried a front-page story, "Definite proof has been found that the much publicized fascist march on Washington . . . was actually contemplated."[15] But by then, public and congressional interest in the affair had evaporated.

Two years after the first overthrow plot was revealed, Smedley But-ler reported on a second effort to recruit him as a "Man on a White Horse." Special agent Tom Dawsey, in a memorandum on August 8, 1936, told of the visit to FBI offices the day before:

> General Butler stated of his own free will and accord that he had something on his mind and that he would like to get it off. . . .
> The Director stated he would appreciate knowing the same, and General Butler stated that quite a while ago Father Coughlin telephoned him and asked Butler if he would command an army of approximately 260,000 men to march to Mexico and over-throw the Mexican government that was at that time picking on the Catholic Church, that the Mexicans had kidnapped the arch-

bishop, and that Coughlin stated he had financial backing and the
men and the arms, and all he needed was a leader. He stated that
he thought Butler was the man.[16]

Butler was quoted as saying that as soon as he recognized Coughlin's
voice, he asked a friend, the editor of the *Philadelphia Inquirer,* to go to
an extension phone and listen in on the conversation. The general stated
that he had refused Coughlin's offer because it "amounted to treason, that
he was employed by the Federal government, and that, moreover, 'If
Coughlin started such a movement the President of the United States
would assemble the militia and stop such a movement.'" The priest was
reported by Butler to have replied: "I should not worry about President
Roosevelt because they would take care of him on the way down." General Butler then told his caller again that "this amounted to treason, and
that he would not talk to him about it over the telephone."[17]

According to Dawsey's report, Butler's next move was to await further actions from Coughlin, although he "was afraid that some of Coughlin's men would bump him off" if the priest's offer was made public or
that "it might cause some disturbance and that people would call him a
fool." There was a follow-up contact:

> The other day a member of the Executive Committee of the
> Catholic organization that is backing Coughlin came to him and
> asked if Coughlin made such a proposition to him. The man from
> Coughlin's faction informed General Butler that he had previously asked Coughlin whether or not he had requested Butler to
> head this movement and Coughlin refused to deny it and told this
> man to go and ask Butler.[18]

Butler offered further details in which "an ex-marine came to him
and showed him a Chinese ring which was a certification that he was a
dope-smuggler, and told him that he had just smuggled one hundred
brownie automatic rifles from one of the arsenals for this group of men
and that they had hidden them on the estate of John D. Rockefeller." The
general confessed to be quite disturbed over this, and so he decided to
check the information out by going to a friend, who was a quartermaster
at a nearby arsenal. Butler told the FBI agent that the friend had confirmed the theft of the one hundred rifles. The general reiterated his belief
that it was Coughlin's "intention of starting an armed revolution in the

United States, and that Coughlin had made the statement that the voters of the United States would not have another opportunity to vote after the next election." FBI director Hoover told Butler to report any further contact with the radio priest. The general then asked the FBI director not to say anything about the situation to Attorney General Homer Cummings.[19]

The moment Butler left the FBI offices, Hoover telephoned Attorney General Cummings and sent a memo to President Roosevelt. The FBI director also authorized an investigation of missing M-16 rifles at the U.S. Army armory in Raritan, New Jersey, but no further investigation was undertaken.[20] Butler's biographer, Hans Schmidt, told the author he felt Butler had been hoaxed; "the entire Coughlin-Mexican affair played on a gullible, but patriotic soldier."[21]

The alleged Coughlin-inspired overthrow attempts led FDR to call for a systematic surveillance of individuals and groups deemed ready to use illegal methods to undermine the U.S. government. In a confidential memo to the files in September 1936, Hoover reported that Roosevelt was not only concerned about plots on his own life but "had been considerably concerned about the movements of the communists and of fascism in the United States [and] was interested in . . . obtaining a broad picture."[22]

By the time Charles Coughlin arrived in England on September 5, 1937, for what his newspaper, *Social Justice,* called "a leisured tour of England and France," he had already been the subject of media gossip. A front-page headline in the Hearst Sunday newspapers was quoted as denying that "Father Coughlin had 'danced on shipboard with an actress.' "[23] There is a hint that the priest returned the following year under even more fascinating circumstances.

In April 1938, Frank Murphy, seeking a second term as governor of Michigan, warned a close family friend, Ruth Ellery Treglown, against investing in Coughlin's publishing projects. Treglown, married to an Englishman born of American parents, was known as a woman of extraordinary charm who for a time traveled in the most exclusive social circles of Detroit's auto industry elite. According to Frank Murphy's sister, she was "very, very beautiful . . . a free spirit, willing to break rules, a woman who, in her stylish way was a down-to-earth person, someone who would be enamored with the idea of doing a little espionage work."[24]

Murphy saw Ruth and Edward Treglown as part of the so-called Clivedon set—upper-class British who supported a policy of accommo-

dation with Nazi Germany.[25] In February 1938, the Treglowns visited
Murphy while he was seriously ill in Detroit, and they discussed the political climate of Europe, including fascism and trade unionism. Edward
later sent Murphy a newspaper clipping telling of Oswald Mosley's denial that he sought the destruction of unions. Murphy wrote back politely
cautioning the Treglowns about fascism.[26]

Coughlin was more than simply an early supporter of and adviser to
Frank Murphy when he began his Michigan political career as mayor of
Detroit in 1930. He was, in fact, for a period of years, a key member of
the inner circle of people who were treated as part of the Murphy household. The summer home of the Murphy family at Harbor Beach, Michigan, was close to West Branch, where Coughlin had one of his first
assignments after coming across from Canada. Through the Murphys,
Coughlin met Ruth Treglown, then married to her first husband, Steve
Hannagan. Although they lived in Palm Beach, they journeyed north frequently and became immersed in Detroit's social world. But from the beginning, there were problems in the marriage.

In an attempt to save her marriage, Ruth converted to Catholicism.
During a six-month sojourn in Detroit for the purpose, she secretly took
religious instruction from Coughlin. According to Frank Murphy's sister,
she became "a devoted, excited, crusading disciple . . . an active worker
in the social justice movement." She also spent a lot of time with the
Murphys: "She was more or less living with us, in the next suite at the
Whittier Hotel." Though there was some hint of romance between Ruth
and Frank Murphy, the general suspicion was that the new convert was
Coughlin's mistress.[27]

Within the Murphy family a legend of international intrigue grew up
around Coughlin's visit to England. It began with Coughlin's confinement in England:

> Ruth was living in England . . . out in the country, and Father
> Coughlin made a trip to England. When he arrived there, the
> British government wouldn't let him land and have free move-
> ment in the country. She [Ruth] appeared as the wife of a British
> citizen and said that she would be his sponsor. The authorities
> did permit him to go to her house under house arrest. He stayed
> as her guest . . . and he wore tweeds and . . . took off his collar.[28]

The story continued with a remarkable proposal the priest was said to have made to Ruth Treglown: "He told her that she would have to come with him on a secret mission. She would have to do it and that he had the tickets and that it was on a small steamer going over to Hamburg, leaving from a North England town. He had tickets under the name of man and wife and that she would have to go with him to carry out the role. Anyway, he was trying to get to Germany."[29] There is no evidence that Ruth accepted the ultimatum or that Coughlin ever embarked on such a journey. The offer, however, was clearly in Coughlin's style; he frequently traveled incognito in the United States.[30] In 1993, Lady Diana Mosley, widow of the British fascist leader, recalled her husband mentioning that a woman by the name of Treglown was accompanying Coughlin around England during one of his visits.

If Charles Coughlin did stay at the Treglown homestead just north of Brighton in Sussex, Ruth's young sister-in-law, a teenager at the time, does not recall such an event, although she remembers that family members "with the exception of my mother discussed the politics of Father Coughlin" and that her father was "quite pro-Coughlin."[31] There was certainly a continuing relationship between Treglown and Coughlin. Frank Murphy's correspondence with Ruth confirms that the radio priest approached her for help in financing a new initiative, which included the hiring of Hilaire Belloc to write for *Social Justice,* and the upgrading of the newspaper's format and overall quality, an effort, according to former writer Joseph Wright, that was meant to give it a broader market but also carried with it "a more pro-Nazi line."[32]

An overhaul of Coughlin's newspaper in February 1938 followed a new printing contract for increased size, multicolor, rotogravure-quality printing, and the use of a finer-quality paper similar to that of *Life* magazine. When, within a few months, Coughlin was sued by the new printer, Frank Murphy composed (but apparently never sent) a note to Ruth Treglown enclosing the news clippings of the damage suit and recalling his advice of the previous year: "I stated that you would save our friend perhaps a half million if you could keep him from getting in too deep with his publication."[33]

Among Coughlin's inner circle at the Royal Oak Shrine, the priest's European travel became a source of pride and fascination, leavened with a good deal of mythologizing fed by the cleric's own penchant for exaggeration. One fellow priest remembered that "Father Coughlin had tried to get to England, but was not allowed to." He recalled Coughlin's telling him that he was able "to cross into France and Germany by private plane from England."[34]

Coughlin apparently spun the tale of a Hitler meeting as a way to impress his inner circle. On numerous occasions, he wove exaggerated tapestries of drama around his contacts with the famous and powerful. When interrogated in 1942 about the alleged visit to Germany, Stanley Boynton, Coughlin's business agent, told of the priest having taken an overseas vacation "at the end of a thirteen-week contract in 1938 at which time . . . the priest went to Scotland and returned directly to the United States."[35] Boynton told the FBI that Coughlin had never mentioned any secret travel to Germany.

On September 29, 1941, Charles Coughlin was refused a passport and his application was referred to the fraud section of the State Department. A terse explanation was typed under Reason: "reported pro-Nazi."[36]

As Charles Coughlin increasingly immersed himself in a global context of political advocacy and even direct political action, his identification with fascism and then Nazism became hallmarks of his public career. Yet within American society, a major fault line was emerging that would become a focus for the radio priest. It divided Catholics and Jews. It was the choice between fascism and communism. When posed in this stark manner, the Gallup survey found that Catholics chose fascism over communism by a two-to-one margin: 36 to 18 percent. For Jews, there was an opposite response: communism, 49 percent, versus fascism, 18 percent. This disparity was no surprise to Coughlin. Privately, he had shared the view of his closest confidants and advisers: Jews were at war with the Catholic church and its most basic teachings, including its economic and social doctrines. Moreover, the battle lines were growing more distinct as Europe moved toward a showdown between left and right.

Coughlin now embarked on a campaign of warning and education for his vast radio audience. It would be a major turning point in a career few had anticipated, and most found it fearfully destructive.

9

"Jewish Actions Which Cause Cruel Persecution"

Throughout the Centuries, the "Unwritten Law" Code of Jewish Leaders has forced Their People into Actions which Create Conflict and Persecution In One Nation After Another

"Ben Marcin," *Social Justice,* December 12, 1938

WHAT MIGHT BE TERMED formal discrimination against Jews in the United States can be traced to the 1870s, when, says historian John Higham, "Jews as a group pressed most heavily upon a limited field of opportunity."[1] A pattern of social anti-Semitism emerged along the eastern seaboard, particularly in New York, the U.S. city with the largest Jewish immigration. Gentlemen's agreements served to exclude Jews from private clubs, summer resorts, and neighborhoods, and quota systems were ultimately established in colleges and universities. An especially virulent strain of anti-Semitism flourished in the 1920s, reinforced by new "scientific" racist theories. Historians have argued frequently over the exact causes for the sharp rise in American anti-Semitism during the 1930s. Much of the debate centers on whether it was indigenous, springing from native populism, or was imported from Europe.[2]

By the time of the Great Depression, America had a flourishing anti-Semitic folklore. Hostile stereotypes focused on the power of Jews to corrupt the cultural, political, and, especially, economic life of America. In May 1934, former president Hoover's friend Poster Bain circulated an article titled "Consider These Jewish Accomplishments":

The old-time Gentile Journalism of Horace Greeley, of Charles Dana, of Schurz, of Lawrence, of Whitelaw Reid, was mired in the gutter by the inventor of Scareheads, Sensationalism, Muck-Raking, Filth-purveying, a New York Jew.

The old-time merchandizing of A. T. Stewart & Co; of Wanamaker; of Hilton, Hughes and Denning; Lord & Taylor; . . . Was not this debauched into the Bait-advertising, bargain-swindling of the Lichtensteins and the Blums?

The old-time drama was polluted and debauched, and Movies, controlled from their start, were added to the Jewish armamentarium for Gentile pollution. And, this is the race now astutely preparing the Gentile mind for subserviency itself!

Unpleasant, unfriendly, but inescapable is the conclusion that it's a case of FIGHTING BACK against ANTI-GENTILISM. A fight for FAIR PLAY; a fight for decency; a fight for LIFE![3]

The nation experienced a flood of anti-Jewish organizations, known as "native American fascists." One such organization that flourished in the Midwest and was a violent force within the Detroit auto industry was the Black Legion. It was exposed in a trial that included this testimony:

William Guthrie, one of the accused [member of the executive committee of the Legion], confessed today that he had received an order from leaders of the Legion telling him to place his cellar at his business premise at their disposal. The cellar was to be used for the production of typhus bacillus cultures. Members of the executive of the Legion, among them a chemist and a bacteriologist, he said, had decided to execute seventy-three Detroit Jews with the aid of the typhus bacillus. . . . The typhus bacillus were to be mixed in the milk and cheese. . . . Shortly before the execution of the plan, pangs of conscience prompted him to prevent it. "I realized that the mass-murder of these condemned Jews might easily result in wiping out the whole of Detroit."[4]

The assassination plan was said to have been inspired by a German brochure, *A Few Practical Proposals for the Solution of the Jewish Problem.*

The Legion, founded by a Ku Klux Klan leader, dressed its members in black robes instead of the Klan's traditional white. Candidates for membership in the group had to take an oath in which those who violated its tenets would have their heart torn out and roasted over flames of sulfur, "his head can be split open and his brains scattered over the earth; and his soul may be given into torment." An additional punishment was to have one's body submerged in molten metal.[5]

Besides the Black Legion, there were native fascist organizations such as William Dudley Pelley's Silver Shirt Legion, founded the day after Hitler took power in March 1933. Pelley frequently spoke and wrote about his aspirations of being an "American white king" and the "American Hitler."[6] When he ran for president in 1936, however, he garnered only 1,000 votes. Another would-be American führer, Kansas-based Gerald B. Winrod, the "Wichita Jaybird," became a leading advocate of American Nazism. Winrod's crude anti-Semitism was printed each month in his *Defender* magazine, which reached a peak circulation of 110,000.

In addition to the overtly pro-Nazi and fascist groups, a host of anticommunist, "Christian," and "patriotic" organizations were active in the 1930s. Whenever testimony about communist infiltration of labor or schools was needed, such figures as Elizabeth Dilling came forward with her scattergun inventory of left-leaning individuals and groups, *The Red Network,* which became a virtual classic for business and government leaders concerned with communist subversion. Henry Ford subsidized her work. The cluster of professional left hunters included Joseph Kamp and James B. True, with his *Industrial Control Reports,* indefatigable pamphleteers who received funds from major corporations such as Sun Oil, Remington Rand, and General Motors.[7] Another publicist who stressed the Jewish-communist basis of labor unrest was Harry Augustus Jung, who, like Coughlin, had been a key witness at Congressman Hamilton Fish's hearings on the red menace in 1930. Jung testified that Jews made up two-thirds of the cadre of persons seeking to destroy American society.[8]

On December 31, 1935, James True, formerly a reporter for the *Chicago Tribune,* filed a patent in Washington for a uniquely designed personal defense club he called a "kike killer." In August 1936, True was interviewed by a British journalist and explained that he expected a major pogrom against Jews to commence the next month. True explained that his wife owned a "Kike Killer, lady's size because the regular size might be too heavy. It can crack even a negro's skull wide open." He added that "Father Coughlin will soon let loose on the Jews" and confided approvingly "that Coughlin's secretary had been doing research and taking notes on 'Semitic pressure in America.'"[9]

The consensus view of Charles Coughlin developed by historians ascribed his intense anti-Semitism of the late 1930s to a bitter, irrational, and desperate gamble to reclaim a lost popularity after the poor showing of the Union party in 1936. It was an effort to ride a rising tide of opinion that considered Jews a group with excessive power in business and politics. Yet examination of the views of his close associates and backers—ecclesiastical and secular—overturns this view, for they say that the priest's private anti-Semitism persisted unmistakably, relentlessly, and fanatically throughout his career. Antipathy toward Jews was probably nurtured during his theological training. In borrowing from a rich variety of sources, some of them anti-Semitic, Coughlin saw himself as a dedicated student of history.

As a media personality, the radio priest touched on a variety of themes initially, seldom dwelling in any direct or specific manner on the issue of Jewish power or subversion. In reflecting on his radio career decades after it had ended, Coughlin explained to a priest colleague, "I never said anything on the air that I didn't believe was true at the time."[10] In this, at least, he was probably close to the mark. But did he have views that he did not express on the air? And if he did, why did he decide finally to broadcast anti-Semitic sermons in the late 1930s?

Given his compulsive energy, once Coughlin set on any course of action he pursued it with a single-mindedness that could often be self-destructive. When he encountered any form of opposition, his hair-trigger response was to elevate each dispute to a final battle between good and evil. Those who would dare challenge him became not only his mortal enemies but the enemies of God as well. In this way, his private obsession could become a major public crusade. We can see this happen by tracking anti-Semitic comments throughout Coughlin's career.

An early, subtle, and indirect indictment of Jews as the cause of contemporary social and economic problems came in a radio sermon Coughlin delivered on February 2, 1930, prior to his having a national network affiliation. On this occasion, he traced the origins of Marxist socialism to the eighteenth-century figure Adam Weishaupt, founder of a mysterious cult known as the Order of the Illuminati.[11] Coughlin declared that Weishaupt's creed was "that of an avowed atheist," who "taught that all human ills and errors were due to civilization and to Christianity." The priest went on to quote Weishaupt: "Therefore, destroy Christianity and civilization will be happy." Coughlin explained that "such is the thought of the 'Old Testament,' if I may call it such, of Socialism. Such is the religion of its author."[12]

In a radio sermon in fall 1930, Coughlin discussed "the majority of the working class," whom he described as being exploited by "billionaires, the bulk of their money having been made through the revival of this usury or abnormal compound profits so openly condemned by the fundamental laws of justice." The priest invited his listeners to draw an analogy to Shakespeare's character Shylock: "a vagrant tear of pity to shed for the old man because his Jewish gabardine was spat upon; because he had been rated on the Rialto for his usury." Coughlin asserted, "We have lived to see the day that modern Shylocks have grown fat and wealthy, praised and deified, because they have perpetuated the ancient crime of usury under a modern racket of statesmanship."[13] For his address the following week, Coughlin turned to the subject of internationalism and attacked communism, alluding to "Trotsky from New York, Lenin from Germany, Béla Kun from Hungary—men from every nation who long since had devoted themselves to the anarchy, the atheism and the treachery preached by the German Hebrew, Karl Marx."[14]

Nearly two years elapsed before anti-Semitism appeared in another broadcast, this one in the throes of the nation's most serious monetary crisis. In February 1933, a month prior to Franklin Roosevelt's inauguration, Coughlin entitled his radio sermon "Gold—Private or Public!" He presented the listening audience with an elaborate and paranoid version of the role of Jews in European history and in the world of contemporary finance. According to the priest, "the story of the modern Jew" was based on "the Rothschilds of Frankfurt [and] the Napoleonic Wars," and "it is all related in one sense to our present misery." Coughlin explained that the "Christian nations learned that the commercial gold of the world had found itself controlled by private individuals" and that to "carry on their wars [they] went to the Rothschilds for gold." He was recounting these events "not with acrimony . . . but simply outlining . . . a fact of history." Next he offered a prophecy: "I know that this thing is not going to last much longer," then, seeming to catch himself in what might be interpreted as a threat to Jews, added, "Not that I intimate that force shall ever be used. God forbid!" His powerful voice now rising in volume, Coughlin reached the apogee of his homily: "I am advocating the national confiscation of all gold. . . . Things that are for the development of a country . . . must belong to the nation alone and must not be permitted to rest in the hands of the Morgans and Kuhn-Loebs and central banks and Rothschilds who have grown fat by the billions at the expense of the millions of oppressed people."[15]

In his address the subsequent week, "The Suicide of Capital," Coughlin hammered away at what he called the exploitative Rothschilds of Europe, describing them as "disparaging the teaching of their forebears, despising the precepts of their great leader Moses, mocking the doctrines of the Talmud and the precepts of the Old Testament," and as men who "re-established in modern capitalistic life the pagan principles of charging interest on productive, or destructive debts." Coughlin charged, "Under the flag of their leadership, there assembled the international bankers of the world. . . . The horrible, hated word spelled W-A-R was the secret of their success."[16]

A key theme of Coughlin's economic and political philosophy can be readily discerned in these radio sermons: Jewish manipulation as the cause of both economic crisis and U.S. entry into World Wars I and II. His stock phrase "international bankers" served as the key slogan of his public career. For many in his audience, it was a code word for Jewish economic exploitation and world power.

The priest's anti-Semitism came to the attention of movie censorship czar Will Hays, who was especially concerned that Coughlin might target his industry because of the visible role of Jews. In the wake of charges of fostering lewdness and disrespect for decency, Hollywood filmmakers agreed to a form of self-discipline. When Hays heard that the radio priest planned a major attack on Hollywood in an address at the Chicago Coliseum in the summer of 1934, he arranged to visit the Shrine of the Little Flower to head off the critical salvo.

When they met, the tenor of Coughlin's remarks convinced Hays that the proposed address was aimed at "using the motion pictures as a means of an attack on the Jews, claiming that they dominated the business, and blaming evils on them."[17] In reflecting on the incident, Hays recalled that he had misgivings about Coughlin: "He seemed to me to express some distinctly good judgments [about the movie industry] . . . and I somehow still felt in the dark. Something seemed out of key." Remarking about "the strength of the man, his clarity and even brilliance of expression," which Hays said "were undeniable," he added, "I do not feel quite so sure that in every case, as the Scriptures put it, 'Out of the heart the mouth speaketh.'"[18] Within a few months of this behind-the-scenes skirmish, the radio priest was defending himself in a public forum against charges of anti-Semitism that appeared in a newspaper of the Detroit Jewish community.

By the late 1930s, Coughlin's attacks on the economic, political, and cultural role of Jews in American society and the rest of the world had become more blatant and frequent. Like most confirmed anti-Semites, he prided himself on his expert knowledge of Jews—their history, religion, and economic behavior. (In the last years of his life, Charles Coughlin offered to donate his extensive collection of anti-Semitic literature to the Detroit Catholic archdiocese. It refused the offer.) Interviewed in 1973, Coughlin responded: "You accomplish nothing by being anti; you accomplish only by being pro . . . Christ and the Apostles were Jews. And the first thirty-three popes were Jews. Among the last ten popes we've had, three were predominantly Jewish. I can't be anti-Jewish."[19] Moreover, in forming the NUSJ, he drew a constituency mainly from non-Catholics, including a significant number of Jews, and had attracted many Jews on the basis of his concern for economic suffering and exploitation. As one Detroit resident remembers it, "Jews in Detroit were divided about whether he was an anti-Semite. How could he be anti-Semitic if he had the Ten Commandments carved in Hebrew on the Tower of the Shrine of the Little Flower?"[20] At the same time, the thread of anti-Semitic rhetoric that was woven occasionally into Coughlin's radio sermons had alarmed certain Jews.

When Hitler came to power in March 1933, Coughlin's taunts, perceived as unfortunate deviations, came to be taken more seriously. Suddenly words seemed capable of triggering violent persecution.

News of Coughlin's anti-Semitism was circulated by those who attended his Shrine Lectures, a weekly Tuesday evening event in which the priest staged mock debates on current social issues and controversies. Often these took place before two or three thousand visitors who were jammed into the Shrine of the Little Flower.[21] To reports that Coughlin was ridiculing and showing hostility toward Jews, he and his supporters vehemently denied that he was attacking Jews as a group. He proclaimed in radio broadcasts and sermons throughout the 1930s that he wanted "good religious Jews" to join him in an anticommunist drive against "apostate" or "atheistic" Jews. In November 1934 when the priest was asked to address the issue of his alleged anti-Semitism, he described the effort as a smear campaign: "Those who are hired to defend the tainted interest of the exploiting class both by innuendo and by malicious suggestions have endeavored . . . to arouse resentment in the hearts of the

Jewish people because of imaginary slanders supposed to have originated from this microphone."[22] Two weeks later, when interviewed by the editor of the Detroit Jewish community newspaper in which his earlier remarks appeared, Coughlin offered his assurance of being a "friend and champion of the Jewish people."[23]

Indeed, since the early 1930s, the radio priest had been enlisting the support and financial backing of the Detroit Jewish community. Dr. Leon Fram, leader of the national reform synagogue movement and chief rabbi of a major local congregation, was among those who supported Coughlin. Recalling his relationship with the priest, Fram spoke of a time beginning in the 1920s as one in which "he and I were both young, liberal clergymen. We were quite good friends. . . . We would be invited to various groups, Rotary and Kiwanis . . . to have sort of an ecumenical program. First I would speak on the misunderstandings that Judaism suffers from . . . [and] he would speak of the misunderstandings of Catholicism. We would travel all around town together. We were pals."[24]

By 1934, Charles Coughlin was using these personal contacts in the Jewish community as a highly public means of garnering support for NUSJ and as a means to answer his critics. In the spring of 1935, he played the role of Jewish compatriot by inviting two highly respected rabbis—Fram and Dr. Ferdinand Isserman of St. Louis—to speak at a large NUSJ rally being held at the Olympia stadium in Detroit. Both accepted the priest's invitation.

Social justice was a cause with which many Jews identified. The previous fall, in the face of criticism from prominent members of the Jewish community, Rabbi Fram had praised the newly formed NUSJ. Rabbi Isserman's address at Coughlin's rally confirmed the support Fram had offered, stressing the affinity between Judaism and the principles of social justice enunciated by the radio priest. "I am not a member," the clergyman noted, "but [I am] in sympathy with its goals though not all of its program." In his closing remarks, the rabbi seemed hopeful about Coughlin's newly created mass movement though wary too:

> If this National Union for Social Justice will rally to maintain democracy, and if it will endeavor to secure social justice for men and women of all creeds, of all denominations, of all races, if its program will equally include black and white, Catholic and Protestant, Jew and Christian, native and foreign born, if it will be animated not with malice but with mercy, not with hate but

with faith . . . if this will be its hallowed purpose, from which it will allow no temporary advantage to swerve it, then it may become a historic movement and gain the acclaim of history and the blessing of God.[25]

Writing to Rabbi Isserman shortly after the NUSJ rally, Coughlin was thankful: "Your presence on the platform and your excellent address on the fundamental principles of social justice accomplished much in reducing the criticism of those who consistently have been trying to build up a spirit of antipathy between members of your race and religion and myself."[26] Yet just a few months earlier, in January, the priest had admonished his Shrine audience: "While we love each other, we're so open-minded [to] Jews [and] Mohammedans . . . remember this is a Christian nation! Let's not overwork this democracy!"[27]

As a condition for speaking at the NUSJ rally, Coughlin had promised Rabbi Isserman to print the following statement: "As long as my voice is on the air, I shall fight any attempt to inaugurate anti-Semitic movements in America." Though he never printed these words in any publication or spoke them over the air, he did repeat them in a letter to the rabbi dated the month after the rally.

In his dramatic final address to the National Union Convention in Cleveland in August 1936, Charles Coughlin did more than break that promise:

We are a Christian organization only in that we believe in the principle of "love thy neighbor as thyself." With that principle in mind I challenge every Jew in this nation to tell me that he doesn't believe in it! I'm not asking the Jews to accept Christianity with all its beliefs, but since their system of a tooth for a tooth and an eye for an eye had failed, I challenge them to accept Christ's brotherhood![28]

At the end of this speech, Coughlin collapsed and was escorted out of the hot summer sun, presumably suffering from extreme exhaustion.

In 1939, *Social Justice* briefly alluded to Rabbi Isserman. He was described as "long a foe of the Detroit radio priest."[29]

In 1970, in an unpublished interview, Coughlin blended conspiracism and anti-Semitism in a new way: "Roosevelt is Jewish. Rosenfelt was the first name and he wasn't regarded as one of the first founders of

Jewry in this country either. I have a book out there with the pedigree of all the Jews in it written by a Jew which I can show you . . . some of them more famous Jews than he."[30] This hindsight paranoia was not just a product of old age but the natural end point of Coughlin's conspiratorial antibanking, suspicious mind, steeped in the paranoia of his day.

When former Pennsylvania congressman Louis McFadden died of a stroke in October 1936, anti-Semitic groups circulated rumors about what they saw as the real circumstances of his death: Jews had killed him. McFadden's association with Charles Coughlin was close. A substantial portion of Coughlin's famous "Versailles" speech had come from a speech delivered by the Pennsylvania representative, and three years later, McFadden ensured his place in history in one of the most blatantly anti-Semitic speeches ever delivered on the floor of Congress. He repeated his remarks in a radio broadcast the same evening, May 2, 1934. On the following day, the *Congressional Record* printed his claims about FDR and the Jews:

> Since the election of Franklin D. Roosevelt in 1932 this country has been educated to a new phase in government. . . . Or shall we say that which it is? It is assuredly "Freedom and planning" adapted to the United States. . . . Stripped of all its camouflage, it is a guild form of government. . . . The guild form of government is directly the opposite of the constitutional form of government. It is the Jewish plan of a world estate.[31]

Congressman McFadden had echoed one of the standard anti-Semitic clichés of the day: FDR's "New Deal" was the "Jew Deal." A bit of colloquial doggerel about Franklin and Eleanor Roosevelt made the rounds:

> Can you answer the $64 question:
> What man said to "That" Woman,
> "You kiss the niggers,
> "I'll kiss the Jews,
> "We'll stay in the White House
> "As long as we choose"?

By the mid-1930s, anti-Semitism had risen to such a fever pitch that its proponents were able to offer a quite simple explanation for FDR's willingness to serve the cause of Jewish domination: his own "Jewish" ancestry. George Deatherage of St. Albans, West Virginia, head of the Knights of the White Camellia, which used the swastika as its insignia, wrote to FDR in the fall of 1934 to explain why he no longer took pride in tracing his roots to the president's bloodline. Instead of telling his son to be proud of their family lineage, Deatherage now would "take the first opportunity I can to kick it out of him."[32] The reason was that the pro-Nazi activist had allegedly discovered the Delanos were Jews.

Gerald Winrod, another professional anti-Semite, told his *Defender* magazine, "From the viewpoint of eugenics it [FDR's Jewish background] explains his [FDR's] natural bent toward radicalism . . . and proves unmistakably, that the Roosevelt administration offers a biological, as well as a political problem." According to Winrod, "It is therefore, as natural to him to be radical as it is for others to be true Americans. . . . HE IS NOT ONE OF US!"[33]

When, early in 1935, the former governor of Michigan, Chase Osborne, told reporters that Theodore Roosevelt had once confided in him about his Jewish ancestry, the revelation immediately became the subject of a nationwide wire story. FDR responded promptly to an inquiry on the issue when it was raised in a letter written to him by *Detroit Jewish News* editor Philip Slomovitz. Roosevelt indicated that he had "no idea as to the source of the story which you say came from my old friend, Chase Osborne," adding, "All I know about the origins of the Roosevelt family in this country is that all branches bearing the name are apparently descended from Claes Martenseene Van Roosevelt, who came from Holland sometime before 1648." FDR then cautioned that "even this fact was not certain" and that "where he came from in Holland I do not know, nor do I know who his parents were." Finally, Roosevelt noted, "In the dim distant past they may have been Jews or Catholics or Protestants—what I am more interested in is whether they were good citizens and believers in God—I hope they were both."[34]

In a letter marked "Strictly Personal and Confidential" that was written to Slomovitz in March 1935 but not published until 1985, Rabbi Stephen S. Wise, one of the key leaders of the Jewish community in the 1930s, related an incident at his home where Eleanor Roosevelt had been a guest: "Mrs. Wise reported to him a conversation she had had with the First Lady: Mrs. Franklin D. Roosevelt said, 'Often Cousin Alice and I say that all the brains in the Roosevelt family came from our Jewish great-grandmother.' She added a name which, as I recall it, was Esther

Levy. Then she said, 'Whenever mention is made of our Jewish great-grandmother by Cousin Alice or myself, Franklin's Mother gets very angry and says, 'You know that is not so. Why do you say it?' " According to Mrs. Wise, "Mrs. Roosevelt spoke with knowledge, conviction, and authority. You must not, however, make use of this." Given the climate of anti-Semitism at the time, Rabbi Wise reinforced his injunctive by posing to editor Slomovitz a rhetorical question: "Do you not think that what President Roosevelt wrote to you is more or less the statement of a man who knows what I have just written to be true but deems it wiser and more expedient not to make any public mention of it at this time?"[35]

Slomovitz might have believed in the truth of the basic charge. No doubt when he wrote to Teddy, it was in the hope of using the truth (whatever it was) to combat anti-Semitism. In his treatment of the original Chase Osborne story, Slomovitz told readers of his skepticism over the matter, given that a fire had destroyed the former Michigan governor's books. In reply, Osborne chided the *Detroit Jewish News* editor: "What was in my mind was that if he [FDR] was a Jew, he is an apostate. If he is an apostate, he is a reflection upon your race . . . President Roosevelt knows well enough that his ancestors were Jewish."[36] In reflecting on the incident half a century later, Slomovitz put the matter quite simply: "It would have been adding fuel to the fires of anti-Semitism."[37]

A leading anti-Semite of the 1930s, Robert Edmondson, argued that Roosevelt's genealogy explained his using the eve of the Jewish New Year in 1939 to call a special session of Congress "to jam through repeal of the existing strict neutrality laws." Moreover, noted Edmondson, FDR displayed "incontrovertible Jewish action-traits." The litany contained thirteen, including these:

1. Roosevelt appointed to office more Jews than any other administration in American history.
2. He has broken practically all his pre-election platform promises.
3. He constantly meddles in the affairs of other nations—just as individual Jews continually butt into the personal relationships of Gentile individuals.
4. He is America's Hitler-Hater No. 1—because Germany expelled Jewish Communists, who have wrecked the Reich. He welcomes Jewish refugees.
5. He is a typical Jewish "show man."[38]

The issue of FDR's Jewish ancestry was a favorite theme of Axis broadcasts and newspaper articles. This item appeared in a Roman newspaper in July 1940, warning of the world danger if FDR were elected to a third term:

> President Roosevelt intends to repeat the "Pax Judaica" of Woodrow Wilson who led the United States into the World War because he acted on behalf of Morgenthau, Warburg, Jacob Schiff, Louis Brandeis, Kuhn, Loeb & Co., all Jewish bankers of New York and masters of the world. President Wilson was able to put across his scheme because 20 per cent of America's population was Jewish then, but it is easier now, because the number of Jews number 40 per cent of the total population today and because Roosevelt himself is a Jew.[39]

Nearing his eightieth birthday, Charles Coughlin explained, when asked by a local journalist in an unpublished interview, why he had broken off his alliance with FDR: "Mr. Roosevelt made up his mind that he was going into this war. He was determined to down Hitler. 'But why do you want to do this?' I asked him. 'Oh, but he's persecuting the Jews!' was his answer. . . . I sat with Mr. Roosevelt telling him my version of why he shouldn't get into this, no matter what faith it was it would have to explode against both Christians and Jews. You know . . . Roosevelt is Jewish."[40]

When Charles Coughlin turned to the topic of the "money question," he relied on the advice and ideas of a coterie of men and one woman, Gertrude Coogan, the daughter of a wealthy Illinois farm family who in 1922 became the first woman to receive an M.B.A. degree. She became wealthy as a business consultant in her own right in Chicago. What drew the careers of Coughlin and Coogan together was a book on the evils of the federal reserve system and its argument that the institution was a mechanism by which international financiers controlled the U.S. economy. Cooper sought out the popular radio priest in order to use him as a vehicle to apply her analysis in solving the problems of the depression.

As the depression settled over the nation, Coogan began writing what she believed was an important book, *The Money Creators,* explaining the causes of and solutions for the nation's economic crisis. She then set out on a national lecture circuit that was crowded with pundits and theories to explain the nation's economic plight. A pamphlet issued in 1935 offered this summary of Cooper's main idea:

> *Money Creators* cites powerful examples from history which are carefully omitted from all works and discussions by eminent "economists." The POWER TO CREATE MONEY IS THE POWER TO TAX. This paramount power BELONGING ONLY TO CONGRESS has been SECRETLY USURPED BY MONEY CHANGERS. "Money Creators" explains how depressions are created and how the money changers WIN by creating depressions.[41]

In the promotional material for her book, Coogan was credited with having "unearthed appalling proof that the trickery of the money changers is but part of a vast plan to bring all countries under subjection to a small group of financiers—men who are cursed with an insatiable ambition to rule others." The author identified herself as a representative of Lawful Money Pilgrims, an organization whose aims "were endorsed by Professor Frederick Soddy of Oxford University, who had received a Nobel Prize in physics."[42] Coogan's book, by virtue of its reliance on Soddy's work, placed it squarely in the conspiracy tradition of anti-Semitic literature. Soddy's *Wealth, Virtual Wealth and Debt,* published in 1926, argued that "Jewish international finance" was the root of modern capitalism's failures.

According to an interview conducted in 1943 with her cousin, a Jesuit priest teaching at the University of Detroit, "Gertrude really indoctrinated Coughlin with anti-Semitism. . . . She is the most violent and hysterical Jew-hater I have ever known. . . . She talked nothing but anti-Semitism until we held a family conference and advised her to go up to the Wisconsin lakes for a long rest and forget all about the Jews."[43]

Coogan first contacted Charles Coughlin through Bishop Michael Gallagher, the radio priest's superior. According to her close friend Mary Larkin, she was called to Detroit to provide some financial advice: "He [Gallagher] probably knew her through some of the priests she was very active with down here [in Chicago]. She helped many priests and parishes. Many times I heard her say that Father [Coughlin] could not say anything on finance unless she was in the room." Coogan would stay with Coughlin's mother, traveling to Detroit every Saturday and remaining until Sunday afternoon.[44]

Coughlin relied on Coogan's writings in creating a third party. The idea he presented to her was to follow up on her successful general treatise on world economic patterns with a more down-to-earth primer, one that could serve as a kind of economic bible for the NUSJ. Early in 1936, in time for the campaign, Coogan ghost-wrote a book that bore Coughlin's name as the author (the only book to bear his authorship until his retirement in the 1970s). The 180-page paperback, *Money! Questions and Answers,* contained a series of questions and responses:

> *Are the international bankers the rulers of the world?*
> Yes. When they are able to manipulate the money structure of the various nations, they *dominate* and *control* both the *economic* and *social* life of any nation wherein they carry on their manipulations. . . .

> *Are the international bankers themselves unpatriotic and greedy men?*
> While some individual men may be honorable, their policies are unsound and unmoral and were conceived by persons by [*sic*] patriotism, democracy, justice and charity are not understood.[45]

The publication of *Money* led to serious problems between Gertrude Coogan and Coughlin. Interviewed in 1986 a few months after Coogan's death, her companion, Mary Larkin, bitterly assailed the priest: "They had an agreement and then he broke it. . . . He republished it and made a lot of money from it . . . $50,000. . . . I don't think she ever got any of it. She made all the trips up there every week. . . . Gert would ask only what would cover her expenses." Coogan had complained to her relative that after the project was completed, "Coughlin thanked her and told her that he proposed to sell the book at cost. . . . Then he marked up the price and made over $50,000 selling at a profit. She got nothing for it."[46]

More was at stake for Coogan then authorship. She angrily wrote to Coughlin's superior, Bishop Gallagher, explaining that the radio priest had "urged me most vigorously to begin writing" and that if she did so, "I was to become Financial Editor of the Newspaper [*Social Justice*]." According to her meticulously maintained records, she and her secretary were entitled to divide some $1,065 in salary, and they had incurred $977 in expenses preparing *Money.* Coogan also reminded Bishop Gallagher that Coughlin had told his radio audience of having spent two years preparing the ghost-authored book, and she pointed out that he had written in *Social Justice* of having "'spent more time in the research and drafting . . . than he had spent in any twenty radio discourses put together.' You know this was not the truth."[47]

Coogan went public with her charges of plagiarism during the height of the Union party campaign in the fall of 1936. The priest was quick to respond, firing off an urgent telegram to Bishop Gallagher accusing Coogan of having "misused your influence evidently to destroy me. . . . I do not plan to let Coogan get away with the statement and with the quotations accredited to you relative to her authorship which makes me nothing more than a pirate."[48] In a press conference, Bishop Gallagher spoke in vague terms about the dispute and did not offer any challenge to Coughlin's version of what had occurred.

For her part, Coogan assailed Bishop Gallagher, charging that "your continued failure to take real and effective steps to right the wrongs caused by Father Coughlin's violations of the trust and confidence placed in him is a source of great disappointment and disillusionment." She asserted that "with your full knowledge at the time . . . I bowed to his obvious extreme egotism and selfishness."[49]

Coogan withdrew from the Union party and avoided any public attacks on Coughlin, although for many years she privately pursued her grievance with church officials, including bringing her suit to the Vatican. No action was ever taken. According to Mary Larkin, Coogan never forgave her church. As blindness overtook her, Coogan gave away most of her private library and became reliant on a companion to read for her, yet she managed in 1974 to publish a new book, *Only You Can Stop Inflation,* and she kept up an active career of lecturing.[50]

Recalling her recently deceased companion, Mary Larkin pointed out that Coogan "was terribly upset about the Jewish influence. She said our country was sold. And Gert was a personal friend of Nancy Reagan's mother, Edith Luckett Davis. She came into Gert's office about once a month. 'Reagan knows the situation.' But she says, 'They're all held. They can't do anything.' She said 'If you only knew the intrigue in Washington that the Jews have the country.'" And Larkin added, "Gert never believed that business about the Holocaust at all."[51]

One must search hard in the career of the radio priest a public figure who, once identified as an ally, did not at some later point become an enemy.

The only one was Henry Ford. Their first encounter was bitter, when Coughlin red-baited Ford to the Fish committee, yet there were both personal and political reasons for Ford and Coughlin to be drawn together. Both men shared a number of common passions, including a visceral hostility toward banking and communism. In the 1970s, Coughlin recalled that he and Ford "were great friends. I had lunch with [him] at least once a month . . . he was a sincere man who knew the truth when he saw it."[52] Despite the priest's penchant for exaggeration, there were indeed a number of occasions on which he and Henry Ford communicated both directly and indirectly. There were as well good reasons for Ford and Coughlin to maintain a careful arm's-length relationship, at least in the public media. Religion was one. Ford was greatly angered when his grandson, Henry II, agreed to convert to Catholicism as a condition of his marriage to Anne McDonnell in 1940.[53]

One of Coughlin's most trusted aides and a key staff writer for *Social Justice,* Joseph Wright, remembers several contacts between the auto industrialist and the priest. A recounting of one such event, which occurred in the late 1930s, offers a glimpse of their relationship at a time when the radio priest was under attack by an old foe: "Malcolm Bingay [managing editor of the *Detroit Free Press*] attacked Coughlin, he hated him, called him a congenital liar. . . . Coughlin wanted Henry Ford to call the *Free Press* and use his influence and tell them what he thought. So Ford says, 'Come out.'" Wright recalls:

> We were met by Harry Bennett, who had a loaded lugar pistol on his desk. He always had one. And his bow tie on. He always wore a bow tie. He was afraid if he wore a four-in-hand tie somebody would come up from behind and strangle him. Ford greeted us very cordially. On the phone he says to Bingay, "Bingay, you God-damned old bald-headed sonofabitch, you got Mickey Cochran [manager of the Detroit Tigers] fired and you got Harry Kipke [University of Michigan football coach] fired and now you're trying to get Father Coughlin fired!"[54]

Coughlin's relationship with Henry Ford appears to have emerged via an intermediary, Ernest G. Liebold, Ford's longtime personal secretary. Described by one historian as "a squat, heavyset, bullnecked man with short-cropped hair," he was an enthusiastic supporter of the "New Germany." A devout Lutheran, he seemed to epitomize the modern Prussian military man: "At dinner time, his eight children would march around the table in military style and no one could sit down until he gave the word."[55]

Liebold's role at the Ford Motor Company was a powerful one.[56] He was a central figure in Ford's infamous campaign against Jewish influence in American business, culture, and politics, which, after its serialization in the *Dearborn Independent* in 1921 and 1922, later became a worldwide reference work for anti-Semitism, entitled *The International Jew*.[57] Within the company, Liebold was certainly the main influence pressing Henry Ford toward a sympathetic view of Nazi Germany. On one occasion at a festive event, he passed out miniature Nazi swastika-flag pins to Ford personnel.[58]

It was during the Detroit banking crisis of 1933 (partly through his own initiative but with the blessing of Ford) that Ernest Liebold developed ties with Charles Coughlin. Ford's key aide recalled that "one evening we discussed the encyclicals of Pope Leo [and] Coughlin tried to compare how closely they lined up with Mr. Ford's ideas." Liebold found that line of comparison "very interesting" and called the radio priest "a man of a very high degree of intelligence." He was particularly impressed that Coughlin "knew what he was talking about" and had command of "facts and figures that could not be refuted." Commenting further, Liebold noted that "Mr. Ford was always interested in anyone who was following along within his principles." In particular, Liebold remembered that "Coughlin came out and talked about Wall Street money interests controlled by Jews. He touched upon the currency issues. . . . They were all matters that Mr. Ford was more or less interested in."[59]

Beginning in the mid-1930s, acting on both his own initiative and that of key Ford aide Harry Bennett, Coughlin was implicated in a series of bizarre and sometimes ludicrous efforts to prevent an independent union from organizing the Ford Motor Company. This was shortly after having served as a fund-raising and morale-boosting speaker for the fledgling American Industrial Workers Union (AIWA) when it formed late in 1934.[60] Leaders of the organization soon broke with the priest, while he accused them of harboring communist leanings.

By the spring of 1937, a new effort was under way to unionize Ford workers. The focus of the United Auto Workers (UAW) campaign was to organize the sprawling Ford Rouge complex outside Detroit. The company, under the leadership of "Service Director" Harry Bennett, was determined to stop it. Under Walter Reuther, the UAW defied the prohibition against union activity and the result became a milestone in U.S. labor history, known as the "Battle of the Overpass."

> On May 26, 1937, a brisk spring day, six union distributors came . . . to pass out handbills. . . . Not knowing that the overpass was restricted to Ford workers, they [were] ordered off. . . . Before they could obey . . . several former prizefighters and a couple of plant foremen grabbed the four union men and brutally beat them. . . . It was really an organized and well-handled beating. . . . They pulled Richard Frankensteen's coat over his head and then proceeded to lambaste him. They kicked him and knocked him out. While he was on the ground, the toughs held his legs apart with their feet, put their heels in the pit of Frankensteen's stomach and twisted, then kicked him several times in the groin. . . . All four men [including Walter Reuther] were pushed, rolled, and finally thrown down the metal steps of the overpass.[61]

The confrontation took place just a few weeks after a new labor organization, the Workers Council for Social Justice, had been announced with a front-page ad in all the major Detroit dailies. This was an attempt by the company to co-opt the union movement. The individuals named as officers were Ford employees, on a two-week leave of absence for this purpose. The new company union's vice president was Robert Montieth, a member of Father Coughlin's Shrine, who secured a position at Ford Motor through the help of Louis Ward. Coughlin touted the labor organization as a boon to Ford workers, including, he noted, the establishment of company stores that would sell food and clothing at cost.[62] But within a few weeks, the priest's newly created enterprise failed for lack of support by rank-and-file workers.

Shortly after the demise of the Workers Council for Social Justice, Coughlin was again implicated in a scheme for a company-sponsored union. This new initiative allegedly involved efforts by the radio priest to help "buy" the president of the UAW. A partner of the abortive undertaking was a parishioner in Coughlin's church, a vice president at Ford, Ed "Pete" Martin. One of the first production and engineering officials of the company, Martin's tough discipline had been a focus of union grievances.

Because of the bitter factionalism within the UAW, Bennett had been able to pursue a strategy of divide and conquer, sowing distrust among potential leaders and between leaders and rank-and-file workers. In the summer of 1937, he reputedly sanctioned a meeting between Coughlin, UAW president Homer Martin, and secretary R. J. Thomas. In hosting the tryst at the Shrine with several key personnel of the divided union, Coughlin appeared to many in the autoworker organization to have betrayed his initial support for workers in the Detroit auto plants.[63] At the alleged secret meeting with UAW representatives, the priest was charged with having offered what was, in effect, a bribe to a key union leader, an offer made on behalf of Henry Ford I.[64] In fact, there is no hard evidence regarding any financial arrangements. Ford's help to the radio priest is rumored to have occurred in two forms: subsidization of Coughlin's organizations with direct contributions and purchase of various publications, specifically *Social Justice.* In testimony before the National Labor Relations Board, a UAW vice president mentioned the purchase of ten thousand copies of *Social Justice* for distribution by Harry Bennett.[65]

Rumors of Ford's underwriting of the political activities of the radio priest were rife even in President Roosevelt's cabinet room. Interior Secretary Harold Ickes mentioned in a 1939 diary entry that "rich people in the country who are said to include Henry Ford and other automobile manufacturers . . . are helping to finance Father Coughlin. . . . He is making a particular drive in New York City and undoubtedly someone is financing him heavily."[66] Roosevelt's son James told me that his father was certain that Ford was subsidizing Coughlin.[67]

On his seventy-fifth birthday, July 30, 1938, Henry Ford, dressed in an immaculate white suit with a red sash draped across his jacket, was photographed having the Grand Cross of the German Eagle pinned to his lapel by the Honorary vice-consul of the Third Reich in Detroit, Fritz Hailer.[68] Ford accepted the medal, he said, from the German people, who "as a whole are not in sympathy with their rulers in their anti-Jewish policies. . . . Those who have known me for many years realize anything that breeds hate is repulsive to me."[69] A year later, after Hitler's invasion of Poland, Ford confided to a young acquaintance, "There hasn't been a shot fired. The whole thing has just been made up by the Jew bankers."[70]

Henry Ford's promotion of anti-Semitism in the early 1920s reflected his rural midwestern upbringing, steeped in Shylock and Fagin images of Jews. It was not difficult for Ford—or for Coughlin—to conclude that international Jewish banking power had started World War I and kept it going and that Jews were seeking to destroy Christian civilization. That these two prominent personalities—one Protestant and the other Catholic—identified Jews as a common foe had an enormous impact in legitimizing anti-Semitism in America.

Throughout 1937 and into early 1938, Jewish financial control became a regular theme in *Social Justice.* Up to this point in Coughlin's public addresses and broadcasts, he had been careful to include a mix of Jewish and non-Jewish individuals and firms when he spoke of "international bankers." Nevertheless many Jews and non-Jews interpreted this reference as meaning "Jewish international bankers." Then, during the summer, as fears over war breaking out in Europe became more intense, Coughlin adopted explicit language and printed his own version of the very centerpiece of anti-Semitic literature at the time, the notorious *Protocols of the Elders of Zion.*

These forgeries have had a remarkable history since they first appeared shortly before the 1905 uprising against Czar Nicholas II of Russia. At the time, the *Protocols* were circulated in Paris, probably by agents of the czar's secret police. They documented a common conspiracy theory then spreading like a social epidemic throughout Europe: an unholy alliance of Jews in league with Freemasons was at the heart of war and depression. The *Protocols* purport to be the minutes of an allegedly secret meeting among Jewish leaders to seize control of the world. Significant parts of the document, however, are virtual word-for-word copies of an obscure French satire, John Robison's best-selling *Proofs of a Conspiracy,* which popularized the role of Freemasons in causing the French Revolution.

When Masonic lodges began admitting Jews and including the symbol of the six-pointed star, fertile ground for paranoia was sown. The Masons' penchant for secrecy and esoteric rituals, and a general promotion of Enlightenment ideas by secret societies, had drawn sharp criticism from the Catholic church, beginning with a declaration by Pope Clement XII in 1738 objecting to the anticlerical attitude of Masons.[71] After the Bolshevik Revolution of 1917, anti-Semitic monarchists began circulating their own translations of the *Protocols* in countries around the world, including the United States and Britain, and they were used as a key source for Hitler's *Mein Kampf.*[72] During the 1920s, Henry Ford published a two-year series in his newspaper, the *Dearborn Independent,* seeking to update the classic *Protocols* with his own investigative sources. Although he made an apology in 1927 for introducing this material, it was widely circulated under the title *The International Jew* even after this recantation.[73]

Coughlin's obsession with the manipulative role of "international Jewry" was closely linked with his preoccupation with Masonic machinations. He saw Masons as a secret force opposed to the Catholic church. He liberally sprinkled references to Masonic covert power in his personal correspondence with such fellow Catholics as members of the Frank Murphy family, Joe Kennedy, and Jim Farley, and the role of Masons in undermining Mexico, Spain, and England was a commonplace conversation topic among Coughlin's close associates.[74]

In the summer of 1938, Coughlin crossed the Rubicon of political anti-Semitism by identifying himself with the *Protocols*. He introduced an extensive series of articles by invoking the authority of Henry Ford. In his "From the Tower" signed editorial column, he quoted with approval Ford's evasive answer to a reporter's inquiry as to whether he believed in the authenticity of the infamous writings: "The only statement I care to make about the Protocols is that they fit with what is going on." Coughlin quoted Ford that "the vast masses of Jewry know little or nothing about them" and that "it is likewise fair to assert that the vast mass of Jews entertain no organized hostile thought against either gentiles or Christians." Coughlin then proceeded to note that "whether the *Protocols of Zion* are as spurious as the Knights of Columbus so-called oath—these questions do not contradict the accord which is evident in the context of the *Protocols* with the very definite happenings which are occurring in our midst. . . . *Social Justice* holds no enmity for the Jews but desires to extend a hand of assistance to every son of the race, we call upon the righteous Jewish leaders to campaign openly, in season and out of season, against these communistic attempts to overturn a civilization."[75]

At the time of their publication and in later years, speculation about how Coughlin came to publish the *Protocols* centered on his friendship with Henry Ford. It was Ernest Liebold who supplied most of the data used in the Ford *Dearborn Independent* series on world Jewish machinations. Ford gave Liebold special research responsibility for the project, and Liebold hired private detectives to gather information and keep files on the business dealings and political views of prominent Jews.[76] Given Liebold's contention that he met with Coughlin frequently in the 1930s, Liebold seems to be the most logical source for the "authentic" *Protocol* series published in *Social Justice*. His views of the *Protocols,* as expressed in 1921, are virtually identical with those of Coughlin in the *Social Justice* series: "You will find we at no time guaranteed their authenticity. We have merely stated what they contain and have paralleled this with what actually took place and are leaving it to the mind of the public to judge."[77]

Casimir Palmer was a member of Henry Ford's investigators of Jews and a member of the Russian czar's secret police. He testified in a 1934 federal court case regarding the origins and nature of the *Protocols* and their importation into the United States via a network of Russian émigrés. Angered by Coughlin's republication of the notorious documents, Palmer wrote to him insisting that "you must know . . . they are clumsy forgeries . . . the most dastardly lies in existence." Chiding the radio priest for his actions, Palmer observed that "every editor in this country knows it. . . . If an ignorant house painter like Hitler falls for stuff like that it is not surprising, for he does not know, but if an educated man like yourself, pretends not to know . . . then it is time that you vacate the editorial chair of Social Justice."[78]

Leaders of the Jewish community, both local and national, were shocked and deeply disturbed by Coughlin's action. When the first installment of the *Protocols* appeared, Philip Slomovitz in Detroit was incensed and immediately telegraphed a detailed protestation: "You are grossly misled, Father Coughlin, regarding the *Protocols* and many other phases of Jewish life which you have undertaken to criticize at this juncture when dictators are destroying every vestige of human decency and freedom for Jew and Catholic alike. . . . Because I still consider you a man of decency, I urge you to meet with a small committee who will supply you with basic facts proving to your complete satisfaction the libelous character of *Protocols* and other charges contained in your periodical." Slomovitz closed by saying he was prepared "to meet with you and any committee or associates you may designate tomorrow morning."[79]

Slomovitz received a reply from Coughlin's office telling the editor that the radio priest would meet with him at ten the next morning. Present at the unusual meeting were Slomovitz and two prominent leaders of the local Detroit Jewish community. Reminded that Henry Ford had retracted his support for anti-Semitism and the publishing of the *Protocols,* the Jewish community representatives argued that regardless of any evidence for or against their authenticity, the publication of the *Protocols* did great harm. Slomovitz recalls that when he entered Coughlin's office, the priest was pacing angrily—"puffing and flushed," not upset by his having been called an anti-Semite, but by the Jewish editors' reference to the priest as a "sadist," a remark Coughlin deemed anti-Catholic.[80]

Coughlin called in one of his secretaries and asked to read her notes regarding the second article of the *Protocols,* already in press. To the great dismay of the Jews present, the priest told them that "there are Jews who are not Jews but who belong to the synagogue of satan." Asserting that there was no danger of anti-Semitism in America and that "it can never happen here," Coughlin further advised that "ridicule" was the best antidote for hatred and that "Jews ought to be less fearful and less sensitive." He added that his statements about Jews' being dominant in international finance could be easily proven. By mutual agreement, a follow-up meeting for two weeks later was proposed to "clarify the issues which have hitherto aroused so much bad feeling."[81] It never took place.

Before the group departed, the priest invited Slomovitz to write his own reply to the *Protocols* article and promised that it would appear in the next issue of *Social Justice.* Two months later, under the headline "The Jewish Answer: The Truth about the Protocols," the detailed rejoinder did appear. Readers were informed on the same page that "Mr. Ben Marcin, whose research articles disclosed the untold 'story behind the story' has consented to comment upon Mr. Slomovitz's article."[82] There was no Ben Marcin. The name was created by combining letters from the name Bernice Marciniewicz, one of Coughlin's secretaries.[83]

Week after week *Social Justice* reiterated the litany of political, cultural, and economic manipulation perpetuated by world Jewry as a conspiracy to undermine Christian civilization. Finally, with "Protocol Sixteen," published Thanksgiving 1938, Coughlin's months-long campaign of exposing a nefarious and threatening Jewish conspiracy climaxed: "We shall abolish every kind of freedom of instruction . . . the purpose of which is to turn the goyim into unthinking submissive brutes." In a signed editorial, Coughlin added a note of explanation: "When we resume printing the *Protocols* we are not attributing them to the Jews. We are simply insisting upon their *factuality* be they plagiarized or not plagiarized, be they satires—or not satires."[84]

Three weeks later, "Ben Marcin" offered an even broader historical assessment of the "Jewish question." In an article entitled "The Talmud as a Cause of Persecution," the imaginary author (almost certainly Coughlin himself) opined that "Jewish spokesmen plead for suppression of facts in the name of 'religious persecution.' Let it be clear that no one

Charles Coughlin as a young boy, probably age six or seven. He is dressed in the "Little Lord Fauntleroy" attire fashionable for middle-class families at the turn of the century. (UPI/Bettmann)

Coughlin's childhood home in Hamilton, Ontario. His mother was especially proud of the front parlor, which contained a piano at which her only child was given lessons.

St. Mary's Cathedral in Hamilton, with Coughlin's home visible in the background. "Sitting at table, the [Coughlin] family could hear the sound of the Cathedral organ," wrote biographer Ruth Mugglebee in 1933.

Undated photo of Charles Coughlin in his late teens. The robes he is wearing are probably those for his 1911 graduation from St. Michael's College in Toronto. (UPI/Bettmann)

(Below) Coughlin celebrated his first Mass in thi wooden structure, the original Shrine of the Littl Flower, on June 26, 1926. According to Coughlir the pews were actually old theater seats.

Sketch of the massive masonry tower and octagonal church that became the new Shrine of the Little Flower, completed in 1936. That same yea the old church was destroyed by fire. (*Shrine of the Little Flower Souvenir Boo* printed by the Radio League of the Little Flower, 1936)

In Madison Square Garden, New York City, Coughlin addresses a rally of his National Union for Social Justice, May 22, 1935. Beyond the capacity crowd of more than 30,000 that paid to hear him speak were thousands more who were turned away but allowed to stand outside listening on the loudspeakers. (UPI/Bettmann)

The so-called Hilltop House, overlooking Lake Mansfield in Great Barrington, Massachusetts. Owned jointly by Coughlin and a key financial backer, Francis Keelon, it served as headquarters for the Union Party. Its library concealed a private altar behind sliding bookcases. (Courtesy Bard College)

Coughlin and his parents in July 1936, when he visited Buffalo, New York, on his way to confer with political officers of the National Union for Social Justice. (UPI/Bettmann)

Coughlin playfully ruffles General L. K. Smith's hair after addressing the Townsend Club convention in Cleveland, August 1936. He is without his cassock and clerical collar, which he had removed in the course of his impassioned speech; Francis Townsend looks on impassively. (UPI/Bettmann)

Coughlin kisses the ring of his religious superior, Bishop Michael J. Gallagher, September 3, 1936. Returning from the Vatican on the ocean liner SS *Rex,* the Bishop dismissed reporters' questions about whether he had been reprimanded regarding his politically active subordinate. (UPI/Bettmann)

A photo seized by FBI agents following a raid on the Christian Front militia chapter in Brooklyn, New York. Shown in the photo are, left to right: Michael Vill, Macklin Boettger, Frank Malone, John Viebrock, and John Graf. Viebrock hanged himself before the conspiracy trial began. National print media included this picture in front-page stories on January 14, 1940. (UPI/Bettmann)

(Above) Eleven of the seventeen accused "Brooklyn boys" pose with their attorney, Leo Healy (seated, second from right), April 9, 194▮ John Cassidy, the designated leader of the Brooklyn "sports club," is seated, smiling, to Healy's right. (UPI/Bettmann)

May 14, 1940

Brigadier General Edwin M. Watson
Secretary to the President
The White House
Washington, D. C.

Dear General Watson:

I thought you and the President would be interested in information which has reached me from a confidential source heretofore found to be reliable. According to my informant, August C. Gausebeck, who is the head of the Robert C. Mayer Company of 50 Broadway, New York City, which is a firm of investment bankers who handle much of the German business in this country, some time ago contacted my informant and told him he wanted to donate $500,000.00 to the Republican Presidential Campaign. The informant inquired of Gausebeck why he wanted to do this, whereupon Gausebeck gave as his reason the fact that if a Republican were elected, there would then be established favorable trade treaties between the United States and Germany, whereas if President Roosevelt were reelected this would be impossible. In view of the international aspect of this situation I thought the President should be informed of it.

My informant advised Gausebeck that such a donation would be impossible because the law prohibited donations in such sums, whereupon Gausebeck stated that he would arrange to have the donations made in small lots from a number of different people, adding that "they" had contributed to Father Coughlin in amounts of $100.00 to $500.00 at a time, which had been sent by office employees in $5.00 and $10.00 bills.

If I receive any further information about this situation I will advise you.

Sincerely yours,

J. Edgar Hoover

69

Resp'y forwarded to the President:

E.M.W.

Letter from FBI Director Hoover to Brigadier General Watson. It was a duplicate of the lette▮ sent to Assistant Secretary of State Adolf Berg▮ who scrawled across his copy: "I hope Hoover really goes to town on this." (Courtesy Franklin D. Roosevelt Library)

father and son, Alexi and Igor Pelypenko, in 1942. The father—a Russian Orthodox priest who converted to Roman Catholicism—was the author of a controversial affidavit describing Charles Coughlin's direct contacts with, and receipt of funds from, German diplomatic officials. Both Pelypenkos were held on Ellis Island during World War II on charges of lacking proper immigration papers.

This montage of headlines in Coughlin's weekly newsletter, *Social Justice,* suggests the controversial nature of its contents. Its demise was a key action in the "silencing" agreement Coughlin signed in May 1942.

On a national speaking tour in 1952, shortly after losing his military command in Korea, General Douglas MacArthur shakes the hand of Father Coughlin at the Shrine of the Little Flower. (Courtesy of Father Cyril Keating)

The Jews Started World War II!
The Proof!

✿

Text of Samuel Untermeyer's
"Sacred War" Speech
August 7, 1933
Upon his return from the World-wide International Jewish
Boycott Conference at Amsterdam, Holland

+

Father Coughlin's Comments
March 16, 1942
The Publication of this Speech in Father Coughlin's Newspaper,
SOCIAL JUSTICE on March 16, 1942, *was the reason the Zionist
Occupation Government [ZOG] under FDR suppressed SOCIAL
JUSTICE!* And Raped the First Amendment to the U.S.
Constitution protecting our God-given Rights to Free Speech and
Free Press!   (Reprinted as a Public Service by TRUTH Books)

Unsolicited flyer received by the author in 1991. Since the 1980s, a variety of persons and organizations at the political fringe have come forward to claim affinity with Coughlin's belief in a Jewish conspiracy.

imbued with the true American spirit would or could condone, hinder, or even remonstrate with any Jew *on account of his religious faith.* We merely assert that according to *The Talmud* the Jewish people are *victimized by the Elders of Zion,* because by the actions therein prescribed, the Jewish people are forced to actions which create the inevitable friction which cause such cruel persecution."[85]

For more than a decade Coughlin had gambled that his natural sense of timing and instinct would let him survive. In 1938, his public anti-Semitism was partly a calculated gamble. The moment he chose for what he saw as his crusade of truth was fraught with disturbing world news. Europe tottered on the brink of war; the leaders of Britain, France, Italy, and Germany bickered over the fate of Czechoslovakia; the Munich crisis was in full swing; and many Americans came to fear that their own nation might soon find itself embroiled for a second time in a world war.

Up to this point in his career, Coughlin had been cautious in his nationally broadcast messages not to say what those in his inner circle and many in his local Shrine had heard in sermons and informal talks. Now he decided to speak more openly of an anti-Christ conspiracy and of the enemies of the Catholic church. Once set upon this course, there would be no way to turn back or to cleanse himself of its consequences. From this day forward he would be labeled as one who brought opprobrium to his church and profound anxiety to America's Jews.

Germany was now engaged in a dress rehearsal for the Holocaust. On October 28, a brutal deportation of thousands of Polish Jews living in Germany warned of the horrors to come:

> They snatched children from the streets without notifying parents and jammed them, along with thousands of others, including the aged and infirm, into trucks and trains bound for the Polish border. The Jews were allowed to take only 10 marks ($4) and the clothes on their backs. About ten thousand were dumped across the border. In bitter cold they sought refuge in empty railroad cars, in the open no-man's-land between the German and Polish borders, or in abandoned, heatless barracks.[86]

Among the families snatched in the deportation was that of Zindel Grynszpan of Hanover. A son, Hershel, seventeen, had fled to Paris earlier. When his father wrote to tell what had happened, the son, who had been deeply upset since he had left Poland, brought a pistol and, on November 7, 1938, went to the German embassy in Paris intent on assassinating Ambassador Johannes von Welczeck. He demanded to see the ambassador but was shunted instead to a lesser official, Ernst vom Rath, and shot him. Ironically, vom Rath was at the very moment walking to his death, under investigation by the Gestapo because of his opposition to anti-Semitism. When French police arrested Grynszpan for the shooting, he broke down in tears, sobbing, "Being a Jew is not a crime. I am not a dog. I have a right to live and the Jewish people have a right to exist on earth. Wherever I have been I have been chased like an animal."[87]

As vom Rath lay dying from the shots inflicted by Grynszpan, the German press launched a drumbeat campaign asking for reprisals against the Jews. On the afternoon of November 9, vom Rath died of his wounds. At two o'clock the next morning, November 10, a wave of arson, looting, murder, and mass arrests occurred throughout Germany. Two hundred sixty-seven synagogues were partially or totally destroyed by fire, and at least thirty-nine Jews lost their lives. Mass arrests resulted in thirty thousand Jews going to concentration camps. A collective fine, the equivalent of $400 million, was levied on the entire Jewish community of Germany. The streets of Germany were littered with shattered glass. Thus came the name "night of the broken glass"—Kristallnacht.

Both British and American newspapers reported that twenty thousand Jews rounded up during that night were being held in three concentration camps, Dachau, Oranienburg-Sachsenhausen, and Buchenwald:

> More poignant than loss of work or business is the news of friends who suddenly disappear and are engulfed into the great concentration camp of Buchenwald. From this dread spot in the heart of beautiful Thuringia, the relatives of those interned there have sometimes received a curt official intimation that the prisoner has died on a certain date, that he has been cremated, and the ashes may be collected.[88]

The Nazi press reported that the Kristallnacht was a spontaneous response of the German people, not an official action. In fact, the Nazis had staged and sponsored the destructive orgy, but then began to realize that the German insurance industry would be ruined by the claims that would be filed. Reporters in Munich had taken note of the fact that police were diverting traffic a half-hour before any looting broke out.

News of German atrocities soon resulted in a barrage of outraged messages from religious and civic groups across the United States. Demands for aid to the refugees and for some official protest action against the German government were echoed in newspapers across the country. The press, described as "nearly a unit in denunciation," wrote that the country had not been so aroused "since the Lusitania."[89]

Coughlin now raised his voice in a most deliberate and detailed fashion. His audience, although reduced in size from the tens of millions at the height of his popularity, still numbered several millions.[90] As they listened on that Sunday afternoon of November 20, the somber yet gentle organ music so familiar to loyal listeners now gave way to the portentously intoned voice of the radio priest's local announcer: "Ladies and gentlemen . . . Father Coughlin will discuss one of the most vital and burning questions of our day—the question of the Jew and of the Christian, and of persecution." As if to build anticipation or perhaps to offer a caution, Coughlin's announcer foretold, "Undoubtedly it will do much to clarify a vexed [sic] problem in our midst."[91]

The priest stepped to the microphone and in his rich baritone intoned, "At long last a callous world has come in personal contact with a persecution which it understands . . . bear with me while I add my voice in protest against persecution—that murderous weapon of hatred; bear with me while I endeavor to trace to its lair the fanged serpent of hatred whose sting has struck once again to spew poison and deal out death over the face of the earth." Warming to his topic, he inquired: "Why is there persecution in Germany today? How can we destroy it?" Describing Jews as having minority status in many nations of the world, he observed that, despite having no "nation of their own . . . no flag, they are closely woven in their racial tendencies." Changing cadence and intonation (which had fallen to nearly a whisper), the priest, as if shouting to wake up slumbering listeners, declaimed, "A powerful minority in their influence; a minority endowed with an aggressiveness and initiative which, despite all obstacles, has carried their sons to the pinnacles of success in journalism, in radio, in finance, in all sciences and arts."

With an ironic edge, the radio priest then arrived at the crux of his disquisition: "No story of persecution was ever told one half so well, one half so thoroughly, as the story of the $400 million reprisal. . . . Perhaps this is attributable to the fact that Jews, through native ability, have risen to such high places in radio and in the press and in finance. Perhaps this persecution is only the coincidental last straw which has broken the back of this generation's patience." Answering the rhetorical question as to why "Nazism is so hostile to Jewry," Coughlin replied, "It is the belief, be it well or ill-founded of the present German government, not mine, that Jews not as religionists but as nationals only, were responsible for the economic and social ills suffered by the Fatherland since the signing of the Versailles Treaty."

Describing Nazism as a "defense mechanism against Communism," Coughlin then declared that the "rising generation of Germans regard Communism as a product not of Russia, but of a group of Jews who dominated the destinies of Russia." He asked, "Were there facts to substantiate this belief in the minds of the Nazi Party?" and then offered "official information and uncontradictable evidence gleaned from the writings and policies of Lenin." Specifically, he referred to a 1917 list distributed by the Nazi party within Germany showing that "of 25 quasi-cabinet members" of the Soviet government, "24 of them are atheistic Jews." Further, "By 1935, the Central Committee of the Communist Party, operating in Russia, consisted of 59 members, of whom were 56 Jews; and that the three remaining non-Jews were married to Jewesses."

Lest anyone draw the conclusion that the priest was offering his statistical recitation as a brief in favor of Germany or Nazism, Coughlin described his motivation as simply that of a "student of history . . . endeavoring to analyze the reasons for the growth of the idea in the minds of the Nazi Party that Communism and Judaism are too closely interwoven for the national health of Germany." He then directed his remarks "to the good Jews of America," advising that they should not be "indulgent with the irreligious, atheistic Jews and gentiles [who] promote the cause of persecution in the land of the Communists. . . . Yes, be not lenient with your high financiers and politicians who assisted in the birth of the only political, social, and economic system in all civilization that adopted atheism as its religion, internationalism as its patriotism, and slavery as its liberty."

Coughlin expressed his "sincere sympathy to the millions of humble, religious Jews both in America and elsewhere who have been persecuted by a thoughtless world," one that "does not always distinguish between good Jews and the bad Jews; a world which lashes at the pillar of persecution the innocent Jews for the misdemeanors of the guilty Jews." As if to offer a positive note, Coughlin observed that "despite all this, official Germany has not yet resorted to the guillotine, to the machine gun, to the kerosene-drenched pit as instruments of reprisal against Jew or Gentile."

Reiterating his core thesis, the radio priest warned that "Nazism, the effect of Communism, cannot be liquidated in its persecution complex until the religious Jews in high places—in synagogue, finance, in radio and in the press—attack the cause, attack forthright the errors and the spread of Communism, [for] Jewish persecution only followed after Christians first were persecuted." Describing the murder of "more than 20 million Christians . . . between the years 1917 and '38 . . . by the communistic government of Russia," Coughlin denigrated the Kristallnacht indemnity imposed on German Jews: "Between these same years not $400 but 40 billion . . . of Christian property was appropriated by the Lenins and Trotskys . . . by the atheistic Jews and gentiles." In a tone rising with anger, he demanded, "Ask the gentlemen who control the three national radio chains. Ask those who dominate the destinies of the financially inspired press. Surely these Jewish gentlemen and others must have been ignorant of the facts of Russia, Mexico, and Spain." Dropping his voice to somber authority, he cited a British government white paper, which he claimed had printed "the names of Jewish bankers, Kuhn Loeb & Company of New York, among those who helped finance the Russian Revolution and Communism." He went on to quote from a Jewish periodical, the *American Hebrew,* that "the achievement, the Russian Jewish Revolution destined to figure in history as the overshadowing result of the World War, was largely the outcome of Jewish thinking and Jewish discontent, of Jewish effort to reconstruct." In a climax filled with sarcasm and facetiousness, Coughlin proclaimed: "By all means let us have the courage to compound our sympathy not only from the tears of Jews, but also from the blood of Christians—600,000 Jews whom no government official in Germany has yet sentenced to death."[92]

The owner of New York's station WMCA, Donald Flamm, recalled this broadcast fifty years later:

When Crystal Night took place I urged him to do something, to say something . . . that would eliminate once and for all this idea that he was anti-Semitic.

I offered the suggestion [to] Coughlin, through his representative, Mr. Boynton. I said, "As far as I'm concerned, Father Coughlin, you may be issuing and writing anti-Semitic words [but] I haven't seen it and certainly you've never said anything over my station that was anti-Semitic, because I can tell you now it would be the last time you'd ever say anything over my station

if you did." And he said, "Well, now, Donald, you're right. I will
do something and I will send you a copy of it in advance."[93]

Coughlin was being carried on Flamm's station only because its
competitor, WOR, had refused to renew Coughlin's 1938–1939 broadcast season contract. The station had adopted a new policy of not accepting religious broadcasts on a commercial basis. Coughlin thus found
himself without a New York outlet. Stanley Boynton, the priest's advertising representative, made an offer to Flamm, which Flamm accepted
and which did not require any prior script review. Recalling that an earlier "satisfactory relationship" had been established, "we didn't think it
was necessary." It was in the broadcast of November 13, 1938, that "the
first suspicion entered our mind that Father Coughlin was about to inject
anti-Semitism in his talks."[94]

According to Flamm, when they signed the new contract in New
York, Boynton gave assurances that Coughlin "would not engage in any
anti-Semitic utterances," since the priest had told his agent to point out to
Flamm, "To do so would be sinful." With this impressive guarantee,
Flamm recalls, "I consented to waive further my obligation to inspect
[Coughlin's] talks in advance." Flamm recalls that when he received his
copy of the script for the November 20 broadcast, which the priest had
voluntarily sent to him, he felt "cruel disappointment. . . . Yes, Father
Coughlin added his voice of protest [to the Kristallnacht atrocities], but it
was a protest that can best be likened to the oration of Marc Antony at the
funeral of Julius Caesar." Flamm immediately telephoned the Royal Oak
Shrine and told Coughlin flatly: "The speech cannot go on." The reply
Flamm received was the assurance that "the facts are correct." In rebuttal,
the WMCA owner told him, "No, I'm going to do my utmost to get you
to have this gone over by people who are in a position who know whether
what you say is correct or not . . . you cannot make that speech. Wait until I get you the copies." Flamm recalls that if the original script had been
broadcast without being edited, it might have been less effective since "it
was so full of historical and factual inaccuracies that no further comment
would have been necessary."[95]

Dissatisfied with the slightly edited version, Flamm allowed it to be
aired with one proviso: his station announcer would have to open the
broadcast with the statement: "At this time, WMCA wishes to reiterate its
position that the views expressed by Father Coughlin on these broadcasts
are his own, and do not necessarily reflect the views of the station." At the

close of the radio address, listeners were told by the announcer, "Unfortunately, Father Coughlin has uttered many misstatements of fact."[96]

"We were shocked," Flamm remembers. "It was a violent anti-Semitic speech with all kinds of misinformation and wild charges." Flamm had telephoned Coughlin well in advance of the broadcast and asked that the script be in the station's hands at least forty-eight hours before airtime. "He did not respond to that whatever," Flamm recounts, "neither by telephone or by letter. Finally, I was advised by those who were assisting me to telephone him, which I did. . . . He did not answer the phone. Finally, I sent him a night letter. . . . The strange part of it is that subsequently he made the charge that he never received that telegram."[97]

On the Saturday prior to the radio priest's next scheduled address, November 27, Propaganda Minister Joseph Goebbels made a speech on the "Jewish question" in Germany. He warned that "the anti-German outside world would do well to leave the solution of the Jewish problem to Germans." In words directed to the United States, he declared, "If the outside world wants the Jews, it can have them. If Jews abroad have a heart for their co-religionists in Germany, let them be truthful in what they say about us." The *New York Times* headlined its story of the speech with the words: "Hitler Aide Warns American Jews of More Persecution."[98] In his bombastic tirade, Goebbels spoke of "a final solution to the Jewish question" and called for the rooting out of "Jewish criminal elements . . . with fire and sword." He warned that "the German people are an anti-Semitic people and will not tolerate their rights curtailed or to be provoked by the parasitic Jewish race."

News stories about Nazi persecutions continued to occupy headlines in the U.S. press. The *Detroit Free Press* described the American consulate in Berlin as a "pathetic sight . . . as hundreds of Jews, many in tears, milled around begging for preferred treatment on their visa applications. Many were women, who, when questioned, said that their husbands had been arrested in the anti-Jewish campaign." The same story told of the situation in Vienna, where Jews "went hungry tonight because of drastic orders of the District Nazi Party that coffee houses, restaurants, and grocery stores were not to serve them."[99]

The very day that Goebbels delivered his inflammatory address, Charles Coughlin received a telegram from radio station WMCA in New York stating new ground rules for carrying his future broadcasts. Charging that the priest's November 20 address "was calculated to incite religious and racial strife in America," the letter noted that "when this was called to your attention by this station in advance . . . you agreed to delete those misrepresentations which undeniably had this effect." Citing these facts, the letter went on to say: "We therefore are compelled to require you hereafter to submit all scripts forty-eight hours in advance." If future scripts were deemed to contain material "calculated to spread racial and religious hatred," they would have to be edited severely. The directive further asserted that "failure to live up to any such agreement will result in instant cancellation of your broadcasts."[100]

Between the November 20 broadcast and the following week's, a storm of controversy broke. Comments both in favor and in (unintentionally ironic) opposition to his remarks appeared in letter-to-the-editor columns such as these in the *Detroit News*:

My hat is off to Father Coughlin! He dares to tell the truth in the face of almost certain condemnation over this wave of hysteria over the treatment of Jews in Germany. More power to Father Coughlin, the only broadcaster who has the courage to speak the truth even though it sometimes hurts.

It is not so much a question of whether Father Coughlin is right or wrong in his contentions; but what an inappropriate time to make such statements! Why kick a man when he is down! Such speeches are dangerous to the cause of democracy and are utterly inexcusable and inexplicable from a minister of religion.[101]

WMCA refused to carry Coughlin's next broadcast. The Nazi press termed it "a sample of the mendacity of the so-much lauded freedom of speech in the U.S. [where] Jewish organizations camouflaged as American . . . have conducted such a campaign and that the radio station company has proceeded to muzzle the well-loved Father Coughlin." Under the headline "America is Not Allowed to Hear the Truth," the *Berlin Zeitung* explained that "this attempt at veiling the truth shows not only the enslavement and submission to Jewry, [but is also indicative of] boundless cowardice." The *New York Times* correspondent in Berlin reported that "Father Coughlin is, for the moment, the new hero of Nazi Germany."[102]

10

Charity Begins at Home

Just a few lines to let you know "Robert" has made the
supreme sacrifice for us & country. Also for freedom may I
be granted my request that no harm befall Father Coughlin,
had we & our administration taken all his heed & warning
we might not have been in this terrible blood bath. Robert
knew when he was drafted . . . that he was going to protect
the big interest of the international Jews . . . so maybe their
hands are dripping with the blood of my boy.

Letter to President Roosevelt, April 17, 1942

THE RADIO PRIEST made no new broadcast the week following the
Kristallnacht address. To the surprise of his listeners and critics, the
program announcer explained that a recording of the original broadcast
would be played. At the conclusion, Coughlin himself spoke in defense
of his statements, describing in considerable detail "a vicious campaign
of misrepresentation" that was directed against him. He offered the name
of a scholar from whose works he claimed to have drawn the basic information for his analysis of the financial backers of the Bolshevik Revolution: "Professor Dennis Fahey of Blackrock College in Dublin, Ireland,"
whom he called "one of the most outstanding scholars in Ireland."[1]

Eight years Coughlin's senior, Fahey received his theological train-
ing in France. In the 1920s, he became founder of an organization, Maria
Duce; he already belonged to the strongly anti-Semitic Action Française.
Fahey was professor of philosophy and church history at the Holy Ghost
Missionary College of Dublin and had his own version of Catholic phi-
losophy. He believed that the Roman Catholic church embodied the
"Mystical Body of the Christ" and that Satan represented the "Mystical

Body of the Anti-Christ." According to Fahey's doctrine, all movements and philosophies opposed to the church were instigated by Satan. Furthermore, events such as the Protestant Reformation, the French Revolution, the Bolshevik Revolution, and the formation of the League of Nations were all expressions of modernism orchestrated by Jews.[2]

The broadcast season of 1938–1939 brought the perfectly complementary teaming of the priest-professor with the priest-politician. Fahey provided what in more recent years has become the conspiratorial view of a manipulating "New World Order," and Coughlin provided the obscure Fahey with an international following. Visitors to the Shrine of the Little Flower concession store found the Dublin cleric's books on prominent display.[3] Fahey did not so much serve to create Coughlin's anti-Semitism as to give it a more elaborate form. By providing a veneer of academic legitimacy to the ideas of a Jewish assault on Christianity, Fahey became a critical part of Coughlin's campaign of hate.

After Coughlin's November 20 broadcast it was virtually impossible for Jewish leaders to suspend disbelief about Coughlin's intentions. And for the first time, there was a concerted effort by Jewish organizations to counter his influence. A variety of informal and behind-the-scenes efforts began, including the sponsoring by Jewish organizations of radio talks by a Unitarian minister, Walton E. Cole, aimed at undoing the impact of the radio priest.[4] A pamphlet published by the General Jewish Council stimulated a response by "The Friends of Father Coughlin": an elaborate defense of the source documents and arguments for the November 20 speech, entitled "An Answer to Father Coughlin's Critics."

From Kristallnacht until the middle of 1942, Coughlin's radio addresses and *Social Justice* articles stressed two themes: that allies England and France had no democracy and no claim for moral superiority over Germany or Italy and that subversive forces within America—Jews in particular—were fomenting a campaign to entangle the United States in a war out of a selfish concern for the plight of Jews in Europe. Often the radio priest identified the source of "warmongering" in poetically elliptical ways:

> Vicious propaganda, counter to that pronounced by the angels, sounds over radio and is multiplied in the press. . . . Warmongers who are concerned not with advancing the kingdom of Christ . . . but with expectancy of profits resulting from their policy of Lucifer.[5]

Intriguers . . . who worship the god of gold and through it control propaganda. . . . I recognize that in broadcasting these facts I am on the unpopular side of a question. . . . I am accustomed to condemnation; accustomed to unpopularity with a certain class which has persisted in making a den of thieves of this world by exploiting the masses of every nation.[6]

On other occasions the priest named names:

The chief document, treating the financing of the Russian Revolution, is the one drawn up by the American Secret Service and transmitted by the French High Commissioner to his Government. It was published by the "Documentation Catholique" of Paris on March 6th, 1920, and preceded by the following remarks: "The authenticity of this document is guaranteed to us. With regard to the exactness of the information it contains, the American Secret Service takes responsibility." Jacob Schiff (Jew); Guggenheim (Jew); Max Breitung (Jew); Kuhn, Loeb & Co. (Jewish banking house), of which the following are directors: Jacob Schiff, Felix Warburg, Otto Kahn, Mortimer Schiff, S. H. Hanauer (all Jews).[7]

There was to be no turning back on the lesson Charles Coughlin righteously appointed himself to teach to the Jewish community. In his December 4, 1938, broadcast, he not only failed to temper his earlier accusations or to steer clear of specific Jews or Jewish organizations but sought to strengthen his indictment by referring in even more detail to documents utilized by Father Fahey. He then summed up his argument:

I am criticized for being so bold as to refer to the merchandisers of murder by name—the men who finance revolution and war. . . . I am held up to public ridicule as an untrustworthy purveyor of falsehood although I have supplemented my assertions with documentary evidence which is difficult to disregard. So be it! May I reiterate. . . . There is no anti-Semitic question in America. There is an anti-Communist question here, and there will continue to be an anti-Communist question.[8]

As the controversy over his radio addresses mounted, Coughlin and his supporters stoutly maintained their quarrel was not with Jews as Jews:

> Openly and fearlessly do I admit that my main contention is with the atheistic Jew and gentile; the communistic Jew and gentile who have been responsible and will continue to be responsible, in great part, both for the discriminations and persecutions inflicted upon the Jews as a body.
>
> Thus, the issue is clear. The Jews of America cannot afford to be identified with Communism or with communistic activities. They are asked to disassociate themselves from the atheistic Jews who espouse Communism.[9]

Yet in his next weekly broadcast, Coughlin explicitly argued that the antagonism of Jew and Christian was religiously rooted. Jews, once having been the chosen people, were doomed to persecution for having not recognized Christ as the Messiah. Any effort to sustain a contemporary "chosen people" pride was therefore erroneous:

> My friends, there is no middle ground upon which Christ can be accepted. Either He is the Deliverer, or He is the seducer of mankind. . . . If Christ is not the Messiah, born amongst the Jews and rejected by the Jews as such, then we Christians have been grossly deceived and should join with the non-Christians in searching for another efficacious order or plan which can dissolve our sufferings.
>
> According to the reformed or liberal Jews who have departed from the ancient hopes and aspirations of Judaism . . . the world is waiting for a Messianic Age which will be the result of Jewish national leadership—an age of naturalism which will have for its end the subjection of all nations to the naturalistic philosophy of race supremacy.[10]

Finally, the radio priest offered a prophetic warning:

> Were my advice of any value, I should counsel the Jews to refrain from joining with others in adopting a program— even though constitutional—which breeds resentment to their race. . . . Intolerance towards men is always reprehensible. But

often times intolerance is provoked by injudicious and erroneous policies. . . .

I am giving voice to a sentiment which is expressed in millions of homes and in thousands of gatherings. Thus, for his collective safety, the American Jew must repudiate the atheistic Jew. Communism must be stamped out, else an illogical world will build up a defense mechanism against it in these United States paralleling, if not surpassing, the same illogical defense mechanism which operates under Nazism.

We are concerned, then, with extinguishing this fire before it consumes our inheritance and before its flames of hatred enfold themselves around the millions of innocent Jews and gentiles in a holocaust of persecution.[11]

Shortly after Kristallnacht, Franklin Roosevelt had confided to Joe Kennedy, then serving as ambassador to England, "If there was a demagogue around here of the type of Huey Long to take up anti-Semitism, there could be more blood running in the streets of New York than in Berlin." Throughout late 1938 and early 1939, in both his broadcasts and the pages of *Social Justice,* Charles Coughlin hinted that "good Christians" would have to take action, even to "organize into Platoons," in order to resist the forces of communist subversion in their midst.[12]

When WMCA refused to air the radio priest's follow-up to his Crystal Night address, the moment had come for Father Coughlin's supporters to take to the streets. The consequences would make FDR's comment remarkably prophetic.

On Sunday, December 18, 1938, mass picketing began at the mid-Manhattan studios of station WMCA. In a formal letter to Frank McNinch, chairman of the Federal Communications Commission, owner Donald Flamm summarized what had occurred:

Last Sunday (December 18, 1938) between 3 and 5 P.M. several thousand people encircled the block where our studios are located, denounced WMCA as un-American, and shouted its slogan of "Don't buy from Jews," "Down with Jews," etc. The committee in charge of this demonstration advised the pickets to boycott the advertisers using WMCA and to write letters of protest to the station, to the advertisers, and to the Federal Communications Commission.[13]

Flamm received a report from a private detective authorized to investigate the demonstration that gave graphic details:

There were five thousand people picketing on Broadway and 51st Street, blocking traffic and interfering with the normal business activities of the street. . . . It should be noted that the slogans and banners dealt not only with the barring of Father Coughlin from the air but also to matters that in no way concern the radio station. They consist of anti-communist slogans and anti-Spanish Loyalists slogans with veiled suggestions of anti-Semitism. . . . The remarks uttered by the picketers are more explicit than the legends on the signs:
"Send refugees to Russia where they can be appreciated!"
"This is a Christian country. Who isn't a Christian, throw them out!"
"Jewish bankers barred Father Coughlin from the air."
"Buy Christian! Vote Christian!"
"Send Jews back where they came from in leaky boats!"
"Wait until Hitler comes over here."
"Down with the Jewish war-mongers."
"Heil Hitler!"[14]

Social Justice initially minimized the scope of the WMCA demonstrations and suggested they were not authorized by the radio priest but rather were a spontaneous emergence of a national movement:

Approximately 7,000 persons gained entrance and 3,000 more, according to the police, were turned away. This meeting was not held under the auspices of Father Coughlin. He had nothing to do with it.
However, his patriotic friends, Catholic and Protestant, and representatives of many organizations, proved to calloused New York that they will not permit Donald Flamm or any other Stalin in the field of radio to dictate what can be spoken in this land of the free.
The Manhattan Opera House meeting is only the beginning. Philadelphians, also, held a meeting and similar protests were registered in the name of liberty.

Other meetings will be held. This movement will grow rapidly and will not be stemmed until Congress and the Communications Commission break the monopoly which now controls radio, press and cinema.[15]

The protests of Father Coughlin's supporters in New York became more intense and spread to include advertisers of WMCA, a furniture store, and other shops with Jewish owners in the Bronx and Brooklyn. Picketers assembled and went from store to store. Meetings in Brooklyn had "crowds of five to six hundred people" who "listened to inflammatory anti-Semitic speeches that sound[ed] as though they might have been delivered at a Nazi meeting in Berlin."[16] All the while, mass picketing continued at WMCA's studios:

> Every Sunday around 3:00 in the afternoon, the crowd would begin to gather. Young men, clerics, and whole families, including couples carrying their babes in arms, would appear to demonstrate their commitment to the cause. . . . Thus stimulated, some of the more impassioned Coughlinites remained unsatiated when the afternoon's picketing came to an end. In their restlessness, unwilling to return immediately to the routine of their lives, groups of marchers began to wend their way toward Times Square as they sought new sources of excitement. On one occasion, some . . . accosted a family on a stroll. Taking them to be Jews, the crowd began shouting insults. Suddenly an elderly woman broke from the pack, rushed at the father, and spat, "Dirty Jew!" In the ensuing scuffle, which others joined, the man lost his glasses, was raked with the woman's fingernails, and his wife was set upon and cursed.[17]

Adding to the tensions of the street picketing was the sale of magazines and the distribution of pamphlets. Salesmen for *Social Justice* at first merely shouted epithets at passing individuals who appeared to be Jewish. Then a new technique emerged. One of the young magazine sellers would start crying and shouting that he had been hit "by a big Jew." A strong-arm guard posed by the seller to offer protection would then initiate a fight.

One bystander described what occurred when street meetings in the

Bronx broke up at about 10:00 P.M.: "The mob crowds into the subway, along with the *Social Justice* salesman, and heads for Times Square. They run up and down the subway cars insulting any passenger who looks at all Jewish, and create a considerable amount of terror."[18]

The street disturbances soon provoked a reaction. Various magazines appeared on the sidewalks to counteract *Social Justice*. Some of the publications were Marxist, like the *Daily Worker.* Others were distributed by liberal groups, including a Catholic organization that attacked the anti-Semitism of the radio priest. In response, Coughlin's supporters became even more active:

> More than Saturday and Sunday . . . *Social Justice* is now being sold every day in the week at such congested spots as 42nd and Fifth Avenue and Times Square. Competing magazines proceeded to do the same and the result has been that for a month or more the busiest spots in New York have been compelled to witness the spectacle of dozens of magazines being sold loudly and in many instances offensively. Traffic has been blocked, businesses have been interfered with, and passersby have been molested and insulted, and the streets of New York have witnessed brawls and disturbances to which they have heretofore been unaccustomed.[19]

There was growing evidence that civil order was breaking down and that "the police were failing to keep the demonstrating groups separated. Coughlin's foes felt that the police were far from neutral and that many belonged to the radio priest's organizations."[20] Fistfights spread. A sworn statement taken by the police in April 1939 described one:

> At 1:40 P.M., April 29, 1939, I witnessed the following scene at 42nd Street and Fifth Avenue. A Jewish man slapped the face of a Christian selling the "Social Justice." A fistfight began. A large crowd, most of whom were Christians, assembled. It was a miracle that the Jewish man was not lynched by the crowd. I can hardly describe to you the tense feeling of those present at the scene. When the Jewish man was asked by a plain[clothes] man . . . why he slapped the Christian, he answered: "Because he insulted my race."[21]

The following reported incident described violence and intimidation:

On Sunday, March 12, at about 4:30 P.M., I boarded a Seventh Avenue I.R.T subway train. . . . I noticed a boy about 15 years of age passing through the train shouting "Social Justice, ten cents!" He passed through the car and I returned to reading my newspaper. A little while later he reappeared, trailed, I noticed, by some other youngsters who stopped to speak with a man who was apparently with them. I arose and told the boy he was not permitted to sell those papers in the subway. He replied, "You can't stop me." I said, "No, I can't, but the guard can." At Chambers Street I looked out of the platform, and, seeing no guard on the station, decided to forget the matter. . . .

Then I looked about me. The car was crowded with men and women wearing "F.C." [Father Coughlin] pins and I realized that they must have been returning from the Coughlin picket lines at WMCA. I stood near the door, planning to slip out at the first station which was comfortably crowded. As I stood there, a man moved over in front of me and opened a copy of "Social Justice" in my face, ostensibly reading it, but flaunting at me the headline, "Pope Pius friendly to Germany." Frightened, I said nothing. I looked about and saw the men gathered in a huddle menacingly. I am somewhat hard of hearing and can read lips to some extent, so I could see the words "Jew" and "Communist" framed and could gather that the conversation was generally threatening to me.[22]

James Wechsler's *Nation* article "The Coughlin Terror" provided an alarming assessment of the overall situation:

The city has become a laboratory for carefully developed fascist experimentation, nourished by the heterogeneous character of its population and by the timidity of press and public officials. . . . What the rest of the country can learn from contemporary New York is the failure of the silent treatment. For silence has merely encouraged rumors, half-truths, and bizarre reports which create a panic among Coughlin's foes almost as deadly as the hysteria which obsesses his followers. What is needed is swift official action.[23]

Coughlin's weekly spoke for many Americans when it asserted, in May 1938, that "until America can provide life and the means of life for all her citizens, she has no more right to open her doors to foreign boarders than the unemployed father of fourteen children has . . . in adopting six more, no matter how desolate the orphanage may seem."[24] One of the leaders of a mothers' group working closely under the radio priest's guidance characterized these same potential émigré children as "thousands of motherless, embittered, persecuted children of undesirable foreigners . . . potential leaders of a revolt against our American form of government."[25]

The burden for America's failure to attempt the rescue of European Jewry has been placed by many historians at the feet of Franklin Roosevelt. One wrote, "The individual in whom the Jews placed their greatest trust . . . failed to seize the hour. . . . Roosevelt had information on the Holocaust long before . . . 1942. . . . The administration's silence kept the American public ignorant and therefore unaroused." Another historian declared, "No excuse can be given for Roosevelt's calculated timidity." And historian David Wyman discerned a pattern "of decreasing sensitivity toward the plight of European Jewry" by FDR during the years 1938 to 1945."[26]

One researcher summed up FDR's response this way:

> Much of what Roosevelt accomplished for Jews the world over and for Jewish-Americans had to be planned and executed in private. Public statements of policy favorable to Jews was construed by the opposition as evidence of a "Jew-Deal," and from such comments the ugly head of anti-Semitism rose over America as it had over every corner of Europe. Roosevelt sought to avoid this situation. He did not want a divided country during the war, nor a split in the unity of the Democratic party coalition. Consequently, if a foreign policy demand stemming from the American-Jewish community reached fruition, Roosevelt did not wish to make it public.[27]

Certainly Coughlin's was not the only voice in the chorus demanding that charity begin at home. Nor were the priest's views quoted as openly in the halls of Congress as they were on legislative issues in the early 1930s. Yet Coughlin played a major role in defining the isolationist agenda of the late 1930s and was the most powerful force feeding a virulent climate of anti-Semitism that seemed to intensify as war clouds in Europe darkened.[28] That national mood significantly constrained both Jewish community leaders and FDR as they reinforced each other's caution in seeking bold public action. Coughlin helped mute those in the Catholic community who sought to ally themselves with the cause of fighting Nazism. His campaign of attacks on American Jews served to distract many in that community from focusing their efforts on the plight of their co-religionists in Europe.[29]

In retrospect, 1938 was the defining year for the United States and the other nations of the world that claimed they wanted to aid Jews fleeing Nazi persecutors. In April, Franklin Roosevelt established the President's Advisory Committee on Political Refugees. Only a few weeks earlier, Germany had negotiated its *Anschluss* (annexation) of Austria. Violent anti-Semitic actions foreshadowed the persecutions of Kristallnacht. Arrests, public humiliations, and a wave of suicides occurred in Vienna. Austria closed its borders to Jewish immigration.

In what became known as the Evian Conference, FDR sought a multinational response to the plight of Jews in Europe. The thirty-three-nation meeting, lasting from July 6 to 15, has been adjudged a dismal failure by historians. Chief U.S. delegate Myron Taylor expressed America's opposition to relaxing its immigration restrictions and even suggested that large-scale Jewish refugee immigration to the West would aggravate anti-Semitism: "How much more disturbing is the forced chaotic dumping of unfortunate people in large numbers. Racial and religious problems are, in consequence, rendered more acute in all parts of the world."[30] Taylor only offered, on behalf of the United States, to make the German-Austrian quota of 27,370 persons fully available—in other words, to stand pat. The most significant outcome of the conference was to establish the new, permanent Intergovernmental Committee on Refugees, which provided a mechanism for negotiating some degree of property settlement with Nazi Germany.

By late 1938, immigration had become the hotly debated point at which anti-Semitism, anti-Rooseveltism, and isolationism intersected. Those who favored increasing immigration quotas for Austrians and Germans had to disguise the fact that the aim of such legislation was to help Jews get out of Europe. Roosevelt strategically avoided making any public statements that might lend credence to the belief that he supported

easing immigration quotas. Public opinion and powerful lobbies like
Coughlin's were key factors in the equation. Moreover, loyal New Deal-
ers such as Frank Murphy expressed the feelings of many in the Catholic
community when he opposed taking political risks to rescue Jews. After
the *Anschluss,* Rabbi Stephen Wise wrote to Murphy:

> It is becoming increasingly apparent that the seizure of Austria
> spells the extension of the anti-Semitic front in Europe, and indi-
> cates the further oppression of five million Jews living in Eastern
> and Central Europe. . . .
>   The whole status of Jewry in Europe is jeopardized and col-
> lective action has become imperative.
>   The noble efforts of the government of the United States to
> welcome refugees to this country, *within the limits of the quota
> laws,* are deeply appreciated by American Jews. But there re-
> mains still the grave problem of the millions of Jews who must
> remain in Eastern and Central Europe and undergo an oppression
> whose barbarism has no parallel in the history of living men. It is
> no exaggeration to say that if this oppression is permitted to con-
> tinue, Jewish life in Europe will be destroyed.[31]

At the end of January 1939, Adolf Hitler, in a speech on the sixth anniversary of his ascension to power, made what amounted to a declaration of war against Jews:

> In my life I have often been a prophet and was often ridiculed
> [for it]. In the time of my struggle for power it was primarily the
> Jewish people who received with laughter my prophecies . . .
> among many things, [to] bring the Jewish problem to a solu-
> tion. . . .
>   Today I want to be a prophet again: If international finance
> Jewry in and outside of Europe should succeed in thrusting the
> nations once again into a world war, then the result will not be
> the Bolshevization of the earth and with it the victory of Jewry,
> but the destruction of the Jewish race in Europe.[32]

On the same day as this speech, *Social Justice* ran a lengthy article,
"Exploiting the Refugees," which dealt with the industry of smuggling
and forged passports. The tabloid provided a warning:

There is danger to the peace of the world in this exploitation of refugees, especially in the intensification and misuse of their natural sense of injury. Not only is popular indignation being superheated by the stories of tyranny and cruelty so that the peoples are becoming war-minded . . . but of recent months it [refugee traffic] has grown to a flood reminiscent of a stampede of animals with packs of wolves, jackals and other beasts of prey worrying the flying herds.[33]

Perhaps the best chance to seek American action to help European Jews occurred in the wake of Crystal Night. A vast majority of the nation—94 percent—told Gallup pollsters in January 1939 that they did not see any justification for the German outburst. Yet while a clear majority of 58 percent supported FDR's recalling of the German ambassador as a means to express U.S. indignation, 66 percent opposed a plan "to allow 10,000 refugee children from Germany to be brought into this country and taken care of in American homes."[34]

In February 1939, Senator Robert Wagner of New York and Congresswoman Edith Rogers of Massachusetts introduced identical bills in Congress calling for the admission of 20,000 German refugee children in addition to the regularly allotted quota of immigrants from that nation—the first attempt since 1924 to expand America's immigration laws. The so-called Wagner-Rogers bill was one of several pieces of immigration legislation introduced in 1939, including proposals to reduce as well as increase quotas. Between November 1938 and the outbreak of World War II in September 1939, Coughlin waged a strenuous campaign against expanding refugee quotas, filling the airways and his weekly newspaper's columns with this theme:

It is natural for us to respond to the victims of persecution wherever they may be. But why not permit charity to begin at home? . . . Why shut our eyes to the pleas of 12-million jobless working men whom our undemocratic financial system practically has despoiled of their right to life, liberty and happiness?[35]

How about the New York barges that slide out to clandestine meetings with ships anchored off the 12-mile limit to bring in overall-clad refugees with "W.P.A. shovels" in hand?[36]

"How many refugees will you take?" is a routine question asked of Jewish businessmen. . . . In some cases, the employees have been told how many Christians should be discharged!"[37]

In an April 1939 editorial introduced with the headline "Depart Alien Critics," Father Coughlin indicated his support of a bill by Congressman Dempsey of New Mexico calling for the deportation of any alien who advocated changes in the American form of government: "The Bill is most timely insofar as this nation is being flooded by refugees who, in many instances, participated in the spread of Communism in European nations. It would be intolerable for us to permit these aliens to raise their voices in America."[38]

When the Committee on Immigration and Naturalization of the House of Representatives held hearings in May 1939 on a joint resolution to authorize the admission to the United States of 10,000 refugee children—a watered-down version of the original Wagner-Rogers bill—a string of witnesses from "patriotic" organizations testified in opposition. Agnes Waters, a leader of a Coughlin-inspired women's group, declared:

This bill is just another one of the series of proposed measures signed and supported by Communists as a part of the plan of the Third International to overthrow this Government. . . . There is no reason in the world today why Americans should look after and provide homes and jobs to foreigners. . . . It is not fair to the United States taxpayers for bills of this kind giving special privileges to aliens to be introduced, taking up the time of Congress and the committees that should be spent in working for the American people, especially in view of the present world crisis, and our domestic problem of 12,000,000 unemployed. Charity begins at home.[39]

Proponents of the bill had sought to avoid arousing anti-Semitic forces by suggesting that the children to be aided were Christian as well as Jewish. A number of Jewish leaders and their organizations were reluctant to go on record in favor of the Wagner-Rogers bill for the same reason. Given the evident disunity within the Jewish community and the political hazards, it was difficult for the Roosevelt administration to take any lead. Hearings dragged on into June 1939. One day after the close of hearings, FDR received a request from his aide, Edwin "Pa" Watson, to express his opinion on the pending proposal. Roosevelt wrote across the memo: "File No Action."[40]

As war neared, FDR and his aides increasingly turned toward a land resettlement solution to the Jewish persecutions in Europe. A number of locations were considered, including Palestine, Madagascar, and even Alaska.[41] An Alaska plan developed by Interior Secretary Harold Ickes was treated with disdain by *Social Justice* in an editorial of August 1939, which repeated the idée fixe that "charity still begins at home—where it is needed sadly. America is full of refugees from economic oppression, and few tears are being shed for them."[42]

Ironically, when the United States became the "Arsenal of Democracy" upon the outbreak of the war, a labor shortage rather than any surplus plagued the American economy. Official national unemployment hit a peak of 24.9 percent in 1933 and after several years of decline returned to 19 percent in 1938. Between 1939 and 1942 the figure dropped from 17.2 to 4.7 percent.

Accusations that thousands of legal and illegal immigrants were stealing jobs from native Americans inspired deep fears but were without foundation. Estimates of the number of refugees from Nazi Europe who immigrated to the United States by the early 1940s number approximately 250,000.[43] Approximately 60,000 of these were from Germany and Austria. Out of a total U.S. population of 130 million, this was less than one-twentieth of 1 percent.

Ten months after World War II broke out and the Battle of Britain was yet to be decided, Father Coughlin's newspaper discussed the plight of children in Europe:

> We are informed that England is planning to transfer at least 50,000 children from the bombing scenes. . . . Social Justice Publishing Corporation is willing to play stepfather and stepmother to 500 such children if the American government will interest itself as much in them as it did in the Jewish refugees.[44]

Perhaps this was the best explanation of "charity begins at home."

The volatile anti-Semitism in New York City in early 1939 involved more than the street confrontations between supporters and opponents of Father Coughlin. An organization that had become the very symbol of Nazism in America, the Friends of the New Germany, commonly known as the German-American Bund, staged a massive rally in Madison Square Garden on February 20, billed as "George Washington Birthday Exercises. . . . [A] Mass Demonstration for True Americanism." With a dramatic backdrop of a huge banner with the likeness of Washington opposite the Nazi-like Bund flag, this event was a frightening indication of the invasion of America by Hitlerism:

> That . . . turned out to be the wildest Nazi demonstration so far staged on this side of the Rhine. The great hall was jammed with 20,000 men, women, and many children. High above the speaker's platform towered a huge figure of George Washington, flanked by giant black swastikas. From somewhere in the rear of the hall came the muffled sound of drumbeats as a uniformed Nazi legion, 1200 strong, marched in behind the swastika flags and the banners of the German National-Socialist Party! Twelve hundred brown-shirted arms smartly raised in a Hitler salute![45]

Newspaper and magazine coverage of the rally emphasized its blatant hostility toward Jews. Its most startling moment was recorded on film, which *Life* magazine treated as a feature photo spread. The caption described "a 26-year-old plumber's helper named Isador Greenbaum who rushed Fritz Kuhn, Bund head, as he was vilifying Jews. . . . Newsreel shots of this violent scene were withdrawn from theatres after two days when managers complained they incited audiences to riot." The photo sequence shows speaker Kuhn hearing a noise, "turning to his right as Greenbaum is tackled by a uniformed Bund member. He then falls over the rostrum railing and then four 'storm troopers' jump on him and then start pulling his legs."[46]

This melee, and the Bund meeting, became the stuff of journalistic legend. At one point, the rally was interrupted by nationally syndicated columnist Dorothy Thompson, who broke out laughing. Her removal by Bund officials only underscored the sense that the organization was a danger to the country.

Most disturbing of all was the audience's reaction to the Bund speakers. According to the author of an exposé of native fascism, "Hitler, Mussolini, Franco and the mention of the Reverend Charles E. Coughlin's name received ear-splitting applause, while the President was booed and hissed and our officials slandered as, one after another, high Bund officials paraded to the speaker's stand."[47]

Social Justice suggested that the cheers had come from a number of Father Coughlin's followers who were at the meeting to see what it was about and then naturally cheered when the priest's name was mentioned. Referring to the "overplayed 'Bund Riot,'" the newspaper opined:

> For six years New York's Jews, operating under the more polite name of "anti-Nazis" have conducted a far-reaching and utterly senseless boycott against all things German. . . . Inside the Garden a demonstrative audience cheered patriotic references to George Washington and Americanism. Messrs. Hopkins, Ickes, Leon Blum, Rabbi Wise, Karl Marx and the Rothschilds brought boos and jeers. References to Father Coughlin made by several speakers brought long and profound cheering. . . . To the unprejudiced observer it was an American audience, drawn as much from curiosity as any "pro-German zeal." Its temper was resentful of all un-American "isms," but particularly of Communism and so-called "Jewish internationalism." Regardless of the venom of the speakers, the big audience appeared to be pro-Christian rather than anti-Jewish; and pro-American rather than pro-German.[48]

There was an overlap between the Bund and Coughlin's followers, and given the growing fear of Nazism crossing to America's shores, any prominent public figure identified with the Bund was viewed as unpatriotic. The radio priest had to offer an explanation for his connection with the subversive group, and yet he espoused many of its values and policy stands. Coughlin had begun to walk this tightrope in an earlier address just after the Madison Square Garden rally, "An American Christian Program."

> The swastika and the Stars and Stripes were proudly displayed on the platform which was guarded by hundreds of uniformed Nazis of German, Italian, Irish and Polish extraction. . . .
>
> Considering all circumstances, no sane American rejoices in such meetings. . . . It is unfortunate that such incidents must occur. They are merely the effects of definite causes. For the past ten years Communists have been holding meetings in public places. . . . For years they have been busy boycotting German and Italian firms. Calmly considering all these causes, they were bound to generate the effect of last Monday night. . . .

Meanwhile the vast majority of American citizens are still Americans. They are sympathetic neither with the Nazi Bund nor with the Communist convention. . . .

It is noteworthy that Communist meetings have been in vogue for many years and have created little or no comment. Now Communists are openly opposed—and very vigorously opposed—not only by Nazis, who formed only a small segment of last Monday's meeting, but by thousands of anti-Communists who are not Nazi-minded but who joined with the Bundists in protest. It is a most opportune time for Americans to enter into this contest—a contest which will determine whether Christian Americanism will prevail or some foreign "ism," dominated by an insignificant majority, will be inflicted upon us.[49]

Organized in 1933, the Bund had undergone several shifts in structure and symbolism. At first parading with the Nazi swastika, by 1937 it had adopted a modified logo. Nevertheless, the initial Nazi-like marching and Hitler salute had permanently branded the group a tool of a foreign, and now militarily threatening, power. In its structure and purposes, the Bund was seen as an alien force on American soil. There was great concern that Germany was planting the seeds of a "fifth column" in the United States and every other nation.

Coughlin avoided any formal or official alliance with Kuhn's organization, yet there were several individuals who acted as links between the radio priest and the Bund. One openly boasted of his meeting with the Royal Oak priest:

[William] Wernecke [a German-American Bund member] has been brought involuntarily before federal officials for an exhaustive examination of his bund activities in Chicago and a possible connection with Father Coughlin's organization. . . . Many witnesses, also appearing involuntarily, have informed the government of Wernecke's bund background. . . .

They told the government that at a regular meeting of the bund . . . Wernecke disclosed that he had had a conference with Father Coughlin in the radio priest's office in Royal Oak. They disclosed that when some doubt was expressed to Wernecke that Father Coughlin would meet with known Nazi representatives, Wernecke produced a letter written on Father Coughlin's private stationery and signed by the priest asking that Wernecke come to Royal Oak for the conference.[50]

Investigative journalist John Spivak reported the contents of an affidavit provided to him by a confidential source describing the Wernecke-Coughlin meeting:

On Wednesday night, February 8, 1939, the German-American Bund had a meeting in its headquarters [in Chicago]. After the meeting Wernecke took my informant aside and in high glee said that he had just come back from a very satisfactory conference with the Reverend Charles E. Coughlin at Royal Oak. . . .

Wernecke displayed a letter . . . setting forth the date and time of the conference. "What did you take up with him?" Wernecke was asked. The Nazi Bund leader laughed. "A number of things, but I myself was somewhat surprised at the lengths to which Father Coughlin went during our talk, which lasted over two hours. We met in his office in the basement of the Shrine of the Little Flower. A man whose name sounded like Richards was with Father Coughlin. In the course of our talk this man asked me when we were going to kill off three or four hundred Chicago Jews. I told him that I hadn't thought of that just yet. Father Coughlin laughed and said, "It needs doing."[51]

Wernecke's name would again surface in connection with Nazi activities, in 1943, when a group of seven saboteurs landed by submarine off the New England coast. They were captured, but not before receiving help from friends and relatives, including William Wernecke:

A young, bitterly fanatic anti-Semite who was a volunteer worker for some of the isolationist societies in Chicago whose efforts on behalf of Germany during the war came close to actual treason, Wernecke himself had ambitions to be a Storm Trooper. . . . He had hidden in a farmhouse a small armory of rifles, shotguns, 2100 rounds of ammunition, a collection of duelling pistols, and two cans of blasting powder.[52]

In several radio broadcasts beginning in 1939, Walter Winchell called Charles Coughlin the "Darling of the Bundists." The connection was soon well established. In testimony before the congressional committee focusing on the activities of extremist groups, Fritz Kuhn told of recommending that his group members read *Social Justice.* Front-page headlines screamed: "Fritz Kuhn Says He Cooperated with Coughlin."

In its quest to keep America out of the European war, the Nazi regime came to recognize that its greatest allies were those who were clearly identified as native patriots. Charles Coughlin thus became a far more attractive resource than the German-American Bund. But in the summer of 1937, Pope Pius XI had openly and formally offered theological criticism of the Nazi regime. In his encyclical *Mit Brennender Sorge* [With Burning Anxiety], the head of the Catholic church had attacked Nazi Germany for the same paganism, "naturalism," and violation of Christian values of the family and religious practice that Coughlin had found so subversive and dangerous in the Soviet system. This offered a challenge to both Catholics in Germany and the leaders of the Nazi state.

Coughlin was now in a profoundly awkward position. He had sung the praises of fascism and Nazism, but his followers saw him as the fighting priest who would defend the "Church Militant" against its enemies. He himself had criticized the "paganism" of the German racial laws.

Out of this mood the priest was open to a proposal for "informal diplomacy." It came from a close adviser, Leo M. Reardon, who was the publicity coordinator for *Social Justice.* Reardon suggested contacting leading Nazi officials to obtain a clear statement regarding the position of the Catholic church in Germany. Reardon proposed that he himself visit Germany.

Leo M. Reardon was a talented lawyer and advertising pro whose life had comprised a series of adventurous exploits, including becoming a millionaire at the age of twenty-four by going into the oil drilling business in Montana. He had opened a newspaper in West Palm Beach but, according to a close colleague who worked with him at *Social Justice,* "lost his shirt in the Florida hurricane of 1926." After a short stint in federal prison for mail fraud, Reardon tried his luck at writing dramas. The plot of one play, *Ringtail,* involved two prizefighters—one a Nazi, the other a Jew. The Nazi wore a swastika on his trunks that so enraged his Jewish opponent as to ensure the Nazi's defeat.[53]

Coughlin's emissary was making his trip to Germany at a most opportune time, since Nazi propaganda minister Joseph Goebbels was just launching a new campaign. He was pressing a decisive effort to eliminate the influence of the Catholic church in Germany and promoting the idea that anti-Semitism was just as prevalent outside the Reich as within it.[54]

Reardon's trip was planned with some care. Joe Wright, a key writer for *Social Justice,* remembers the preparations. "He went so far as to hire a German maid to prepare his meals [and] to teach him to speak German." As Wright remembers, "The purpose of the trip was to get a statement. He wanted to soften, to try to make Hitler more acceptable, to make him less obnoxious to Americans than he was. He wanted to defuse the criticism that he was anti-Christian. He knew better than to try to get him to say he wasn't anti-Semitic. He just wanted a statement which would get published that Hitler endorsed Christianity." Reardon kept the whole thing quiet: "He made damn sure it wasn't written up. It had to be secret or it wouldn't be effective at all. And it would wind up smearing Coughlin rather than helping him."[55]

Coughlin's emissary was issued a passport on January 4, 1939, for travel to Hamburg, Germany. That same day, by coincidence, the Nazi press issued a statement to quell fears of its hostility toward Christianity in Germany:

> We are interested in political but not in ideological problems, with the exception of Bolshevism of course. . . . We also do not threaten religion. The Jewish question is not a religious question, and at Field Marshal Goering's Christmas celebrations for children all the old Christian Christmas carols were sung.[56]

Reardon arrived in Germany in the second week of January 1939 and made appointments to see both Goebbels and Hitler's Foreign Office head, Joachim von Ribbentrop. Reardon was initially received by a deputy official, Richard Sallet, who had served several years in the German embassy in Washington and was very familiar with U.S. politics. According to the official German Foreign Office memorandum, included among documents captured at the end of the war, it was Sallet's task "to entertain Reardon and talk to him about German problems." According to the report made by State Secretary Ernst Woermann, "Reardon talked against President Roosevelt and against the Jews, and conveyed Coughlin's suggestion that Hitler personally make some sort of statement that the Nazis were supporters of Christian religion." Woermann noted that "after spending a few days with Sallet, Reardon saw Ribbentrop. To Ribbentrop he repeated the things he had told Sallet." Ribbentrop replied in vague terms that "they would do the best they could on it. At the close of the interview, Ribbentrop said: 'Give my regards to Father Coughlin. I have a high regard for him.' "[57]

On January 21, Goebbels personally replied to criticisms of German treatment of Jews coming from across the Atlantic. In a speech entitled "What Does America Actually Want?" he decried the "distorted picture of Germany that was given by a Jewish-dominated press which did not represent the true views of Americans."[58] His diary for January 24 records:

> The manager of Father Coughlin, the anti-Semitic radio priest in America, tells us that America is basically more anti-Semitic than we give it credit for. He would like us to take a more positive attitude toward Christianity.
>
> I tell the Führer about this. He intends to touch on the question in his speech to the Reichstag. He intends to put out feelings to the Americans and give an outline of Germany's general position. I believe that this speech will be very important.[59]

On the testimony of Joseph Goebbels, it would appear that Reardon not only encouraged a theme in a speech by Adolf Hitler but had potentially encouraged "feelers" of growing anti-Semitism in the United States.[60]

As the first weeks of 1939 unfolded, the Nazi press focused on American anti-Semitism:

Cries of Desperation from the U.S., Growing Anti-Semitism in Roosevelt's Country

> A typical demonstration took place in Washington, which proves anti-Semitism in the U.S. is becoming more and more noticeable. About 20 Americans appeared in front of the "Washington Post" building with posters and pamphlets in which they demanded the deportation of the Jews from the United States.[61]

Meanwhile, *Social Justice* printed a steady stream of letters to the editor and commentary reporting favorably on church-state relations in the Third Reich.[62] Though when interviewed about his opinion on the impact of the death of Pius XI and the accession of Cardinal Pacelli, Coughlin took the occasion to call for "the Hitler government to reconcile itself with views of the Vatican," a few weeks later the radio priest's weekly carried the front-page headline, "Rome-Berlin Axis Is a Firm Rampart against Communism." The article stated that "it should never be forgotten that the Rome-Berlin axis . . . is serving Christendom in a peculiarly important manner."[63]

By late summer 1939, both practical and ideological reasons emerged for the radio priest to back away from Reardon's January initiative. The signing of the remarkable Non-Aggression Pact between Hitler and Stalin in August caught many by surprise and undermined the entire rationale for Reardon's mission. If Nazism, the "defense mechanism" against bolshevism, was now in league with Stalin, there was no point in the radio priest's trying to accommodate such an ideology with Christianity. Furthermore, Coughlin had been reprimanded severely (albeit in private) by his archbishop, who had, after consulting with the Vatican, notified the priest that his actions in attacking Jews were a violation of church doctrine.

Now Coughlin forwarded his delayed response to the Nazi overtures generated by Leo Reardon's visit. Fritz Hailer, an American citizen who was serving as the honorary German consul in Detroit and had apparently been asked by the Nazi high command to approach Coughlin through Reardon, was contacted and asked to relay a message to the German government. It was a diffuse and mildly chiding rejection of any role as mediator between Germany and America:

> Mr. Reardon has detailed to me the conversation you had with him and has also urged me to compose a letter.
> After due consideration these thoughts are uppermost in my mind.
>
> 1. I am not an official either of the State or of the Church. Consequently a letter from me is of little or no value.
> 2. His Holiness Pope Pius XII well understands how necessary it is to combat the international disease of Communism. . . . He is most able and diplomatic and understands how to convey important ideas of state far better than do I.[64]

Coughlin offered a vague observation: "Certainly there is need for a Christian front to operate under the visible head of Christianity in order to overcome the anti-Christian front operating under the invisible directorate of Satan." He then explained that Nazi Germany was not viewed favorably by "Christians in the United States because the officers of the Reich have persecuted Christians, if not physically, at least in other ways." Protesting that he was not being "argumentative or uncharitable" but was speaking as a "simple Catholic priest with no jurisdiction outside my parish," Coughlin reiterated his suggestion that it was the pope who was better suited for diplomacy than himself.[65]

In early August, Hailer was in Germany, and he hoped to again serve as a useful intermediary between the radio priest and German authorities. He told German state secretary Woermann that he hoped a reply to Coughlin's letter could be taken back with him when he planned to leave for the United States in mid-September. In his memo of August 11, Woermann wrote to von Ribbentrop that he had told Hailer "that it probably would be difficult to formulate an official German statement for Coughlin."[66]

Hailer's return to Detroit was delayed one week by Germany's invasion of Poland on September 1. The consul would remain at his post in Detroit until June 1941, when FDR ordered all German embassies and legations closed on the grounds of "activities harmful to the country." By this time, the United States was on the verge of entering the war, and public opinion had shifted so decidedly in favor of helping the Allies that any contacts with Nazi Germany would be viewed as tantamount to treason. In the future, his communication with the radio priest would be conducted on an even more confidential basis.

By March 1939, Hitler discarded the agreement he had made a few months earlier in Munich to annex only part of neighboring Czechoslovakia. Coughlin "responded" in a booklet, *Our Problem Is in America*. Calling the concerns "with the minorities of Europe" a distraction from America's problems, the priest asserted that "no one can stop Hitler or his historic successor in Germany or elsewhere until the injustices against God and men are eradicated from the hearts of diplomats and intriguers." He went on to denounce bitterly those who were calling for U.S. intervention in Europe:

> On every hand there is raised the cry, "Stop Hitler! . . . Who started Hitler?" . . . It was the signatories of the Treaty of Versailles who recognized atheistic Soviet Russia, a menace to civilization. It was they who imposed a $57 billion fine payable in gold upon the outraged German Christian people. . . . It was they

who dismembered the empire, piece by piece, and evolved a program of encirclement so that never again would German commerce, German industry and German goods compete with the victors upon the shores of the seven seas. . . . There is no stopping Hitlerism![67]

Social Justice echoed the standard themes of Nazi leaders. Just after the September 1938 Munich agreement, *Social Justice* had referred to Czechoslovakia as "this new mongrel state." Moreover, "The Germans and Hungarians were ordered into this incoherent State because they were the vanquished of the war. . . . The Czechs, who are cunning propagandists, bamboozled English, French, and American public opinion by their glib talk of their devotion to 'democratic principles.' "[68] Two weeks later, with the resignation of President Beneš, the magazine wrote that Czechoslovakia "should move forward to peace and prosperity":

> The agreement at Munich . . . is a victory not for Hitler and aggression, but for peace, truth, and justice! Dr. Bencš, the ordertaker, and all the leftist promoters of revolution in America [are] charging a "sell-out" and a "rape" of Czechoslovakia. What actually happened was that the long persecuted Sudeten Germans will return to their fatherland.[69]

When all of Czechoslovakia was absorbed by Germany a few months later, *Social Justice* commentator J. S. Barnes offered this postmortem:

> Germany's policy . . . remains . . . the necessary policy of any strong and independent Germany. It was the policy of Kaiser Wilhelm's Germany no less than it is the policy of Hitler's Germany. It is a vital interest for Germany; and it is dictated by geographical reasons. . . . The real trouble that might lead to a general war, is not likely to arise from problems. The real trouble lies in the ambitions of the old school of capitalistic financial imperialism. *It is these people who are the real aggressors* and they are chiefly found in England and America.[70]

Within two weeks of the outbreak of war, Coughlin launched the most ambitious lobbying campaign of his career. Hammering away at the theme of Jews and international financial interests, he now called for a

national expression of resistance to the policies of "cash and carry"—
FDR's plan by which the neutrality rules could be softened to permit
more arms sales to the Allies.

In September 1939, Coughlin told his readers:

> American men and women! The Second World War has be-
> gun. . . . But can there be an oasis in this world of bleeding hu-
> manity? Can there be a country strong enough to withstand the
> infection of war and dedicate itself to a strict policy of neutrality
> and peace? Positively, Yes. . . . There is no valid cash-and-carry
> program. But there is a "credit-and-carrion" program.
>
> ORGANIZE YOUR NEIGHBORS, YOUR FAMILY, YOUR CLUB MEM-
> BERS, YOUR FELLOW CITIZENS, AND NOT ONLY PETITION YOUR CON-
> GRESSMAN TO KEEP STRICT NEUTRALITY BUT DEMAND THAT HE AND
> HIS FAMILY GET OUT WITH YOU TO MARCH ON WASHINGTON IN THE
> GREATEST PEACE DEMONSTRATION OF ALL TIMES.[71]

The priest went on to warn his readers that "our engaging in the merchandising of murder is the first step which leads inevitably to the last
step of war." Coughlin also congratulated his supporters for their "splendid petitioning" and for their letters sent to Congress: "Ten million more
letters from you will insure that victory!"[72]

In the face of a likely confrontation with interventionists, Coughlin
stopped advocating a march in favor of separate constituent pressure on
each member of the Congress. This strategy clearly had an impact. On
September 25, Congressman William J. Miller, a Connecticut Republican who had advocated total repeal of neutrality legislation, told a State
Department official that he now favored retaining the arms embargo.
Miller disclosed that he had received 1,800 letters and telegrams, with
only 76 favoring the cash-and-carry proposal. Describing the response
within the Catholic community, the "Washington Merry-Go-Round" column by Drew Pearson and Robert Allen asserted that

> all members of Congress testify that far and away the strongest
> pressure against them, either Catholic or Protestant, is brought
> by Coughlin.
>
> About one-half of their neutrality mail is from Coughlinites,
> while even more potent are the Coughlin delegates which have
> been storming Capitol Hill. . . .

When Congress opened, delegations from New York . . . and Massachusetts packed the halls in [*sic*] rowdy mood. As they entered the House Office Building to talk to New York Congressmen, one husky young delegate called out: "Don't smash the furniture boys, we're going to take over this place soon."[73]

The U.S. entry into the war would finally put a stop to Coughlin's power, but in the late 1930s, he seemed invincible. One final story from these years, the bizarre tale of the Brooklyn Boys, suggests the frightening reach of Coughlin's oratory and the terrible grasp it might have exercised had not Pearl Harbor intervened.

11

The Trial of
the "Brooklyn Boys"

> If every reader of *Social Justice* formed at once a platoon of
> 25 or more persons dedicated to opposing Communism in all
> its forms, a Christian Front of 25,000,000 Americans would
> already be in operation.
>
> Charles Coughlin, May 1938

A MAJOR FAULT LINE had appeared since the early 1930s between Jews and Catholics in America. It began with events in Latin America (Mexico in particular), shifted to the Civil War in Spain, and opened widest over responses to fascism in Italy and Germany. At their height, these tensions were far stronger than those that would arise between blacks and Jews in the 1980s over affirmative action and job competition.

Coughlin understood this fault line all too well. Indeed, he seemed to encourage it with talk of a "Christian front." As researcher Richard Davis observed in 1974, "Of all his organizations, it was his Christian Front . . . that clearly linked Father Coughlin with the American variant of fascism."[1]

Coughlin claimed that he had borrowed the term "Christian Front" from Franco, to describe the counterforce to the Popular Front, a coalition of Marxists and leftist groups in depression-racked Europe. But after Spain's conflict, the struggle in Europe seemed to be a stark choice between communism and fascism.

Coughlin first referred to a Christian Front when he spoke of forming "platoons of 25 men each into a Christian Front." Among the functions of these neighborhood units was the study of "the principles of social justice, establishment of . . . programs for the poor, and preparation against the day when they will be needed."[2]

The first meeting of any group of this sort occurred in midtown Manhattan at the Paulist Fathers' rectory. A cleric described the setting and the themes of those speaking:

> About 40 or 50 men were present. . . . Corrigan told of the "young Jew girls" collecting funds for Spain in Brooklyn. All down the line there was constant reference to Jews. . . . The first speaker Cooper, went back to the days of Martin Luther and stated that the Jews were behind Luther and now that the Jews have split up the Protestants they were striving to break up the Catholics. . . .
>
> This is going to be a national movement in America, because we have the strength of the Catholic religion with us. We are most desirous of marching side by side with the Protestants.[3]

At a meeting the following month, a commentary given to Coughlin's archbishop in Detroit included this narrative:

> The . . . speaker was a fellow named Hahn, who was introduced as a member of the U.S. Immigration Board, a private organization. "I want to tell you that I am not only a member of the Immigration Board but that I am a U.S. Secret Service agent. Holding the position that I do I am able to tell you that by our records we know that there are thousands of Jews pouring into the U.S. from every direction. . . . I am a tough man. I'll tell you that there is only one thing to do and that is to kill all the Jews." As he said this he deliberately placed his hand on his hip. . . . "I am impatient to use my gun on them. . . ." There was no word of censure from Father Burke or anyone else after Hahn's talk.[4]

By October 1938, Coughlin sounded as if he were menacingly issuing a call to arms: "Our people have passed beyond the point of being satisfied with a mere study club. I am convinced we are ripe for action clubs."[5] In a series of radio sermons the next summer, he hailed the formation of Christian Front units "to look forward to the day, hopefully by 1940, when there would be five million marching under the banner of a Christian Front."[6]

It now appeared that Coughlin had created his own national militia-

style organization. His core of activist supporters seemed poised to respond as his words became wilder and wilder:

> Organized along militant lines, as defense mechanism against
> Red activities and as a protector of Christianity and American-
> ism, the Christian Front is spreading from Greater New York into
> Philadelphia, Boston, and other Eastern centers.
>   Invasion of Cleveland, Cincinnati, Detroit, Chicago, and
> other key cities of the Middle West will begin in August.
>   Sports and athletic prowess are two of the main objectives of
> the Christian Front.[7]

Coughlin was careful to avoid suggesting that he personally was the
official leader of the organization: "First and foremost, let all those who
are interested in either organizing the Christian Front or joining it understand that I am neither the organizer nor the sponsor of the Christian
Front. . . . I must hold myself disengaged. . . . I must act in no other capacity toward you than as a friend and counsellor, whose privilege it is to
address you in your homes each Sunday."[8] But this public announcement
was, in fact, made at the demand of Coughlin's archbishop.

The local groups of the Christian Front were formed from the ranks
of Coughlin's earlier Social Justice Study Clubs, which were established
after the 1936 elections to prepare for the 1940 campaign. Two men
stepped forward as leaders of the Christian Front. Joe McWilliams, a talented and suave public speaker, broke away to form his own "Christian
Mobilizers" when Jack F. Cassidy, a Fordham Law School student, won
Coughlin's endorsement. In Boston, a second Christian Front leader
emerged, Frances P. Moran.

Meanwhile, both Coughlin's own superior, Archbishop Edward
Mooney, and New York's then Archbishop Francis Spellman were receiving private reports as to Coughlin's critical role in the Christian Front
movement:

> Clearly the leaders of each section of this movement, Christian
> Front or Christian Mobilizers, look on Fr. Coughlin as the for-
> mulator of their thought, the ideologue of the movement, the
> Mohammed, their Mecca being Royal Oak. A close study of
> their remarks should shed light and reveal that they employ pat
> phrases of the priest from Royal Oak; his technical social termi-

nology is found in their sentiments, even to a degree in their pamphlet on the movement. A number of his followers who are members of these organizations mimic his speech and intonations.[9]

Other clergy noted the growth of the New York branch of the movement:

The Christian Mobilizers and the Christian Front are openly National American movements. . . . This ideology is being developed and is being used consciously as it has been used in Nazism. The same references to race and blood are being employed. The idea of training the youth in military discipline is being carried out in two ways: 1) by having them join the National Guard as the Communists are supposed to be doing; and 2) by training them directly in thinly disguised "sports clubs."[10]

"Sports clubs," according to one observer, functioned as models of Nazi-like regimentation:

The military leader known as "Bill" called them slaves, asked them to stand and defend their rights, since neither Congress nor the Roosevelt Administration will defend them. Everywhere they see Jews and Communists working to overthrow the government. They act as if Der Tag is the day after tomorrow. They are preparing, actually, to be a counterrevolutionary force.[11]

Membership in the Christian Front stemmed disproportionately from an underclass within Irish and German-American neighborhoods. Many were young. A report circulated to Coughlin's archbishop sounded deep alarm about the "primitive sources" of the Christian Front recruits:

The movement is the result of a sublimation of individuals' financial insecurity, lower middle-class social disillusion and frustration, social unrest and religious subjectivity coupled with racial and national pride. Collected as a brew of hatred, the potion is strong enough to promote a movement of national significance and importance, a threat that can become actual both to the progress of the Church and the maintenance of the Republic in America.[12]

From merely listening to inflammatory speeches, Christian Front members in New York now formed the picketing army that surrounded radio station WMCA. They were also embroiled in the street violence precipitated by the mass demonstrations.

On Monday, January 15, 1940, Americans were jolted by headlines across the nation like this one that catapulted the Christian Front to a disturbing prominence: "18 Seized in Plot to Overthrow U.S."[13]

Since the previous summer, an FBI informer had been planted in the Brooklyn unit of the Christian Front. On the night of January 13, J. Edgar Hoover personally led a contingent of agents who raided several neighborhoods, picking up the members of the club headed by Jack Cassidy and William Bishop, a British émigré and soldier of fortune who had once fought in the army of Francisco Franco. A cache of arms was seized, including homemade bombs, several rifles, thousands of rounds of ammunition, and evidence of an elaborate plan to begin an overthrow effort as early as January 20.

The alleged plot included starting an uprising that would destroy Jewish-owned newspapers and stores and blow up bridges, utilities, docks, and railroad stations in the New York City area. Gold was to be seized from the U.S. Custom House, the general post office, and federal reserve banks. Members of the Congress, including both senators from New York, were to be assassinated, and a terrorist campaign would force the federal government to send in troops. Once that occurred, the public, enraged over the money being spent to protect Jews, would rise up to overthrow the Roosevelt administration and initiate an anticommunist revolution.

The news of the Christian Front indictments brought the threat of prosecution to Coughlin's doorstep. Reporters eagerly sought his reaction to the startling events in Brooklyn. Questioned by the local Detroit newspapers, the priest initially "roundly disavowed" the Brooklyn arrestees and described their activities as a scheme for infiltration by communist agent provocateurs:

These people tried to ride on my coattails. . . . I had an appeal to Cassidy when he planned to have some crazy people march on New York City Hall in my name 8 or 10 months ago. I had to tell him to lay off. There has been an attempt on the part of the Communists . . . to organize a fake Christian Front, solely to embarrass me.[14]

Yet just a few months before the arrests in Brooklyn, supporters of the radio priest had heard him praise Cassidy: "The Christian Front is not a debating society; it is an action society. . . . God bless Mr. Cassidy and the Christian Front!"[15]

In its first issue after the arrests, *Social Justice* described the government action as a plot by Attorney General Frank Murphy to smear a patriotic anticommunist organization. The paper distinguished between the Christian Front and the sports club, saying that only the latter was the focus of prosecution. A week later, the publication said that politics and "warmongering" were behind the plot investigation, all of which was described as an attempt to link Coughlin to the eighteen arrested men. By his January 21 radio address, the priest had shifted ground and now offered a ringing defense of those who had been indicted:

> I take my stand beside the Christian Fronters. . . . While I do not belong to any unit of the Christian Front, nevertheless, I do not disassociate myself from that movement. I reaffirm every word which I have said in advocating its formation; I re-encourage the Christians of America to carry on in this crisis for the preservation of Christianity and Americanism more vigorously than ever despite this thinly veiled campaign launched by certain publicists and their controllers to vilify both the name and the principles of this pro-American, pro-Christian, anti-Communist and anti-Nazi group![16]

This broadcast had been approved by a committee appointed to control Coughlin by archbishop Edward Mooney. The original text was even more strident:

> I congratulate . . . every one of the incarcerated men for the Christian way in which they have conducted themselves!
>
> "I was in prison and you came to me," said Jesus Christ. The spirit of America is on the march and will visit you, be you saint or sinner, innocent or guilty. . . .
>
> Ladies and gentlemen, will you visit these young men too, in the cause of justice, of Christianity and of Americanism?
>
> Today, we, the friends of the Christian Front, will contribute towards your defense through the agency of the Brooklyn "Tablet" and or "Social Justice" magazine.[17]

Three weeks after their arrest, the "Brooklyn boys"—the median age of the group actually being thirty-two—were indicted on one count of conspiracy and one count of stealing government property. Trial was set for April 3, 1940. There were a number of problems with the prosecutor's case, not the least of which was the fact that the chances of the plot's succeeding were so low that it made the entire affair seem ludicrous. This helped lend an air of unreality, which worked heavily in favor of the "boys." The weapons, bombs, and skill of the plot participants seemed more comic than menacing.

The Christian Front case was tried for the government by Harold M. Kennedy with the assistance of O. John Rogge, a Justice Department attorney who would later be the chief prosecutor in a bizarre sedition case against several dozen pro-Nazi activists. Although fifty-one witnesses were called over five weeks, the testimony of Dennis Healy, the FBI's undercover informant, remained central to the case. Healy had written notes on the inside of his shirtsleeves, and these were supplemented by a series of tape recordings of meetings he held with the various defendants.

It was in June 1939 that the plan was first discussed by Cassidy, Healy, and Bishop. Gradually others were drawn into the plot while activities began: stealing ammunition from government armories in the New York area and engaging in rifle practice at a Narrowsburg, New York, firing range on the estate of a friend of Bishop. According to Healy's testimony, the plotters had hoped to trigger a revolution that would rid the nation of Jews and place in power a person widely admired by the anti-Semitic far right of the time, General George Van Horn Moseley. The plot was to be initiated on January 27, 1941, by attacks on the Brooklyn and Philadelphia navy yards as well as Annapolis and West Point. A small quantity of ammunition was turned over to Bishop by a member of the National Guard at Fort Dix. Writing on the Christian Front defendants, Charles Higham indicates that

> Healy was told that he would be tested on his ability with a machine gun. He attended a Sporting Club target practice at Narrowsburg, Long Island, at which he was shocked to see an enormous target consisting of a portrait of President Roosevelt blown up and caricatured out of all proportion. He had to steel himself to riddle it with machine-gun bullets. At one stage in the afternoon, a Sporting Club member brought a replica of a big Jewish nose and put it over the President's. The men gleefully shot it off.[18]

Leo J. Healy, a popular former judge in Brooklyn, served as the main defense attorney. He sought to turn the tables on the government by suggesting that the entire prosecution was a plot to defame the Catholic church and to this end painted a picture of communists seeking to discredit the Christian Front "boys," who were merely playing an active role in defending America, he said. Coughlin's *Social Justice* echoed this theme:

> This is a Christian country. Will you convict these young men because they dared to say so?
>
> These young men were interested in rifle practice. Because they did a little shooting in the country some months ago, they are locked up as revolutionaries. If they did this today, they would be greeted as patriots who were learning civilian marksmanship in preparation against Fifth Columnists and parachutists. They were ahead of their time. . . .
>
> Macklin Boettger is charged with having said he would like to have a rifle with a telescopic sight so that he could "go out and shoot a few Communists." . . . Well, I too, would like to shoot a few Communists. I would like to see every Communist in this country strung up on the nearest lamppost. You cannot, however, convict a person for his likes or dislikes.[19]

Defense attorneys hammered away at informer Dennis Healy, keeping him on the stand for eight days. Conceding that they had discussed the possibility of instigating a revolution that would lead to a "Christian" coup d'état, the defendants protested that they had only been engaging in lighthearted braggadocio.[20] Jack Cassidy testified that he suspected William Bishop was a Nazi or a communist agent but admitted he had not checked on his suspicions. And it got odder. Before the proceedings ended, one defendant, thirty-six-year-old Claus Gunther Ernecke, committed suicide, apparently believing there was a plot to prevent him from returning to Germany and fighting for Hitler.

A noisy crowd constantly milling about the Brooklyn federal court booed and heckled federal agents and Justice Department attorneys as they entered or left the premises but lustily cheered the defendants whenever they came into view.

In his summation, defense attorney Healy told the jury that should the "boys" be convicted, "the jurors would be hailed as heroes by the Communists."[21]

After nine weeks and a million and a half words of testimony, the case went to the jury on June 19, 1940. On the first ballot, nine jurors voted for acquittal. After six days and nights in the sweltering confines of the Federal Court Building in Brooklyn—nearly fifty hours of deliberations and more than three hundred tallies—the jury reached a decision. With one juror still holding out, they declared a mixed verdict: ten of the seventeen defendants were acquitted of all counts; two were acquitted of one count of conspiracy, with no agreement on a second count of illegal acquisition of firearms; and a mistrial was declared for five other defendants.[22] Two months earlier, Claus Gunther Ernecke had hanged himself. One of the defendants, James Prouty, who had given the ammunition from the National Guard Armory to William Gerald Bishop, was court-martialed trial in December 1940. He was cleared of the charge of illegally disposing of military property.[23] Bishop, however, after being sent to Ellis Island, was deported.

The government was publicly embarrassed by the Brooklyn verdict; the Coughlin forces savored vindication. The line taken by *Social Justice* and supporters of the radio priest was to ridicule the case as a failed attempt to link Coughlin to the "so-called Christian Front" trial, claiming that New York papers and the "Jewish press" had engineered the entire affair. This theme even emerged in the summation to the jury by defense attorney Leo Healy:

> Let's get down to the facts. Who were you [speaking to the government attorneys and FBI agents] after in this case, gentlemen? I know you were out to get Father Coughlin and the Christian Front!
>
> The government says that the Christian Front is not on trial. But can we be sure that it wasn't out to get the Number One Christian Fronter in America, and failing that, swooped down upon that "Chocolate-cake revolutionary," 18-year-old William Bushnell and these others.[24]

An editorial in the priest's magazine subsequently asserted: "It was Father Coughlin and the Christian Front whom these anti-Christian radicals wanted to see on trial in New York."[25]

Why were the Christian Front defendants exonerated? Certainly the venue of the case was one factor. Friends and supporters of the "boys" were evident in the local media, particularly the *Brooklyn Tablet,* a widely read Catholic newspaper, whose editor, Patrick Scanlan, was a close friend and supporter of the radio priest. Leo Healy, who had been a magistrate in Brooklyn, was a highly popular public figure, while no one on the federal prosecutorial team was a local. It also emerged after the trial that the forewoman of the jury, Helen Titus, was the cousin of a close aide to Father Edward Brophy, himself a close friend of Coughlin and one of the founding clergy of the Christian Front.[26]

During the trial, Coughlin's name came up occasionally but played no role in the government's case. One of the defendants, a thirty-two-year-old telephone line repairman, testified that he joined the Christian Front because he believed that since Father Coughlin led it, the church had given its blessing. Defendants Cassidy and John Viebrock both stated that they looked to the radio priest as their leader. At one point in the trial, William Bishop mentioned that he was offered leniency if he would tell if Coughlin was financing the organization.

Both the government and the church had discreetly agreed to keep Charles Coughlin's name out of the trial. His archbishop told Vatican officials that "one who occupied a high position [in the Justice Department] told me in confidence that he had taken pains to keep Father Coughlin's name out of the newspaper publicity attention on those arrests." In his own mind, the radio priest's superior had "no doubt" that Coughlin "had been closely connected with the formation and promotion" of the Christian Front, whose activities brought the "Catholic name into disrepute." "In opposing communism," he noted that the group "adopted the technique of the Communists; in meeting social problems incident to the presence of a large Jewish factor in the population of New York, they have made themselves the apostles of an anti-Semitic movement which is utterly opposed to the Christian spirit."[27] In public, though, he made no such condemnation.

Charles Coughlin's career up to the point of the Christian Front trial had made a steady progress toward political extremism. He came to gamble his reputation on world fascism and Nazism, but from the beginning he was anti-Semitic. As the focus of world attention, the Nazi persecution of Jews was a litmus test for many public figures, particularly for those who may have sincerely wanted to keep America free from foreign entanglements. These non-anti-Semitic "isolationists" were faced with a personal and ethical dilemma that did not trouble Charles Coughlin.

   As Coughlin moved from populist protest to ever more direct sympathy for, or at the least benign tolerance of, totalitarian fascism and
Nazism, he besmirched not only his own career but the Catholic church,
for which he claimed to speak. In equating his own political ideas with
Catholic doctrine, he challenged the church to respond. It did so only
slowly, but a response finally did come.

12

Just a Soldier in the Pope's Army

I am bitter against you for your rebuking words about Father
Coughlin. . . . If we lose him there will be a great multitude
of our Catholic people dropping of[f] from going to Church.
Why he's the only one [who] keeps our hopes alive by telling
the truth.

Mrs. John Negil to Archbishop Mooney, October 8, 1937

COUGHLIN'S FIRST CHURCH SUPERIOR was both his mentor and his victim. In this intimate relationship Bishop Michael Gallagher was no different from others whom the radio priest used and exploited. And for his part, Gallagher typified many associates of Father Coughlin who saw him as the means to their own ends.

By temperament, both Gallagher and Coughlin were impulsive. They enjoyed politics in the same mischievous way. They vexed church authorities. One Basilian father put the matter very simply: "He was a fighting Irishman, Gallagher was, and he liked that in Charlie."[1]

Born in Michigan and educated for the priesthood in Ireland and Austria, Gallagher was appointed bishop of Detroit in 1918. He had a reputation as a rabid Irish nationalist and a political radical, with strong Anglophobic attitudes. According to Coughlin, he and Michael Gallagher first met by coincidence:

At Ypsilanti . . . we got on the electric train for the ride back to Detroit. Gallagher shook hands with [Monsignor John] Doyle and said, "Who's this young boy?" "Coughlin." "Glad to know you,

199

Father. Sit down. Sit down." I took an immediate liking to Gallagher, and he to me. I was close to him ever since that day. And next
to my own father, I think he was the most beloved man in my life.[2]

Early in 1926, when Gallagher returned from Rome, where he had
attended the canonization rites of St. Therese, the Little Flower, the mandate for Coughlin's career was firmly established: "Build your church in
the wilderness. Name it the Shrine of the Little Flower. Make it a missionary oasis in the desert of religious bigotry."[3] Coughlin immortalized
Gallagher by using the bishop as the model for the visage of Michael the
Archangel, which is carved on the face of the Shrine of the Little
Flower's Crucifixion Tower, the imposing edifice marking the central focus of the church.

Gallagher's fellow bishops and superior officers in the church disliked him because he indulged Coughlin during his public career. Although criticism of Coughlin from within the ranks of Catholic prelates
did not publicly emerge for several years, when it did come, Gallagher's
response was strong and unqualified. A case in point was the attack
in April 1932 by William Cardinal O'Connell of Boston. He assailed
Coughlin's radio addresses as "hysterical. . . . The individual in Michigan takes it into his head to talk to the whole world. To whom is he
responsible? . . . You can't begin speaking about the rich, or making sensational accusations against banks and bankers, or uttering demagogic
stuff to the poor." To these criticisms, Bishop Gallagher replied: "I have
no intention of interfering with Father Coughlin. . . . Christ was not setting class against class when he rebuked the abuse of wealth. . . . To accuse him [Coughlin] of fomenting class bitterness is to accuse the Popes
and to accuse Christ of setting class against class."[4]

Later in 1932, Bishop Gallagher received via letter from the apostolic delegate in Washington, Archbishop Amleto Cicognani, the first of
many Vatican rebukes directed to him for his unrestrained support of
Coughlin. While politely deferring to the authority of the local bishop—
"I would not wish to diminish in any way any good such [Coughlin's]
talks are effecting, nor to impugn the motives by which they are actu-
ated"—Cicognani indicated that "from reports which have come to me
[such addresses] seriously violate the conditions which should always
characterize a sermon by a priest in the sacred edifice of the Church."[5]
Rome specifically instructed Gallagher to forbid any priest in his diocese
from delivering an address, on "radio or otherwise . . . which is of a po-

litical character" or which was "for the purpose of arousing political partisanship and persuading citizens to vote for one party or candidate rather than another." These conditions, the delegate offered, were to be "fully and faithfully observed."[6]

In fact, the Congregation of the Clergy at the Vatican had begun to hear complaints about Coughlin's conduct as early as 1929.[7] Among the most powerful salvos directed against the radio priest's "radicalism" were those emanating from such conservative lay voices as papal countess Mrs. Nicholas Brady, wife of a leading investment banker and close friend and mentor to Archbishop Francis Spellman.[8] In the fall of 1933, former president Herbert Hoover, then embroiled in a bitter confrontation with Coughlin (and debating whether or not he should publicly reply), heard from his former press secretary that Mrs. Brady had traveled to Rome to express her views on Coughlin directly to the Vatican. "All the heads of the Church are in agreement as to his [Coughlin's] delinquencies," she informed Herbert Hoover's aide, "but the Church is not in a position to discipline except where there is a question of morals and faith involved." Hoover learned that Countess Brady intended to see "if the matter cannot be again be brought to the head of the Church in Rome and some action taken."[9]

The church was wary of criticizing Coughlin's actions publicly. Even Cardinal O'Connell's attacks did not mention the radio priest by name, citing only "the blather from Michigan." Coughlin was not reluctant to take full advantage of this leniency. When he was alluded to for the fourth time in the addresses of the elder statesmen of the church hierarchy, he delivered a defiant reply, reminding the world of the source of his authority: "The Cardinal has no jurisdiction over me . . . it is high time that this bubble be bursted [*sic*]. . . . Every word that I have written has received the imprimatur of my Right Reverend."[10]

Throughout his public career, rumors of an impending Vatican crackdown on Coughlin provided journalistic copy. In mid-1933, when the first fissures began to appear in the FDR–radio priest alliance, media curiosity regarding alleged Vatican pressure to bring Coughlin to heel was significantly fueled. Speculation that Roosevelt was putting pressure on the church was accelerated in the wake of Coughlin's creation of the NUSJ in the fall of 1934.

The official attitude of the church hierarchy in America was expressed by the U.S. National Catholic Welfare Conference (NCWC). Liberal and pro–New Deal, the organization had had its first warning about FDR's efforts to curb Coughlin in a private appointment with Monsignor Michael Ready in the wake of the "Silver List" revelation in mid-1934, when the radio priest's silver investments were exposed. Roosevelt told the NCWC secretary that the "Gentile Silver" attack on Secretary of the Treasury Henry Morgenthau was anti-Semitic and criticized the church for allowing a priest to become so directly involved in politics. Near the end of 1934, in response to these criticisms, the NCWC was on the verge of adopting a formal statement that included a rebuke of Coughlin, but the statement was never issued.[11]

As the firestorm of criticism mounted and church officials questioned his authority behind his back, Bishop Gallagher came to the aid of his controversial protégé during one of Coughlin's broadcasts:

> In numerous letters which have come to me, many questions are asked regarding the position of Father Coughlin as respects his fellow priests, his religious Superiors, the American Hierarchy, the Holy Father, and the Church in General. . . .
>
> His critics say, "If we can get his Superior to own him as their own, then we may frighten timid souls among them with the threat of persecution. We can, in either case, divide his followers." . . . I see in some of the questions this crafty spirit. But I will answer respecting the position of Father Coughlin, and the answer will stand until an authority higher than mine reverses my judgment. . . . "Who is ecclesiastically responsible for the addresses of Father Coughlin?" "Answer: I am, as Bishop of the Catholic Diocese of Detroit."[12]

By 1936, with the National Union third-party campaign becoming a reality, it was evident to many inside the church that between Coughlin and Gallagher, the tail was wagging the dog. One bishop told Vatican officials that Coughlin was being "aided and abetted by his Most Reverend Ordinary, Bishop Gallagher," and was "now quite beyond control."[13]

Gallagher's attitude toward Coughlin's third-party effort was ambiguous. While lending his general support, he kept himself informed of the campaign's developments through his financial adviser, Gertrude Coogan. Although she was a key player in the development of the Union party, she sharply disagreed with the monetary plank of the party, which advocated government regulation of all forms of credit.

Gallagher did make a significant last-ditch effort to pull his protégé back from the brink of a risky adventure. The incident, as recounted by one of Coughlin's former fellow Basilians, occurred during the ordination of a priest in the Detroit diocese in the summer of 1936:

> Gallagher got an apple, and as he was peeling the apple and bending down over it, he says, "What do you priests think about this new party?" Hanick, who was home, he was his host, he says, "It's a bunch of horseshit." He said, "It's crazy and it'll never get anywhere. It can't upset either of the big parties." And Gallagher went on eating his apple. When he finished, he said, "Where is your telephone?" And he phoned and got Charlie. And he was on the platform in a park. . . . "Cancel the third-party thing." So Charlie faked a heart attack.[14]

This stunt, assuming it did occur, was too late. Moreover, there is no evidence that Coughlin's superior opposed the Union party effort once it was in full flower.

In July 1936, in the heat of his intense political campaigning, Coughlin denounced President Roosevelt, uttering the words "liar," "Great Betrayer," and "anti-God" during speeches. As a result, Bishop Gallagher faced more Vatican disapproval. Divided and unable to find a means to curb the radio priest, the American church hierarchy sought help on "this delicate and difficult question" from Vatican representative Archbishop Cicognani.[15] Bishop Gallagher's departure for a summer vacation cruise to Europe occasioned speculation that he was being summoned to Rome for a conference about Coughlin.

Although his name was kept off the passenger list of the ocean liner *Rex,* reporters caught up with the prelate. His answers to press questions were ambiguous, however:

> Father Coughlin is entitled to his own opinion, but I do not approve of the language he used in expressing himself on the President. He should have had more respect for the Executive. . . .
>
> There are a lot of folks who would like the church to discipline Father Coughlin because they would like him out of the way, but so far as I am concerned, and he is directly under my authority, he is working along the right path and he has my support.[16]

Gallagher had assured reporters on his departure for Europe that he did not expect to be discussing Coughlin at the Vatican "unless he was questioned about the matter" and that, in speaking with the apostolic delegate, Cicognani, a few weeks earlier, no mention of the radio priest was made. Such bland denials were reinforced with a press release from Vatican City on July 31:

This morning the Pope received Bishop Gallagher, who, after audience, gave to press the following statements: "My audience with the Holy Father was fully satisfactory. His Holiness was delighted with the report I made on conditions of the Diocese of Detroit, and with very paternal conditions sent his blessing to the clergy and Catholic people of my diocese."[17]

Despite the appearance of concordance among the prelates, an internal note circulated among officials of the National Catholic Welfare Conference offers an insider's view of Gallagher's voyage: "Our correspondent in Cleveland, in a private letter . . . says . . . Gallagher . . . is going to Rome . . . I hear, after being summoned. You know the [U.S.] Apostolic Delegate is in Rome, or was recently, and there may have been a submission to him to the Vatican of a few observations relative to the priest at Royal Oak."[18] Gallagher denied that specific restraints were proposed or that any discussion of Coughlin had taken place at all. Yet the *Osservatore Romano,* the official Vatican paper, published the following extraordinary rebuke:

Some newspapers made Monsignor Gallagher, Bishop of Detroit, say when he was in Rome that the Holy See fully approves of Father Coughlin's activities. This does not correspond to the truth because Monsignor Gallagher knows too well what was said to him thereto. The Holy See wants respect of all liberties but also of all proprieties, and it is well known that the orator sins against elementary proprieties who inveighs against persons who represent the supreme civil authorities, with the evident danger of shaking the multitude in the respect due to these same authorities. The impropriety is greater and equally more evident when the orator is a priest.[19]

The article pointed to Vatican "disappointment," said to be "by no means slight," over the activities of the radio priest, and called the situation "very displeasing and most delicate." Furthermore, it was mentioned that the Vatican had done its best "to arrive at a solution of 'an internal character' in order to avoid the matter being aired in public with inevitable repercussions."[20]

Upon his return from Rome to New York, Gallagher was besieged by reporters and supporters of his famous protégé. When asked about the *Osservatore* article at dockside in New York, Bishop Gallagher retorted: "I want to say emphatically that Father Coughlin's activities will not be curbed. . . . The question of Father Coughlin was mentioned neither officially nor unofficially in my talks with the Holy Father."[21]

Just as the press wires were beginning to cool on the story of the errant cleric and the battle of his ecclesiastical superiors to assert control over the situation, a new cause for Vatican displeasure emerged: Coughlin's speech in which he alluded to President Roosevelt as "anti-God" and declared that if an "upstart dictator in the United States succeeds in making a one-party government, and when the ballot is useless," he would urge "the use of bullets." Rumors now circulated of a second warning from Rome. The archbishop of Cincinnati, John T. McNichols, condemned Coughlin's speech the following day; the radio priest, however, on that same evening in Philadelphia, told reporters he planned to keep going and did not expect any rebuke: "I'll keep on going just the same as I am. I am not going to call him [President Roosevelt] a liar. There are other words in the English language. I am not going to attack him personally, but objectively."[22]

From Rome, the Associated Press reported that "prelates today said they wouldn't be surprised if the Vatican were obliged to give Father Charles E. Coughlin a stronger 'warning' than the one which appeared recently in *Osservatore Romano*." Such a step might be necessary, the prelates added, "if the Detroit priest continues his attacks on President Roosevelt." The prelates reiterated that the *Osservatore*'s previous remarks were not merely those of a newspaper but reflected the opinions of the pope, and that "Father Coughlin, by continuing his personal attacks on President Roosevelt, was going directly contrary to the pontiff's desires." For his part, the radio priest declared that he would not be muzzled by warnings from an "anonymous prelate" who spread the story that he was to receive a warning from the Vatican. Coughlin also defiantly stated that "his political campaigning" had the approval of his immediate superior, Bishop Gallagher, and that he would "not be swerved by reports of a warning coming from anonymous sources."[23]

The Vatican decided not to reenter the media war with Detroit. Gallagher was privately warned, via the apostolic delegate, not to imply that there was any official approval of the actions and discourses of Coughlin and that "the Holy Father spoke definitely and explicitly . . . against the statements made by Father Coughlin to the President of the United States," and to imply otherwise "does not correspond to the truth." This bluntly worded statement also noted, "It is well known that it is the policy of the Holy See not to enter into questions of American politics, and this attitude remains unchanged. The Holy See is unwilling to be thrust into the political arena by any Bishop or priest." In a final word of advice, the apostolic delegate suggested to Bishop Gallagher that he refrain from being interviewed by newspaper reporters and "thus avoid endangering [his] dignity as a Bishop."[24]

One week after this warning, Eugenio Cardinal Pacelli, the papal secretary of state who subsequently became Pope Pius XII, made an unprecedented visit to the United States which included a meeting with FDR. Although it is not clear who initiated the discussion, FDR and Pacelli apparently dealt with the idea of having a U.S. representative to the Vatican. It was rumored that Roosevelt had dangled this jewel of diplomatic recognition as a quid pro quo for restraining Coughlin. Certainly, as the radio priest later put it, "Pacelli was 'no friend of mine.' "[25] Coughlin told his questioner that Cardinal Pacelli refused to meet with Bishop Gallagher, who then allegedly told Coughlin, "Boy, have I got news for you. You're finished!"[26] A letter from Coughlin to Jesuit historian Michael Gannon written in 1954 (and quoted in part in the semifictional book La Popessa, published in 1983) offers the opinion that Pacelli's conversations with FDR "could be regarded as a type of informal pact."[27]

In American Pope, a critical biography of Cardinal Spellman written in 1984, author John Cooney asserts that Spellman was the intermediary between the Vatican and FDR in seeking control over Coughlin. According to Cooney, just prior to Cardinal Pacelli's visit to the United States, Spellman visited the president at Hyde Park, at which time FDR complained about Coughlin. The Vatican felt that U.S. diplomatic recognition was critical to the pope, who needed to strengthen the power of the church in fending off the influences of Nazism in Europe and advancing its own efforts to keep peace. But Roosevelt was cautious about the recognition issue and delayed any action until 1940, when he appointed Myron Taylor, a Protestant business executive, as a personal representative rather than an officially designated ambassador. (It was not until 1984, under the Reagan administration, that full diplomatic relations were established.)

Coughlin's third-party campaign ended in November 1936 with FDR's landslide reelection. In its wake, Coughlin made his radio farewell address on November 7. Claiming that the outcome of the election doomed democracy, he saw himself as "a target for all the slings and arrows of calumny, of jealousy, of libel and vituperation," and said that he would retire "from all radio activity in the interests of all the people." He declared as well that he would follow a policy of silence with regard to political and economic matters. He alluded to healing wounds within his church and said that it would be best "both for you and for me, for the country I serve and the Church I love, for me to be forgotten for the moment."[28] The Shrine told his followers that their leader would be on vacation in Bermuda.

On January 1, 1937, after a retirement of only seven weeks, Coughlin delivered a New Year's radio greeting. Not three weeks later, on January 20, Charles Coughlin lost his strongest supporter when Bishop Gallagher died of a heart attack. Asserting that it was the dying wish of his mentor, the radio priest announced four days later that he was returning to the airways and devoted the February 1 broadcast to a eulogy of Michael Gallagher: "From this great Bishop I gained my inspiration. By virtue of his encouragement I pursued the path that he had blazed for me."[29]

Now Coughlin was to have a new superior. The contest of wills between the two men would take five years to resolve.

There would be numerous occasions in his long and stormy career when Charles Coughlin would be front-page news because of an alleged or actual silencing, but none of these threats of a silencing ever led to a full-scale confrontation while Bishop Gallagher was alive. That changed with the appointment of Archbishop Edward Mooney early in 1937. It was well known that Bishop Gallagher's successor would be encouraged by church leaders to restrain Father Coughlin. The failure of the American bishops to do so had been an embarrassment to Vatican officials and even to the pope himself.[30] Finding the right man to discipline Coughlin was a delicate task, but it turned out to be a crucial step in the eventual curbing of the radio priest's activities.

Born in Maryland and raised in Ohio, Archbishop Mooney became the first native-born American to serve as an apostolic delegate, posted to both Japan and India. He was a bishop in the Rochester, New York, diocese before he transferred to Detroit. Well before assuming his official duties in his new location, Mooney had had to consider Coughlin's challenge to church authority while serving on a key board for the NCWC.[31]

Speculation about the kind of man Mooney was and whether he would move quickly to restrain the radio priest lent an air of dramatic expectation to the colorful pageantry of the archbishop's appointment:

> Sometime during the solemn ceremonies, while hundreds of church dignitaries and thousands of laymen look on, all priests in the diocese [of Detroit], numbering more than 1,000, will approach the archbishop's throne and on bended knee kiss the archbishop's ring in what the clergy know as an act of obedience.
>
> Father Coughlin will be in the line of priests, and this formal occasion will be, in the minds of many of the watchers, the most dramatic moment of the ceremony.[32]

Any silencing of Coughlin by Mooney, it was predicted, would have to be done with diplomatic skill. No direct action could be made. Moreover, asserted one news analyst, "Archbishop Mooney and Father Coughlin . . . both are hard fighters. . . . Mooney is described by his friends as deliberate in making up his mind, but once it is made up he is firm. . . . In contrast, Father Coughlin is a two-fisted orator who pulls none of his punches."[33]

For a few months at least, both men seemed to avoid testing the other. But by early fall of 1937, the uneasy peace ended. In a press interview on October 4, Father Coughlin referred to the "personal stupidity" of President Roosevelt in appointing Hugo Black to the Supreme Court. He also declared that Catholics could not join the fledgling Congress of Industrial Organizations because of its Marxist orientation. After this, the first of a series of strategic duels ensued between the radio priest and his new superior.[34]

The archbishop responded to Coughlin with a statement published in the *Michigan Catholic:*

> No Catholic authority has ever asserted that the CIO is incompatible with Catholicism on the basis of its publicly stated principles. . . .

Of course, priests have the right to disagree with Presidents and they may feel the duty of publicly expressing such disagreement, especially in matters of high moral import.

But a deeply inculcated respect for authority as well as consciousness of the reverence with which their own sacred calling is regarded always makes them, on reflection, impose upon themselves a fine sense of restraint in the language they use.[35]

Just one day later, the office of the radio priest issued a press release: "Father Coughlin will cancel his contract for a series of 26 broadcasts over 35 national stations, scheduled to start October 31."[36] To the archbishop's surprise, the attorney for *Social Justice* wrote, indicating that the publishing company for the paper was a private corporation and was not under ecclesiastical control:

I am directed to inform you, and, through you, his Excellency the Archbishop of Detroit, that while the columns of "Social Justice" are open at all times for any contributions which the officers of the corporation feel will be of interest to its readers, the corporation will continue to edit and publish "Social Justice" without supervision of anyone except its own officers.[37]

This was the culmination of a complicated, behind-the-scenes ecclesiastical chess game. The precipitating event was Archbishop Mooney's withholding of the required imprimatur for a pamphlet Father Coughlin wanted to publish, *Can Christians Support the CIO?* Two censors had reviewed the contents, which were based on *Social Justice* articles printed in August. Coughlin had addressed an "open letter to Ecclesiastics" with the same title. He invited "Your Excellencies Right Reverend, Very Reverend and Dear Confreres" to respond to his assertions that the so-called sit-down strikes and other CIO organizing tactics in the auto industry were the opening salvos in "a social revolution along the lines of what had occurred in the Soviet Union."[38]

One of the censors Archbishop Mooney appointed sent the draft back unrecommended for an imprimatur, concluding that "while it contains nothing intrinsically opposed to the defined doctrines of the Church on faith and morals," the statement nonetheless "presents not merely in a controversial manner but condemns categorically a labor movement which is at the present time in a decidedly *formative* stage."[39] By calling for the involvement of Catholics in the union movement in America, the church hoped to avoid polarizing the working and middle classes. The goal was to have industrial workers organized within the bounds of the capitalist system rather than to have that system rejected by the working class.

In the next phase of the media war, Coughlin appeared to outwit his bishop. On October 18, *Social Justice* headlined a story purporting to reveal the behind-the-scenes reason for the radio priest's canceling his broadcast season:

Would Not Contradict Word of His Superior

In view of a recent statement by the Archbishop . . . Father Coughlin obviously could not go on the air at this time in seeming contradiction to his lawful church superior. . . . Readers of Social Justice will agree that Father Coughlin is wise in refraining from broadcasting at this time lest a spirit of controversy appear to arise between an obedient priest and his church superior. Furthermore, it will be obvious that for the same reason Father Coughlin cannot now comment upon his own case in these columns.[40]

Mooney, angered by the article, wrote to Amleto Cicognani that he "foresaw that this kind of thing would continue indefinitely and would poison the minds of many simple people." He had decided "it was [his] duty to make one effort at least to set before the readers of Social Justice the plain facts."[41] Mooney virtually ordered the managing editor of Coughlin's newspaper to print his version of the controversy, requiring that neither the radio priest nor himself add anything further on the matter.

Now Coughlin and his aides, swinging into action to mobilize a grassroots protest effort, formed the Committee of Five Million, a new group that lobbied heavily to return Coughlin to the air. *Social Justice* readers were told to organize "Father Coughlin's millions of friends" and were instructed to take their protest to the Vatican:

Write Your Own Letter to Pope

To be a member of the Committee of Five Million obligates a person to a series of simple, concerted actions *which cannot be disclosed to any other person.*

It is suggested that each member of the Committee of Five Million will write a polite, simple letter to His Holiness, Pope Pius XI, Vatican City, Rome, Italy (five cent stamp). Each letter must be personal and should cover the subject, "What Father Coughlin Has Meant to Me."[42]

On Saturday evening, November 20, Amleto Cicognani issued a statement only slightly different from the one suggested by Archbishop Mooney three weeks earlier, saying essentially that the archbishop's criticism of Father Coughlin was just and timely. In the interim, the agitation Mooney had hoped to avoid had become a major media event.

In addition to flooding the Vatican with letters and telegrams, Coughlin's supporters began picketing Archbishop Mooney's residence. *Social Justice* featured a story on a large protest meeting, whose keynote speaker was the managing editor of *Social Justice.*

Coughlin's newspaper asserted that the public was being misled by Vatican press releases, arguing that the words "Holy See" do not mean Pope Pius XI "anymore than 'United States government' means President Roosevelt." Catholic papers were assailed: "What the Catholic Church needs in America is the services of a press department with as competent a knowledge of public relations and journalism as the bishops have of theology and Canon law." The statements about Coughlin were said to represent a "meeting of minds of the executive committee of American Bishops at their Washington meeting," not the position of the Vatican.[43]

Instead of moderating the situation, the apostolic delegate's support for Archbishop Mooney now appeared to have produced the opposite effect: Coughlin's campaign to put pressure on church officials intensified. Walter Baertschi wrote:

We Cannot Stop!

I know that Father Coughlin is an obedient priest. He cannot give his consent to our rallies, but in two years of association with him I know how his great heart loves social justice. As chairman of the Committee of Five Million I cannot let the people down. No fewer than 40,000 persons this week have begged me to carry on this fight for social justice and the restoration of our great leader to the radio.[44]

As Mooney sought a stronger backup statement to enforce his control over Coughlin, the radio priest himself directly sought to plead his case before the apostolic delegate: "In the full spirit of obedience and humility I lay these facts before you as a son would to his father because I know that Your Excellency possesses not only marks of high intellectual distinction: if I know human nature when I see it, God has blessed you with an understanding and sympathetic heart."[45]

Coughlin's meeting with Cicognani was a personal triumph over Archbishop Mooney. The delegate, rather than reinforcing the position of the superior, acted as a messenger for the subordinate: "I permitted him to speak his mind fully. . . . His real purpose in coming . . . was to make known his wish to return to the air." Cicognani told Mooney that Coughlin was "anxious to avoid even the appearance that his resumption of broadcasting was under a cloud of ecclesiastical condemnation." The delegate indicated that he told the priest that in order to gain permission to resume broadcasting, he had to make a statement of "clarification" during the first radio address. Cicognani added that such a declaration "must not give any appearance of compromise on the part of ecclesiastical authority, but both be and appear an action expressive of the duty of a loyal priest toward both the Church and his superiors."[46]

On December 7, the NCWC News Service reported that Coughlin would return to the air "in the very near future. . . . All matters have been clarified and will be fully explained in Father Coughlin's first of the year address."[47] A week later, *Social Justice* informed its readers that, "petitioned by millions of his friends and admirers, Father Coughlin will return to the nation's radio network within a few weeks" and that "all differences between Father Coughlin and his superiors have vanished."[48] In his public statement on the matter, Mooney explained that "Father Coughlin's resumption of his radio addresses is an exercise in the liberty of action which he has always enjoyed" and that he was "confident that his series of radio addresses will bring to bear on a nationwide audience his recognized power for good as an exponent of Catholic teaching."[49]

Privately, the archbishop had much more to say to the apostolic delegate about the entire Coughlin incident, which he hoped would turn out to be a "one-chapter story." He mentioned his personal distaste for the priest's character: "I had to tell him frankly that I found his methods of action devious and wondered if he could simply and without qualification accept a correction. . . . [He is] a man who does not view things in perspective—and in a commonsense way. . . . [His] incurable tendency to inaccuracy is, I fear, something we shall have to bear with to the end of the chapter."[50]

The archbishop's struggle to teach his miscreant priest true humility while at the same time upholding the inviolable authority of the church would prove to be a costly one. Mooney's reluctance to make public his differences with Coughlin allowed Coughlin to continue his antics largely without rebuke. What Mooney called Coughlin's "self-willed impetuosity and strategic cleverness" allowed him to deceive Mooney and escape punishment for his disobedience and outrageous behavior. But Mooney's reluctance was not naive. He hesitated because he feared that if he alienated Coughlin, the American Catholic laity would be torn apart, with significant numbers defecting to Coughlin's faction.

From the moment that Father Coughlin organized the NUSJ in November 1934, a number of political commentators anticipated that ecclesiastical authority would be brought to bear on this celebrated parish priest if he strayed too far from the role of popularizer of Catholic doctrine regarding problems of poverty and social inequity. A contemporary journalist summarized the church's dilemma: "Let him go that hair's breadth too far, which would convert his 'lobby' of five million members . . . into a National Catholic Party, or let him presume to dictate a breach between Catholics and the New Deal, and Father Coughlin will be silenced by his superiors." And what if Coughlin resisted his church's pressure? The commentator continued, "Two or three of the Father's closest friends have intimated that he will leave the Church, if necessary, to advance his social principles."[51] That possibility—a schism—was never far from the minds of church superiors and of the priest himself. Philip Johnson, a key aide to Coughlin during the 1936 presidential election campaign, recalls that he urged Coughlin to leave the church: "I asked him and he answered in a way that led me to think he had considered it. . . . He said, 'Do you want me to pull a Martin Luther?' "[52]

There were several interrelated problems posed to the church by the career of Father Coughlin. First, the priest's anti-Semitism was frowned upon since it threatened to engender an anti-Catholic backlash. Second, church superiors began to realize that a bitter anticlerical reservoir had been tapped by Coughlin; attempts to curb his activities threatened to unleash bitterness toward the hierarchy and what many saw as its elitism. Clearly, the radio priest was seen by many church leaders to be exacerbating long-standing social class tensions within the Catholic community. Coughlin also posed a challenge to the order and quietude of the church by creating a cult of personality. Coughlin's street-level politics jeopardized the aloof and insulated calm of the Catholic hierarchy, as well as its unquestioned power and authority.

A typical expression of the hostility Coughlin inspired was offered by the wife of a Detroit autoworker, who complained in a letter to Archbishop Mooney in 1937 about "those big shots . . . [who] earn from $100,000 to $250,000 besides all the extra dividends they get." She continued:

> I have read with the greatest regret your comment on Father Chas. E. Coughlin. The only real follower of God besides our beloved Pope Pious [sic]!! They are the ones who make us keep our Catholic Religion. Yes, I am a Catholic but when I go to Church & hear our pastor say give for this, give for that, yes, give, give, give, but never do they say we will fight for your people like our beloved Father Coughlin does. So you are going to rebuke Father Coughlin and his honesty, at least he tells the truth no matter who is hurt. . . . Dear Bishop I am bitter against you for your rebuking words about Father Coughlin. . . . If we lose him there will be a great multitude of our Catholic people dropping of[f] from going to Church. Why he's the only one keeps our hopes alive by telling the truth.[53]

Coughlin's most openly critical opponent, Monsignor John A. Ryan of the Catholic University, confessed that "if I were in Archbishop Mooney's place, I am afraid that I should be inclined to do as he is doing, namely, tolerate Father Coughlin's ravings as the lesser of two evils—the other evil being that hundreds of thousands of Father Coughlin's followers would quit the Church entirely."[54]

After the major confrontation over the CIO statement and the flurry of protest to the Vatican in the fall of 1937, the archbishop confided to the apostolic delegate: "I fear that . . . [in this] obscured atmosphere of clever misrepresentation, it will become increasingly difficult for Father Coughlin's pride to accept a rebuff as time goes on. And he may unfortunately take himself out of the church just as he so easily took his paper [*Social Justice*]."[55]

Mooney feared rebuking Coughlin too strongly: "It would serve the interests of the Church and render less likely the possibility of defection on the part of Fr. Coughlin, if the Holy See might think it well to take advantage of this first intimation of a mass protest to answer with a mild but clear declaration of the fundamental facts and principles involved." The archbishop felt a deep sense of isolation in his efforts to steer a course between alienating Coughlin's followers and suffering the public criticism of appearing to condone Coughlin's words and deeds. In January 1939, Mooney wrote to the Vatican of the need to "prevent agitations and divisions which could easily become disastrous."[56]

Monsignor John A. Ryan once described the infatuation of millions of Catholics with Father Coughlin as "saddening and sickening to contemplate." The danger posed to the church by the devotion of Coughlin's followers led one Catholic woman to write to the head of the NCWC just a week after Pearl Harbor expressing her view of the ironic impact of that event on Coughlin's career:

> You know the masses—our Irish mostly of the lower classes—treat Father Coughlin as their God. Msgr. Keegan said that some of the heirarchy [*sic*] felt that if something were done to silence him we would lose these souls. . . .
>   If the heirarchy [*sic*] are afraid . . . why can't we the laity use this moment to force an issue?
>   His anti-Semetic [*sic*] seeds of hatred are sown deep—it is rankling in the souls of our rich and our poor Catholics. . . . If this war had not come when it did—we might have had a shism [*sic*].[57]

Charles Coughlin would continue his public career for only a few months following America's entrance into World War II—a time when public opinion, the power of the federal government, and his own ecclesiastical superiors would unite against him. And in the course of his near indictment for sedition, the radio priest would threaten to do precisely what his superiors had feared.

Throughout 1938–1939, there was virtually no broadcast in which Coughlin did not allude to Jewish financial machinations or the fomenting of the bolshevik revolution and, increasingly, in which he did not make bitter personal attacks on leading rabbis and Jewish organizations. Still there was no public denunciation from Father Coughlin's superior. The archbishop's silence in the face of many provocations served to en-

gender both disappointment and a simmering but muted anger in the Jewish community.

The threat that Charles Coughlin posed to America's Catholic community went beyond the issue of his leading an exodus from the church.
Despite the enormous gains Catholics had made as recognized members
of mainstream society, there lurked a potent danger of what Andrew
Greeley described in the 1950s as "America's ugly little Secret": anti-
Catholic prejudice.[58] (Indeed, the residue of nativist depiction of Catholics as an alien group would emerge as late as John Kennedy's 1960
presidential campaign.)

As a self-defined minority, Catholics in the 1930s were vulnerable to
feelings of insecurity not unlike those that all other minority groups
experience as they seek to assimilate, yet preserve their cherished tradi-
tions and values. And although Charles Coughlin at first was hailed by
Catholics and non-Catholics alike for legitimizing a church voice in
America's popular culture (and producing more than his share of converts), his entrance into politics had, by 1936, raised the specter of a
backlash not unlike that which results when a previously low-profile minority asserts itself in a more militant and aggressive manner.

Even Catholics were angry and concerned about Coughlin's behavior. One parishioner wrote to Bishop Gallagher:

> Unless you get Coughlin off the radio, you are going to be re-
> sponsible for one of the greatest anti-Catholic movements this
> country has ever seen. . . .
>
> A book is now being written—a pamphlet with all the fire
> and brimstone necessary to make it inflammable—"COUGHLIN—
> The Menace." . . . Coughlin has put the Catholic Church squarely
> into politics . . . this will not go down the throats of the people in
> this country—the Catholic hating population is too great.[59]

What made the church most vulnerable from Charles Coughlin was
his anti-Semitism. A Catholic laywoman, writing in 1936 to Bishop Gallagher, stated the problem in both theological and practical terms:

> I am writing from a point of view you will not receive often in
> the barrage of letters received. I am an ordinary Catholic girl,
> with a thorough Catholic education. . . . Personally I am in dis-

agreement with Father Coughlin—or, more frankly, disinterested—having read his book—Money and Credit and others of his addresses—without being too much impressed. . . .

But not until the recent broadcast in which he avowedly excused Hitler, and voiced anti-Semitism, did he loom as important on my horizon. . . .

I am constantly on the defense—and I am ashamed that Father Coughlin has not been rebuked. I could repeat all of the reasons why we, as Catholics should be ashamed of intolerance of any sort voiced by a minister of Christ—but this letter has taken enough of your time already. . . .

Please, father, there are many thousands of Catholics like me. We, perhaps, do not make ourselves heard, as followers of Father Coughlin do, but we are your flock too, even though we are not an organized political force. If your own conscience prompts you to rebuke Father Coughlin, please do not yield to pressure and desist.[60]

Finally Archbishop Mooney could no longer turn away from the storm of controversy. Mooney's first public response to the whirlwind of criticism over the series of radio broadcasts begun on November 20, 1938—Coughlin's infamous Kristallnacht discourse—was a formal statement issued through the *Michigan Catholic:* "Totally out of harmony with the Holy Father's leadership are Catholics who indulge in speeches or writings which in fact tend to arouse feelings against Jews as a race."[61] Yet he also attempted to draw what to many seemed too fine a distinction: that his imprimatur granted only permission to speak, not approval of the content of what was said.[62]

On his December 11 broadcast Coughlin accused Jewish community councils of undermining the celebration of Easter and Christmas holidays in public schools and called on "the eminent sons of Jewry who have risen to high in government, journalism, in banking, in broadcasting and in motion pictures to launch an effective, determined campaign against the Red menace." Coughlin, claiming to have received approval for the broadcast, said he had "had a direct telephone conversation with His Excellency one-half hour before it was delivered and deleted from that address the parts that His Excellency held objectionable."[63] Mooney's version of what happened is quite different:

He had refused to follow my advice of two days before and changed the subject entirely and, in the telephone conversation referred to, he practically gave me the option of having him deliver a hastily and partially corrected piece of anti-semitism, or having him read extracts on the protocols from Father Fahey's "approved" book, or of having his radio time taken up by an organ recital.[64]

Deeply offended by the specter of anti-Jewish charges being directed at the church and believing such attacks would be closely followed by anti-Catholic bigotry, Mooney strove to assert his own authority regarding church teachings and anti-Semitism. In a confrontational meeting late in 1938, Coughlin and his superior agreed that the question of whether the radio priest's recent addresses violated church doctrine should be submitted directly to Rome.

In preparing to present his case to the Vatican, Mooney charged that Coughlin had promised to "discontinue talking on the Jewish question" but had "returned to the subject while [Mooney] was absent in Florida." The archbishop had told his priest specifically that "your radio addresses of November 20 [1938] and December 11 [1938] taken in conjunction with your writings in Social Justice during the past year did, in effect, convey an impression of anti-Semitism and were not in harmony with the utterances of Pope Pius XI on the subject."[65]

Hopeful that he would receive backing for his case against Coughlin's anti-Semitic radio broadcasts, Mooney forwarded a letter to the apostolic delegate four days after his confrontational meeting with his subordinate, asking that a judgment be rendered on the matter. The response the archbishop received from Cardinal Pacelli was far from satisfactory. Apparently the gist of the telegram from the Vatican suggested that the Coughlin matter should be resolved at the local level.[66]

Because he had agreed to share with his priest whatever response the Vatican made to the jointly submitted request, Mooney now faced a problem because Coughlin might interpret the vague reply as a victory. In this ecclesiastical poker game, the stakes now appeared to have been raised. Mooney wrote to Pacelli indicating that the lack of action by the Vatican would embolden Coughlin's "numerous but irrational followers" and that the radio priest would claim "his methods and politics" would be vindicated.[67]

Mooney next received word that the pope had authorized the Vatican representative, Amleto Cicognani, to "counsel this priest to follow the suggestions and directions of Your Excellency in a spirit of docility."[68] Coughlin was summoned to the diocesan chancery office to receive the directive from Rome, but he indicated he was too ill, so the letter was delivered to the Shrine of the Little Flower. To avoid a repeat of the letter-writing campaign of the previous year, Mooney forbade Coughlin to discuss or make public the contents of the Vatican missive. A few days later, in a brief note, Coughlin offered his assurance that "I shall abide by the directives contained in the Apostolic Delegate's letter." Specifically Coughlin stated that "with reference to the matter of anti-Semitism with which I am thought to be at variance with the . . . Holy See, I can only protest my entire willingness to be guided by my Archbishop."[69]

The pact of silence that constrained the radio priest also inhibited his superior from defending his private actions through any public explanation. Thus, Mooney felt duty-bound not to speak openly of Coughlin's having been officially warned that his anti-Semitic campaign was incompatible with the views of the church. With Mooney's encouragement, the leaking of the Vatican ruling was to be carried out by a leading Catholic prelate, the highly respected archbishop of Chicago, Cardinal George Mundelein. His sudden death a few days before a specially scheduled radio address on December 11 meant that his words were spoken by Monsignor Bernard Sheil, a close adviser to FDR: "As an American citizen, Father Coughlin has the right to express his personal views on current events, but he is not authorized to speak for the Catholic Church nor does he represent doctrines or sentiments of the Church."[70]

Archbishop Mooney, as head of the administrative board of the NCWC, had some influence over what might be done to counter the deterioration of Jewish-Catholic relations caused by Father Coughlin's broadcasts. One project that Mooney helped initiate was the launching of a monthly newspaper, the *Voice,* sponsored by a newly created organization, Catholics Against Anti-Semitism. Paul Weber, a Catholic labor leader, was a key figure in its formation. The paper featured a number of Catholic celebrities and prominent public officials, including Irene Dunne, Gene Tunney, Don Ameche, and Al Smith, and was headed by Judge Frank J. Hogan, president of the American Bar Association. A July 1939 issue of the newspaper carried the headline, "Bishops Condemn Anti-Semitism." Mooney's picture was displayed prominently on the front page, and the entire issue contained articles showing how incompatible anti-

Semitism was with Catholicism and how the former would inevitably
lead to an attack on the latter.

In April 1939, the NCWC, expressing the views of the Catholic hierarchy in the nation, called official attention to a statement made by Pius
XI that "it is not possible for Christians to take part in anti-Semitism" and
asserted: "We regret and deplore the widespread propaganda in the interests of systems and theories antagonistic to the principles of democracy
and the teachings of Christianity. A Christian people will oppose these
dangerous aberrations with all the might of Christian charity."[71]

This rather nebulous statement was not the kind of call for controlling Coughlin that many observers thought the church needed to assert.
The key question on the minds of many, both within and outside of the
Catholic community, was, "What was happening in Detroit?" Implicit in
such an inquiry were speculations regarding Mooney's ability to tame his
errant subordinate.

The cat-and-mouse struggle between Archbishop Mooney and Coughlin was played out in private face-to-face interviews and in numerous
written "corrections" that flowed out of the Detroit Chancery office to the
suburban Shrine of the Little Flower. Mooney's goal was to harass and
restrict Coughlin to just the right degree without offering the radio priest
a forum in which to make himself a martyr of ecclesiastical suppression.
The spring and summer issues of *Social Justice* contained a number of
irksome and provocative statements, and in one instance, Mooney chose
not to let them pass without comment. One paragraph in the May 29 issue appeared to dare Mooney to take drastic action: "If any priest were
anti-Semitic in the sense that he were a hater of the Jews as a race, it
would be the obligation of his ecclesiastical superiors to demand that he
retract his anti-Semitism or remove himself from all church activities."[72]

Provoked to reply, Mooney rose to the implied dare, reprimanding
Coughlin for allowing "an anonymous letter in Social Justice to interpret
for the public the obligations of ecclesiastical superiors." He added, "It is
definitely your place . . . to prevent publication in Social Justice of this
kind of statement which is so likely to create confusion in the minds of
those who do not know the background as only you and I do."[73] Coughlin acknowledged his review of the original statement, defending himself
by asserting that he "found no fault with it" and indicating that it seemed
to be "merely . . . a well-founded moral principle." The priest added, "I
also know what constitutes an anti-Semite and I am not one of them."[74]
In replying to Coughlin, Mooney seemed almost to apologize for insult-

ing Coughlin, asserting that finding something "not good" in a "course of action" "does not mean that . . . there was nothing good in that course of action."[75] Clearly, whatever their differences, Mooney and Coughlin kept them mostly private and maintained a respectful if sometimes antagonistic distance.

Asked about hard feelings between himself and Edward Mooney, Coughlin told an interviewer in 1972, "He was always gracious, and I always received him graciously. . . . In fact, during his last illness in the last year and a half of his life, I was one of the few persons who used to go down and see him. He knew that I was, of all things, an obedient priest."[76]

In the wake of the 1938–1939 broadcast season, a growing army of Coughlin's critics began a campaign to prevent his return the following year. The Institute for Propaganda Analysis, an organization of liberal educators and academics concerned over the vulnerability of the average citizen to being manipulated by Nazi and fascist ideas, commissioned a booklet, *The Fine Art of Propaganda: A Study of Father Coughlin's Speeches.* Authored by sociologist Alfred McClung Lee and his wife, Elizabeth Briant Lee, the two researchers used the priest's radio addresses to illustrate the principles of manipulation and distortion inherent in propaganda.[77]

Reverend Leon M. Birkhead left his parish duties to devote full-time efforts to publishing a newsletter of his one-man lobbying organization, the Friends of Democracy.[78] In April 1939, he sent a memorandum to the National Association of Broadcasters (NAB), the self-regulatory association of the industry, protesting Coughlin's use of the airways "for the purpose of inciting to riot and civil war and stirring up racial prejudice and hatred among the American people." Birkhead accused Coughlin of abusing the radio "as an instrument of public service." He demanded that all Coughlin's contracts be canceled or not renewed.[79]

In July, the NAB proposed a new rule placing tight restrictions on the use of the radio waves by "spokesmen of controversial public issues." The secretary of the association noted that in revising its code, he meant to restrict such things as Coughlin's broadcasts on the arms embargo. Station WJR in Detroit, Coughlin's flagship radio outlet, with its 50,000-watt range, protested the rule, but it went into effect for the fall of 1939.

Immediately upon the implementation of the new code on October 1, 1939, just a month after World War II broke out, it was clear that many stations were defecting from the radio priest's network: "Inside word in the radio industry is that Coughlin is having trouble buying new time," reported Drew Pearson, although he noted that the priest's followers "are flooding the Federal Communications Commission with protests against his 'suppression' under the new . . . code." Pearson reported that in spite of several contract cancellations, Coughlin nevertheless "was meeting with success in putting together a new lineup of sponsors. A 1939–1940 broadcast season was assembled with forty-eight stations, including fifteen in the populous East Coast area served by the Yankee Network."[80]

As the probability of a new set of inflammatory broadcasts loomed, a confrontation between Archbishop Mooney and Charles Coughlin seemed inevitable. The priest made the opening move, testing the will of his superior with regard to the careful set of constraints issued for the previous year's anti-Semitic campaign. One technique for evading ecclesiastical censorship was to use direct telephone transmissions, so Coughlin delivered several speeches to followers in Boston, Philadelphia, and New York using this method, his voice being amplified in an auditorium from his Shrine office phone. He also used outright evasion, not sending the head of the censorship board the radio script until the day after his Sunday program.

On February 5, 1940, listeners around the country tuning in to Father Coughlin were surprised to hear not his voice but organ music, with a brief announcement that the priest would not deliver his sermon that evening. The announcer then suggested that listeners write or telegraph the Detroit Chancery of the Catholic Archdiocese, offering their support: "Father Coughlin knows why neither he nor any other person is speaking over this microphone today. Probably events transpiring this week will enlighten you."[81] The organ music resumed, and no more was heard that evening from either the announcer or the priest.

Mooney's board of censors had rejected the entire script on the basis of its anti-Semitic content. Coughlin had intended to broadcast these thoughts:

We may say that very little of any consequence is taking place in Jewish life in this country without the participation, or even the initiative, of the Jewish communists. . . .

Is there actually the "control" over the press that a small but powerful minority group boasts that it wields? . . .

If I address the following remarks to the intelligent Jews of this nation, do not accuse me of endeavoring to act the part of proselytizer. . . .

In this crisis when the pillars of civilization are being shaken from under us; when the trend has turned from individualism to an over-emphasis on collectivism, I still maintain that whether or not you believe in the divinity of Jesus Christ, you must believe in His principles or else accept the inevitabilities of the errors of Communism.[82]

There was little doubt that Coughlin's days of radio broadcasting were numbered. Many stations wanted to cancel him, and the newly adopted stringent NAB code would have permitted them to do so. However, the regulation contained one loophole: all existing radio contracts had to be honored through the 1939–1940 broadcast season.

On September 15, 1940, the Pearson and Allen Washington "Merry-Go-Round" column dropped a minor political bombshell by claiming that "Father Coughlin is quietly planning to stick his oar into the presidential campaign with a new radio series to begin around October 15." The two journalists noted the priest's difficulties in lining up radio outlets: "Since the controversial nature of his talks bars him from the big networks, under the National Association of Broadcasters code, the only course open for him is to buy time on individual stations for purely political speeches." Commenting that Coughlin was engaged in such efforts, the columnists asserted that "he is encountering a lot of coolness among station owners."[83]

Archbishop Mooney was confident that he had effective strategies to keep Charles Coughlin out of the political community of 1940. He described his approach as one that used ecclesiastical power "to restrain unobtrusively but consistently [any] manifestations of unpriestly conduct." Sensing the growing pressures operating on the Vatican from the Roosevelt administration, Coughlin's superior stressed to Rome that he was prepared "to meet any violations of this prohibition with a prompt and public reprimand of the offender. Thus I have had no real fear that even if Father Coughlin resumed his broadcasts he would have attempted to repeat what he did in the campaign of 1932 in support of Mr. Roosevelt or in the campaign of 1936 against him."[84] Mooney's confidence in his efforts seemed confirmed when a *New York Times* article quoted Coughlin in September as saying that he "could not in good conscience support either candidate."[85]

The broadcast season that ended in May 1940 brought down the curtain on Coughlin's radio career. The *New York Times* reported:

The Rev. Charles E. Coughlin has abandoned his plan for a new series of weekly radio talks. . . . In an interview in the current issue of Social Justice, the priest asserted that "men in powerful positions in the field of radio and other activities" had "forced the decision upon me." The article said that in response to Father Coughlin's petition for a half hour of time every Sunday for a year, most of the large stations declined "for various reasons" although many small stations accepted. . . . He added he would not broadcast again "until we cease to be war-minded—it may be ten months or it may be ten years."[86]

A day earlier, Archbishop Edward Mooney had reported privately to the Vatican that Charles Coughlin "is not now openly engaged in any activities beyond the duties of a parish priest in a suburban district," and rumors of a resumption of his radio broadcasting were unfounded. As for the inflammatory newspaper, *Social Justice,* Mooney claimed that it no longer posed a problem, since Coughlin "has no ownership or responsibility for it and neither contributes articles to it nor publicly promotes its circulation."[87]

Mooney now felt assured that his frustrating struggle to curb Father Coughlin was at an end. As for Coughlin's attitude, one might only surmise it from the tenor of a comment in *Social Justice* made at the beginning of 1941 when the last charges against the Christian Front "boys" were finally dismissed: "Possibly, his [Coughlin's] period of watchful waiting has terminated. Possibly, those who think they have silenced him will now begin to experience the fact that he is still alive—and more vigorous than ever!"[88] Indeed, for two more critical years, Mooney would continue to deal with a variety of creative evasions and denials regarding *Social Justice.*

Since it was not a Catholic publication, Coughlin managed to shield *Social Justice* from ecclesiastical control. Mooney did not challenge Coughlin's assertion that he was attached to *Social Justice* as an "editorial counsel" when Coughlin had presented this as a fait accompli in December 1937. The arrangement was acceded to as a sop to Coughlin's pride.[89] But with the publication of excerpts from the *Protocols of the El-*

ders of Zion in the summer of 1938 and the proliferation of violently anti-Semitic issues in the first months of 1939, Mooney sought to assert some kind of control over the contents of *Social Justice*. He began with a mild letter of reprimand sent in mid-April 1939 in which he cited his specific concerns. One of these was a back-page set of pictures in the April 10 issue dealing with Hollywood stars favoring help to Republican Spain. The magazine stated, "The 'new Hollywood' is as notorious for its free use of Anglo-Saxon names as it has been for its abuse of Anglo-Saxon moral standards." The article then listed the names of stars whose altered names had replaced Jewish names. The April 17 issue, published immediately following Mooney's critical letter, featured an article entitled "The Jewish Problem," with at least one reference to Jews on every page of the tabloid. The back page of the April 24 issue contained a drawing of Moses Montefiore, Anselm Rothschild, Sir Marcus Samuel, Sir Victor Sassoon, and Bernard Baruch under the headline, "If war, what for?" Above the caption references were made to "owners of the world" and suggested that it "was high time that we identified the warmongers."[90]

Mooney suggested no disciplinary action, and Coughlin's reply was a masterly exercise in polite denial of malevolent intent: "May I assure you that I heartily agree with your constructive criticism. It is regrettable that the articles to which you refer found a place in the pages of 'Social Justice.' Naturally, I accept all the blame because I feel it was my place to have prevented their appearing."[91] Ten months later, in February 1940, as bitter controversy swirled around the radio priest, Archbishop Mooney moved decisively but privately to require his priest to make a choice: either place *Social Justice* under full ecclesiastical censorship or totally divest himself of any connection to the publication.

The radio priest balked. Eight days later, he asked Mooney for details of what the proposed supervision would entail. When the archbishop cut short further discussion on the grounds and details of how the publication would be regulated, he fully anticipated a negative response, but on March 9 Coughlin agreed to the directive.[92] The new agreement required that copy be presented to a board of review appointed by Archbishop Mooney. Additionally, although there was a right of appeal, "deletions made by the board had to be accepted." Furthermore, there was to be no public mention of the agreement "pending mutual agreement as to its successful working." The first sheets were to be submitted for review on March 20.

Up to this point, Coughlin had claimed that he himself did not edit the contents of *Social Justice,* and had thereby evaded Mooney's control. A year earlier, Coughlin, in response to one of Mooney's rebukes regarding the anti-Semitic contents of an issue of *Social Justice,* proffered the apology that "post factum I severely criticized the editor who included so many references to the Jews which was not only a mark of bad taste, but of poor editing."[93]

E. Perrin Schwartz, official editor of *Social Justice* since its inception in 1936, was a quiet, almost shy, pipe-smoking man in his late forties and a person who, out of deep loyalty to Coughlin, was not one readily to challenge any directive from the priest. Schwartz had previously worked as editor of the highly respected *Milwaukee Journal.* Recruited to take the job with Coughlin's weekly, he and his three daughters did the research and writing, often without byline credit. Louis Ward, as editorial director, and Schwartz, as editor, were now directly responsible for reporting to the Detroit archdiocese. They received a taste of what the new arrangement would be when they met for the first time with the board of censors. Notes made by the reviewers gave a clear sense of what was involved in the control process:

> Story of Mayor La Guardia being supported by "Communistically inclined group of teachers"—completely deleted
>
> Two full page spreads of Farley [James] were successively submitted and rejected: the first because of bigotry angle; the second, because of patent plug for candidacy in spite of contrary printed assurances.[94]

A deleted portion of the April 29 issue was a cartoon depicting a large octopus representing "money based on debt." The captioned story under it was the basis for a subscription solicitation that was to have begun:

> Like a gigantic, life-sucking octopus, a false and pernicious monetary organism straddles the United States.
>
> With currency based upon Government obligations instead of real wealth, this monster is slowly but certainly drawing from the great heart of America its last vestiges of vitality.[95]

Two months after the detailed censorship began, Coughlin was ready to throw in the proverbial towel:

May It Please Your Excellency:

Due to reasons which, in my judgment, are substantial I will not be responsible for "Social Justice Magazine" beyond the issue of the date of May 27, 1940.[96]

With a sense of guarded satisfaction, Mooney informed the Vatican that *Social Justice* was no longer a Catholic publication since Coughlin had withdrawn from any participatory role in it. While admitting that his subordinate was unlikely to abide by the new agreement, Mooney nevertheless stressed the effectiveness of his most recent efforts at control: "that it was because the exercise of supervision—though it was by no means overly rigid—made it impossible for the paper to indulge in the personalities and to advocate the extreme views which sustain interest on the part of the type of readers to which it appeals."[97]

Coughlin's apparent withdrawal from control over *Social Justice* was to prove a sham that was far more transparent than Archbishop Mooney was willing to admit, perhaps even to himself. To its last days of publication in April 1942, the magazine carried in its lower-left-hand corner a small, round visage of the radio priest. Although no signed editorials or articles appeared after the summer of 1940, a steady flow of Coughlin's past radio addresses were reprinted on its pages. In December 1940, however, during an evening's visit from the well-known British writer, debater, and publicist Arnold Lunn, Coughlin was caught in his lie:

The . . . visitor challenged C's disclaimer of responsibility for the savage attacks of Social Justice on the Bishop. . . . "I do not own it; I have sold it; I am not editor; I have nothing to do with it anymore," Father C stated. . . . But the vigilant eye of the clerical visitor prompted him to ask C: "What is that you have in your hands?" It happened to be the proof sheets for that next issue of Social Justice.[98]

On the occasion of Father Coughlin's silver jubilee in the priesthood, *Social Justice* devoted a special edition to a celebration of the event. In addition to several pages devoted to the career of the priest, Rev. Edward F. Brophy of Long Island offered a glowing commentary, including a quotation from Thomas Moore:

The harp that once through Tara's halls,
    The soul of music shed,

Now hangs mute on Tara's walls
    As if that soul were fled.
So sleep the pride of former days,
    So glory's thrill is o'er,
And hearts that once beat high in praise,
    Now feel that pulse no more![99]

From the beginning of Coughlin's career, church officials saw in him a force that might strengthen and popularize Catholic doctrine, and so his unorthodox methods of publicity were accepted uncritically at first. Yet eventually his flaws of personality and character seemed to overshadow his talents. Shortly after the Christian Front coup episode, Mooney, in a letter to the Vatican, offered a thoroughgoing condemnation of the man, calling him a "master of confusion" and a "born opportunist who realizes that the common people have a short memory. . . . I do not find him a person of balanced mind or of unselfish good will. . . . In my judgment he is inaccurate, fanciful and illogical; he is proud, stubborn and vengeful." Recognizing in Coughlin a supreme egotist, Mooney had sought to encourage good behavior by avoiding severe public reprimands and holding private scoldings. Now he felt that Coughlin could be controlled "only by prompt, firm but kindly use of authority. . . . He is suspicious and crafty, and incapable of being dealt with confidentially."[100]

13

"Sentenced to the Silence
of a Sealed Sepulchre"

The Servant is not above the master. Nor is Father Coughlin
above his Christ who was sentenced to the silence of a sealed
sepulchre after He had driven the money changers from the
temple.

Coughlin Silver Jubilee, A Life-Motif Recorded, 1941

IN OCTOBER 1940, months after Hitler had overrun the Low Countries
and France, with England the only remaining obstacle to his total mastery of Europe, *Social Justice* argued that perhaps the German dictator
had not been completely honest about his intentions, but he posed no
threat to America. In fact, it argued, the reverse was true: "The American
government has attacked Hitler, Mussolini, France, and the Japanese
government, either directly or indirectly; either through shipment of arms
or the imposition of economic restrictions." Moreover, added the editorial, "we have done our level best to invade Germany through the cat's-
paw of the British navy and the Royal Air Force."[1]

Ten months later, in August 1941, Coughlin's publication characterized the war as one "between the 'haves' and the 'have-nots' . . . between
the gold nations and the non-gold nations." The conflict was derived from
a desire for "world domination. In plainer language: because Jewish International bankers own or control the gold of the world, *it is their war.*"
Two months earlier, at the time of the Nazi invasion of the Soviet Union,
Social Justice prophesied that if Hitler "did not vanquish his . . . foe, no
nation or combination of nations can hold Stalin. . . . The Red army will
certainly move on to world conquest and world revolution." By contrast,

229

Hitler's aims would lead "to a United States of Europe. . . . This would appeal to Americans despite all the propaganda aimed at disparaging it."[2]

As England fought the Nazi onslaught, *Social Justice* provided its readers with a unique view of the causes and consequences of the Battle of Britain:

England Is Faced with Revolution

England is on the verge of revolution. . . . The English have not thus far seen any results of their sacrifices and sufferings. Naturally, they are resentful. . . . The Chamberlain "appeasement" was a popular—and necessary—move. . . . If the war continues, in spite of the many efforts to make a Christmas peace, Britain will surely undergo a revolution.[3]

A few months later it ran this story:

Poor England!

England, indeed, is poor.

And there is no poverty like unto that poverty suffered by a person, or a nation, devoid of friends. . . . They are starved.

Millions are forced to dwell in caves and dugouts and subterranean shelters. . . .

Thousands of homes with their precious furniture have been demolished.

Incalculable debts have been piled up against future generations. . . .

Piece by piece, England is being demolished. Her citizens are being shell-shocked into voicelessness.

In one word, the mighty British Empire—*to save its gold, its international bankers and its puppet King and Queen*—is sacrificing 45 million Englishmen![4]

With England facing the threat of invasion, a dominant theme of *Social Justice* was the inevitable triumph of the Axis nations due to the errors and provocations of U.S. foreign policy. "France and Spain to Join the Axis," declared Coughlin's newspaper in May. In a subsequent issue it claimed that the United States was "almost despairingly behind the Axis powers. It would require years for us and Great Britain combined to catch up with Adolf Hitler. A few months later, it wrote: "Russia is whipped—just as much as Belgium and France and Greece were whipped; just as surely as England will be whipped!" In October, it asserted in bold headlines: "Fall of Reds Leaves New Deal Stranded."[5] Somewhat prematurely, the editorial proclaimed:

> The three major Soviet armies have collapsed. . . . Eclipsing the achievements of Alexander the Great; surpassing the startling performance of Napoleon, the disparaged paperhanger from Munich toppled over the colossus of 13 million Soviet troops. . . .
>
> In 1917 German international bankers and warlords invited a pants-pressing, radical Jew from the East Side of New York to join with the flotsam and jetsam of continental society in overthrowing the czaristic government of Russia. . . . Rising to power, like a meteor from the East, came the paperhanger from Munich.
>
> He rallied round him millions upon millions of Germans and Austrians as he orated against the injustice of Versailles. . . . When Chamberlain was ousted from power in Britain, Churchill proceeded to do battle against Hitler against the provisions of common sense. . . .
>
> Communism, as a political force, is as dead as Yorick's skull. . . .
>
> Roosevelt and Churchill say that they cannot do business with Hitler.
>
> Possibly, Hitler is saying that he cannot do business with them. . . .
>
> Meanwhile, victory is on the side of Adolf Hitler, though gold is on the side of Churchill and Hitler.[6]

The December 8, 1941, issue of *Social Justice* had gone to press without news of Pearl Harbor, but the publication had its own startling story:

Revolution in the U.S.A.!

Congressmen of the United States have been reduced to the stature of school boys. Their master stands over them. Fearing the sting of a political whip, like school boys they acquiesce. . . .

Hitler has preached against the iniquities of parliamentarian government which, according to his viewpoint, became the servant of the privileged classes. Is our Congress supplying an argument to the contentious radicals in their present behavior? . . . Perhaps, so-called democracy has run its crooked course insofar as democracy is represented, or misrepresented, by men who, perchance, think more of retaining their office than their honor.[7]

The same edition also carried an article attacking those who relied on *Mein Kampf* "as indispensable evidence that Hitler intends to conquer the United States. . . . We are not concerned with whether Hitler wrote in letters two feet high that he was going to invade America with 10 million men."[8]

With the United States now at war, the danger loomed that *Social Justice* might overstep the bounds of freedom of the press in its incessant criticism of America to the Allies. But rather than erring on the side of caution, the newspaper became even more vituperative, offering a dismal view of the Allied and U.S. war effort. Its ceaseless attacks on the Roosevelt administration coupled with an even more virulent anti-Semitic focus seemed to mirror major themes of Nazi propaganda. Charges that the radio priest had turned his publication into a mouthpiece for the enemy placed him and his publication under governmental scrutiny.

In 1940, John Spivak had published in book form a set of investigative articles he had written the year before for the *Daily Worker*. He claimed that "the figures which I had from Father Coughlin's own books showed that neither the Radio League of the Little Flower nor *Social Justice* magazine, which back the weekly broadcasts, clears that much money." According to his probe of official records filed with the state of Michigan, Spivak found that Coughlin had, in fact, been running a significant deficit. A reduction in the number of staff used to open mail suggested that "a good portion of this money did not come from small public donations." Spivak hinted that funds might be coming from a "sinister source" and that, "logically the radio time and the magazine's deficits must have been and are now being met by persons other than the general public—persons who are interested in promoting Father Coughlin's pro-Nazi, anti-semitic and anti-union activities."[9]

At the time of *Social Justice*'s campaign of anti-Semitism and its opposition to aiding the Allies (and particularly its defeatist propaganda once the United States was involved in World War II), many people wondered whether Coughlin had been "taking Nazi money to run his machine."[10] Now, more than a half-century later, new evidence strongly suggests that Coughlin did receive funding from Nazi sources. It was done indirectly and in conjunction with Coughlin's efforts to impress, if not influence, the Hitler regime. To reconstruct the undisclosed story, one must journey through the circuitous routes the priest traveled, all of which offer glimpses into a world of aborted informal diplomacy, personal intrigue, and ego-driven puffery.

From the start of the war in Europe, the general public as well as those in positions of power—members of the Roosevelt administration, journalists hostile to Coughlin, leaders of the NCWC—felt sure there was a smoking gun in the Coughlin case. Late in 1940, after Secretary of the Interior Harold Ickes met with the distinguished Catholic priest Reverend Dr. Maurice S. Sheehy to discuss the Coughlin problem, Ickes noted in his diary that "he [Sheehy] believes that Coughlin is getting his ammunition for his pro-Nazi propaganda from Germany and that Germany is also financing him." Attorney General Frank Murphy had his own reasons for telling Ickes that the priest was "a dangerous man."[11] Murphy, of course, had become estranged from the priest as their politics diverged, but specifically he may have had in mind the Treglown connection in England and Coughlin's ties with fascists there.

Among the most promising of smoking guns was George Sylvester Viereck, who had been convicted of not registering that he was a paid German agent. Not only was Coughlin in contact with this well-known writer and Nazi sympathizer, but *Social Justice* had published a series of his articles in 1938 and 1939. Moreover, the publication of the writings coincided with a brightening financial picture for the newspaper. Its format, print quality, and paper were improved, and for the first time, colored inks and more photographs were used. These improvements may well have been made possible by Nazi funds, filtered through someone who had close ties to Nazi diplomats and propaganda outlets. Viereck was paid directly by the German consulate and its outlets to write and disseminate articles endorsing Nazi policies.[12] No evidence has ever come to light, however, that Coughlin received German funds through Viereck.[13]

Within the Jewish community and under the aegis of such organizations as the Anti-Defamation League and the American Jewish Committee, a number of efforts were made to see whether Coughlin might be receiving funds to reprint or use Nazi propaganda materials.[14] In May 1940, the executive secretary of the Minneapolis Anti-Defamation League, Samuel Scheiner, wrote to the Chicago branch office of his organization, reporting what he considered a significant discovery. For some time he had been sending small contributions to Coughlin and asking that books in which he had an interest be sent to him. (When Scheiner sent his requests to Coughlin, he changed the spelling of his name to the more German spelling, "Schreiner," to see if this might affect how quickly his requests for materials were filled.) Along with the books he ordered, he received one additional item: a book entitled *Polish Acts of Atrocity against the German Minority in Poland,* bearing the return address of the German Library of Information, located in New York City.[15] And the name to which the book had been addressed was identical with the one he had given to Coughlin: Schreiner. He concluded that the German Library of Information "somehow or other is acquiring a mailing list directly from Father Coughlin. . . . This is the tie-up that we have been looking for for some time."

Other evidence of Coughlin's possible links to the German government officials came to light in the middle of World War II. In 1943, during the course of a deportation hearing in Detroit's federal court, one of seven individuals being stripped of their U.S. citizenship for being members of the Nazi party, Fritz Ebert, gave testimony that he had regularly delivered mail to a friend in Germany. Among the materials were copies of Coughlin's radio addresses, which the friend told him would be "forwarded . . . to the highest [Nazi] party office, which will see that they are properly distributed."[16]

A far more direct indication of Coughlin's having been in receipt of Nazi funding was interviews I conducted with former Third Reich officials. In 1987, Dr. Otto Ernst Braun, who had been an official of the German Foreign Office, told me that a close friend and colleague, Paul K. Schmidt (writing after World War II under the pen name of Paul Carrel), had told him that his office did send funds to Father Coughlin. Braun also explained that Schmidt did not answer my letter requesting information about such transactions for fear that revealing information would be harmful to our side [those sympathetic to Nazism]."[17] Schmidt had been a key official of the Nazi Foreign Office in charge of public information and propaganda relative to the United States. (In his capacity he had helped arrange Leo Reardon's visit to Germany in January 1939.) Schmidt, when interrogated at the end of World War II, indicated that

Coughlin was discussed "with extraordinary frequency" by his department in the Nazi government.[18]

No more bizarre figure is included in the exploration of Charles Coughlin's alleged ties to Nazi Germany than Alexi Pelypenko, a Ukrainian Orthodox priest who converted to Catholicism and entered the United States as a paid agent of the FBI. How this chain of events occurred and the implications for the Justice Department case against Coughlin stand as a remarkable example of bureaucratic inertia, personal and organizational expediency, and interagency squabbling.

This tale of two priests begins in the chaos of the Ukraine in the wake of the Bolshevik Revolution and World War I. Born in 1893, Pelypenko was shaped by the political and religious uncertainties that plagued a region chronically buffeted by the shifting frontiers of Russia, Poland, and Austro-Hungary. Tall, with penetrating dark eyes, Pelypenko was described as "obsessed with the goal of freeing the Ukraine from Soviet Russia . . . [and he] combined a sense of imagination with a flair for melodrama."[19]

The pertinent thread of Pelypenko's story begins with his arrival, accompanied by his twenty-two-year-old son Igor, in New York in March 1941. They had sailed from Argentina, where both had been spying for the British and the Americans. Because Father Pelypenko's daughter was enrolled in a French-language private school in Buenos Aires, the priest had met the British ambassador, whose daughter was also a student in the same institution.[20] (He began his clerical career in the Ukrainian Orthodox Church but early in the 1930s, after the death of his wife, he was ordained a Roman Catholic priest.) Recruited to work for the British government, Pelypenko, with some help from his medical student son, provided regular reports on the subversive work of Nazi agents and sympathetic priests in the Argentine Catholic community.

With the growing concern in the United States over the activities of the German-American Bund and pro-Nazi Ukrainian nationalist organizations, Pelypenko seemed ideally suited for a special American mission. Eager to visit North America, Pelypenko and his son sailed north and were met in New York harbor by the FBI.[21]

Eventually they settled in Chicago. Because they were fluent in German, Russian, Polish, Ukrainian, and Spanish, father and son proved to be highly useful agents for the FBI, and so arrangements were made for them to stay in the United States. Living with a Ukrainian family, the Pelypenkos were accepted for what they appeared to be: strongly anticom-

munist and supportive of Ukrainian nationalism. Often Alexi Pelypenko
would be gone for a day or two and return without explaining the purpose
of his travel.[22] Throughout the summer of 1941, one of the places he frequently visited was Detroit.

While spying on the German-American Bund in Chicago, Pelypenko
befriended one of their leaders, Otto Willumeit, who had encouraged him
to make a variety of contacts in several cities, including Detroit.
Willumeit told Pelypenko that when he traveled to Detroit, he should
"look up Father Coughlin. . . . Visit the German Consul in that city, Fritz
Hailer, and he will direct you to Father Coughlin." Pelypenko later reported to the FBI that Willumeit told him, "Father Coughlin collaborates
with Nazi representatives in Detroit and receives financial support from
them. You will learn all the details in Detroit from the German Consul,
who will furnish you with Father Coughlin's address."[23]

The Ukrainian priest arrived in Detroit the next morning, July 8,
1941, and immediately contacted Hailer, the German consul. In the affidavit given to the military intelligence officer who interviewed him in
September 1942, Pelypenko wrote:

> Promptly at 1:00 I met Heile [Hailer] in his office. . . . We con-
> ferred for at least two hours. I told Heile that Dr. Willumeit sug-
> gested that I visit . . . Father Coughlin in Detroit. Thereupon,
> Heile [sic] stated to me, "Yes, it is imperative that you confer
> with Father Coughlin, he is one of our collaborators." I said to
> Heile, "I understand that you work with Father Coughlin." He re-
> sponded in the affirmative. I then said, "I understand that Father
> Coughlin is our agent for the spreading of anti-British and anti-
> Semitic propaganda, and that he also carries out for us a program
> amongst the Washington warmongers." He said that this was
> true.[24]

When Pelypenko asked how he might get in touch with Coughlin, he
was given Coughlin's Royal Oak address and taken to the priest's home:

> I arrived at Father Coughlin's home at about 5:30 in the after-
> noon. The man who accompanied me left me at the door and
> went away. I was taken into a parlor and the priest asked me to
> wait a few minutes, saying that Father Coughlin had a visitor and

would be with me shortly. Within a few minutes Father Coughlin appeared. In mixed English and Latin Father Coughlin immediately apologized for having made me wait and asked me to stay for dinner.[25]

Pelypenko noted the presence of "five of us priests" and that at first the conversation dealt only with "trivial matters of no importance." After dinner Pelypenko stated that he and Coughlin drove through the Detroit suburbs. Pelypenko reported that he gave background information on his life in Europe, to which Coughlin replied, "That is very interesting. You probably have a good deal of information concerning the Jews and the communists which I can use against them in this country." Pelypenko indicated that he would bring material of this kind with him on a return visit to Detroit. They agreed to meet again at Coughlin's home at nine on the morning of July 28.[26]

At the appointed time . . . I appeared at Father Coughlin's home. . . . Thereupon Father Coughlin stated to me that he needed anti-Semitic and anti-communist material very badly and that he was ready to compensate me well for this material. He stated that "We have ample to compensate you with, from our funds." . . .

Father Coughlin stated to me that President Roosevelt was "a war monger who was trying to embroil the United States in a war and to bring about a catastrophe." Father Coughlin said that President Roosevelt was doing this because he was nothing more or less than a "hireling" of the Jews.[27]

The conversation, reported Pelypenko, turned to the topic of mutual associates: "Coughlin said he was in touch and cooperated with all the anti-administration groups in the country." At this point Coughlin was reported to have focused on his contacts in the Ukrainian community: "He was cooperating with the anti-British groups in Canada and also with the Ukrainian Nazis operating in the United States" and was "working very closely with a prominent member of the Ukrainian Hetman organization in Detroit," and he had "become intimately connected with various Nazi Ukrainians in Detroit including among others an attorney by the name of Ivan Koos who, he said, occupied an important job at Henry Ford's factory."[28]

In the fall of 1942, Pelypenko had managed to raise funds for himself and his son by selling to the Anti-Defamation League this same affidavit that designated Coughlin as a Nazi supporter. Included in it were details of Pelypenko's conversations with German agents and Nazi diplomatic representatives. He stated that the source of Coughlin's German funds was the first secretary of the German embassy in Washington, Kurt von Heyden.

Prior to meeting with Coughlin in July 1941, Pelypenko mentioned that he had met with von Heyden "on many occasions" and that following the Detroit visit "on or about the 7th day or 8th day of August 1941" he had gone to Washington, where he met with the German official at the Harrington Hotel:

> I told Heyden about my meeting with Coughlin. I asked . . . if it was right for me to have talked freely and frankly with Father Coughlin. Von Heyden said to me, "Certainly, he is our man, we help him financially and we give him material to use." Von Heyden said to me that I should "cooperate with Coughlin and help him in any way" that I could "because that would be helping Germany."[29]

Pelypenko also stated in his affidavit that six months later, in January 1942, he had conferred with Baltimore steamship agent Karl Klein, "who actually, as he stated to me, was a Gestapo agent, who until the closing of the German Embassy, operated under the supervision of Baron Ulrich von Gienanth, the U.S. Gestapo chief." The Ukrainian priest added, "In the course of my conversation with Klein, I asked him about Coughlin. Klein confirmed to me what von Heyden had said." Klein also told him that a hardware merchant in Baltimore, Eric Arlt, was "the liaison man between Father Coughlin and the German Embassy in Washington." In describing Arlt's role, Pelypenko indicated to the FBI that he had taken on the task of the go-between following the closing of the German embassy in June 1941. He stated that Klein had told him, "When money or material had to pass from the German Embassy to Coughlin, Beyer was the contact man who handled the transaction. He received it from von Gienanth, commercial attaché at the German Embassy, and passed it along to Coughlin."[30]

By the time Pelypenko met with Coughlin, he was no longer in the

FBI's employ.[31] While his testimony was used in one case to convict several Bund officers and two collaborators with German espionage efforts, his penchant for telling newspapers about his undercover spying had resulted in J. Edgar Hoover's designating him as a "potential enemy agent." Though there was no proof that Pelypenko had been a double agent while in the United States, nevertheless he and his son were interned at Ellis Island from 1943 to 1944 and subsequently deported to Argentina.[32]

Ellis Island was also the place where another individual with an alleged money trail to the radio priest spent his last days on American shores. At about the same time as the Pelypenkos were detained, August Gausebeck and his wife were awaiting repatriation to Nazi Germany under a diplomatic exchange arrangement.

Since early 1940, the German government, through its U.S. consulate offices, had received substantial funds from Berlin to influence the direction of American foreign policy. In effect, the German government was undertaking a major covert effort to affect the outcome of the presidential and congressional elections later that year. A message marked "top secret" was sent in July 1940 from the German chargé d'affaires in the United States to the Foreign Ministry in Berlin. It referred to the necessity "in our information activities in America to employ a great variety of methods, for which it will probably be possible to render normal accounting after the war." Reference was made to an earlier secret directive, which had described "special methods" for "prevent[ing] the country from entering the war and to exert direct political influence."[33]

O. John Rogge, a Justice Department attorney who traced the documentation of this effort following the end of World War II, described this investment as "The biggest single scheme the Nazis had involving the United States." It included an effort to influence labor leader John L. Lewis to support FDR's 1940 opponent for the presidency, Wendell Willkie.[34]

The multimillion dollar campaign launched by the Nazi regime included the subsidizing of magazine, pamphlet, and newspaper articles, along with creating new publications aimed at shaping American public opinion in the direction of isolationism. The ultimate goal was to defeat Franklin Roosevelt. Toward this end, a number of Republican members of Congress were particular targets of the special methods devised by Third Reich officials under the auspices of Hans Thomsen, Germany's chargé d'affaires to the United States:

An effective and particularly favorable opportunity presented itself in connection with the Republican Party Convention, which takes place next week, and the election organizers with whom I am in constant touch. As I have already reported . . . in strict confidence some 50 Congressmen will be going to Philadelphia to explain our views to the delegates at the party convention. . . .

I have recently initiated the following propaganda campaign. . . . Speeches [of isolationist congressmen] will be printed . . . in the *Congressional Record* . . . and then an edition of 50,000 to 1 million copies will be sent . . . to specially chosen persons.[35]

The ambassador explained that because of the congressional franking privilege, "German influence is not visible to the outside . . . [and] the cost of this large-scale propaganda can be kept disproportionately low."[36]

A few months later, Thomsen had occasion to send another secret communication indicating that one particular segment of American society might be a receptive target of German propaganda, given their antipathy to England: Irish Catholics. He had already made efforts in this direction: "By spending considerable sums from the War Press Fund we make use of the Irish-American newspaper, the *New York Enquirer*, whose circulation we have in various ways greatly increased." Thomsen then added this reference: "We maintain relations with Father Coughlin and his newspaper, *Social Justice*."[37]

In the spring and summer of 1941 the Nazi government engaged in elaborate money laundering and secret funding of superpatriotic Americans and organizations that had no taint of foreign domination. They attempted, and to a degree succeeded, in infiltrating the major isolationist organization of the time, the America First Committee. In May, FBI director Hoover sent a letter to special State Department aide Adolf A. Berle, Jr., referring to "information that reached me from a confidential source heretofore found to be reliable." The FBI head provided the name and address of a German investment banker in New York, August T. Gausebeck, who "according to my informant . . . some time ago contacted my informant and told him he wanted to donate $500,000 to the Republican Presidential campaign." The informant inquired as to the reasons and was told that "if a Republican were elected there would then be established favorable trade treaties between the United States and Germany, whereas if President Roosevelt were re-elected this would be impossible."[38]

Hoover's informant advised Gausebeck that the idea of a large donation "would be impossible" because of laws prohibiting such large political contributions. In response, the questioner explained that he already knew of a way around these restrictions: "the donations need to be made in small lots from a number of different people." He went on to say that "they" had contributed to Father Coughlin in amounts of $100 and $500 at a time, which had been sent by office employees in $5 and $10 bills. The FBI director forwarded his informant's letter directly to Roosevelt via Edwin "Pa" Watson and, on the same day, to Adolph A. Berle in the State Department. A full investigation of the German banker was then initiated by the FBI.[39]

Three days after receiving Hoover's letter, Fletcher Warren of the State Department had a meeting with FBI officials. A memo on the meeting quotes Warren as hoping that "the bureau goes to town on this."[40] Considering what ensued in its investigation, no such outcome ever materialized.

Gausebeck, in addition to being a director at the investment banking firm of Robert C. Mayer and Company, was also the honorary German ambassador to Bolivia. Born in Munster, Germany, in 1893, he had emigrated to the United States from England in 1915. Since arriving in New York, he had been associated with a number of financial businesses. Credit reports obtained by the FBI showed him to be "a man of considerable wealth, having his residence at East Orange, N.J." According to "confidential informants," Gausebeck was "an extremely active Pro-German" and had "close connections with the N.Y. German Consulate office."[41] One investigator recalled seeing an article in the *Nation* from the early 1930s that described him as "Hitler's Banker."[42] There was no record of Gausebeck's having registered himself as "an agent of a foreign principal" under the 1938 legislation requiring persons to do so if they received income for such lobbying activities.

Despite the fact that J. Edgar Hoover pressed for results on the Gausebeck inquiry, information was assembled at a snail's pace. Even after Pearl Harbor, when the United States was formally at war with Germany, no definitive picture of the financial dealings of the banker with German espionage or propaganda activities had been formed. FBI background reports did detail Gausebeck's connections in Washington, including being on "close and friendly terms with U.S. Senator Reynolds [Robert R.] and also the late Senator Ernest Lundeen, as well as other Senators and Congressmen."[43]

The banker knew a Berlin lawyer, Gerhardt Alois Westrick, who had been sent from the German Foreign Office in 1940 on a special mission, ostensibly to build up goodwill among U.S. industrialists. According to Hoover's informants, Gausebeck was holding the funds that were to be used for Westrick's tour.[44] Westrick's visit was given a great deal of publicity, and accusations that he was attempting to undermine American interests and was engaged in "fifth-column" activities led him to alter his plans and return abruptly to Germany. While in the United States, however, he met with a group of prominent business officials who were led by James D. Mooney, General Motors vice president.

Eventually the FBI learned that not only was Gausebeck in the business of funneling funds to representatives of the German government, but he was also an active member of the Nazi party. (This fact was revealed in an alien registration form that was not discovered until after he had left the country.) Moreover, a 1937 trip he had financed for thirty members of a Bund Youth Group to visit Germany was actually a Nazi indoctrination effort. And on April 20, 1938, at Koenigsberg Castle, East Prussia, an oath of personal loyalty to Adolf Hitler was administered. There were two representatives from the United States: Severin Winterscheidt, an editor of the German-American Bund newspaper, and August Gausebeck: "They wore uniforms resembling the Brown Shirts and were trained in Nazi racial theories."[45]

Walter H. Schellenberg was a partner with Gausebeck in the R. C. Mayer and Company investment banking firm. Schellenberg was a mysterious figure, generally cited as the coordinator of Nazi espionage in the United States.[46] He had participated in the abortive "Kapp" putsch of 1920 in Germany and then joined the Nazi party as a leader of special street fighting detachments. Shortly before Hitler came to power, Schellenberg came to New York and began organizing Nazi intelligence specifically with a focus on financial institutions suspected of evading German foreign exchange restrictions. Ironically, Schellenberg had given testimony in 1934 before the McCormack-Dickstein congressional committee investigating Nazi party activities in the United States. When questioned about a high-level meeting he attended in Germany with Rudolph Hess and the coordinator of overseas Nazi party members, he offered no explanation for his activities and was not called back for further testimony.[47] FBI files would eventually describe Schellenberg as the chief coordinator of Gestapo activities in the United States and his banking firm as "a cleverly disguised blind for Nazi financial transactions."[48]

In August 1941, the FBI was told by a business acquaintance of the banker that "Gausebeck and his associates are in constant contact with the German Consulate. . . . Walter Schellenberg has boasted that he is an officer in the Nazi Party and has made numerous trips to and from Germany within the past few years."[49] Over dinner, Gausebeck confided that "he was going to leave the country as soon as the Great White Father (President Roosevelt as Gausebeck calls him) signed the bill to freeze the foreign currency. . . . He had sent most of the firm's funds to Buenos Aires in the Argentine which was thoroughly pro-German and he would open his main office there." Gausebeck noted "he had dined with the Bolivian Ambassador to Germany who was on his way back to Bolivia. They had asked Gausebeck if he would be the financial adviser to the Bolivian Government."[50]

Walter Schellenberg was last seen in public in the United States on the platform in Madison Square Garden on March 22, 1941, where leading isolationist spokesmen Charles A. Lindbergh and Senator Burton K. Wheeler were giving addresses. On July 15 Schellenberg departed the United States aboard the liner *West Point*. A warrant for his arrest was sworn out only a few days after his surreptitious departure.

Two weeks after the bombing of Pearl Harbor, Fletcher Warren of the State Department received a communication from the Bolivian foreign minister inquiring about the former honorary consul. Noting that he was "married to a United States citizen . . . who comes from a well-known and highly respectable family in Bolivia," the U.S. official was told that "the Bolivian Government, in its personal capacity, would be interested in ascertaining whether Gausebeck might be released for confinement either on his arm or in his town house." The State Department's reply was blunt: "The only thing that would be done for Gausebeck would be to expedite his hearing," since the information the U.S. government had indicated that Gausebeck was "an economic and financial, and perhaps a political agent of the German Government."[51]

One month later in a confidential memo, Secretary of State Cordell Hull informed Attorney General Francis Biddle of a dispatch from the American Legation at La Paz, Bolivia, that Gausebeck had attempted to flee to Bolivia. In 1943, Gausebeck and his wife were allowed to sail on a Swedish liner to be repatriated to Germany. By the time the FBI finally had enough evidence on the foreign agent actions of Gausebeck to seek his arrest, he was already out of the country.[52] Gausebeck's possible links to Coughlin were never made public.

The FBI's interest in Charles Coughlin began with the Smedley Butler incident of 1936 and the alleged coup to overthrow the Mexican government. (At that time, FDR had initiated his mandate to the agency for investigation of far-right and far-left political organizations.) In 1938, in connection with the radio priest's attacks on Jews, and subsequently in the months just prior to World War II, when Coughlin was a key lobbyist against revision of the neutrality laws, letters began flowing to the FBI and officials of the Roosevelt administration questioning Coughlin's patriotism.

On November 27, 1939, Assistant Attorney General O. John Rogge addressed a memorandum to J. Edgar Hoover, director of the FBI, requesting records from the Criminal Division regarding the Social Justice Publishing Company, Radio League of the Little Flower, National Union for Social Justice, and the Social Justice Poor Society. Rogge's investigation had been stimulated by a series of newspaper articles written by muckraking journalist John Spivak. The general focus of Spivak's allegations was Coughlin's diverting of funds earmarked for religious and charitable purposes to finance political activities, but Rogge's concern was the link Spivak made between the radio priest and the subversive activity of disseminating Nazi propaganda. Some of Coughlin's writings followed speeches of Joseph Goebbels word for word.

The fall of France in May 1940 and the possible imminent Nazi takeover of Europe raised fears about U.S. security, and Americans who appeared to support Hitler, including Charles Coughlin, became increasingly anathema to the public at large. Dorothy Thompson, the widely read liberal daily columnist, began beating a drum for a government investigation of the radio priest. Shortly after the verdict in the "Brooklyn boys" case was rendered, she asked in her "On the Record" column why Congressman Martin Dies and his Un-American Activities Committee, along with FBI director Hoover, were not pursuing the link between Father Coughlin and the Christian Front.[53] But by the fall of 1940, with Charles Coughlin's radio broadcasting career at an end, attention began to focus on *Social Justice*.

In June 1940, the FBI had been authorized by the president, with the advice of Attorney General Francis Biddle, to proceed with a plan for "custodial detention" of individuals suspected of sympathies with potential enemy nations of the United States. This program, later scrapped as unworkable and unconstitutional, caught up in its web both the publisher of *Social Justice*, E. Perrin Schwartz, and Coughlin's longest-serving secretary, Eugenia Burke. An investigation of Schwartz was ordered in September 1940. Coughlin's secretary, erroneously listed as an alien of German descent, was cited as a Nazi agent. When the priest was contacted to provide evidence as to her subversive activities, he became enraged. Informed by the agent in Detroit as to what had occurred, the FBI supervisor in Washington told him that more discreet methods would have to be found to pursue the investigation.[54]

By March 1941, the U.S. military had banned the distribution of *Social Justice* on military bases. The magazine examined its own future in May:

Is Social Justice in Danger?

This comment is inspired by a letter from a young man who works in Washington, D.C. . . . "I do not believe you are aware of, or fully appreciate, the hatred which a powerful minority here in Washington holds toward your publication. . . . Except for their fear of public opinion—and they quake in holy terror of that—these foes of the social truths which you expound *would have acted long ago to have you suppressed!*"[55]

A retired navy official urged in a December 15, 1941, letter to the Justice Department: "This paper should be suspended for the duration of the present war as it does not serve the best interests of the Country being detrimental to the morale of not only the men in service but to the citizenry as a whole. It so happens that I am a Catholic but . . . I feel it should be banned."[56]

Two months after America was at war, *Social Justice* was forecasting a gloomy future, with the United States fighting with no allies. It drew a biblical analogy between Roosevelt and Moses: "America, even though your new Moses leads you to victory through the waters of a Red Sea of blood, there is a desert beyond—a desert of scorpions, serpents, poverty and death; a lifetime of sorrow."[57] In mid-March, Coughlin's newspaper asked in blaring headlines, "Who Started 'Scared' War?" Its conclusion was that the "Jewish boycott of German goods in 1933 [was] started by

Mr. Samuel Untermeyer, an American Jew . . . nine years ago. . . . This high Jewish official . . . has the effrontery to ask Christians of the world to join with his nationals throughout the world to destroy not only Hitlerism and the 2 million Nazis but also the more than 40 million Christians in Germany. . . . What price Jewry!"[58]

A spate of journalistic assaults on the radio priest and his newspaper soon appeared. In March 1942, the *New York Times* warned that "Pro-Nazi Weeklies Flourish Unchecked," adding that the "Coughlin sheet leads." Five days later, the *Florida Catholic* called *Social Justice* "an un-American paper" that was "following the latest methods evolved for use in the United States by the general staff of Axis propaganda. With unwearying repetition, it details week by week the insinuation, the false pervasions of truth, which issue from the studio of Dr. Goebbels."[59]

The most powerful attack came from *PM,* the liberal newspaper of New York. An editorial in March, written by publisher Ralph Ingersoll, was entitled "Denouncing Charles Coughlin":

> We have no issue with any spiritual leader in his pulpit. We are fighting a total war to defend man's right to seek God as his conscience dictates. . . . When Father Coughlin steps down from his pulpit, leaves his church and goes to sit at his editorial conferences, he ceases to be *Father* Coughlin and he becomes . . . one of us journalists. . . . As a publicist, Charles Coughlin is a slanderous, foul-mouthed, dirty-minded liar. . . .
>
> Charles Coughlin is malicious, contemptible and wholly irresponsible. In turning the innocent against their Government, in filling their poor bewildered heads with lies, half-truths, perversions of the truth—in inciting the unstable to hatred and violence—he fails in the most elementary obligation of one human being to another. . . .
>
> Your brother and your son are going forth to risk their lives to destroy the threat of what this man Coughlin openly advocates. Do you want your son to fight next to a soldier whose mind Charles Coughlin has poisoned?[60]

Although the newspaper made no specific recommendation, it argued that "the Government has the facilities to collect evidence and the power to act. All a newspaper can do is to give the facts to the public and to call for action."[61] *PM*'s article provoked a deluge of letters to FBI director

Hoover. Many of them handwritten, the citizen missives called for the investigation and suppression of *Social Justice* and its creator, Charles Coughlin.

> In these times of suppression of enemy propaganda and sabotage, the Government is overlooking the most nefarious and insidious type of anti-American weapon in this country.
>
> Unless Silver-Charlie Coughlin and his miserable gang of rats are thrown in jail and their yellow Nazi paper is suppressed, we may soon find mobs of people taking him and the rest of his degenerate crew and lynching them.
>
> Personally I would like to see it happen as he bleeds the poor and ignorant and preaches racial religious and national hatred. Please do something to eliminate his cancerous growth.[62]

A clear shift in mainstream public opinion now condemned as un-American and subversive any concerted attacks on minority groups. Consequently, once America was at war, what *Social Justice* had proclaimed its patriotism became, in the eyes of the public, the very opposite—blatant enemy propaganda.

On January 22, 1942, Adolf A. Berle of the Department of State, in a personal and confidential letter to J. Edgar Hoover, called for a full-scale investigation of Charles Coughlin and his weekly newspaper. One week later, the FBI director sent a memo to Attorney General Biddle enclosing various quotations summarized in a privately circulated newspaper, the *Hour,* edited by investigative journalist Albert E. Kahn.[63] Hoover asked Biddle for guidance on the Berle information. On February 7, Hoover notified the special agent in charge of the Detroit office, John Bugas, that he was to "immediately review the files of your office with respect to Father Charles E. Coughlin and to initiate the necessary investigation to determine whether his present activities are in any way inimical to the present war effort." Bugas was further instructed that

> the investigation of this case, as you can well realize, should be conducted in a careful and discreet manner, however thoroughness is of the essence. All available confidential sources that may in any way be able to furnish information regarding the current activities of the subject should be thoroughly exploited. I shall

consider it your personal responsibility to supervise this matter
in a way that the maximum results can be obtained in the short-
est possible time.[64]

In late March 1942, Associate Justice Frank Murphy of the U.S.
Supreme Court, in an action that violated the separation of governmental
branches, sent a memorandum to FDR aide "Pa" Watson, forcefully expressing his opinion that *Social Justice* constituted an example of "giving
aid and comfort to the enemy." He wryly concluded that "Father Coughlin is trying to work himself into jail."[65] Murphy enclosed the March 23
and March 30 issues of the priest's publication, which Roosevelt forwarded, with a memo, to the newly appointed attorney general, Francis
Biddle, stating: "Will you speak to me about this?"[66] On April 7, FDR,
J. Edgar Hoover, and the attorney general met. A week later Biddle wrote
Postmaster General Frank Walker, recommending that the second-class
mailing privilege of *Social Justice* be suspended or revoked.

The front page of the March 30 issue of Coughlin's newspaper informed its readers that something was afoot with the banner headline,
"Jews Plot to Ban Social Justice!"

Since May 1941, a special grand jury had been sitting in Washington
hearing testimony about a host of pro-Nazi, anti-Semitic "small fry" individuals and groups. Coughlin was clearly a hot potato and yet a tempt-
ing target for investigators. The grand jury probe was headed by a special
prosecutor, flamboyant trial attorney William Power Maloney. An Irish
Catholic, he was the ideal choice to handle the case of Father Coughlin.
Moreover, Maloney had just successfully tried a suit against George
Sylvester Viereck, who had carried on paid propaganda activities for
Nazi Germany. (Viereck was convicted despite a subsequent challenge in
the Supreme Court.)

Pursuit of the Coughlin case frequently fell victim to the intense rivalry between J. Edgar Hoover and Maloney. This exacerbated interagency jealousies typical of any large bureaucracy, but it also engendered
bitter personality clashes between key players in the unfolding investiga-
tory process. Attorney General Francis Biddle described Maloney as
"tough and ambitious, his eyes never off the headlines."[67] Maloney was
sincerely devoted to rooting out pro-Nazis, and to this end he was frequently advised by a coterie of talented undercover investigative journalists.[68]

Meanwhile, although Hoover's assay against the Christian Fronters and their militia "coup" attempt in 1940 was praised initially by liberals, it was criticized later when the case failed to produce any convictions. Jealously guarding the crime-fighting reputation of his agency, Hoover was suspicious of outsiders and saw special prosecutor Maloney's one-man independent investigation as an amateur effort that misused FBI personnel. He and Maloney clashed frequently on procedural matters and competed over who would get credit for exposing pro-Nazi activities. Maloney, for his part, was impatient with Hoover's plodding approach and felt that going by the book was not the way to eradicate the danger of seditionists. When FBI agents were asked to carry out specific tasks, Maloney was often dissatisfied with their performance and did not keep his views to himself. Such conflicts created delays and missed opportunities to obtain evidence, and little headway was made against Coughlin and others sharing his sympathies with the Axis cause.[69]

There was more than a little suspicion that perhaps Hoover did not have his heart in the Coughlin investigation. In a letter to the prominent majority leader of the House of Representatives, John McCormack, the FBI head pointed out that "the FBI's jurisdiction is strictly limited by federal statute to investigation of possible violations of certain federal laws. In the absence of these grounds, we are without authority to act."[70] Coughlin's seditious words were disturbing and perhaps dangerous to wartime morale, but denying his right to speak was troubling to many in the White House. Confidentially, columnist Drew Pearson told a top FBI official, "Some time ago the Treasury Department had developed a very good case of income tax evasion against Father Coughlin. However, this was squashed by Secretary of the Treasury Morgenthau on the basis that it would be impolitic for a Jew to inaugurate prosecution against a priest."[71] Publicly, Pearson and his writing partner, Robert Allen, reported on March 28, 1942, that "Attorney General Francis Biddle is finally going to get tough—on direct personal orders of the President." Biddle himself recalled the pressure:

> The President was getting a good deal of mail complaining about the "softness" of his Attorney General. After two weeks, during which FDR's manner when I saw him said as plainly as words that he considered me out of step, he began to go for me in the Cabinet. His technique was always the same. When my turn came, as he went around the table, his habitual affability

dropped. . . . He looked at me with his face pulled tightly together. "When are you going to indict the seditionists?"[72]

Washington was now rife with rumors about what would be done
with Coughlin. Both the Justice Department and the FBI seemed to be
searching for the most promising avenue to achieve the president's goal.
In the race to make a case against Coughlin that would stick, the competition between Maloney and Hoover became increasingly intense. In February 1942, Hoover had found an informant who provided an inside track
to the Royal Oak priest. Without immediately sharing this information
with Maloney, the FBI had obtained some background on the operation
of *Social Justice* from the editor, E. Perrin Schwartz. He provided a
wealth of information that was crucial to the government's case.[73]

John Bugas, agent in charge in Detroit, met Schwartz, "who had appeared quite affable and sincere." At a lunch meeting in downtown Detroit, Schwartz told Bugas that "there is nothing in the Social Justice
magazine that Father Coughlin doesn't want, and if it can be predeter-
mined nothing is put in there he would not want. . . . He spoke of the title and ownership of *Social Justice* as being just a legal fact." Schwartz
also told agent Bugas that Coughlin had "a truly great mind."[74] The investigator indicated "clearly that Coughlin was the author or purported
author of the vast majority of the material" that appeared in *Social Justice*:

> From the testimony it is apparent that Coughlin ruled the destiny
> of Social Justice with an iron hand and was in absolute control of
> the paper at all times. E. Perrin Schwartz, the ostensible editor of
> the paper, was in reality nothing more than a copy reader and
> make-up man for the sheet and took all of his instructions from
> Coughlin. All employees were hired and fired by Coughlin and
> the rate of their salaries was fixed by him.[75]

Based on Schwartz's testimony and an examination of the style of
letters to the editor, investigators concluded that most were written by
Coughlin himself.[76] In a memo to Attorney General Biddle, Justice Department investigators, in coordination with the Internal Revenue Service, reported progress on tax audits of various Coughlin enterprises.
Among other things, they discovered that the Radio League of the Little
Flower had recently loaned large sums to Father Coughlin and to something called the Valdan Corporation, controlled by E. Pruitt Semmes, the

priest's attorney. The unsecured loan to Coughlin was $25,000, and another loan for twice the amount went to the Valdan Corporation. According to one of Coughlin's bookkeepers, "Both of these loans were made with the understanding that the money was to be used by Coughlin and the Valdan Corporation to speculate in the stock market."[77]

Coughlin's finances were not the only concern. A portion of the Justice Department's internal case memorandum prepared by Maloney was devoted to "The Use of Nazi Propaganda in Social Justice":

> Entirely aside from the consistently pro-Nazi policy of the articles . . . there is at least one occasion upon which Social Justice reprinted in almost identical form a speech delivered by Goebbels. The Social Justice article gave no credit to Goebbels and did not in any way indicate that it was a reprint of Goebbels' speech. In addition to the Goebbels article we have testimony from one witness, the Reverend Dr. Cole of Boston, that on one occasion when he visited Coughlin at Royal Oak he saw Nazi propaganda leaflets stacked upon the shelves of Coughlin's library. Dr. Cole can specifically identify the Goebbels speech in pamphlet form, printed in English, as having been on Coughlin's shelf.[78]

The memo to Biddle stated as well, "We have seen a reproduction of *Der Sturmer* published by the notorious Jew-baiter, Julius Streicher, in Germany, which reproduction sets forth an entire page of the March 21, 1938, issue of *Social Justice*." Included in the case memo were various excerpts from articles that had appeared in *Social Justice;* the memo argued that, after the U.S. entered the war, the magazine began giving "aid and comfort to the enemy."[79]

Among the most important evidence of links to the Axis powers the investigators thought they had uncovered was the hiring of *Social Justice* foreign correspondent James Strachey Barnes. Since the beginning of World War II, Barnes had been working for the Italian fascist government as a radio propagandist—the male counterpart to Germany's "Axis Sally"—and was broadcast by shortwave to Allied troops. When Justice Department investigators first obtained, via British intelligence on Bermuda, intercepted correspondence to Coughlin, Barnes's use of the initial "M" led them to think that the priest was receiving communications from Mussolini.

Yet another line of inquiry was brought to the attention of the FBI. Agent Percy Foxworth of the New York City office told his director about a follow-up to a tip offered by Ralph Ingersoll, editor of *PM*. "He was most desirous of personally meeting you at an early date on a matter he considered of importance," the agent wrote Hoover. Ingersoll had told him that "he was under obligation to pass on the information given to him only to Mr. Hoover, for which purpose he was willing to proceed to Washington at any time."[80] In his meeting with Hoover held in mid-April 1942, Ingersoll indicated that he was acting at the behest of *PM*'s owner, Marshall Field III. The FBI transcript of the interview relates Ingersoll's tip as follows:

> He stated that he had ascertained from reliable sources that Father Coughlin at the present time was being treated by a reputable Detroit psychiatrist for certain sexual difficulties. He also stated that Father Coughlin had in his employ a maid or secretary, with whom Father Coughlin had had relations, and who was also being treated by the same psychiatrist. Ingersoll did not know the name of the psychiatrist.
>
> Ingersoll stated that Mr. Field and he were desirous of having me suggest the name of a woman investigator, preferably a Catholic, who could be sent to Detroit . . . to join Father Coughlin's Church and endeavor to obtain the true facts concerning this particular situation. I advised Ingersoll that this Bureau did not employ women investigators and that off-hand I did not know of anyone who could be suggested for such an assignment, but I would think the matter over and communicate with him later.[81]

Hoover instructed special agent Foxworth to telephone Ingersoll and inform him that "I have been unable to find anyone that I could recommend for the assignment which Ingersoll had in mind." The FBI director took Ingersoll's suggestion seriously enough to pass on the essence of it to Attorney General Biddle, who apparently did not follow up on the matter, since no further reports are found in the FBI's files.[82]

Coughlin's intimates retain vivid recollections of the day that federal investigators arrived at the Shrine of the Little Flower. One recalled that "papers and records were strewn about the grounds. . . . They came in a long line of black limousines." Coughlin told an interviewer in 1972 that it "was a horrible thing. They came up to the Shrine with Army trucks and took all my files away, a million names of the mailing list, all the papers and the letters, wagonload after wagonload, and I've never received them back. I guess they junked them in Washington someplace."[83]

By late March 1942, Attorney General Biddle considered using grand jury information to develop a case against Father Coughlin as an Axis agent. Under the Foreign Agents Registration Act, passed in 1938, failure to report income from a foreign government while acting in a lobbying capacity would subject a person to a fine or even a jail sentence. In fact, one of Coughlin's closest associates, Louis Ward, was being investigated on this basis. Ward, who had been a key organizer in the 1936 Union party campaign (he narrowly missed winning a primary bid for the U.S. Senate nomination), played a variety of key roles in Coughlin's career. Designated editorial manager for *Social Justice* in 1940, he stood as a virtual second in command to Coughlin.

Ward was essentially a public relations professional whose ties to members of Congress, along with his consulting work for the Ford Motor Company, kept him close to Washington as the nation moved closer to war. In July 1940, it came to the attention of J. Edgar Hoover, from "very reliable sources," the Office of Naval Intelligence, that Ward was doing paid lobbying work for the Japanese government. Through the ONI's top-secret program of decoding Japanese diplomatic messages, known as MAGIC, details of Ward's activities came to light because of his ties to an American being tracked for illegal lobbying:

> [Vincent P.] Walsh's name appears frequently in official Japanese dispatches. . . . Walsh receives funds from the Japanese government and from these funds makes payments to Ward. . . . Recently . . . ONI agents in New York made illegal entrance into the offices of the Japanese Consulate General and there made photographic copies of the stubs of the Consul General's check book. . . . Both Walsh and Ward's name appeared as payees.[84]

Evidence was found that Ward had received $1,000 from the Japanese Chamber of Commerce in February 1938 for "publications." In August 1939, Ward was paid another $2,650 for 15,000 copies of an article entitled "Regaining Our Market," written for and distributed to members of the Japanese Chamber of Commerce in New York. The consul general paid Ward another $13,000 on May 4, 1940, and $1,300 on May 28.

While still employed by Father Coughlin, Ward received approximately $26,000 from the Japanese government.[85] In secret cables, the Japanese explained to their diplomats the importance of Ward's work: "The goal was to create a break in diplomatic relations between the US and the USSR." Japanese officials noted that the project was filled "with dynamite" and "urged caution" but gave the go-ahead signal. A second purpose of Ward's work was directed to members of the U.S. Congress. Naval intelligence reported that in early October 1940, " [Vincent] Walsh and Ward went to Washington and conferred with Senators Nye, Thomas, Wheeler, Byrd, Johnson of Colorado and others, and made undercover investigation which was forwarded [to Tokyo] by the Japanese Consul of New York."[86]

The government's formal charges against Louis Ward for illegal activities on behalf of a foreign government—one that was about to go to war with his own nation—were fraught with political and evidentiary problems. In October 1941, a few weeks before Pearl Harbor, FBI director Hoover was advised that the War Department did not want to proceed with the case against Ward because of his close connection with Coughlin. The Justice Department was balking because of "the fact that reports and other sources have indicated that [Ward] is well acquainted with high government circles in Washington D.C. being intimately acquainted with numerous Congressmen and Senators and Stephen Early of the White House."[87] John Bugas, the FBI's agent in charge in Detroit, was told that Hoover would not give the go-ahead "in view of the fact that a local arrest would mean considerable publicity."[88] Bugas was advised that if an investigation went ahead, it "would have to be open and aboveboard . . . due to the strong connections which [the] subject [Ward] had in Washington."[89]

One week after bombs fell at Pearl Harbor, Ward was summoned to the FBI's Detroit field office for an interview. He was allowed the courtesy of accompanying agents as they searched his home. He made a statement for the record:

My interest in foreign trade dates from my school days when I majored in economics. . . .

My interest was retained . . . when I taught American History and Government to the largest classes, perhaps, ever assembled in this subject.

My interests continued during the years. . . . I was associated with the late Theodore F. McManus, Detroit advertising and sales counsel of such accounts as Cadillac, Packard, Fisher Body, Dodge, all Divisions of Chrysler and many other nationally known accounts.[90]

Despite the accumulation of evidence, the Ward case contained a major flaw: its source of information could not be revealed. Even years after the close of World War II, the extent and character of the MAGIC intercept program remained classified. To try Louis Ward would have compromised one of America's major war secrets.

In early 1942, with America on the defensive in the Pacific and the Axis powers of Europe remaining unchallenged, the investigation of domestic groups sympathetic to America's enemies continued. The special grand jury in Washington that had been looking into *Social Justice* moved ahead in calling witnesses, one of them Louis Ward, but on April 21, he suffered a fatal heart attack. Newspaper accounts of his death note that his heart attack had occurred just after receiving a subpoena to appear as a witness before the grand jury. For the *Detroit Free Press*, it was a front-page story, with its headline, "Ward's Career Tied Closely with Priest's," followed by a detailed review of his public career and the impending *Social Justice* investigation.[91]

Despite the enormous pressure on Attorney General Francis Biddle to indict Charles Coughlin, the exact line to take was unclear. With regard to the charge of serving as an unregistered agent of a foreign power, no agency had turned up evidence that linked Coughlin to any receipt of funds. It was suggested that by hiring others who were clearly in the pay of enemy nations—such as *Social Justice*'s John Strachey Barnes—the employer of such persons (Coughlin in this instance) might then be charged under the 1938 statute. But Biddle was advised by Justice Department attorneys that "the Foreign Agents Registration Act does not include a person who employs another who is, or may be, an agent of a foreign principal. . . . There must be proof that Father Coughlin . . . knew or had reason to know" that Barnes was "acting as an Axis agent."[92]

Another direction Biddle considered led to the Christian Front. Was it still operating? And, if so, was it "dominated by Reverend Charles E. Coughlin to such an extent that he [could] dictate its policies and direct members into civilian defense organizations or to any other organizations which due to the overwhelming numbers of Christian Fronters [would] be considered as potentially dangerous to the internal security of the

United States?"[93] This line of investigation did not prove fruitful either because it became clear that Coughlin was not in any official leadership position, although he was in contact with key leaders of Christian Front offshoot organizations in Boston and New York.

On April 14 Attorney General Biddle informed Postmaster Frank Walker that *Social Justice* had, since December 7, 1941, "made a systematic contribution and unscrupulous attack upon the war effort of our Nation, both civilian and military, and reproduces in this country the lines of the enemy propaganda war being waged against this country from abroad."[94] And three days later Biddle announced publicly that a special federal grand jury would begin an investigation of *Social Justice*.

The day after Biddle's announcement, newspapers printed a picture of Father Coughlin standing next to his aging parents, captioned with the fact that ownership of *Social Justice* was in their names. That same day, Attorney General Biddle hinted that there might have to be an early appearance of the priest before the grand jury in Washington. He said that the investigation would look into "the ownership, policy, policy-makers and financial set-up" of the magazine. Biddle added that the grand jury, over the next few months, "would be asked to look into the possibility of a tie-up with Axis propaganda sources" and that he thought the relationship was "quite clear" and that there was evidence of "systematic seditious utterances."[95]

Next, the attorney general inquired about the possibility of revoking the second-class mailing privilege of *Social Justice* on the grounds that it was violating section 3 of Title I of the Espionage Act of 1917. Under this legislation, penalties could be levied for obstructing the war effort by conveying false information to aid enemies of the United States. Under section I, Title XII, any matter in violation of the statute was "nonmailable matter and shall not be conveyed in the mails or delivered from any post office or by any letter carrier." Postmaster General Walker issued two directives regarding *Social Justice*. The first stated that the post office in Royal Oak would not dispatch future issues but would refer them to the solicitor of the Post Office Department for review. The second order, called the "show cause" order, required the publishers of *Social Justice* to make a cause for why the paper should not be permanently excluded from the mail.

When he was reached for comment after the post office orders, Coughlin told United Press, "I am neither editor, owner, nor publisher of *Social Justice*." If the attorney general wished to summon him to come to

Washington, he would "not only be happy to do so, but will challenge him on the invitation."[96] Just two days later, though, Coughlin changed course:

> I do here and now publicly state, that I, Father Charles E. Cough-lin, pastor of the Shrine of the Little Flower, alone am responsible for and do control the magazine, its policies and contents. This sole responsibility and control over the policy-making and content of the magazine I have exercised personally and officially by my effective moral and spiritual influence and direction over the editors, publishers and owners of *Social Justice.*
>
> If *Social Justice* . . . is "clearly sedition" the responsibility is mine alone.[97]

That same day it was rumored that subpoenas for the owners of record, Mr. and Mrs. Thomas J. Coughlin and E. Perrin Schwartz, were to be issued. If the goal of Coughlin's statement was to alter the plans of the grand jury, he succeeded. On April 22, a *Detroit Free Press* story countered the news in other papers by announcing that Coughlin would not be called before the grand jury, nor would his parents. Service was sought only on editor Schwartz. On April 26, however, Drew Pearson and Robert Allen's column claimed that Coughlin would be cross-examined in the following week about two "mysterious associates, Philip Johnson and Alan Blackburn."[98]

Now the spotlight turned to the grand jury. Here, William Power Maloney swiftly grabbed national headlines by announcing that ten employees of *Social Justice* were to be called for testimony, starting with Schwartz, the editor. He was followed by a virtual parade of the radio priest's staff, including his personal secretary. Thirteen witnesses were called by the end of April 1942, and several were asked to return, to testify in early May. Among the witnesses were the key backer of the Social Justice Printing Company, Francis Keelon; Philip Johnson, former aide and foreign correspondent of *Social Justice;* bank officials; and representatives of the printers of *Social Justice.*[99] An indictment against Charles Coughlin now appeared imminent.

Lieutenant Edward J. Hickey was a young Justice Department staffer on loan from his naval intelligence duties. He now found himself designated to try the case against perhaps the most famous individual in the far-right politics of the day. As a devout Catholic, Hickey had misgivings about participating in the prosecution of a Catholic priest and sought counsel from the NCWC in Washington. He recalled receiving the advice that he should feel no conflict of faith over the case: "God bless you, my boy" was the admonition he recalled.[100] Then, just as it seemed that government officials were ready to move decisively on the radio priest and his magazine, the case was brought to a halt.

Action on the Coughlin sedition case was suspended due to a variety of factors, including Biddle's deep sensitivity to the question of civil liberties. Shutting down *Social Justice* as a seditious publication was not an action he contemplated with any enthusiasm. Of all the public officials dealing with subversion from extremist groups, Biddle was the most alert to violations of First Amendment guarantees. The American Civil Liberties Union, through its highly respected head, Arthur Garfield Hays, went on record expressing its concern too. Opinion makers in the media, despite their general distaste for Coughlin's politics, were concerned about the precedent that would be set in the curbing of his newspaper. The *New York Times* ran an editorial, "The Case of 'Social Justice,'" in which it agreed that the magazine had been guilty of "outrageous provocation" but that this should not be a cause preventing its publication:

> We must remember that the American people in the past have had a way of answering lies with truth, hate with tolerance, incitements to civil strife by a united front to the enemy of mankind. . . .
>
> In these circumstances we must ask ourselves how far we can go in the direction of the suppression of opinion, even opinion as filthy as that expressed in *Social Justice*, unless the facts of the case warrant the direct charge of sedition and prosecution on that ground.[101]

The trepidation within the Justice Department was not quite so lofty in nature but did reflect the delicacy of the situation. Even the FBI was preparing an excuse to withdraw from the investigation. In a key strategy meeting held April 22, FBI officials complained to one another that the State Department's original request for an investigation of Coughlin was not specific and had not indicated under what statute prosecution was to be conducted. Still other problems were raised: the logistics of trying to tap Coughlin's private switchboard, the lack of space for storing the bulky list of more than 200,000 *Social Justice* subscribers secured in the raid at the Shrine, and the need to show that *Social Justice* had in fact been delivered at military establishments and bases.[102] In a memo generated after this meeting, the FBI stated its reasons for withdrawing from the case:

> It is recommended that the Bureau go on record as stating that no further investigative steps are being taken in this case, pending a specific request of the Department as to the exact inquiries desired. The basis for the bureau's withdrawal of investigation would be that the Post Office Department has taken action against "Social Justice" by banning it from the mails, and that Father Coughlin and "Social Justice" are being investigated by a grand jury. Consequently, it would be duplication of effort to continue the inquiry until such time as a definite outline of what is desired is made by the Department and the outcome of the grand jury proceedings is known.[103]

On April 24, Coughlin sent a telegram to FBI assistant director E. A. Tamm asking to appear before the grand jury. After receiving an evasive reply, the priest asked again three days later. The next day, he was sent a brief note from the executive assistant to Attorney General Biddle saying that he would "be advised in due course of the date upon which your appearance as a witness is required."[104] No April 27 issues of *Social Justice* were mailed; its second-class postage privilege had been suspended. The show-cause hearing for the ban on *Social Justice* by the post office was postponed from April 29 to May 4, but on that date, no one showed up to challenge the decision. Postmaster Walker did receive two telegrams that day: one from editor E. Perrin Schwartz stating that "the publisher-owner and editor abandon the second class mail privilege" and the magazine would no longer be published, and the other from Charles Coughlin approving the "action of the publisher-owner of *Social Justice* abandoning the second class mailing privilege."[105]

On May 11, 1942, under the signatures of Edward Hickey and William Maloney, a detailed case outline memorandum was forwarded to Wendell Berge, now transferred from the State Department to the post of assistant attorney general. The document started by reviewing the testimony of the grand jury witnesses regarding the authorship of articles appearing in *Social Justice* from July 1940 to the most recent issues, when Coughlin was not formally associated with the magazine. When I interviewed him, Hickey recalled that the grand jury was "very anxious to bring in an indictment, and it would not have been difficult to do so. They were ready to go forward with the cause. . . . The woman who was foreman of the jury was Catholic, as was the majority of the grand jury."[106] William Power Maloney's son remembers that his father told him, "It took a lot to convince them [the grand jury] to vote for a true bill, but finally sufficient evidence was presented and a vote was prepared. My father told Biddle he could have an indictment whenever he wanted."[107]

But there was to be no trial. An arrangement was negotiated that would finally silence Charles Coughlin. Some thirty years after the event, Coughlin boasted to one interviewer:

Biddle couldn't have tried me for anything. If Biddle had ever tried me for sedition, he would have been tried for a lot of other things, because I had an attorney stronger and smarter than Biddle. He knew perfectly well that if he had ever tried me, a case would be brought against him personally that would have put him in limbo forever.[108]

Over the span of just three weeks, from April 14 to May 4, 1942, Coughlin traveled the gamut from defiance—daring Attorney General Francis Biddle to allow him to testify in defense of *Social Justice*—to meek acceptance: "I approve the action . . . of abandoning the second class mail privilege."[109] Certainly the radio priest had made dramatic reversals before, but the reasons for his final silencing in 1942 have remained a subject of speculation for decades.

From May 1940 onward, both the priest and his bishop maintained the public fiction that *Social Justice* was no longer the voice of the radio priest. In the face of violent attacks on *Social Justice* for its pro-Axis editorial line, Archbishop Mooney seemed withdrawn and detached from the controversy swirling across the news media. As bishops around the country felt the pressure to respond to critics of the Royal Oak priest, Mooney studiously avoided any public statement; in private, written communications, he was cautious in expressing his reaction to what was occurring.[110] Yet this outward facade belied a mounting pressure directed to Coughlin's superior by both his church peers and the federal government.

When Coughlin made his public admission on April 20 that he had sole responsibility and control over *Social Justice*, he was violating the agreement he had made with his bishop two years earlier. Within three days of the event, the priest received a stinging indictment from Archbishop Mooney:

> Let me recall what I wrote to you on November 7th, 1940. . . . "I desire the requirement of previous review by proper ecclesiastical authority to extend to all interviews or signed statements which you give to the press. . . ." In view of that precept of your bishop, your action in releasing this statement [of April 20, 1942] to the press without submitting it to ecclesiastical authority for previous review is, in itself, a definite act of disobedience.
>
> So much for the fact of the statement. To consider its contents, it is clear that your acknowledgment of full responsibility for and control of "Social Justice," its policies and contents, reveals a continued course of disobedience to the injunction of complete dissociation from "Social Justice" which I laid upon you in my letter of May 23rd, 1940.[111]

Mooney added that Coughlin's public statement brought him "into conflict with the general law of the Church" and that "the assumption by a priest, without the consent of his bishop, of 'sole responsibility and control over the policy making and content' of a magazine involves a violation of Canon 1386 of the Code of Canon Law." The archbishop warned, "If you do not desist forthwith from a course of action which I, as your bishop, hold to be in violation of the injunctions I have given you . . . I shall be obligated to proceed, however reluctantly, to canonical measures designed to enforce clerical obedience."[112]

Coughlin's superior demanded an admission that the priest had contravened injunctions of his bishop and called for "a clean-cut renunciation . . . of responsibility for *Social Justice*." Mooney pointed out, "In view of the public character of your statement of April 20th, I shall have to make this assurance public." Although he softened his demands by saying that "I shall do everything possible to save your feelings," he added, "I must likewise do all I can to safeguard the faith of many Catholics whose minds are sadly confused by your course of action."[113]

The next day Mooney reported to the apostolic delegate: "I cannot any longer defer proceeding in this case if Father Coughlin refuses to give the assurance I have asked. . . . To do so would be to let him flagrantly flout ecclesiastical authority." If this approach failed, the archbishop suggested turning the case over to a diocesan tribunal "for appropriate decision and sanction."[114]

Now the tempo of events quickened. Coughlin called his superior the following morning to request a personal interview and was granted an appointment for April 28. It was to be one in a short series of confrontations. As he entered Archbishop Mooney's office, Coughlin asked permission to read what he called a "hurried" reply to his superior's letter of April 23. In fact, it was a sixteen-page typewritten statement in which he denied that he had violated the 1940 agreement with his bishop and claimed that he had avoided "whatever might lead the public to identify the magazine [Social Justice] with me." He asserted that he had warned the publication's editor not to print anything that might lead the public to think otherwise and as to his picture appearing in a small circle at the bottom of the front page, Coughlin drew the analogy of the Saturday Evening Post, which has Benjamin Franklin's picture on its front cover. Finally, he asserted, "My conscience would not permit me to live with myself if I sought freedom from such responsibility [for Social Justice] by confessing to what I consider to be a lie—namely—formal disobedience to my Archbishop. . . . Though no longer a young man I should prefer to live in a penitentiary with peace of mind for twenty years than to live in the world a self-confessed coward, liar, and ecclesiastical rebel for a lifetime."[115]

When Coughlin had finished, Mooney suggested they collaborate in framing a definite agreement that could not be evaded. Coughlin responded, "You do not think I am honest, do you?" Mooney replied that "he certainly did not," to which the priest conceded that Mooney had expressed such an opinion three years earlier but not "so brutally." The archbishop then handed Coughlin a draft letter—a "canonical admonition"—that required "a clear-cut renunciation, from this date," of any involvement with Social Justice. The penalty for violation would be immediate suspension from the priesthood. By accepting the statement, Coughlin would be admitting he had been formally sanctioned by his superior.

At this point Coughlin brought up the implication of receiving an ecclesiastical reprimand on his possible indictment by the grand jury and ultimate conviction under the Sedition Act of 1917. Fearing that he might receive more than a heavy fine, perhaps "a prison sentence of twenty years in the Federal penitentiary," Coughlin asserted that he would be denounced in the eyes of laymen as a traitor to his country. More important, if he received a religious punishment, this would lead to a civil conviction, since during any trial, the evaluation by his superior as to his standing in the church would be brought up. The priest declared he would refuse to sign Mooney's directive if it would harm his future trial: "It is easier to get in the Church than out of prison." It was a matter, the priest argued, that forced him into a choice between the priesthood and what Coughlin called the "law of self-preservation." At this, Mooney asserted that the priesthood should be the paramount consideration. Disagreeing, Coughlin said that " 'in point of urgency' his life comes first."[116]

In speaking about the prejudicial effect of accepting an admonition from his superior, Coughlin stated that Mooney would be "the chief witness at his trial." He told his superior he needed to consult his lawyers about whether making the statement presented to him by Mooney would have a deleterious effect on his coming trial. He asked that the ecclesiastical action be deferred until after the civil case had been settled.

Throughout the meeting, Coughlin had delivered what Chancellor Edward J. Hickey called "both veiled and open" threats to Mooney. Not only might the archbishop be blamed for Coughlin's civil conviction, but more important, "C repeated at least two or three times the idea of leaving the Church."[117]

Mooney gave Coughlin a short time—"three or four days"—to accept or reject the public admonition and agreed that Coughlin's lawyer could be at their next meeting. On April 30, Coughlin, E. Pruitt Semmes (Coughlin's lawyer), and Mooney met. Semmes agreed with his client that a permanent second-class mailing ban of *Social Justice* would result from the grand jury's deliberations and proposed that he would see whether, if Coughlin's newspaper "would quietly and definitely cease publication and abandon its mailing privileges," the "Attorney General would drop proceedings against C [Coughlin] before the grand jury."[118]

The following day, Coughlin and his superior signed an agreement that contained several components, one of them an admission by Coughlin that he "violated objectively but not intentionally the legitimate precepts of [his] ecclesiastical superior . . . and also the canons of Church law." Mooney agreed not to publish his paragraph "pending final disposition of any charges against Father Coughlin" arising from the Washington grand jury investigation. He pledged "to keep the ecclesiastical forum and the civil forum separate and to do nothing in the ecclesiastical forum which might, through public misunderstanding of its purport, prejudice Father Coughlin's case in the civil forum." The priest also had to pledge that "he would not have anything to do with any other publication in the future unless he had explicit permission from his superior." If Coughlin violated any of the pledges, he would be found in "contumacious disobedience to the legitimate precepts" of his superior. He also had to formally acknowledge that "such disobedience incurs the penalty of 'ipso facto' suspension from my priestly functions."[119]

On May 2, Mooney formally acknowledged by letter Coughlin's renunciation of future ties with *Social Justice* and the other conditions, with the exception that he could write and edit the parish bulletin "on condition that its circulation be limited to your parishioners and that a copy of each issue be mailed to the Chancery."[120]

The stage was now set for the end of Charles Coughlin's national political career. Chancellor Hickey had cryptically recorded that during the final climactic confrontation between Coughlin and his bishop, despite the government's having "uncovered a mass of evidence involving his connections with Axis embassies, his writing for the magazine and his incomplete tax returns . . . the [archbishop] knew Washington officials did not want to press anything against C."[121]

As early as the "Merry-Go-Round" column of April 26, Drew Pearson and Robert S. Allen had hinted that some backdoor arrangement was being worked out between church officials and the federal government to avoid going to trial with the Coughlin case. They claimed on May 11 that church officials favored the government's action in closing down *Social Justice* but felt it was going too far to indict Coughlin. A "Broadcast Memorandum" prepared for Drew Pearson a few days later was much more explicit about a deal having been worked out.[122]

At the time of the 1936 election, it was widely believed that Franklin Roosevelt had pressured the church to silence Coughlin because of Coughlin's political activism in opposition to the president, and the myth of Vatican conspiracy with Roosevelt to silence Coughlin has persisted in a variety of forms.[123] In fact, direct efforts by the Roosevelt administration to influence Coughlin's superior did not emerge until the fall of 1941. Myron Taylor, the unofficial U.S. representative to the Vatican, contacted Roosevelt indicating that Archbishop Mooney would be in Washington on October 23 and that "it would be a good idea if, without publicity, the President could have a talk with him."[124] Roosevelt's secretary replied ten days later: "The President desires an off-the-record appointment, Thursday forenoon with Myron Taylor, who will bring with him to the White House a member of the Catholic Hierarchy."[125]

After his off-the-record meeting with Taylor and FDR, Mooney was kept apprised of progress in the federal government's investigation of the radio priest through intermediaries. At the beginning of March 1942, a particularly urgent signal arrived by way of the New York archdiocese. Chancellor J. Francis McIntyre wrote to Mooney that "Mr. Lawrence C. M. Smith is the chief of the special defense unit of the Department of Justice . . . [and] is investigating, officially, the affairs of 'Social Justice.' . . . [He] has made inquiry through Catholic friends as to how he might approach the Church authority for the best information on the Church's position in the matter." McIntyre indicated that he had told Smith to contact Mooney.[126] Three weeks later, Mooney was given a rather explicit warning via the archbishop of New York, Francis J. Spellman: "I wish to confirm that a gentleman occupying one of the highest positions in the Federal Government and one who is deeply interested in the Catholic Church as well as the welfare of the country, came to tell me quite frankly that measures will soon be taken against subversive publications and among these publications is listed *Social Justice*."[127]

Mooney complained to Spellman about a lack of support from his fellow bishops but at the same time was annoyed by governmental pressure and did not want to offer "a *carte blanche* to federal investigators." He was still reluctant to challenge Coughlin "on the basis of suggestions conveyed indirectly and without the accompaniment of factual data that would save any action on my part from being futile and probably harmful to the Church," and given his experience in dealing with Coughlin, he did not want to have to back down again.[128] Yet despite all of his misgivings, Mooney's attitude was unmistakable: he welcomed a strong intervention by the federal government, almost as a compensatory mechanism for the lack of support from his ecclesiastical peers.[129]

On April 30, while awaiting a reply to the ultimatum of April 28 from Coughlin and his attorney, Mooney received word from yet another source regarding overtures by the federal government regarding an ecclesiastical settlement of the Coughlin affair. The Vatican's U.S. delegate, Amleto Cicognani, had been telephoned by Leo Crowley, chairman of the Federal Deposit Insurance Corporation and a prominent Catholic, who had been asked by FDR to serve as a troubleshooter on a variety of delicate negotiations missions:

He spoke of the desirability of avoiding a public scandal and of
the opportuneness of the Church's treating the matter as an ecclesiastical question. I avoided passing judgment on his proposal, although I agreed with him on the desirability of avoiding
scandal. He said he had no difficulty about speaking of the case
to Your Excellency and I understood that he will soon try to
arrange a meeting with you.[130]

At virtually the same moment that Crowley was flying to Detroit to
assure the archbishop of the willingness of the administration to avoid
putting Coughlin on trial, E. Pruitt Semmes was being received by key
administration officials who had been given Mooney's assurances as to
the bona fides of this special emissary:

Postmaster Walker and Attorney General Biddle took the matter
directly to the President, who directed that the proceedings of the
grand jury in regard to C be quashed quietly. At the same time
these men saw that they could not in public place reliance on C's
own word of honor. They therefore felt that . . . the [archbishop]
should issue a statement expressing gratification over the way
the post office case was settled and informing the public that he
and C had reached a broad and firm understanding which would
preclude any repetition of this embarrassing situation.[131]

On May 4, the post office declared the permanent suspension of *Social Justice*'s second-class mailing privilege and the archbishop issued a
press statement: "I am gratified to learn that the question between the
Post Office Department and *Social Justice* magazine, involving a priest
of this diocese, has been disposed of as reported in today's paper. . . . My
understanding with him [Coughlin] is sufficiently broad and firm to exclude the recurrence of any such unpleasant situation."[132]
Earlier that same day, Coughlin's attorney, E. Pruitt Semmes, had met
with Postmaster Frank Walker, Attorney General Francis Biddle, and Leo
Crowley. Word of what happened was sent back to Archbishop Mooney
via Monsignor Michael Ready, the general director of the NCWC in
Washington: Crowley "took the matter to the President." A few days
later, Mooney penned a personal note to FDR:

Mr. Crowley had occasion to consult me by telephone in connection with his unselfish interest in seeing the "Social Justice" case disposed of in a quiet but thoroughly effective way.

It is, of course, evident to me that no such happy solution of a problem embarrassing alike to civil and ecclesiastical authority would have been possible but for your own high-minded and magnanimous attitude.

May I not, therefore, use the liberty you gave me some months ago and tell you that I think this is fine statesmanship as I know it is real Christian charity? Let me add that the delicate consideration shown in this instance strengthens my own hand immeasurably in dealing with a situation in which I am fortunate, indeed, to have your sympathetic understanding.

This whole lamentable affair gives striking confirmation to the wise observation you made in our conversation last October. The arena of politics is no place for one whose ecclesiastical character surrounds him, in the minds of good men, with a protective consideration he personally could never claim.[133]

Two days later, President Roosevelt sent his own expression of gratitude:

I am, indeed, grateful for your note. I am happy, too, in the outcome of what might have hurt the Church and the Government equally. May I say that I think that both you and I can well have sympathy with our mutual problems! In this case I really feel that both of us have shown true Christian Charity.[134]

Just three days after Archbishop Mooney wrote to FDR, the prelate reported to the apostolic delegate on what he called "this sorry chapter in the life of a misguided priest." Saying that "we can write 'finis' . . . to this longstanding and nerve-wracking difficulty," the archbishop described his attitude as one of "cautious optimism." He believed that Coughlin "sees that those whom he worked against or deceived are the only ones who could save him from the penalty of his unpriestly folly and save the Church from the results of his wrongheadedness."[135] Interviewed forty years after the event, a clerical aide to Coughlin tersely summed up his assessment: "Mooney got the red hat for silencing Charlie."[136]

Whatever the price, clearly both the church and the Roosevelt administration avoided what might have been a protracted legal struggle in which public opinion might have been deeply divided. Given the military setbacks of America's first year of involvement in World War II, there were strong reasons for the Coughlin case to be laid to rest quietly. Nonetheless, Coughlin's millions of followers were occasionally encouraged by persistent rumors that Coughlin would return to radio broadcasting. Vigilance would be needed. For those who were disappointed that the priest did not receive any punishment for sedition, the silencing agreement remained a source of anger and frustration.

14

"And the Truth Shall
Be Known"

A broad and firm understanding has been reached between
myself and Father Coughlin and he has made a definite and
explicit commitment that his severance of all connection,
whether direct or indirect with Social Justice or any other
publication would be absolute and complete.

Press statement of Archbishop Mooney, May 5, 1942

THE SILENCING AGREEMENT worked out in May 1942 resolved nothing
except the most basic issue of the moment: the ending of Charles
Coughlin's political career. Within the Catholic community, the reaction
to Archbishop Mooney's "broad and firm understanding" with Coughlin
was decidedly mixed, ranging from hearty congratulations to bitter denunciation. For Mooney, the most pressing question centered on future
events: Would the priest honor the secret agreement or attempt yet another dramatic public comeback? Coughlin's superior did not have long
to wait. Within four months of formally agreeing to these strictures,
Charles Coughlin creatively circumvented them.

In April 1942, Private William J. Lutz, serving in Hawaii, received this
letter, addressed to "My Dear Friend":

You are better aware than I am of the solicitude your friends entertain for your welfare.
    Because of this solicitude, your name was sent to me with
the request that we at the Shrine say some prayers for your

269

safety. So here is the story: At the Shrine there is a beautiful altar dedicated to St. Sebastian, the patron of soldiers. The names of all the boys in the army, navy, or air service—that is the names sent to me—are printed legibly and fastened to the marble walls of St. Sebastian's altar. Every Tuesday a Mass is said for the safekeeping of these men. Every day thousands of school children and others are asked to pray for that same cause. I thought you would like to know about this, namely, that we stay-at-homes recognize the sacrifices and dangers that are yours; and that we are praying for you with all our might.

God bless and preserve you!

Cordially yours,

Charles E. Coughlin

P.S. If there are other men in your outfit who want us to enroll their names at St. Sebastian's altar, feel free to send them along, together with address of nearest relative.[1]

Lutz passed on the letter to military intelligence, where it started making its way through the system, eventually becoming the basis of a memorandum from Hoover to Assistant Attorney General Wendell Berge:

There are attached copies of a letter addressed to Private William J. Lutz. . . . This letter was made available by the Military Intelligence Division, with the comment that Private Lutz does not approve of Father Coughlin or his political ideas and that his father probably furnished his name and address to Father Coughlin. . . . This letter probably represents an effort on the part of Father Coughlin to develop a mailing list comprised of men of the armed services. . . .

The postscript in this letter deals with the submission of additional names. . . . The purpose of this particular portion of the letter is not known, but it is obvious that the names and addresses of men in the armed forces, as well as their nearest relatives, can be of considerable interest to an organization desiring to distribute material detrimental to the war effort.[2]

Archbishop Mooney learned of the breach of his agreement with his priest by reading the New York liberal tabloid newspaper *PM*. For several months earlier in 1942, the publication had waged a formidable campaign to have the radio priest indicted for sedition. "I began to fear," wrote Mooney to the Vatican representative, Cicognani, "that PM . . . would now seize this occasion to bring strong pressure on the government to reopen the [Coughlin] case." Now fully alerted and angered by the attention given to the Coughlin missive, Archbishop Mooney resolved to nip the problem in the bud. He was determined "to forestall . . . any public letter writing activities on the part of Father Coughlin which might create the unpleasant situation of last May." He ordered the priest to submit "all circulars or group letters" that were sent out under his signature to prior censorship by the chancery office. Mooney confided to Amleto Cicognani: "Formulating hole-proof regulations" for his priest was "one of the most difficult tasks I have ever assayed."[3]

On December 11, 1942, an FBI agent interviewed the chancellor of the Detroit archdiocese, Edward J. Hickey:

The informant advised that Father Coughlin had not sent him a copy of the letter in question. . . .

The informant stated that this matter was discussed with Pruitt Semmes, attorney for Father Coughlin, who appeared to be in agreement with the letter [the precept from Mooney] and personally discussed with Father Coughlin.

The informant said that he believed sometime back that Semmes had influenced Father Coughlin against principles of the Archdiocese, but that it had since been believed that Semmes is more or less of a "brake" upon the activities of Coughlin and has several times prevented the Subject from proceeding to the extent of involving himself in more serious matters.

The informant when questioned as to his opinion in regard to Father Coughlin's idea behind the request for the names of men in the service, advised that Father Coughlin was a very clever advertiser and used that method of appeal to the parents of men in the service, knowing that when they sent back the names of a relative in service they would include with that a check. . . . Informant did not believe that Father Coughlin had in mind . . . any subversive activity.[4]

John Spivak, in his interview with Monsignor Hickey, chancellor of the archdiocese of Detroit, probed further:

"Am I to understand that so far as Church authorities are concerned there is no recognized saint of soldiers?"

Msgr. Hickey sat quietly for a long while. Finally he said: "I think that is true. I have not been able to find one so recognized."

"Has a priest authority to pick a saint and announce him as the patron saint of soldiers?" . . .

"The answer depends upon what authorities he found to support it. Otherwise he could not." . . .

"Was the Diocese informed that St. Sebastian's Brigade was originally started in the guise of a subscription-getter for *Social Justice* magazine?"

"Not to my knowledge. . . . It's what you might call an extra-curricular activity. The Diocese isn't particularly interested in it." . . .

"All right," I smiled, "but there is an aspect of this extracurricular activity as you politely term it, about which I should appreciate an answer: 'Is the church interested when one of its priests . . . is now quietly building a powerful potential army within the armed forces of the United States?' "

He looked at me gravely and thoughtfully quoted a Latin phrase.

"I gather that the phrase means that an empire within an empire isn't good business?"

"An empire within an empire would not be good religion—nor good patriotism," he said slowly and emphatically.[5]

In the middle of the war, a clerical visitor to the Royal Oak Shrine reported on the success of Father Coughlin's entrepreneurship:

Several women were kneeling before the popular, exquisitely beautiful Shrine of St. Sebastian. . . . The number of members [of the Brigade] became so huge that it covered all the walls of the Shrine, obscuring the beauty of the marble and carving. . . . After 80,000 had been recorded, there was no more room for another name. All the names were taken down, and now they are kept in a special St. Sebastian room in the tower. There are now some 130,000 names recorded.[6]

The visitor drew these conclusions: "Of much greater significance [than treason] is the political value of this. . . . It ties several hundred thousand parents with Father Coughlin. When their sons return, at least out of respect for the old parents, many of the sons will join a society of St. Sebastian. This can well be a new and powerful pressure group."[7]

According to Spivak, Coughlin had obtained the names of 160,000 service personnel; "donations accompanying the request for prayer, averaged $3 each."[8]

In January 1944, J. Edgar Hoover marked the investigation of the St. Sebastian Brigade closed. John Spivak's article was never published. He had agreed to edit his interview with Monsignor Hickey to exclude what the prelate called "your interpretation of my facial expressions—raised eyebrows, whispered responses, and all those dramatics which leave a sinister impression upon the mind."[9]

Throughout the war, demands that Coughlin be prosecuted arose regularly—as regularly as he challenged the constraints of May 1942. The FBI feared the political consequences of prosecuting Coughlin, so it relied on the church to discipline him privately. Alleged Coughlin plots and subversive enterprises dotted the records federal agencies until World War II ended, but they were never made public.

In addition to organizing the St. Sebastian Brigade project, Coughlin was believed to be fishing once again in the troubled waters of Latin America. Since the mid-1930s when he had sought to involve Smedley Butler in an attempt to overthrow the Mexican government, reports had occasionally surfaced that he was working with right-wing revolutionaries who had been active in the Gold Shirts and their successor organization, the Sinarquistas. The FBI was aware of such rumors. Two days before Pearl Harbor, J. Edgar Hoover received an anonymous note with this cryptic warning: "Father Coughlin is up to something in the Latin Americas. It would be a good idea for authorities to check his activities on this important front."[10] Left-wing magazines circulated stories such as that which appeared in the New York–based *People's World* in July 1942 with the headline: "Coughlin Conspires with Axis Agents in Mexico." Referring to several exiled terrorists of the right, the article described a "Nazi inspired, Coughlin-backed" political movement:

> In Mexico Sinarquismo has won the nickname of "Falange en Huaraches"—the Barefoot Falange. Roughly, Sinarquisto is a

Mexican counterpart of Charles Coughlin's Christian Front, but far bigger, rougher and more immediately menacing. Sinarquist propaganda—canned for export in the Ibero-American Institute in Berlin—is simple, crude and effective among tens of thousands of Mexicans in the Southwest whose long-standing, justified grievances make easy sailing for trained agitators whose job is to crystallize discontent and promote disunity.[11]

Early in June 1942, memoranda began flowing between the State Department, the FBI, and the Department of the Treasury. The cause was a form letter Coughlin was sending to various Latin American consulates:

Beginning with this current scholastic year, [Coughlin's parish] high school will emphasize a junior course in commerce and finance stressing particularly a relationship with your esteemed country.

There are two services which your Embassy can supply and for which we will be deeply indebted: First, kindly put our high school on the mailing list for all literature published through your Embassy for general consumption; second, kindly supply our high school with the names of high schools in the principal cities of your Republic so that I may correspond with them immediately with the object in mind of obtaining names and addresses of young ladies and gentlemen attending your high schools in order to have them correspond with young ladies and gentlemen attending our high school.[12]

On June 15, Adolf Berle, assistant secretary of state, asked Hoover to report on "the activities of Reverend Coughlin in this matter as soon as possible." Four days later, *PM* bannered the story: "Coughlin Is Running Loose Again: Rabble-Rouser to Open Fascist School for Boys." Walter Prendergast, an assistant director of the Inter-American Affairs Office for President Roosevelt, sought advice on the article from the NCWC general director. Father Michael Ready replied that "PM blew the announcement of the Little Flower High School into a Father Coughlin plot to aid Generalissimo Franco and all that sort of nonsense. . . . The whole business was typically PM. In my opinion the PM story implied and insinuated a lot of stuff that some PM reporter wished were true." He concluded by saying that Coughlin had financed the school and "there is no more to the story than just that."[13]

By October, the FBI agent had concluded his probe of Coughlin's new educational venture:

Father Coughlin . . . proposed [the] plan. . . . Due to transportation difficulties the small boys of Berkeley, Michigan, who had been attending his Elementary School, were no longer attending and three rooms of the Elementary School located at the Shrine of the Little Flower were vacant and available for use. In addition, Father Coughlin stated that a great amount of bookkeeping equipment was available in the basement of the Shrine since the Social Justice magazine had ceased publication. Father Coughlin established a high school for boys to teach accounting as Father Coughlin felt that there would be a great demand for Certified Public Accountants. . . . Father Coughlin . . . sought to prepare students . . . so that they would . . . enter the South American market after the war.[14]

In January 1944, the director of naval intelligence communicated with the FBI about Coughlin's links to the Union Nacional Sinarquista. The bureau reported allegations that the priest supported the organization, but that "in each instance these reports have originated with Communist Front periodicals in the United States and Mexico." Released documents from federal agencies also reveal no pursuit of rumored links between Coughlin and Mexican politics or Hispanic groups in the Southwest United States.

By the spring of 1944, a new Latin American scare had emerged, this time preceded by rumors that Father Coughlin intended to resume broadcasting from a Mexican station. This news came from indicted ultra-right-wing publicist Court Asher, who proclaimed in his *X-Ray* publication, "Thank God, with Father Coughlin back on the air, it will be just too bad for the double-dealing, crooked-tongue, New Deal deceptive sons of Satan. The truth will make us well and give the Jew Deal a headache."[15]

By April 1944, for reasons unrelated to any Latin American forays, the FBI found itself entering the Shrine of the Little Flower to eavesdrop on Coughlin's parish talks. Word had leaked out about a series of the priest's special Lenten sermons. Beginning in February 1944, Coughlin was reported by the editor of the *Hour,* Albert Kahn, to be mixing religious statements of the Lenten services with "some very startling statements which show why it was to the interests of certain groups in America to keep the Father off the air."[16] The FBI was given reports on Coughlin's remarks that included these notes:

> In a sarcastic vein he spoke of England's entry into the war to save Poland and now "Churchill is giving Poland to Bloody Joe. . . . I say that compared to Stalin Hitler is a piker. . . . Many of you workers were led around like sheep by the Marxists. . . . At the end of this war there will be 30 millions of unemployed in this country. Are you going back to soup lines? Do you want to again sell apples to each other?"
> The attendance was about 1300 persons.[17]

It did not take long for the national news media to return to Coughlin as a subject. Noted labor columnist Victor Riesel was the first to write a lead story, on March 16, 1944, asserting that "Father Coughlin is coming back":

> I sat with 1,000 of his followers last night in the auditorium of his marble-studded $5,000,000 Shrine . . . and heard him attack Britain, Russia and the war.
> I heard him charge, in his old blood-and-thunder Coughlin style, that "It matters not what military force wins this war."[18]

Not to be outdone, *PM* followed the next day with its own story on the Coughlin speeches, which included a lengthy review of the career of the radio priest and again calling for his indictment on sedition charges. Four days later the same newspaper carried a story entitled, "Agents to Hear Coughlin Talk," and reporting, "In addition to government agents the audience [will] contain representatives of several patriotic and anti-Nazi organizations, [and] reporters and observers from Archbishop Edward Mooney's offices. Though silent on the reemergence of Coughlinism, the Chancery is known to be deeply perturbed."[19]

There was now a special air of expectancy surrounding the priest's next Lenten talk. Would Coughlin offer any openly seditious remarks? The *Chicago Sun* correspondent filed this story:

It was like turning the calendar back six or eight years to hear Father Charles E. Coughlin return to the oratorical wars. . . . Within the handsome church structure, largely built by radio donations, his audience listened reverently and attentively to a talk that would in this place have brought an uneasy, queasy feeling to many not his flock.

We should love Hitler, he said in effect, for Christians love their enemies instead of hating them. "God made Hitler," he said, "just as he made you. Do not follow the easy path of hatred. . . .

"Americans at present are being air-conditioned, no I haven't just the right word there, they are being radio-conditioned, to give Russia's legions too much credit," he said. "Meanwhile those of us who would like to tell another version are forced into a modern catacomb."[20]

Two days later, Drew Pearson reported on "a barrage of pressure on the Justice Department to indict him [Coughlin] . . . for sabotaging public opinion."[21]

In the wake of the outcry, Attorney General Biddle ordered the FBI to monitor all of Coughlin's sermons "for the next several Sundays." A teletype summary was to be forwarded "with a detailed air mail letter just as soon as [the local agent] could get it out."[22] Hoover was informed a day later that Coughlin would deliver no Sunday sermons but would continue the Wednesday Lenten addresses. He was also told in the same telegram, "One previous Wednesday Sermon covered, nothing subversive noted."[23]

The intense coverage of the Shrine was received with a decidedly mixed response by Archbishop Mooney. He had been informed indirectly of the government action in his Royal Oak parish by his close friend and colleague Michael Ready. Mooney penned a handwritten note expressing his concerns:

I was surprised to learn, through your recent letter, that Mr. Biddle is taking seriously the agitation started by the New York Post and P.M. . . . Personally I think that the Post and PM are playing right into the hand of our friend—and probably trying to embarrass Mr. Biddle as well. . . .

I do not like to spy on church activities in R. [Royal] O.

[Oak]. But if I get definite information about anything wrong there from the F.B.I. or any other reliable informant I will not hesitate to make the boy submit in advance the text of every pronouncement he dares to make in the routine of church activity. That is about the only thing now in which he does not have to submit copy.[24]

As the war moved to its conclusion, each successive incident exposed the fragile nature of the 1942 silencing compact.

Outbreaks of violent anti-Semitism occurred that could be traced to Coughlin's influence. National surveys over this period showed an increase in hostile attitudes toward Jews.[25] Because the mobilization for war brought together large numbers of otherwise isolated listeners and former Coughlin supporters, there was now a critical mass present in military units, which brought to the surface widely held anti-Jewish prejudice. At various times and in a number of letters to editors of local newspapers, Coughlin's supporters in the armed forces praised his name. One example surfaced overseas in England, in the London-based Catholic *Herald,* written by a U.S. Army corporal:

Like all great characters in history, he has experienced victory and defeat; loyalty and betrayal; leadership and obedience; eloquence and silence. . . . We shall defend his personality against the world. . . . We shall beg God to hasten the day when once again his voice may ring out over the airways to protect our Church, our country, our priesthood and our fellow citizens against all our enemies.[26]

Coughlin was a wartime threat not simply because he could poison the minds of inductees but because civilians, amid the curtailments and sacrifices of the war, seemed to have become more anti-Semitic as well. Strongholds of the Christian Front were still active, and among them, Father Coughlin's influence was still being felt.

The Royal Oak priest's undertow on civilian and military morale concerned the Roosevelt administration. This wave of hate reached its crest in the last full year of the war, 1944, and it occurred in Coughlin's mightiest stronghold: Boston. In October, *PM* ran a detailed story:

Christian Front Hoodlums Terrorize Boston Jews

In Dorchester, an overwhelmingly predominant Jewish area with about 6,000 Jews living within its borders, violence today has reached such heights that its people have taken matters into their own hands. OCD [Office of Civilian Defense] air raid wardens and auxiliary police are patrolling the streets at night to protect children of Dorchester from attacks by groups of young anti-Semitic hoodlums who rove the area apparently unmolested by police or local officials.[27]

Referring to a "blanket of silence" over the past fourteen months, the *PM* journalist criticized the "hush-hush, hands-off" policy of police and political leaders in Massachusetts such as Governor (later Senator) Saltonstall and Mayor Maurice Tobin of Boston. The reporter noted:

I have seen affidavits written and signed in the scrawling hand of Dorchester's Jewish children. I have copies of these statements in which they recount how they were beaten by gangs of toughs, beaten because they were Jewish. . . .

Franklin Park . . . is unsafe today, for Jewish children to play in. A neighborhood roller skating rink is unusable by Jewish children because according to local Jewish leaders, young anti-Semites—girls as well as boys—have made it their headquarters from which they sally forth nightly to go "Jew hunting" as they call it. . . .

These gangs of marauders roam the streets of Dorchester at night screaming imprecations against its residents. . . .

Miss Frances Sweeney, director of the American Irish Association, a leading anti-fascist group here, says: "These attacks on Jewish children are the complete responsibility of Gov. Saltonstall, Mayor Tobin, the church and clergy—all of whom have for three years buckpassed and ignored this tragedy."[28]

Warning that the attacks would lead to riots if not stopped, the *PM* correspondent described them as "a manifestation that the Christian Front still thrives and is encouraged in Boston."[29]

The key figure in the Boston front was Francis P. Moran, a former seminarian whose role closely paralleled that of "Jack" Cassidy. He had been in contact with the German consul in Boston and had shown films depicting the overwhelming power of the Wehrmacht and had counseled a number of his followers to avoid complying with the military draft. Father Coughlin was in close contact with Moran and had praised him highly, calling him in 1939 the "National Director of the Christian Front."[30]

Luther Conant, a journalist who had written extensively in Boston's leading newspapers, became so deeply concerned about the threat posed by Boston's Christian Front that he asked to conduct extensive investigative work on the group and to pose as a sympathizer:

> The City Editor of the *Herald,* on his own initiative, gave me the go-ahead [to] act as a "mole." Under this guise I sought out the Front's aggressive leader, Francis P. Moran. . . . I stayed on good terms with Moran and one day, while he was out of his office on an errand, I did a quick search. The files, disappointingly, were locked; but his desk drawers were open. In the middle drawer— face up—was a letter to him from Father Coughlin. The letter staring at me from Moran's desk drawer gave the complete lie . . . to his [Coughlin's] disavowal of Christian Front connections. . . .
>
> Moran, in his office, was a quiet-spoken, well-mannered person. Moran, on the platform of a Christian Front meeting, was evil incarnate, with the ability and technique to arouse his audience to a frenzy and a fanaticism of hate. One favorite ploy of his was to wait until he had gotten his audience to the proper pitch . . . dramatically stop talking . . . wait for silence in the hall . . . and ask: "Who are the blood suckers plotting to send our boys to die in England?"
>
> The crowd would roar back: "The Jews."[31]

Christian Front agitation in Boston was of no small consequence to the Roosevelt administration as it geared up for the 1944 election. War weariness coupled with a revival of isolationist sentiments offered a clear danger to both FDR and the Democratic party leaders in Massachusetts. Several months before the *PM* story had been published, at the suggestion of Myron Taylor (FDR's special representative to the Vatican), Monsignor Michael Ready was asked to meet with Benjamin Cohen, a

Roosevelt adviser, regarding outbreaks of anti-Semitism. Taylor told Ready that "representatives of the Jewish faith have brought to my attention what they consider to be a very serious opposition which is developing in Boston and even at Harvard."[32]

A few days after meeting with Cohen, Ready reported to Archbishop Mooney on the conversation:

> Mr. Cohen said he had spoken to Myron Taylor soon before he left for the Vatican and expressed grave fears about many anti-Jewish campaigns in strong Catholic centers. Mr. Cohen said to Mr. Taylor that there was a current belief "in his group" that Fr. Coughlin was influencing his old centers of loyalty and that he was preparing to make an active campaign against the administration this year on the basis of its Jewish control. Mr. Cohen thought the Holy Father and others at the Vatican should know these fears of Jewish leaders in the U.S.A. and take preventive measures before great harm is done not only to the Jews but to the Catholic Church in the U.S. Mr. Cohen was sure that the reaction to "Coughlinism" this time would be a vigorous anti-Catholic campaign.[33]

Ready, however, only suggested to Cohen that the media outlets that were raising the name of Coughlin were owned by Jews. He then wrote to Archbishop Mooney and hinted that "our people in Detroit" were thinking of giving Coughlin a chance to "answer his lying critics."[34] Once again, the church was hardly unified in opposition to the rogue priest.

In September 1942, Alexi Pelypenko provided a naval intelligence officer with a copy of a deposition detailing his meetings with Coughlin. J. Edgar Hoover was later to write off Pelypenko as an unreliable agent because he violated a prime rule of his agency: no outside publicity of its activities. From almost the moment Pelypenko landed in the United States, he was under surveillance as a former German agent and was so indiscreet as to tell an Immigration Department official that he was withholding information from the FBI. This fact, coupled with the Ukrainian priest's effort to sell a book on his espionage activities, *How I Captured German Agents,* led to him and his son being kept at the alien detention facility of Ellis Island.[35]

Pelypenko's 1942 deposition found its way into the hands of special prosecutor Maloney, several journalists, and a book agent. The FBI soon learned of this. Retrieval of all of the Pelypenko-Coughlin affidavits involved a six-month effort. Finally, with the leak plugged, Coughlin silenced, and the war over—the Pelypenkos having returned to Argentina in 1945—it appeared that the troublesome affair of the two priests had ended.

But suddenly word got about in 1946 that the Pelypenko affidavit was about to be published in George Seldes's widely read muckraking newsletter, *In Fact*. The FBI director sought strong backing from the Criminal Division of the Justice Department and called for a united front against any unfavorable publicity: "I do not intend to permit the activities of this individual to embarrass the Bureau and I expect you to be guided accordingly."[36] When T. Lamar Caudle, assistant attorney general, seemed reluctant to spring to the defense of the bureau, Hoover was more than perturbed.

Assistant Attorney General Caudle had only a few days to review the complex set of files and make a recommendation; there was no time to gather any new information. He made two proposals: that Pelypenko, described in internal FBI memos as "an unfrocked priest," had proven to be "utterly unreliable" and that "the matters contained . . . were investigated in detail and found to be without basis in fact sufficient to justify any action against Coughlin."[37] These assertions were leaked widely to the press.

That same day, February 11, 1946, the Coughlin evidence appeared in George Seldes's *In Fact* newsletter, bearing the headline, "Suppressed Dep't of Justice Document First Evidence Father Coughlin Was Paid Nazi Agent." In the introduction of the reprinting of the entire Pelypenko affidavit, Albert Kahn noted, "On two occasions during the Nuremberg Trials the name of Charles E. Coughlin has been mentioned." The first occurred when "the obscene pogromist Julius Streicher said he wanted Coughlin as one of his defense witnesses. The second was when the British prosecutor, Sir David Maxwell Fyfe, quoted a confidential memorandum of Joachim von Ribbentrop, head of the Foreign Office in the Nazi regime, in which Coughlin was cited as an example of the far-reaching influence of Nazi propaganda."[38] Following the publishing of the *In Fact* story, there was a campaign by New York's *PM* asking its readers to vote on whether they wanted the Coughlin case reopened. But Hoover's public relations campaign succeeded. Several journalists, including Drew Pearson, ignored the story. Just two members of Congress bothered to write to Hoover seeking further assurance that the evidence against Charles Coughlin was without foundation. But when Pelypenko had first surfaced, he had genuinely worried Hoover, and the Coughlin supporters were always prepared to make trouble for the bureau.

Midway through World War II, the Michigan Civil Rights League, a liberal organization serving as a watchdog over far-right activism, received a confidential report from a Catholic clergyman who had met with Charles Coughlin at the Royal Oak Shrine. It revealed a mood of resignation and pessimism by the silenced priest: "Things are now so bad that if I give my name openly to any kind of movement, it ruins the movement." The visitor's report went on to note that Coughlin felt "resigned to the fact that he can work only indirectly, that is, through his friends. But even with them he confesses that he has to be extremely careful that through some unfortunate oversight his emissary not be exposed." In reporting that he was "strictly confined to dealing with matters of his parish," Coughlin spoke of his isolation and the fact that "his occasional visitors no longer get political opinions out of him. . . . He complains that he is 'persecuted' and 'must bide his time.' "[39]

Coughlin's strongest political influence had always been in the East, and his supporters remained active there. A rally in New York City in the fall of 1945 was described as follows:

> [They] stood in reverence as the hall darkened and spotlights played on a picture of Coughlin, hung over the center of the state. . . . The rally . . . attracted some 600 persons. They paid $1 admission. During the evening it was announced that all funds raised would be sent to Father Coughlin. It was broadly intimated that this money was to be used to get him back on the air. . . . One of the prominent speakers said . . . "We are friends of Father Coughlin in his silence, and we will be friends of Father Coughlin when he again speaks over the air . . . he will be stronger than ever."[40]

When, a few months earlier, a petition had begun circulating in several Midwest communities calling for the return of Father Coughlin to radio broadcasting, Coughlin himself was quick to mollify his ecclesiastical superiors, albeit in somewhat ambiguous terms: "I totally disavow this circular and consider its issuance a semifraud."[41]

The priest did what he could after the war—which was not much. In the spring of 1947, at the exclusive Detroit Athletic Club, he attended the twenty-fifth wedding anniversary of station WJR owner George "Dick" Richards. Kim Sigler, the governor of Michigan, K. T. Keller and William Knudson of General Motors, Henry Ford II, and Eddie Rickenbacker were also in attendance. Crowning the group were William Paley, president of CBS, and FBI director J. Edgar Hoover. The radio priest delivered one of the congratulatory speeches to his longtime friend and media mentor. One labor newspaper sounded an alarm about the gathering—"Coughlin Plots Return to Air; Meets Sigler; Are Auto Moguls Grooming Coughlin for Comeback?" But nothing resulted from the evening's events.

There was, however, one last occasion when Coughlin received, for a brief moment, the kind of national media attention he had enjoyed at the height of his fame. Surprisingly, in this final episode of notoriety, the priest received the united support of both his ecclesiastical superiors and the Catholic lay community. As with virtually every other critical event in his career, Coughlin became entangled in a highly personal and bitter dispute with another public figure.

Muckraking newspaper columnist Drew Pearson had made Charles Coughlin a target of his political attacks for many years. From Huey Long in the early 1930s to Robert Welch, head of the John Birch Society in the 1960s, Pearson had mounted scathing denunciations of his rogues' gallery of public villains. According to the late columnist's son-in-law, choosing Coughlin was a singularly courageous act, since other commentators "feared to tangle . . . because of his cloth."[42]

While Pearson was a supporter of FDR's New Deal, when the columnist accused General MacArthur of seeking special influence to aid his promotion, Roosevelt was so angry that while addressing the cabinet, he threatened to put Pearson and his newspaper out of business. MacArthur sued Pearson and the Patterson newspaper chain for $1,750,000.[43]

In 1949, Pearson believed he had uncovered another piece of scandalous information—an affidavit on file in the Internal Revenue Service, the contents of which Pearson made public on his weekly radio program:

The Justice and Treasury Departments have ordered the prosecution of Dr. Bernard F. Gariepy of Royal Oak, Michigan, in a strange income-tax case indirectly involving Father Coughlin. Dr. Gariepy's defense is that Father Coughlin gave him $68,000 because of alienation of affection of Mrs. Gariepy by the radio priest. The Justice Department plans to prosecute Gariepy anyway.[44]

In effect, Gariepy was claiming that the money was not taxable because of the purpose for which he had received it.

When the columnist's program aired, local Detroit newspapers headlined the item on their front pages: "Commentator's Love-Payoff Story: Coughlin Denies Charge" and "Heart Balm Payoff by Coughlin Denied."[45] One day before the story hit the headlines, Coughlin issued a formal press statement on the story:

> Without any endeavor to verify his scandal-mongering, Mr. Pearson was instrumental in smearing my reputation before the American public. . . .
>
> It is a Pearsonian lie to affirm that I transacted any financial business with or bestowed any funds upon or paid any hush money to Dr. Bernard Gariepy. . . .
>
> As for alienating the affection of Mrs. Bernard Gariepy, I happen to be the Pastor of the Shrine of the Little Flower and enjoy the assistance of four curates, one of whom listened to the cause of Dr. Bernard Gariepy some years ago when he was seeking to divorce his wife. Once and just once I listened to Mrs. Bernard Gariepy who protested the divorce. On no other occasion have I ever met the lady either officially, socially or privately. The Gariepys are not and never have been members of the Shrine of the Little Flower.
>
> As yet I do not know if Dr. Bernard Gariepy was responsible for the lies and filthy insinuations broadcast by Drew Pearson. All I do know is that the Federal Communications Commission is inviting charges of Supineness in permitting the type of Drew Pearson to assail not only me by innuendo but the whole American Catholic clergy and laity.[46]

Three days later, the *Michigan Catholic,* expressing the official view of the Detroit diocese, published "Time to Clear Air of Pearson Poison," an article that asked: "How much longer are the American people going to tolerate Drew Pearson?" Angrily, the article noted:

Pearson's vicious slander upon Father Charles E. Coughlin . . . was an insult equally to Fr. Coughlin, to all Catholic priests and to the Catholic people who revere their priests.

Pearson's charges have been proved a lie by the testimony of Dr. Bernard Gariepy and his former wife. . . . If American Catholic and other decent-minded citizens of this land do not effectively demand that the author of this malicious slander be debarred from the air, then they deserve to be victims of whatever other scurrilous falsehoods Pearson may see fit to utter.

We call upon WXYZ, the American Broadcasting Co. and the program's sponsor, the Lee Hat Co., to disavow and repudiate Drew Pearson by canceling their business arrangement with him.[47]

In his diary, Drew Pearson recounts that "everyone I talked to figured that Coughlin had an affair with Mrs. Gariepy and also with various other women." The journalist added an explanatory note: "He is the most powerful man in the community [of Royal Oak] and was considered the most unscrupulous."[48]

The Gariepy situation was remarkably ironic. The same silencing tactics that had been used against Coughlin in his broadcasting days were now being used against Pearson on Coughlin's behalf. In his response to Pearson, the priest had called for Catholic solidarity, and for the first time since his earliest days of national prominence, he was able to rally it. Monsignor Maurice Sheehy, who had delivered a biting attack against Coughlin a decade earlier, now wrote to Frank Lee, owner of Lee Hats, the company sponsoring Pearson:

The charge made . . . is not only false but it will probably be the basis of a libel suit against your company as sponsors of the broadcast. I do not know where Pearson picked up this misinformation. I used to disagree with Father Coughlin on some public issues but, since he has ceased to broadcast, he has done a superb pastoral job in Royal Oak and he does a great deal of charitable work in addition. . . .

I think you should suggest to Pearson that he either send a special investigator to Detroit to rectify his mistake or that he publicly apologize.[49]

In response to the outpouring of criticism, Pearson struck back, as one close associate put it, as a "Quaker with a conscience":

> Certain religious leaders have been trying to persuade my sponsors to take me off the air because I accurately reported the income tax case of Dr. Bernard Gariepy . . . whose defense indirectly involved Father Coughlin. I would like to say to these clerics and my sponsors that all my life I have opposed Father Coughlin and the intolerance he stands for and I do not propose to change now.[50]

When the initial story broke, both Mrs. Gariepy and her husband had made statements to the press. Bernard Gariepy asserted that "neither in . . . testimony nor in any memorandum or brief filed by me or on my behalf has any charge of any kind been made against Father Coughlin nor mention made of his name in connection with the receipt by me or the payment to me of any money, at any time, or for any reason." For her part, Mrs. Gariepy declared, "When I lived in Royal Oak I attended Father Coughlin's church, although I was not a parishioner. I spoke to him only once and that was when the question of divorce came up. I don't think Father Coughlin would know me if we passed on the street."[51] In response, Pearson told his radio audience that "despite denials, the income tax case of Dr. Bernard F. Gariepy, indirectly involving Father Coughlin, will be brought to trial. When the trial takes place we will see who was really telling the truth."[52]

The newly appointed U.S. attorney in Detroit, Edward T. Kane, issued a statement at the beginning of May 1949 that "there was absolutely no evidence that Father Coughlin was mixed up in the Gariepy tax case."[53] Pearson was incensed and demanded action to retract this effort to keep Coughlin out of the case. John Beltaire, the sales and advertising vice president of the Lee Hat Company, stated that he was neutral on the controversy but urged that "the matter be settled once and for all. If Father Coughlin was involved, let's bring it out into the open." He also advised Pearson that if the story was a mistake, "I personally believe this should also be acknowledged."[54]

On June 8 Pearson confided to his journal, "The Lees are getting nasty. They served me with another ultimatum that I was to get off the air by June 12, though I have a two-year contract yet to run. They want me to cancel with no compensation." A now deeply worried Pearson noted in his diary on July 17, "My last broadcast for Lee Hats." He contacted Supreme Court Justice Frank Murphy and asked for help, but none was forthcoming. Murphy later quipped: "The Church was almost down on him as it was on me." On July 30 Pearson noted in his diary: "[I was] warned Spellman might ban column [sic] for all Catholics."[55]

The trial of Dr. Bernard Gariepy for tax evasion commenced in Detroit federal court on October 15. Despite the strenuous efforts of defense attorney John Babcock to forbid the admission of statements by his client made to IRS agents and his accountant about the involvement of "a prominent Royal Oak person," the issue was raised at the trial. Clarence Kitchen, an IRS investigator, testified that Bernard Gariepy had shown him a cold air duct [where money was hidden] and "other money he had in his pocket. There were four $1,000 bills and a check for $10,000." Kitchen told the court that Gariepy had said, "Why don't you take it with you and apply it on what I owe." Kitchen testified that he told Gariepy he could not accept the money. Statements obtained in the preliminary tax investigation given to both Kitchen and an attorney for Gariepy contained a number of references to "another party." Kitchen had asked Gariepy whether the person who furnished him the money owed it to him. The reply was: "He did in a way. It was a way of easing his conscience."[56]

Charles Coughlin, neatly attired and wearing white gloves, was called as a witness. No, he testified, he had never had any relationship with Mrs. Bernard Gariepy, except to counsel her once about her marriage. This, he stated, had occurred in his office at the Shrine of the Little Flower. Coughlin also mentioned that he had been treated by Dr. Gariepy, as had his mother. In her testimony, Mrs. Gariepy corroborated the priest's testimony. On November 8, Gariepy was found guilty of two counts of tax evasion and was later sentenced to two and one-half years in federal prison. The sentencing judge, Frank A. Picard, offered what one local paper called a "withering 20 minute rebuke":

> It was your duty to bring the facts to this court if Father Coughlin had done these despicable things. . . . It was your duty as a Catholic yourself to be a good citizen. . . . You told others that you received this money [$60,000] from Fr. Coughlin, but you would not tell this court or a jury. . . . When confronted by rev-

enue agents, you gave an explanation which would have been a good defense if it were true.

Now, Dr. Gariepy, in my opinion, after you had brought in the name of Father Coughlin, through others, in an attempt to justify the increased net worth of your assets, there was only one fair, decent, honorable course for you to pursue—either before the case came to trial or during the trial. . . .

In neither testifying against Fr. Coughlin nor clearing his name you have given comfort to every anti-Catholic bigot in the country.[57]

One year after the original radio broadcast, Mary Gariepy sued Drew Pearson for libel. The case was a marathon one, spanning dozens of procedural motions, two jury trials, and more than five years. In his own defense, Pearson paid for private investigators and made a number of trips to Detroit to obtain evidence. An internal memo from the columnist's attorney noted that "the chief difficulty in lining up character witnesses will be that no one will want to testify in a way that might arouse the enmity of Father Coughlin."[58] One potential witness against Mrs. Gariepy changed her mind largely because, as a maid and a black woman, she was afraid that she would not be believed and would be unable to work again.

On February 2, 1955, the jury found Pearson innocent and required Mrs. Gariepy to pay his court costs. A motion to set aside this judgment was filed one month later but was denied. Despite the victory, Pearson was still uncertain about the core issue of the libel action:

This case has now gone . . . to the Supreme Court, has lost me a sponsor, has required innumerable trips to Detroit, plus various depositions; and I still don't know where we are. I have talked to various people in Royal Oak, including the police force, but still don't know whether Mrs. Gariepy was intimate with Father Coughlin or not. Lots of people in Royal Oak suspect it.[59]

But the lesson of the Gariepy affair was clear for all to see: Charles Coughlin had been returned to the bosom of his church. For the priest, it was a moment of affirmation and a tangible acknowledgment that his fidelity to the silencing agreement of 1942 had brought him a legitimacy he had not enjoyed since the earliest days of his national fame.

Years later, the former Mrs. Gariepy was adamant in her denial that any love affair had occurred with Coughlin and laid the source of the story to her brother-in-law, Edward Gariepy, a member of the Shrine church who "had sought employment from Father Coughlin at one time." When he did not get the work, Mrs. Gariepy said he turned against Coughlin. Mrs. Gariepy referred to the role Edward and his wife had had in breaking up her marriage to Bernard—the "rotten brother" who "cooked up this idea of me and Father Coughlin. . . . I never knew him! I saw him up on the altar and that was it. I never had a word with him!"[60]

During my interview with the former Mrs. Gariepy, she told of being married twice since her divorce from Gariepy and of having to move frequently to avoid publicity and harm to her son as he was growing up. She mentioned that she received help from friends of Father Coughlin in pursuing her suits against Pearson and said her only reason for taking these court actions was her concern about the welfare of her child.

15

The Ghost of Royal Oak

Christ and the Apostles were Jews and the first 33 popes were Jews. Among the last 10 we've had three were predominantly Jewish. I can't be anti-Jewish!

Charles Coughlin, *Religious News Service,* August 15, 1973

If Christ Himself was assassinated by His own people and betrayed by one of His closest friends, what should any priest expect?

Charles Coughlin to Edward J. Hickey, May 19, 1976

A FTER THE SILENCING, the Shrine of the Little Flower became a kind of prosperous manorial estate for Coughlin. It was a haven and retreat—the very core of a splendid miniature religious kingdom. One journalist from the loyal *Royal Oak Tribune* who had observed the priest for his entire career described Coughlin as "living in oriental splendor."[1] Across the street from his church, Coughlin enjoyed the hospitality of Cotter's Inn, a popular roadhouse-style restaurant. He dined either at his own curtained-off table or a private room in the rear of the facility. He was part owner of the establishment.

Throughout his lifetime, Charles Coughlin enjoyed speculating in stocks and exploring avenues of profitable investment, for his own personal benefit and to enhance the financial position of his various enterprises, including his beloved Shrine, and he acquired significant wealth. A $900,000 bank account at Barclay's in England had been located by Justice Department investigators just a few days after the silencing agreement in May 1942.[2]

In February 1935, Congressman John Lesinski of Michigan had charged that Sylvester J. Christie, manager of the State of Michigan Home Owners Loan Corporation (one of the New Deal agencies set up to stimulate the buying of real estate), was running "the grandest racket on the part of real estate sharks." Lesinski noted that "Mr. Christie is Father Coughlin's appointment, and Mr. Christie is, by the way, an usher in Father Coughlin's church."[3] In later years, Christie remained a friend and source of indulging the radio priest's lifelong passion for real estate investment. Up to almost the last minute of his life, Coughlin kept in touch with his investment broker regarding local market values. That same friend and business adviser was but one of several people who over the years provided the priest with information and advice on land investments. Coughlin acquired homes in Arizona, Florida, and suburban Detroit.[4] One attorney who worked with the priest on his business investments estimated that at this time he was "well on the way to being a millionaire."[5]

In the decades following the silencing, as had been true before it, few who worked at the Shrine of the Little Flower were neutral toward Coughlin. Parishioners and priests ranged from extravagant praise to bitter denunciation. There was an inner circle of deep loyalty, honed through decades of service, and they wielded a special kind of personal power that defined life at the Shrine. During the last years that Charles Coughlin served as its pastor, they were nicknamed "The Holy Ghosts." Ever vigilant lest a new criticism emerge in print, they steadfastly shied away from interviews and kept in the shadows. Their anonymity had been severely breached just once: each had been subpoenaed and testified before the Washington grand jury investigation in the spring of 1942.

A great deal of Charles Coughlin's pride and energy in his later years was devoted to two high schools, one for boys and the other for girls, that had been built at the Shrine in the late 1930s and early 1940s. An attorney who was associated with most of the Shrine's social and business enterprises recalls that Coughlin "was very demanding. . . . He was a disciplinarian. When things didn't go right with the senior class . . . he dressed them down. I remember parents were crying [when] their [children's] conduct and so forth was not what it should be."[6] One former parishioner described an incident that drove him away from the Shrine school:

My dad didn't pay the tuition one year. I didn't know it. . . .
[When] they used to give the report cards out . . . they had the se-

niors, juniors, sophomores [there, and] I was a freshman. . . . It was in the gymnasium of the girls school. I was pretty far back. Father Coughlin used to give out the cards for the whole high school. Every name was called and you walked up . . . and I marched up that aisle, and he said, "Mr._____, you have a delinquent tuition bill and therefore you will not be receiving your report card." I just made a left turn in front of one of the classes, right out the exit. Never went back to school again. I wouldn't go back into school. I told my mom. It was a bad embarrassment. I never went back to Shrine.[7]

Charles Coughlin was also a demanding priest for the altar boys of the Shrine church: "He was a domineering, highly meticulous, precise individual. Almost to the point of fright. . . . It was as if we were a couple of male servants. Our job was to serve him."[8] There was much fear and trembling at the Shrine, recalled the former groundskeeper: "I remember his assistants . . . they used to shake, physically shake in front of him. They really didn't say a word when he was around. . . . The nuns used to cower in the corner. He had such a dominant personality . . . you felt there was a kind of militariness about it, too. I think he liked that. He saw himself as a Prussian general."[9] One of the priests who worked with Coughlin at the Shrine offered a more graphic description: "Father Coughlin would pin your chest full of medals and then, as time went by, he'd pick them off you one by one."[10]

The Shrine's groundskeeper told of an incident that left an indelible impression of Coughlin's dangerous impulsiveness. One day he was summoned to the priest's office and found Coughlin pacing and looking outside at a gas station that had, in the heyday of Coughlin's fame, been the location for "Shrine Super Service" and had offered a convenient fill-up for parishioners, visitors, and passing tourists. After World War II it had been leased to Standard Oil, and it continued to earn revenue for the Shrine. The station, he said, was scruffy and was going downhill.

Coughlin then exclaimed: "I want you to blow the bastard up!" When the groundskeeper asked what would happen if he were caught, the priest reassured him, "Don't worry, I'll make sure nothing will happen to you." After leaving for the day, "I went home and told my wife, I was shook." The groundskeeper added that "nothing came of it because he never called me back. . . . And whenever we met thereafter, he kind of avoided me. . . . I think he figured, 'I went a little too far.'"[11]

*   *   *

Edward Mooney was made a cardinal in February 1946 and died on Coughlin's sixty-seventh birthday, October 25, 1958. In the interim between Mooney's promotion and his death, Coughlin managed a rehabilitation from disgrace as a soft-spoken and contented parish priest. It was hardly an easy transition. In 1952, the radio priest gave his first public address outside his parish at his place of birth, Hamilton, Ontario. *MacLean's* magazine demonstrated the type of press coverage that Coughlin could forever expect—a feature article entitled "Hamilton's Holy Terror Returns for a Visit."[12] That same year, there was an unannounced visitor to the Shrine of the Little Flower who also did a little to help Coughlin's rehabilitation. Douglas MacArthur deviated from his itinerary to motor from downtown Detroit out to Twelve Mile Road and Woodward in Royal Oak. He had just given his famous "Old Soldier's" farewell address and was contemplating running for the presidency. A crowd of admiring parishioners gathered around his convertible. He was photographed shaking hands with Coughlin.

In December 1953, Coughlin made his first public address in the Detroit diocese since the silencing. Here, finally, came some protective support by chancery officials:

> Approximately a week ago, Father Coughlin telephoned to inquire whether or not it would be necessary . . . for him to have a manuscript. . . . After consultation with Cardinal Mooney, Father Weier advised him that, although he would not be asked to submit the manuscript for previous review, he should nevertheless have a manuscript for his own protection just in case the newspapers might misquote him.[13]

Coughlin submitted an advance manuscript anyway and was asked to reword some passages that speculated about future trends, to indicate that they were merely his own opinions. The talk made local headlines: "Fr. Coughlin's Old Fire Blazes on Eve of Trip."[14]

Talk of a guaranteed annual wage was in the news, and Coughlin cast himself once again in the role of a prophet, reminding his listeners that he had advocated such a policy back in 1931. (He mentioned that the idea appeared in a book he published that year, *The Red Serpent*.) The priest did deliver radio addresses with that title, but no such book ever was published.) Coughlin touched rather generally on several other domestic and foreign policy issues:

> In my opinion every factory worker who has the responsibility of a family should come first in our consideration when we begin talking of tax reduction. Some legal way must be discovered to free the working man from taxes on food, on clothing, on housing and necessary transportation.
>
> Those ideas are twenty-three years old. It is to be hoped that, within the next twenty-three years, the brilliant minds of the brilliant Americans can translate them into realities. . . . Quickly the day will arrive when Satan-ridden Russia will succumb to the Masses you offer, the Communions you receive, the good deeds you perform, the prayers you say.[15]

The talk was favorably received, mainly for its support of autoworkers. The media attention remained local.

Nearly two years passed before news media outside Detroit picked up the threads of the priest's career. A *New York Post* story became a prototype for many subsequent "Where are they now?" news articles. The lead to the piece read: "Father Coughlin Has Mellowed." The priest was quoted as saying that he was "delighted to be out of public life. If I had to do it over again, I don't think I'd go in for radio broadcasting. You can only reach people superficially that way. Besides, I don't think a priest should go into politics." Coughlin was described by the *Post* columnist as sometimes sounding "downright bored. . . . No longer can his utterances be remotely regarded as 'controversial.' Indeed, among his admirers there is some doubt whether he cares to orate any more."[16]

When asked about his talks dealing with Jews and communism, the priest told his interviewer: "I know most of the Communist leaders were Gentile. But I was trying to prod the Jews in America to attack Communism . . . the same way they were attacking Nazism in Germany." The writer swallowed the rehabilitated Coughlin wholly, noting that the priest appeared to offer some regrets about the past and that "he would have been wiser if he had repudiated the frenzied Christian Front, but it was hard to let his friends down." He offered mild support for Truman and Eisenhower but when asked about Joseph McCarthy replied testily, "Now please. Why should I stick my neck out? Haven't I had enough trouble?" The columnist remarked that "politics, one gathered, just did not interest him too greatly. He spoke without fervor and with the relaxation of a man who does not have to make headlines."[17]

Two months later, *Life* magazine carried a brief story on Coughlin, entitled "Calm for a Stormy Priest." He was pictured by his famous Shrine tower, surrounded by happy-faced young children. Here was a grandfatherly figure, a subdued firebrand. The article read:

> The Coughlin of the 1950s and 1960s appeared to be a man who had mellowed considerably, a man at peace. . . . "It was a horrible mistake to enter politics. . . . If I had it to do over again I would not talk about economic and political change, but would speak in terms of ethical changes and Christ's way of life . . . every man has to mature a little bit, and make an act of contrition sometime during his life."[18]

Coughlin's influence nevertheless persisted through the civil rights era. During the Kennedy presidency, he offered consistent praise of the young Catholic chief executive, but following an explicit warning given to him by Joseph Kennedy's close associate, Philip Smith, he made no open endorsements in the 1960 campaign. A priest serving in Coughlin's Shrine dubiously claims that the Kennedys visited the Shrine often after the election and that Coughlin's advice was solicited:

> President Kennedy was more or less a victim of his job in the White House. He had a lot of enemies and his wires were tapped all the time. He couldn't make a phone call with complete security that it would remain confidential. Someone was listening. So to get information from Father Coughlin, when he thought about this he would use his relatives as messenger people. . . . They [the Kennedy family] came to the 9:00 Mass on Sunday which Father always said, and then Father invited them to breakfast after, or brunch. They'd go down in the dining room and Father could communicate his ideas to them. They would go back to the White House and communicate personally.[19]

Until Kennedy's death, Coughlin seemed to have accepted his muted public role gracefully, but in the wake of the liberal developments of Vatican II, the priest once again sought to test the limits of ecclesiastical tolerance. In the early 1960s, the civil rights movement precipitated action to desegregate public and parochial schools. Under then Archbishop (later Cardinal) John Dearden, the Detroit metropolitan area explored ways to carry out the reforms of Vatican II and to reduce the racial tensions that had flared up in the wake of the 1967 Detroit riot. Bitter strife in the Shrine parish accompanied efforts to carry out diocesan policies. Paul Weber, a Catholic Trade Union leader, recalled that Coughlin inspired some activism in those years that was violent and disruptive. A meeting at the Shrine High School ended with a pelting of Dearden by some of Coughlin's most ardent supporters: "They rode Cardinal Dearden, the newly named Archbishop of Detroit, off the rostrum up here at the Shrine High School. A bunch of Coughlinites . . . came in . . . they booed . . . they threw eggs and tomatoes at him. . . . Finally the Cardinal had to pick up his paper and leave."[20]

When the American Catholic Trade Union came down in favor of the passage of the 1964 Civil Rights Act, every church was required to read a letter of endorsement at Sunday Mass. According to Weber:

> Charles Coughlin did not read it . . . because I was standing there waiting to hear what was going to happen. . . . So I came back on Monday morning and called the Chancery, and I said: "Well, he didn't do it." "Well, he's got to do it, we can't afford to have anybody left out. Let's call him up." So the next Sunday it was read, but it was read in a rapid monotone by an old Franciscan who you couldn't understand anyway.[21]

On May 26, 1966, Charles Coughlin formally announced the end of his two-decade-long silence, an event that brought a full-scale news conference attended by a large number of reporters and media representatives from around the nation. The *New York Times* took note of "twenty-five years of church-enforced silence" and published the priest's denial that he was about to retire. The paper recorded "a flash of his renowned temper for a brief second" when one of the journalists at the press conference asked the priest if he had been accused in recent months "by some of his own parishioners and some Detroit archdiocesan officials of being anti-Negro."[22] The next day, Coughlin's old nemesis, the *Detroit Free Press*, told of a "rumored revolt in his church to oust him as pastor." He denied that any such move was afoot, referring to "a few little pipsqueaks who were ordained for three years [who] thought they knew more than the rest of us, but they didn't. This church, this parish, is one house."[23]

Then, suddenly, three days after his twenty-fourth year of "silence" had supposedly ended, Charles Coughlin publicly announced his retirement. Deep divisions had opened at the Shrine of the Little Flower. Many parents were opposed to what they considered Coughlin's racist attitudes and his martinet style of interacting with school students and parents. Pressure was applied to Coughlin to be named pastor emeritus of the Royal Oak Shrine. One month later, Father Coughlin's name was quietly removed from the masthead of the Shrine of the Little Flower *Bulletin*. He told the public he was on sabbatical in the West and was considering settling permanently in Arizona. In fact, his ecclesiastical superior, Archbishop Dearden, had acted to force his retirement and now sought to remove his influence on his former home base.[24]

The following year, a *Detroit News* journalist wrote that "Fr. Coughlin's long dormant political nature sprang to life last fall when he wrote long essays in his parish paper in support of the candidacy of Barry Goldwater, and in which he issued grave warnings about the Communist conspiracy."[25] In all the remaining years of his life, Coughlin vainly sought some means to raise his voice beyond the confines of his local parish. Few were listening or cared to listen to the long-forgotten firebrand. He published nevertheless.

The opening salvo in this virtually private war (only a few hundred copies were distributed, to close friends) was a fifty-four-page booklet in late 1968, *Helmet and Sword*. It targeted "the loud-mouthed clerical advocates of arson, riot, and draft-card burning. . . . It is regretful their demeanors, escapades, excesses, manners, vocabularies, sweat shirts, disobediences and disloyalties have warped the faith, culture and gentility of the laity."[26]

A book-length exposition of Coughlin's opinions, *Bishops Versus Pope,* soon followed. It contained four individual essays attacking philosophical and social trends in his church. Coughlin took aim specifically at his immediate superior:

> Definitely, Archbishop Dearden has placed the individual's conscience, although it is well informed, beyond the Papal teachings. In other words he has authentically determined for the members of the Archdiocese of Detroit that their conscience is their guide despite what the Pope may say or has taught. . . .

Probably Martin Luther is more solid in his theology, even from a Catholic viewpoint, than is Cardinal Dearden in the matter of subjective sin.[27]

In the same book he condemned as well the president of Notre Dame, Theodore M. Hesburgh, declaring that "the honorary degree which I received from that institution many years ago has lost its meaning, as I bow my head in shame. Never again shall I boast that I was a recipient of such an honor."[28] Coughlin was angered over what he saw as a form of Marxism being expounded at Notre Dame.

Coughlin regained his voice at a time of national crisis in which the same divisiveness and uncertainty that marked his entry into the national stage at the beginning of the Great Depression was prevalent once again. It was the height of national agony over the Vietnam War:

> Now that we have failed to overcome the Communist aggression in Vietnam; now that we are witnessing the onrush of the Red tide which threatens to deluge our institutions and liberties, let our ecclesiastics re-inspire the youth of America to fight for God and country when the battle for survival is only a few short years away. . . . There can be no compromise with the enemy who already has seduced at least 50-million Americans to sympathize with their bastard philosophy [Marxism] a philosophy sired by Satan and wombed by theistic atheists.
>
> Therefore, were I able physically; were I permitted the usage of television and radio, I would appeal to the youth of America and of the world . . . to put aside their contempt for authority, their unintellectual mobsterisms, their seizure of properties . . . and particularly their cynicism.[29]

The antidemocratic sentiments that had so energized the radio priest in his heyday reemerged and were directed against a liberalized ecclesiastical authority he now saw engulfing both his church and America. In *Bishops Versus Pope*, Coughlin attacked the theology of French Jesuit Pierre Teilhard de Chardin and denounced as scandalous those who abandoned the priesthood. Coughlin described bishops as "a pitiful, lamentable college of sociologists, raceologists, slum-diggers and would-be ecumenists . . . headline seekers in the science of racism." Attacking "one-worldism and Ecumenism," he asserted that bishops had "forsaken their divine calling" and that the "Church militant" had surrendered to the topic of communism, and he again equated it with trends in America:

> Probably the most disastrous doctrine Satan has disseminated through his earthly leaders was "government by the people." Never in history has government by the people been actualized. Always it has been a will-o'-the-wisp. For one short year only (1917) the blandishments of Karl Marx relative to the reign of the proletariat were cheered to the high heavens; then (1918), following Kerensky's defeat, Stalin [sic] . . . instituted the reign of dictatorial oligarchy. Here was the beginning of the end of democracy. Dead in Russia, 1918; dead in the United States, 2000.[30]

Twelve Timely Essays on Antichrist offered readers an essay entitled "The Militiamen." In it, Coughlin spoke of "the Sacrament of Confirmation . . . as a conduit to convey supernatural gifts. These are the gifts which transform a citizen into a soldier; these are the militiamen's courses in strategy, tactics and military training which are bestowed on baptized persons who are old enough to realize they are making a choice . . . to forgo the comforts of their domestic pursuits and to assume the rough army life with hardships, privations, wounds and even death in defense of Christ and Christ's constitution and flag."[31]

In the last of the *Antichrist* essays, Coughlin returned to an old theme: federal reserve banks as part of an age-old "tyranny of privately created and controlled money . . . a major evil whose curse has fallen upon the underprivileged citizens of the United States and the world." He concluded by stating, "My public career, so much expended upon disclosing this form of satanism, is at an end. Younger and more forceful men have taken up Excalibur to wield in these days of mortal combat."[32]

Coughlin eschewed extensive allusions to the role of Jews. In fact, in one address delivered during Pentecost 1973, he proffered that the new anti-Christ was "no longer . . . the Jews . . . but apostate Catholics" plus "cowardly Christians, cowardly bishops, cowardly priests."[33]

In 1976, on the fortieth anniversary of the completion of the Shrine of the Little Flower, Coughlin made his "last hurrah" (as one parishioner described it) in order "to thank his people—to say goodbye." In his ceremonial remarks, Monsignor Edward Hickey, who had been chancellor during Cardinal Mooney's tenure, looked back on problems the church had with Coughlin:

> We think he made mistakes in economics and in his international relations . . . we condemned his attitudes toward the Jewish people. But when the showdown came, what so edified us all was his obedience. . . . I used to say if the bishop had told him to stand on his head . . . he would have done so.[34]

Charles Coughlin died Saturday, October 27, 1979, six days after his eighty-eighth birthday. He had already suffered several heart attacks; he finally succumbed to heart failure. Media coverage was extensive in the local Detroit area, and news stories about the priest's life circulated among the leading national press services and newspapers. The treatment was often forgiving. The right-wing Catholic publication *The Wanderer* wrote, "It matters not whether his words were right or wrong. . . . He stirred millions and impacted private and public opinion as to the events of history as it was being lived."[35] Coughlin's old nemesis, the *Detroit Free Press*, provided two distinct views of the man, the first as a loyal son of the church: "God is a giver and a forgiver, so why should we hold anything against one of our brothers? We remember not so much what Father Coughlin said, but what he believed. In his priesthood he had a deep loyalty to the Church he served. He never set himself above it. His joy was to be a faithful priest."[36] The second article issued a warning: "It would be pleasant to forget the excesses of the strident voices that rose during the hard times of the '30's of which that of the late Father Charles Coughlin was the loudest. Except there is truth in the saying that those who forget history are doomed to relive it."[37]

Within a few years of his death, Charles Coughlin was granted the status of an elder statesman of the populist right. In 1982, *Liberty Lobby* published *Profiles in Populism,* a series of biographical profiles, edited by Willis Carto, originally written as articles in his *Spotlight* political tabloid. The book described "thirteen leading American populists" starting with Thomas Jefferson and Andrew Jackson and including Henry Ford, Charles Lindbergh, Jr., and the radio priest. A decade later, the antiblack and anti-Semitic monthly tabloid *The Truth at Last* devoted an entire "50th Anniversary Commemorative Edition" to reprinting excerpts from Coughlin's radio addresses and *Social Justice* articles. In celebrating the event, the editor invited his readers to "Step back in time . . . to

study the life and writings of one of the greatest Americans in history."
He added, "It is amazing how little things have changed from 1940 to
1991!"[38]

In May 1992, a special effort was made in Detroit's Catholic and
Jewish communities to exorcise the ghost of Charles Coughlin. The event
was a joint fund-raising reception held at the Shrine of the Little Flower
on behalf of an ecumenical organization directed by a Protestant clergyman. The occurrence was newsworthy enough to receive an item in the
New York Times. The article quoted the pastor of Coughlin's church: "I
would change history if I could." In his remarks on the special occasion,
the Catholic official included an apology in the name of the church: "We
need to find forgiveness in our lives whenever possible."[39]

Across the street from the Shrine, it was reported that "a lone man
stood . . . holding a sign that read: 'Father Coughlin was on target concerning the Jewish Communist Conspiracy.' "[40]

Appendix

Chart 1
Coughlin Radio Audience Before and After "Kristallnacht" Broadcast, November 1938
(Listened to at least one broadcast during the past month)

	April 1938	December 1938	Change
Total Audience	16,000,000	14,500,000	-1,500,000
Approve/Agree	51.9%	46.2%	-5.7%
Estimated Number	8,300,000	6,700,000	-1,500,000
Total of U.S. Sample	12.8%	10.3%	-1.5%

NOTE: Between the spring of 1938 and the following mid-December—three weeks following Coughlin's Kristallnacht broadcast—the radio priest's audience declined by 5.7%, or 1.6 million persons.

Overall, those favorable to Coughlin's radio addresses declined from 1 in 8 adults to 1 in 10.

SOURCE: The estimates indicated were calculated by the author on the percentages found in the samples for Gallup surveys #118 and #141 and do not take into account any sampling error. *They are not actual audience counts.*

Chart 2
Religious Affiliation and Coughlin Audience Approval Size, December 1938
(In millions)

	Listen	Approve
Catholics	4.0	2.4
No Denomination Given	3.2	1.2
Methodist	1.6	0.65
Protestant: No Specific Denomination Named	1.3	0.4
Baptist	1.1	0.45
Presbyterian	1.0	0.5
Lutheran	0.9	0.56
Jewish	0.8	0.2

Chart 2 (continued)

	Listen	Approve
Episcopalian	0.4	0.25
Congregational	0.25	0.11
TOTAL	14.5	6.71

NOTE: More than 2 in 5 who listened to and 1 in 3 who approved of Coughlin's radio addresses were Catholic. Yet the large majority of listeners—7 million—reported that they belonged to a Protestant denomination, and 3 million of those respondents reported favorable attitudes.

SOURCE: Gallup survey #141, conducted December 12–18, 1938. The large number of persons indicating "No religious affiliation" is an artifact of the mode of interviewing, which allowed many persons sampled not to be categorized unless they chose to answer the question. Most of those respondents should be assumed to have had a Protestant religious background.

Chart 3
Approval of Nazi Treatment of Jews and Reported 1936
Presidential Vote, December 1938
(Percentage approving)

Voted for Lemke		15.8%
Voted for FDR in 1936		5.4%
Voted for Landon		5.4%

SOURCE: Author calculations based on Gallup survey #139, in response to the question, "Do you approve or disapprove of the Nazis' treatment of Jews in Germany?"

Chart 4
The Catholic-Jewish Chasm, Late 1930s

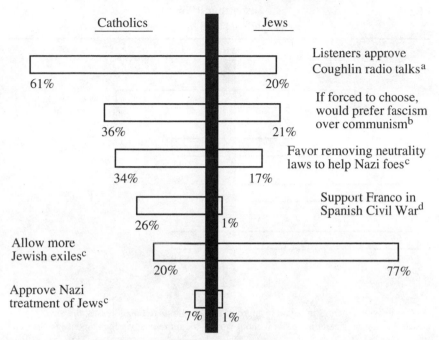

Catholics · Jews

Listeners approve
Coughlin radio talks[a]
61% · 20%

If forced to choose,
would prefer fascism
over communism[b]
36% · 21%

Favor removing neutrality
laws to help Nazi foes[c]
34% · 17%

Support Franco in
Spanish Civil War[d]
26% · 1%

Allow more
Jewish exiles[c]
20% · 77%

Approve Nazi
treatment of Jews[c]
7% · 1%

SOURCES: [a]Gallup survey #141, December 16, 1938; [b]Gallup survey #145A, January 20, 1939; [c]Gallup survey #139, November 22, 1938; [d]Gallup survey #141, December 16, 1938.

Chart 5
Coughlin and Class Division in the Catholic Community, December 1938
(Occupational level of listener)

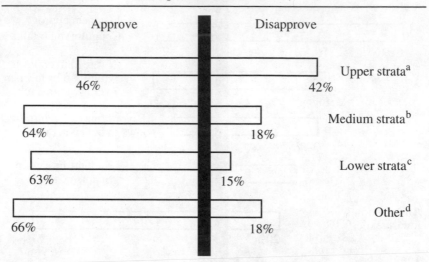

| Approve | | Disapprove |

A clear division emerges in regard to approval of Coughlin's radio addresses: the lower the occupational status—including those without work—the more positive the response to the radio priest's broadcasts.

SOURCE: Gallup survey #141: [a]"Professional" and "Business" categories; [b]"Skilled white collar worker," "Unskilled white collar," "Skilled blue collar"; [c]"Unskilled worker"; [d]"Unemployed," "No occupation," "On WPA assistance."

Chart 6
Awareness of Anti-Semitic Groups and Individuals, August 1940
(Percentage of those answering yes to the question: "Have you heard of any organizations or men who are trying to stir up feeling against the Jews in this country?" If yes: "Name it (them).")

German-American Bund	50
Ku Klux Klan	25
Charles E. Coughlin	20
Silver Shirts	10
Christian Front	9
Germans	5

NOTE: Respondents totaled 22 percent of sample.

SOURCE: Opinion Research Corporation Survey, N = 3,101.

Notes

Introduction: Vox Populi

1. *New York Times,* January 14, 1940; *Detroit Free Press,* January 14, 1940.
2. Alfred McClung Lee and Elizabeth Briant Lee, eds., *The Fine Art of Propaganda: A Study of Father Coughlin's Speeches.*
3. Quoted in the *Detroit Free Press,* April 28, 1995.
4. "What Radio Is Saying," *New York Times,* November 18, 1986.
5. Murray B. Levin, *Talk Radio and the American Dream,* xiii.
6. Ibid., 151. Levin recognizes that talk radio serves several social purposes, including developing a sense of "class consciousness." He points out that the medium could serve as a democratic forum, but instead, "the host is a professional talker and manipulator. . . . Political talk radio is structured by the ideology of the host" (17).
7. Excerpt from a radio broadcast of Father Coughlin, May 17, 1937, aired on National Public Radio in 1986 as part of a special segment dealing with the radio priest, whose broadcasting had begun six decades earlier.

Chapter 1: A Child of Circumstance

1. According to Charles Coughlin's close confidant Louis Ward, Daniel Coughlin found a residence above an undertaking establishment run by a local family. The location on Seneca Street is just around the corner from what was his son's home and the birthplace of his grandson Charles. See Ward, *Father Charles E. Coughlin: An Authorized Biography,* 6.
2. Regarding the version Coughlin gives of his father's work, see Harold Schachern, "Fr. Coughlin's First Interview in 20 Years," *Detroit News,* December 16, 1962. In the subsequent biography by Sheldon Marcus, *Father Coughlin,* 20, Coughlin mentioned that his father held a job of chief examiner of steel for the Imperial Munitions Board of Canada. When he was investigated in the 1940s by the Justice Department, FBI Freedom of Information Act files quote the priest as explaining some investment in property in Colorado as having been given to him in his father's will.
3. Coughlin's university transcript gives the erroneous date of October 24, 1890, for his birth. In all passport applications and a gun permit, the date given for Coughlin's birth is October 25, 1891.
4. Alan Brinkley, *Voices of Protest,* 84. Richard Davis, "Radio Priest," 6, describes Coughlin's upbringing as "pervaded by the aspirations and attitudes of a highly religious and upwardly mobile working-class family." Marcus, *Father Coughlin,* 12, indicates that Thomas Coughlin was "the owner of a comfortable 4-room home . . . in the heart of a middle-class Irish neighborhood."
5. Davis, "Radio Priest," 7, speaks about Amelia Coughlin's arraying her son "in the ruffles and kilt which she thought complemented his long, blond curls. For-

          tunately for the boy, his mother abandoned the kilts and curls when she heard how he was taunted by a priest on the first day of school."

6.   This incident was reported in "The Holy Terror from Hamilton," *Macleans Magazine,* October 1, 1952. In the same article, another incident is mentioned: the seven-year-old Coughlin's reciting verses at St. Mary's Cathedral school with his peers. After announcing that he intended to become a stonemason, he "received a polite round of applause. But instead of running off the stage the moment he finished, as the others had done before him, the boy stood in place and continued bowing."

7.   Several incidents recounted by Coughlin's biographers suggest he was very dependent on his mother and her support and care packages while he attended high school and college. Amelia would bring not only clothing but cakes and pastries as well. Because he spent most of his time in a private dormitory room, he was able to make regular long-distance calls to his mother. His motivation was "sustained in part by his mother's devotion and in part by his own dedication to his studies." Davis, "Radio Priest," 10.

8.   Brinkley, *Voices of Protest,* 86, refers to Coughlin's college career as "a classic campus success story. He earned excellent grades, played starting fullback for the school's rugby team, served as president of his senior class, [and] developed a reputation at St. Michael's as an unusually talented public speaker." Ruth Mugglebee, *Father Coughlin,* indicates that Coughlin was selected as both class president and valedictorian. Davis, "Radio Priest," found no evidence for either claim.

9.   Interview with Father Dwyer, 1987.

10.   Ibid.; Mugglebee, 66–67.

11.   According to Mugglebee, *Father Coughlin,* Charles sought out a former teacher at St. Basil's, where he had been a high school student—Father Thomas Roach—for advice. By this account, it was Roach who persuaded Coughlin to enter the priesthood. Davis, "Radio Priest," 13, indicates that "in so doing, Coughlin could later realise . . . his ambitions in the fields of politics and sociology."

12.   Author interview with Margaret Flood, 1987, a cousin of Charles Coughlin. In regard to Coughlin's European trip, which Mrs. Flood recalled having been an uncle's gift, author Sheldon Marcus was told by Coughlin that it was a gift from his parents.

13.   Mugglebee, *Father Coughlin,* 84, mentions the significance of Amelia Coughlin's chronic ill health on her son. She was hospitalized on a number of occasions, sometimes near death. Coughlin told Mugglebee that, when he was age four, he visited his hospitalized mother and announced his commitment to the priesthood; at age nine, "during the delirium of a bout with typhoid, the boy saw religious visions."

14.   According to Brinkley, *Voices of Protest,* 87, the idea of a "just community" as a major Catholic doctrine, derived from the teachings of Thomas Aquinas, "resonated particularly clearly with Coughlin and his contemporaries. . . . Social justice required neither rigid collectivism nor laissez-faire individualism; it required, rather, a system of private ownership tempered by recognition of the individual's obligation to his community."

15.   The ordination ceremony took place in Toronto, with Bishop John M. Mahoney, a second cousin to Coughlin's mother and the bishop of the Hamilton diocese. Coughlin told biographer Louis Ward that it was this same figure whom he sought to imitate in speaking style. Another would-be biographer, Farley

Clinton, was told that Mahoney had been appointed as assistant attorney general in the Canadian government. Official records fail to support this assertion.

16. Interview with Father Dwyer.
17. Interview with Father Dwyer.
18. Ibid.
19. Ibid.
20. Mugglebee, *Father Coughlin,* 38. While her effusive praise is reflected throughout her extensive biography, first written in 1933, by the time of the revised edition in 1935, she saw her previously revered subject as a "serious threat by becoming a leader of the mob."
21. Author interview with Father Dwyer.
22. Brinkley, *Voices of Protest,* asserts, "There could hardly have been a less hospitable setting for an ambitious young priest attempting to establish a new church." He describes Royal Oak, Michigan, as having remained "until recently . . . an isolated, largely rural community . . . no longer countryside and not yet city, but a sort of intermediate, urbanized wilderness. Dotted with the cheaply built, shingled homes of newly arriving automobile workers, made even more desolate by large, unkempt vacant lots. It offered a bleak and forbidding landscape." (89).
23. Ibid., and Davis, "Radio Priest," put the loan figure at $79,000. Mugglebee (186) and Marcus (23) used the figure of $79,000 as well. There are no diocesan or other records to verify a particular figure, nor is it even fully clear that the loan was repaid.
24. According to the uncredited publication *Shrine of the Little Flower, Golden Jubilee 1926–1976* the original Shrine, "a simple russet brown wooden building . . . rose quickly." The date of June 26, 1926, is given for the first mass. The same book indicates that "even before it was completed, Father [Coughlin] moved his residence from St. Francis's home in Detroit to the unfinished and unheated church, using its small sacristy as combination living room, dining room, kitchen, bedroom, and office, and relied on the invitations of parishioners for his dinner each day" (6).
25. *Shrine Herald,* May 17, 1936. Coughlin's church, located at the intersection of Woodward Avenue and Twelve Mile Road, would eventually become a striking landmark. Woodward, a main thoroughfare that runs directly to the Detroit River twelve miles away, was already becoming an avenue of outward expansion of the city's population. In the 1920s Twelve Mile was merely an unpaved road and "muddy ruts and ditches were everywhere."
26. John C. Cahalan, Jr., "The Hour of Power," *Commonweal,* January 28, 1931, reports that Coughlin began his broadcasting career with a surplus from the original diocesan loan following the completion of the church. Coughlin himself mentions a figure of $5,000 that was left over in the church's account.
27. See Robert S. Gallagher, "The Radio Priest," 99. Brinkley, *Voices of Protest,* 90, states that "the Catholic population of Royal Oak was simply too small to bear the financial burden of the church." In fact, the community had had a Catholic church, St. Mary's, founded decades earlier.
28. Marcus, *Father Coughlin,* 23–24. Marcus quotes Coughlin as recalling that Ruth "gently but firmly, assisted me to the altar and told me to keep the hell out of the way" (24).
29. Almost from the very first days of his Shrine church, Coughlin was a master at tie-in sales. For example, for the purchase of a membership in the Radio League

of the Shrine of the Little Flower, an individual would receive a subscription to *Shower of Roses,* the small magazine Coughlin published, and enclosed would be a medal with the inscription "Blessed and touched with an authentic relic of the true cross." The quotation is from a form letter addressed to A. L. Overton, December 17, 1933, Franklin D. Roosevelt Presidential Library.

30. Author interview with Father Dwyer, 1987.

31. Ibid.

32. Ibid.

33. These passages are found in Coughlin's tenth anniversary issue of the *Shrine Herald* for May 1936. The fiftieth anniversary volume, published by the Shrine in 1976, mentions that while the priest "lived in the sacristy . . . a flaming cross was burned only a few yards from the church. This outrage gave impetus to Father's efforts to erect a more permanent monument to the innocence of the Girl Saint of Lisieux and to carry Christ's doctrines of charity beyond the limits of his own parish." *Shrine Golden Jubilee,* 11.

34. This dialogue is from the pilot film produced in 1933, with the cross-burning scene having been shown in a PBS documentary in 1986. In 1933, both Mugglebee and Ward had just completed their biographies of Coughlin. Ward makes no mention of any cross-burning incident. By contrast, Mugglebee offered a fulsome and sentimental account: "The priest vowed that he would build a cross so high . . . that neither man nor beast can burn it down" (quoted in Marcus, 23). Davis, "Radio Priest," 18–19, relies on the Mugglebee story: "One night word came that a cross flamed in the churchyard. Coughlin rushed to the scene to find the cross still burning; he was convinced that he must now work also to erase the then prevalent anti-Catholic bigotry."

35. Brinkley, *Voices of Protest,* 90. While recognizing that the priest "embellished for dramatic effect" the alleged cross-burning incident, the historian comments that Coughlin's "vibrant and prestigious church" attracted Catholics to Royal Oak in such numbers "that the Ku Klux Klan could no longer terrorize the community" (91). Marcus, *Father Coughlin,* 23, states that "barely two weeks after the completion of the church, the Ku Klux Klan burned a cross on the lawn of the church along with a sign that read, 'Move from Royal Oak.'"

36. Gallagher, "Radio Priest," 98. This distinctive variation on the Klan story would suggest that the three-day weekend would have been late in May—the Memorial Day period—and not the July 4 weekend. The first mass at the Shrine was held on June 26, 1926; it is puzzling to try to figure out what three-day weekend would have occurred earlier in the month. There are no Oakland County court records related to any KKK injunction mentioned by Coughlin.

37. Marcus, *Father Coughlin,* 28. This alleged incident "in May of 1927" might be linked to a KKK parade that was held on Twelve Mile Road in mid-November 1926. Throughout the 1920s, the *Royal Oak Tribune* carried stories describing local and national Klan activities. No mention of Coughlin's involvement with the fall event occurs or for any other Klan story carried in the newspaper.

38. Kenneth Jackson, *The Klu Klux Klan in the City, 1915–1930,* originally published in 1967 by Oxford University Press. The 1992 edition contains a new foreword. The analysis focuses on the Klan's opposition to Al Smith's 1928 presidential bid. The study provides extensive content analysis of newspaper coverage and details Klan activity in the Detroit metropolitan area.

39. Author interview with Grant Howell, 1985.

40. *Royal Oak Tribune,* November 15, 1926. The story appeared on the front page and was titled, "Klansmen Parade and Hear Speeches."

41. Rasmussen showed me the cross in his upstairs storage area, where he posed for a picture standing next to it. He said he had bought the cross for ten dollars and identified the person who claimed to have been present at the scene of the burning and had taken the cross away. Rasmussen gave me the telephone number of the daughter of the Shrine parishioner, but she could offer no authentication as the original incident and, in fact, seemed to demur with regard to her own knowledge as to what had actually occurred.

Chapter 2: Inventing the Political Soap Opera

1. In 1920, Fisher Body became part of the General Motors Corporation. The five Fisher brothers had a voting trust in the du Pont Corporation, which owned a controlling interest in GM.
2. According to James Quello, whom I interviewed in 1984, "The Fisher brothers were very close to [Coughlin]. . . . Larry Fisher and Richards [George A., owner of WJR] were very good friends. They used to go to the DAC [Detroit Athletic Club] and get loaded and throw bottles at the chandelier and say, 'What the hell do you care, we'll pay for it!'"
3. Quoted in Sheldon Marcus, *Father Coughlin,* 26.
4. One description of the priest's speaking style was described approvingly by a supporter as "a combination of Mussolini and Will Rogers." *Social Justice,* November 9, 1936.
5. The evaluation and anecdote come from Charlie Park, a longtime WJR announcer. The final scene of the hat-throwing incident was that Richards sent an aide downstairs "to buy . . . a couple of new hats at the haberdashery."
6. Announcers were instructed to slant news items against the Roosevelt administration and liberal public figures. Richards' strident anti-Semitism was reflected not merely in his hiring virtually no Jewish employees but in his views regarding Jewish political machinations. In a series of actions dealing with Richards carried out in the late 1940s and early 1950s, the Federal Communications Commission sought a suspension of his broadcaster's license. Prominent personalities such as Eddie Rickenbacker and Bing Crosby testified to Richards' good character. For a detailed discussion of the licensing controversy, see Erik Barnouw, *The Golden Web.*
7. Author interview with Frank Stanton, 1984.
8. *Detroit Free Press,* January 17, 1927.
9. Sociologists Alfred McClung Lee and Elizabeth Brian Lee were the coauthors of a book published in 1939 by the Institute of Propaganda Analysis, *The Fine Art of Propaganda: A Study of Father Coughlin's Speeches.*
10. Ward, *Father Charles E. Coughlin,* 38, 42.
11. Ward, 47. In the sermon, Coughlin also offered practical advice to the kidnapper: "In your anxiety and in your nervousness, perhaps you are afraid to contact the police. . . . If you look in your telephone directory . . . wherever you are, you will find the name of some Catholic orphanage." *Father Coughlin's Radio Discourses,* 224.
12. Ward, 37, 46.
13. Wallace Stegner, "The Radio Priest and His Flock," 234.
14. Ibid.
15. Mugglebee, *Father Coughlin,* 320, 269.
16. Author interview with Frank Stanton, 1984.

17. Author interview with longtime Shrine of the Little Flower parishioner Clarence Grix, 1984.
18. *Detroit Free Press,* March 29, 1933.
19. Author interview in 1985 with Joseph Wright, a former writer for Coughlin's weekly newspaper, *Social Justice.* In an unpublished taped interview in 1970 with journalist Eric Thuma, Coughlin referred to his earliest broadcast in the 1920s, "The Children's Hour," a series of catechism classes, as being "so formulated that it would appeal to all Christian children and non-Christian [children] because I avoided bigotry, and I avoided specifications." Coughlin offered that " 'The Children's Hour' became very fruitful, very attractive to adults and pressure was put upon me after that, after two years, to raise my voice and raise my sights to the adult age."
20. Ward, *Father Charles E. Coughlin,* 32, 35.
21. Mugglebee, *Father Coughlin,* 184.
22. Quoted in ibid., 184.
23. Quoted in ibid., 185.
24. Ibid., 186.
25. Ibid., 187.
26. See Caroline Bird, *The Invisible Scar,* 45.
27. Quoted in Ronald Steel, *Walter Lippman and the American Century,* 290.
28. Quoted in Ward, *Father Charles E. Coughlin,* 58.
29. By the fall of 1929, Coughlin's mail had increased to "some three thousand letters a week." Marcus, *Father Coughlin,* 30, 60–70.
30. Ward, *Father Charles E. Coughlin.* Ward comments that Coughlin "was startled by the number of professors and of seemingly well educated persons who wrote to him in defense of communism" (58).
31. Coughlin broadcast of January 26, 1930, quoted in Ward, *Father Charles E. Coughlin,* 65, 66. The broadcasts about the "red serpent" concluded on March 9, 1930. Ward concludes that "Father Coughlin had aroused the American people to the imminent danger which this new radicalism was creating" (71).
32. Coughlin radio address, February 9, 1930.
33. U.S. Congress, House, *Investigation of Communist Propaganda,* Hearings, 1930, Part IV, Volume No. 1, 18, 19, 22, 24, 25.
34. Ibid., 25.
35. When the investigating committee's chairman asked whether Ford's actions were "done on purpose," Coughlin replied: "Not at all. It was done through ignorance." Ibid., 21.
36. *Detroit Free Press,* July 26, 1930.
37. Quoted in Mugglebee, *Father Coughlin,* 214–15.
38. In response to Coughlin's broadcast, Ward, *Father Charles E. Coughlin,* 86, boasted, "on January 4, 1931, before the court of public opinion, more than 1,250,000 Americans made the law of the radio in the greatest single flood of letters ever sent in protest to radio stations."
39. According to David Burner, *Herbert Hoover, a Public Life,* 318, McFadden's action was "one of the first measures introduced in the December [1932] 'Lame Duck' session of Congress." Coughlin and McFadden remained close for a number of years. McFadden was not reelected to Congress in 1934.
40. Coughlin radio address, January 11, 1931.
41. Mugglebee, *Father Coughlin,* 212.
42. Ward, *Father Charles E. Coughlin,* 84.

43. Ibid., 85.
44. Quoted in William S. Paley, *As It Happened: A Memoir,* 115. In his 1979 auto-biography, Paley writes that "Coughlin appealed to his radio audience to write me personally in protest against the restrictions imposed on him. Almost 400,000 letters poured into CBS, almost all of them in protest against our action. Nevertheless we canceled Coughlin immediately, but allowed him to finish his contract through the spring of 1931." Evidence emerged later that NBC also refused airtime to the priest. See *New York Times,* March 21, 1934.
45. Robert S. Gallagher, "The Radio Priest," 100.
46. These comments were made during the highly attenuated interview I was granted with Paley in 1984. The former CBS official angrily explained, "This [the subject of the radio priest] is personal! . . . and it's a subject I don't want to get into. . . . I had many other problems on my mind and I put this matter away. Of course you know for the record, CBS came out with a public statement taking him off the air and the reasons for it: his views were too controversial."
47. Jeffrey Dorwart, *Conflict of Duty.* The head of the Herbert Hoover Library at the time his study came out was quoted as saying that Dorwart's charges were "a bunch of crap . . . it's so foreign to Hoover's personality . . . honesty, integrity and morality. He never authorized any clandestine operations." Quoted in the *Iowa City Press-Citizen,* February 24, 1983.
48. The Herbert Hoover Presidential Library's file on journalist William Allen White contains the Ferber letter written in May 1934. She recounts that while staying at the Drake Hotel in Chicago, her friend noticed an extra telephone, apparently disconnected, "sitting on the floor." After hearing occasional rings "she picked up the phone and heard what was apparently a conversation between you [White] and Pat Hurley [Hoover's cabinet member]. . . . She listened for ten minutes or so, to be sure there was no mistake. . . . Apparently a wire was tapped somewhere along the line."
49. Charles Coughlin, *Father Coughlin's Radio Discourses, 1931–1932,* 186–187.
50. Joslin to Hoover, March 21, 1931, Hoover Library.
51. Coughlin interview with Eric Thuma, 1970.

Chapter 3: A Player on the New Deal Team

1. Eric Thuma interview with Coughlin, 1970.
2. Coughlin radio address, November 30, 1930, in *Father Coughlin's Radio Discourses, 1930–1931,* 91.
3. Coughlin to FDR, July 15, 1931; J.J.M. to Louis M. Howe, memo, July 24, 1931, Democratic National Committee Papers, Franklin D. Roosevelt Library (FDRL).
4. Gracie Hall Roosevelt to FDR, May 5, 1931, Governor's Personal File 147, FDRL.
5. Alan Brinkley, *Voices of Protest,* 107, indicates that a year passed after FDR was sent the letter about contacting Coughlin and then "Frank Murphy interceded. . . . He and Coughlin met for a conference in Roosevelt's town house in New York." In 1972, in reply to the query on how he first was introduced to FDR, Coughlin recalled that "my good friend Joe Kennedy . . . had me get very close to him." Gallagher, "Radio Priest" (40).
6. Quoted in Sheldon Marcus, *Father Coughlin,* 46.

7. Quoted in Robert Gallagher, "Radio Priest," 98.
8. *New York Times,* April 27, 1931. The address was aired on two radio stations. Mayor Walker paid a surprise visit, and he and Coughlin were lustily cheered by the 2,000 firemen present. Walker embraced the priest and whispered, "Thanks." According to historian Brinkley, *Voices of Protest,* 105, the publicity Coughlin received moved him "more directly into the center of the city's, and to some extent the nation's, political consciousness."
9. Quoted in Gallagher, "Radio Priest," 99.
10. Eric Thuma, interview with Father Coughlin, 1970.
11. Coughlin to FDR, August 12, 1932, Democratic National Committee Papers, FDRL. Walker's resignation occurred one month later.
12. Gallagher, "Radio Priest," 100.
13. Brinkley, *Voices of Protest,* 109
14. Eleanor Roosevelt to Charles Tull, March 16, 1960. I am grateful to Dr. Tull for allowing to have a copy of this communication. Brinkley, *Voices of Protest,* argues (107–123) that the early decision to win over Coughlin was based on FDR's efforts to build a coalition of urban Catholics and rural Protestants.
15. Quoted in Davis, "Radio Priest," 46.
16. The priest indicated that while "in no manner" could he take sides in the upcoming election, he was prepared to give four broadcasts praising FDR and condemning Hoover. See Coughlin to FDR, September 12, 1932, Official File 306, FDRL.
17. *Public Papers and Addresses of Franklin D. Roosevelt, vol. 1, 1928–1932,* 771. FDR's adoption of the "Social Justice" rhetoric Coughlin employed was clearly aimed at the followers of the radio priest, but despite a call for the president to mention him by name (Coughlin to FDR, July 2, 1934, Democratic National Committee Papers, FDRL), FDR's only personal reference in his remarks was "to my friend, Frank Murphy."
18. In one telegram, Coughlin described FDR as a "natural born artist" on the radio and counseled him on the use of the airways to counter the Republican press. Coughlin to McIntyre, March 13, 1933, Official File 200B, FDRL.
19. Eric Thuma interview with Coughlin, 1970.
20. Ibid.
21. Author interview with Father Peter Wiethe, 1984. Marcus, *Father Coughlin,* 49, quotes the priest as saying that FDR asked Coughlin to prepare a draft. James Roosevelt, in my raising once again what he called "this old saw," told me, "I think I could say just from memory, that as far as any direct contribution [to the inaugural address of 1933] it just doesn't exist. Whether there was indirectly through Mr. [Joe] Kennedy . . . I'm not sure I could say that, except that it might have been possible that there was an indirect conversation about it." Author interview, 1984.
22. Coughlin to Mrs. Chase, form letter, November 1933, Herbert Hoover Presidential Library.
23. Theodore Joslin to Hoover, April 5, 1933, Hoover Library.
24. *Cleveland Press,* December 22, 1933.
25. Author interview with J. Mills, 1987. Mills was a close family member of Coughlin. Davis, "Radio Priest," 53, suggests that an estimate of $500,000 a year in contributions is a low figure, "given the size of his expenditures and the solvency of his organization."
26. Mugglebee, *Father Coughlin,* 323.

27. Rev. A. M. Hutting, *Shrine of the Little Flower Souvenir Book,* 30.
28. Ibid., 54.
29. A confidential report indicated that title to the park surrounding the Shrine and Crucifix Tower was in the name of Coughlin's parents, with other property, except the church itself, remaining outside the financial control of the local archdiocese. "Coughlin families Activities," September 19, 1943, Michigan Civil Rights League file, Labor History and Urban Affairs Archives, Walter Reuther Library, Wayne State University.
30. Ibid. The report also mentions that lottery tickets were offered to worshipers. It was estimated that $16,000 in tickets were sold each week. A service station owned by the Shrine dispensed gasoline during World War II to 200 or 300 cars each Sunday.
31. Author interview with T. Franco, 1987. Confidential reports seeking to gauge Coughlin's sources of income and activities in the 1940s focused on the souvenir shops located at either side of the entrance to the Shrine sacristy. One noted that four salespeople were needed to dispense the pictures and articles bearing the Shrine stamp, and that "Old Man Coughlin presides. At the time he is selling trinkets at 10 times their cost." Michigan Civil Rights League Report, September 10, 1943, Walter Reuther Library.
32. Author interview with Father Edward Balczak, 1984.
33. Insider commercial withdrawals at the Guardian Group decreased deposits by $15.1 million between December 31, 1932, and February 11, 1933. See John J. Holland, "The Detroit Banking Collapse of 1933," 228.
34. Quoted in the *Detroit Free Press,* March 27, 1933.
35. Ibid.
36. Ibid., March 28, 1933.
37. Ibid.
38. Ibid., March 29, 1933. Calling the priest "a religious Walter Winchell," the paper quoted from Ruth Mugglebee's biography, in which Coughlin had said, "If I didn't believe in religion and a happy beyond, I would get everything for myself that I could lay hands on in this world."
39. Malcolm Bingay, *All Around Detroit,* 111–112. Bingay wrote, "I never knew his [the informant's] name and have never have seen him since" (112).
40. *Detroit Free Press,* April 1, 1933.
41. Ibid., March 31, 1933.
42. Louis Ward, *Father Charles E. Coughlin,* 336. The *Free Press* story of March 31, 1933, quoting from a police report, indicated that the "bomb" was little more than a large firecracker, clearly not a threat to life or limb. Ward criticized the newspaper for poor reporting and even suggested that it falsified what Coughlin had to say about the incident: "The truth is that Father Coughlin never regarded the bomb as anything different from what the police described it, an 'intimidating bomb,' not intended to kill, not designed even for an undue destruction of property" (236).
43. Quoted in Ward, *Father Charles E. Coughlin,* 250–52.
44. Ibid., 212.
45. Coughlin to Jesse Jones, June 4, 1933, FDRL.
46. Bingay, *All Around Detroit,* 113.
47. *Detroit News,* August 23, 1933.
48. Ibid., August 24, 1933.
49. *Detroit Times,* August 24, 1933; *Detroit News,* August 24, 1933.

50. Herbert Hoover to Foster Bain, August 28, 1933; Hoover Library.
51. Herbert Hoover to Patrick J. Hurley, August 30, 1933, Hoover Library.
52. Hurley to Hoover, August 24, 1933, Hoover Library.
53. Roy Chapin to Hoover, August 27, 1933, Hoover Library.
54. Marcus, *Father Coughlin,* 59, quotes these remarks from former key FDR aide Jim Farley in a telephone interview in 1970.
55. Quoted in Brinkley, *Voices of Protest,* 118. Coughlin had suggested that McIntyre had authorized him to speak for the Roosevelt administration: "[William] Woodin [Secretary of the Treasury] asks me to tell this audience" (116).
56. Marcus, *Father Coughlin,* 60. Marcus also quotes Coughlin as telling him in 1970 that [he and FDR] "were supposed to be partners. He said he would rely on me. That I would be an important adviser. But he was a liar. He never took my advice. He just used me" (70).
57. The investigation by Ferdinand Pecora, which involved hearings of the U.S. Senate Committee on Banking and Currency, did bear out some of the general criticisms leveled by Coughlin, but those directed specifically to E. D. Stair and the Guardian Group were not. See Ferdinand Pecora, *Wall Street Under Oath,* 238–257.

Chapter 4: Off the FDR Bandwagon

1. *Literary Digest,* December 9, 1933.
2. Alan Brinkley, *Voices of Protest,* 120.
3. Louis Ward, *Father Coughlin,* 107. The allusion to "racial psychology" is apparently meant as a polite code word for the claim that Jews held particular control over international banking, a contemporary theme of anti-Semites.
4. *Fortune* (February 1934): 38.
5. Ibid.
6. Ibid.
7. Coughlin's close associate Father Peter Wiethe told me that Harriss "owned half of Texas." Edward Voss's name was finally taken off the "Forbes Wealthiest Men" list in 1985. In the late 1940s, he was linked to a commodities exchange scandal regarding alleged inside-trading. An indictment was instituted against the two and their trading colleagues, but no prosecution took place.
8. During the 1950s, Harriss's name emerged nationally because he wrote a letter to the editor suggesting that George Marshall had communist leanings. See *New York Times,* August 4, 1954.
9. Thomas was a key figure linked to the cotton commodities cornering charges that were levied against Robert Harriss's business partner, Edward Voss.
10. Arthur M. Schlesinger, Jr., *The Coming of the New Deal,* 252. The so-called Thomas amendment was passed into law as part of the Agricultural Extension Act on May 12, 1933. See Robert S. McElvaine, *The Great Depression,* 149.
11. *New York Times,* April 29, 1934. Coughlin had told his radio audience early in 1934: "Here is a prophesy: I believe the president is about remonetize silver!" See David H. Bennett, *Demagogues in the Depression,* 47.
12. Coughlin, *Series of Lectures on Social Justice,* 222.
13. Monsignor Michael Ready to Amleto Cicognani [apostolic delegate], April 30, 1934, National Catholic Welfare Conference Archives. Ready also quoted to the Vatican representative FDR's views, which condemned Coughlin's "gentile Silver" metaphor as religious bigotry.

14. *Nation,* March 15, 1934. Childs tells of an alleged incident in which a foreign government sent its attaché from Washington to Royal Oak, under the impression that Coughlin spoke for the president.
15. Brinkley, *Voices of Protest,* 120
16. Ibid., 119, reports that by 1934 Coughlin "was receiving more than 10,000 letters every day (65 percent of them, he claimed, from non-Catholics), and after some broadcasts his weekly total surpassed a million."
17. Ibid., 109, characterizes the policy suggestions of Coughlin to the White House as "unsolicited advice and offers of unwanted assistance."
18. Quoted in ibid., 124.
19. Sheldon Marcus, *Father Coughlin,* 64, FDR's private secretary, Marvin McIntyre, did not bother to send Coughlin an acknowledgment of his request for FDR's endorsement.
20. Quoted in ibid.
21. Ibid., 60, 70.
22. These are the core extracts of each item that were recited as part of Coughlin's November 11, 1934, radio address. Following a preamble, each principle was phrased as a pledge: "I believe . . ." The exact wording is found in Marcus, *Father Coughlin,* 72–73. On December 2, 1934, Coughlin announced additional "principles" dealing with the functions of government to limit profits, to institute a minimum wage, to limit private competition, and to prevent strikes and lockouts. Ibid., 74–75.
23. Coughlin radio address, November 11, 1934.
24. Coughlin radio address, "The Menace of the World Court," January 27, 1935.
25. Ibid.
26. *New York Times,* January 30, 1935. Because of a typographical error, the newspaper reported the number of telegrams as 400,000. This erroneous figure was repeated in a number of subsequent articles on Coughlin.
27. Senator William Borah to Coughlin, January 30, 1935, Borah Manuscripts, Library of Congress.
28. Coughlin radio address, February 6, 1935.
29. Roosevelt to Elihu Root, February 9, 1935, in Elliott Roosevelt, ed., *The Letters of Franklin Roosevelt,* 1:45. FDR to Henry L. Stimson, February 6, 1935, quoted in Arthur Schlesinger, Jr., *The Politics of Upheaval,* 243.
30. Horace G. Knoles to Howe, January 31, 1935, Official File 202A, FDRL.
31. *New York Times,* May 23, 1935.
32. Coughlin, *Series of Lectures, 1934–1935,* 198.
33. Ibid.
34. Ibid, 230.
35. Ibid.
36. Frank Murphy to FDR secretary Missy Le Hand, May 12, 1935, quoted in Sidney Fine, *Frank Murphy: The Detroit Years,* 221.
37. Coughlin to Murphy, September 5, 1935, Frank Murphy Papers.
38. Ibid., August 30, 1935, Murphy Papers.
39. Quoted in Michael Beschloss, *Kennedy and Roosevelt,* 118. "Kennedy made periodic visits to Royal Oak and, on one occasion, brought his son Jack along to meet the celebrated radio priest." Eric Thuma's unpublished interview with Coughlin in 1970 includes the recollection by Coughlin of Jack Kennedy sitting in the chair that "once was owned by Admiral Sims of the Confederate Navy."

40. Beschloss, *Kennedy and Roosevelt,* 117–18.
41. Joseph Kennedy to FDR, September 4, 1935, FDRL.
42. Coughlin to Frank Murphy, September 5, 1935, Murphy Papers, Bentley Historical Library, University of Michigan.
43. Marcus, *Father Coughlin,* 99.
44. Quoted in Beschloss, *Kennedy and Roosevelt,* 120.
45. Ibid., 119.
46. Ibid.
47. Ibid., 99.
48. Interview with Coughlin in Robert Gallagher, "The Radio Priest," 103. Coughlin mentions a version of the "Mexican check" issue in his interview with Sheldon Marcus in 1970. In my own interview with Marcus in 1985, he told me, "Coughlin lied to me. . . . He just told me a great many things that were lies."
49. Unpublished Coughlin interview with Eric Thuma, 1970.
50. Coughlin to Frank Murphy, November 13, 1935, Murphy Papers.

Chapter 5: "I Know the Pulse of the People"

1. *Berkshire Courier,* September 12, 1935.
2. Ibid., October 16, 1935.
3. Author interview with Joanna Keelon, the younger sister of Francis, 1985. According to Great Barrington real estate records, the home was owned by Francis Keelon and Edward Kinski, a key distributor for Coughlin's newspaper, *Social Justice,* which was published between 1936 and 1942.
4. Author interview with Joanna Keelon. According to Joanna, Francis never paid back his mother even though he became a multimillionaire. Joanna recalled that on one occasion when she asked her brother for money for herself and her mother, "he looked like a murderer," shouting, "I wish I could carve the name of Keelon out of your heart!"
5. Ibid.
6. Ibid.
7. Ibid. During World War II, rumors that there was a secret Nazi transmitter at Hilltop circulated among the estate's neighbors. When I visited the site in 1986, by then being used by Bard College as a student dormitory, Dean Ba Wan agreed to aid me by asking college workmen to pry open the bookshelves to see what lay behind. When the shelves were opened, whatever contents had formerly been occupying the space had been removed.
8. M. Morton Blumenthal to "Marty," May 10, 1935, Herbert Hoover Presidential Library.
9. In Lewis's novel, Coughlin is frequently mentioned by name and is well depicted in the fictional character of "Bishop Paul Peter Prang," who is ultimately imprisoned by the native fascist dictator, "Berzilius Windig." When asked about his novel and the political reality of 1936, Lewis described Coughlin as "fast losing his influence." *New York Times,* October 4, 1936.
10. See Raymond Gram Swing, *Forerunners of American Fascism,* 49–50.
11. Lawrence Dennis, *The Coming American Fascism,* 257, 256.
12. Ibid., 3.
13. In March 1935, FDR explained to his adviser, the friend and biographer of Woodrow Wilson, Colonel Edward M. House, that "individual psychology cannot, because of human weakness, be attuned for long periods of time to a

constant repetition of the highest notes on the scale." Quoted in Arthur M. Schlesinger, Jr., *The Politics of Upheaval,* 10.

14. Quoted in the *New York Times,* March 31, 1935.
15. Coughlin, *A Series of Lectures on Social Justice, 1935,* 230.
16. William Norton to Coughlin, June 22, 1936, Franklin D. Roosevelt Library (FDRL).
17. Ruth Mugglebee, *Father Coughlin,* 357. Her new volume contained two chapters testifying to her disillusionment.
18. Westbrook Pegler, *Washington Post,* July 16, 1936. The conservative columnist accused Coughlin of fascism on another occasion. *New York World-Telegram,* October 12, 1936.
19. *New York Times,* January 16, 1936.
20. See David H. Bennett, *Demagogues in the Depression,* 71.
21. *New York Times,* May 22, 1935.
22. *Social Justice,* August 10, 1936.
23. *New York Herald Tribune,* December 18, 1934. Lawrence Dennis was a major inspiration for Johnson's party. When interviewed in 1985 on a National Public Radio special dealing with Coughlin, Johnson said that he and many other people were attracted to the ideas of National Socialism. National Public Radio broadcast, October 19, 1985.
24. Author interview with Johnson, 1984.
25. Ibid. Johnson was called to testify when Coughlin's *Social Justice* newspaper was being investigated in 1942 for alleged seditious content. He had served as a foreign correspondent for the publication and was present at the German invasion of Poland. His close association with those having foreign agent links to the Third Reich brought him under government scrutiny. An FBI report dated February 1, 1945, described him as a rather harmless dabbler in political fads: "He just has a lot of money with nothing to do but travel around and spend it being a nuisance to himself and everyone else." Charles Coughlin cross-reference file, U.S. Justice Department, Freedom of Information Act (FOIA). Johnson was inducted into the service in 1943 and served in an intelligence capacity but remained under close surveillance because of his pro-Nazi ties.
26. Quoted from National Public Radio broadcast, October 19, 1985.
27. See Franklin Welch, "Memorandum Re. Reverend Chas. E. Coughlin's Special Network," June 28, 1934, Official File 1761; also File Memorandum, "L.L.M.," May 23, 1935, FDRL.
28. Coughlin offered various estimates of the NUSJ membership, including a figure of 8.5 million who had "expressed support for the sixteen principles." In January 1936, Coughlin announced that "at least" 5,267,000 new members had been recruited. In August, he mentioned that 1.6 million "active" members and 6 million "passive" members had been recruited. See Bennett, *Demagogues in the Depression,* 71.
29. Coughlin radio address, December 15, 1935.
30. *New York Times,* October 27, 1934.
31. "National Whirligig" column, *Detroit Free Press,* June 25, 1936.
32. Coughlin broadcast, June 4, 1935.
33. E. E. Lincoln to Herbert Hoover, March 11, 1935, Hoover Library. As early as December 1933, Republican backers of Hoover saw Coughlin as a potential golden goose: "His natural talents along with his acquired talents could be a

greater force for good if he would guide his talents in the right direction." Dixon to Richy, December 24, 1933, Hoover Library.

34. M. M. Blumental to "Marty," April 23, 1935, Hoover Library. One year later a "dyed in the wool Republican," after hearing Coughlin speak, wrote to him asking if "somehow the tremendous ability of Mr. Hoover and the vast influence which you can assert . . . could . . . return the nation to the path of social and economic sense." Charles P. Sisson to Hoover, April 1, 1936, Hoover Library.

35. Unsigned memo to Herbert Hoover, June 4, 1936, Post-Presidential File, Charles E. Coughlin, Hoover Library.

36. Drew Pearson column, August 14, 1936.

37. Unpublished interview of Eric Thuma, 1970. Coughlin told Thuma that years afterward he visited with Hoover, who, according to the priest, allegedly confessed that his hands were tied in doing anything about the depression. In 1972, he told another interviewer that Hoover was "one of the finest gentlemen I have ever met." Richard Gallagher, "Radio Priest," 101.

38. Unsigned memo to Herbert Hoover, June 4, 1936, Post-Presidential File, Charles E. Coughlin, Hoover Library.

Chapter 6: "Two and a Half Rival Messiahs"

1. Quoted in Alan Brinkley, *Voices of Protest,* 72.

2. Long's plan called for what would have been, in effect, a guaranteed annual wage, since with the federal government's "capital levy tax," families would receive a "house-estate" of $5,000, "enough for a home, an automobile, a radio, and the ordinary conveniences." Ibid., 79.

3. Smith's career is carefully examined in a biography by historian Glen Jeansonne, *Gerald L. K. Smith: Minister of Hate.* Until his death in 1981, Smith was a tireless far-right and anti-Semitic pamphleteer. His publication, *The Cross and the Flag,* a racist and anti-Semitic weekly, was published from the 1940s to the 1970s.

4. Brinkley, *Voices of Protest,* 251, indicates that "after 1935, the Share Our Wealth Society survived only in his [Smith's] own hopeful imagination."

5. Ibid., 213, stresses that Long's Share Our Wealth and Coughlin's NUSJ were similar and that "by the spring of 1935, a strong impression was growing in the public that indeed the two movements were one."

6. The prevailing view of FDR's advisers was that Long posed much the greater threat because of his legislative experience and perceived greater political acumen. A carefully constructed sampling of voters conducted a few months before Long's assassination in September 1935 by Emil Hurja underscored the danger. Ibid., 207–209, 284–286.

7. Sheldon Marcus, *Father Coughlin,* 86. According to T. Harry Williams, *Huey Long,* 801, Long frequently entertained Coughlin in his Washington, D.C., suite at the Broadmoor Hotel.

8. *Life,* November 14, 1955; Marcus, *Father Coughlin,* 105.

9. Quoted in Arthur M. Schlesinger, Jr., *The Politics of Upheaval,* 30.

10. Marcus, *Father Coughlin,* 103, indicates that "in November [1935] Townsend visited Father Coughlin at his home and they agreed to form a loose alliance." The meeting was reported in the *New York Times,* November 25, 1935.

11. Quoted in Schlesinger, *Politics of Upheaval,* 555.

12. Quoted in the *New York Times,* June 21, 1936.
13. See Brinkley, *Voices of Protest,* 256–261 passim. When interviewed by Sheldon Marcus in 1970, Coughlin denied he had ever been "allied with either Smith or Townsend." *Father Coughlin,* 105.
14. FBI report, March 7, 1941, Louis Ward File, U.S. Justice Department, Freedom of Information Act (FOIA).
15. This was the time that Coughlin's newspaper was being closely censored by the Detroit archdiocese. See Chapter 12.
16. An FBI report noted, "When in Washington, Ward entertains congressmen and senators in a lavish manner; he is well-known on the 'Hill' and for this reason has gained some success in lobbying activities." March 7, 1941, Ward File.
17. In his authorized biography of Coughlin, Ward comments, "After spending weeks of study of the man personally and of his works, I prefer to think . . . that this man's source of strength is from above; that a Divine Providence directing the destiny of this nation of ours has chosen him." Ward, *Father Charles E. Coughlin,* 351.
18. Author interview with Father Peter Wiethe, 1986.
19. "Memorandum for the files," January 28, 1936, Marvin McIntyre, Official File, Franklin D. Roosevelt Library (FDRL).
20. Quoted in Edward C. Blackorby, *Prairie Rebel: The Public Life of William Lemke,* 221.
21. David H. Bennett, *Demagogues in the Depression,* 192.
22. Blackorby, *Prairie Rebel,* 208.
23. Geoffrey S. Smith, *To Save a Nation,* 40.
24. Quoted in Marcus, 114.
25. Smith, 40.
26. Quoted in Milton Crane, ed., *The Roosevelt Era,* 193.
27. *New York Times,* July 17, 1936.
28. Quoted in Crane, *The Roosevelt Era,* 194.
29. Roosevelt to Josephus Daniels, March 1, 1935, in *Roosevelt and Daniels: A Friendship in Politics,* ed. Carroll Kirkpatrick, 195–196.
30. Coughlin's finances had been tracked for some time earlier. See W. L. Slattery to James A. Farley, March 19, 1935, Official File, FDRL. One loyal supporter sent Farley the first copy of Coughlin's new weekly newspaper, *Social Justice.* With a circulation of several hundred thousand, it became a major tool for political mobilization in 1936 and in later Coughlin activities.
31. See Richard D. Lunt, "Frank Murphy's Decision to Enter the 1936 Gubernatorial Race," 330–331.
32. Rep. John McCormack to Roosevelt, September 26, 1936, President's Personal File, FDRL.
33. James Roosevelt to Jim Farley, September 17, 1936, National Committee Correspondence, FDRL.
34. Quoted in Bennett, *Demagogues in the Depression,* 222.
35. John Lesinski to Farley, August 21, 1936, National Committee Correspondence, FDRL.
36. John L. Mikelich, September 10, 1936, National Committee Correspondence, FDRL.
37. *New York Times,* August 6, 1936.
38. Steve Early to James A. Farley (letter of Dean Alfange), September 25, 1936, official file 306, FDRL.

39.   Copy of Joseph Kennedy address, October 5, 1936, Thomas Corcoran Papers, Library of Congress, Manuscripts Division.

40.   Farley to Bowers, October 23, 1936, Thomas C. Corcoran Papers, Library of Congress.

41.   *New York Times,* August 3, 1936.

42.   In a confidential memo to FDR, Stephen Early quoted a Democratic party worker in Indiana, saying, "He is convinced Coughlin [*sic*] so-called union party is operating on 'a shoestring.'" Early to Roosevelt, June 22, 1936, Official File 306, FDRL.

43.   *New York Times,* October 30, 1936.

44.   Ibid. In the same address, Coughlin, partly in the light of the erroneous *Literary Digest,* which predicted a Republican victory with Alf Landon, was quoted as declaring the election would go to the House of Representatives, where John Nance Garner would become president. Richard Davis, "The Radio Priest," 228, notes that such a view shows the priest's statement "stemmed from his ignorance of the Constitution."

45.   Quoted in Blackorby, *Prairie Rebel,* 232. Lemke later rejoined the Republican party, but at first unsuccessfully tried to sustain an independent party organization on his own. See Bennett, *Demagogues in the Depression,* 276.

46.   Quoted in Robert S. Gallagher, "The Radio Priest," 102.

47.   *New York Times,* November 6, 1936.

48.   Ibid., September 26, 1936. There is some dispute as to whether Coughlin was correctly quoted in his Cincinnati speech. See Davis, "Radio Priest," 224. The quotation regarding the White House appears in the *New York Times,* September 3, 1936.

49.   Coughlin radio address, November 7, 1936.

50.   Mencken to Dreiser, May 17, 1935. A few months earlier, Mencken recorded in his diary for January 18, 1935, that Fulton Oursler, the editor of *American Mercury* magazine, was informed by a friend, "Coughlin, after a few drinks, began speculating about his future. He said, 'If I am dictator for five days, even though I be killed afterward, I'll live in history.'" Quoted in Charles A. Fecher, *The Diaries of H. L. Mencken,* 84–85.

51.   Author interview with Father Peter Wiethe, 1984.

52.   Ibid., 1986.

53.   *New York Times,* April 8, 1938.

54.   Author interview with Father Peter Wiethe, 1986. Coughlin had written to his archbishop, Edward Mooney, on April 11, 1938, that he had been warned by "a certain Congressman [who] visited me" that the reorganization bill was going to be reintroduced by Representative John McCormack of Massachusetts. United States Catholic Conference Archives.

55.   *New York Times,* March 25, 1938.

56.   *New York Journal American,* April 6, 1938.

57.   Harold Ickes, *The Secret Diaries of Harold Ickes, 1936–39,* April 11, 1938. FDR to J. David Stern, April 20, 1938, FDRL.

58.   *New York Times,* April 29, 1938.

Chapter 7: All the World's a Stage

1.   Early in FDR's administration, the need to send U.S. delegates to the London Economic Conference dealing with setting new guidelines for international

currency values in June 1933 provided congressional supporters of Coughlin an opportunity to suggest he be named one of the American representatives. Among the more prominent of the fifty-nine members of Congress who petitioned the president on the priest's behalf were Huey Long, Elmer Thomas, Emanuel Cellar, Pat McCarran, Wright Patman, Burton K. Wheeler, Everett Dirksen, and William Borah. Roosevelt did not follow their suggestion.

2. *New York Times,* September 15, 1935.
3. Major C. H. Douglas, quoted in John Finlay, *Social Credit: The English Origins,* 103.
4. Ibid., 104.
5. John A. Irving, *The Social Credit Movement in Alberta,* 6–7.
6. As a political theory, social credit stressed individual economic rights as the basis of political rights. Any representative elective body was seen to have been prone to manipulation by financial (i.e., Jewish) interests. Existing political parties were seen in this light and had to be replaced with a single party committed to the principles of social credit.
7. Alvin Finkel, *The Social Credit Phenomenon in Alberta,* 60.
8. The focus on this theme in Pound's *Cantos* 12, 14, and 15 is presented by E. Fuller Torrey in *The Roots of Treason: Ezra Pound and the Secrets of St. Elizabeths.*
9. Ezra Pound, *Jefferson and/or Mussolini,* 125, 128.
10. Pound to Coughlin, November 30, 1934, Pound Collection, Yale Collection of American Literature, Beinecke Rare Book and Manuscript Library, Yale University.
11. *British-Italian Bulletin,* March 14, 1936.
12. Pound to Coughlin, October 26, 1936, Pound Collection.
13. Ibid., December 1, 1936, Pound Collection.
14. In one letter to Coughlin, he mentioned being asked to write articles for the Vatican's official newspaper, *Osservatore Romano.* Despite opposition to this work, he expected it would be going ahead, since "the canonists are against USURA." Pound to Coughlin, January 20, 1936, Pound Collection.
15. Pound to Lewis, September 11, 1937, Pound Collection. Torrey, *Roots of Treason,* 155–156, notes that "H. L. Mencken wrote repeatedly to Pound telling him that Roosevelt was trying hard to get the United States in the war, reinforcing Pound's views that the President was a tool of Jewish financial interests."
16. Pound told Louis Zukofsky, "Father Coughlin speaks regularly to millions of Americans." Humphrey Carpenter, *A Serious Character: The Life of Ezra Pound,* 561.
17. Pound broadcast of February 19, 1942, in Torrey, *Roots of Treason,* 468. Torrey argues that Pound's decision to pursue radio broadcasting was inspired by Coughlin.
18. Diary entry of Hugh Walpole, September 12, 1937, quoted in Rupert Hart-Davis, *Hugh Walpole, A Biography,* 386–87.
19. Author interview with Father Peter Wiethe, 1986.
20. A. N. Wilson, *Hilaire Belloc,* 257.
21. Ibid., 258. Wilson notes that the rhyme is from the oral tradition.
22. Belloc asserted that his aim in writing *The Jews*—"my admirable Yid book"— was to reduce distrust and fear between Jews and non-Jews: "I have written it as an attempt at justice." Wilson, *Belloc,* ix. The phrase used to describe his writing is quoted in Wilson, *Hilaire Belloc,* 258.

23. Belloc to Mells, February 5, 1937, quoted in Wilson, *Hilaire Belloc,* 344–345.
24. *Social Justice,* February 28, 1938.
25. Ibid., April 11, 1938.
26. Wilson, *Hilaire Belloc,* 348. Belloc found the "nigger jazz band with the niggers making loud animal barks and yelps" a major annoyance on his return voyage to England.
27. When the corruption accusations were not supported in a government investigation of the Marconi contract, Chesterton felt he had been labeled an anti-Semite. In an open letter to the prosecutor, he coined a classic argument against such a charge: "I have made many friends among the Jews, and some of these I have retained as life-long friends." Chesterton sarcastically commented, "If we are lovers [pro- versus anti-Semitic], we will not kill ourselves for love." Frances Donaldson, *The Marconi Scandal,* 258.
28. Chesterton, *The New Jerusalem,* 221.
29. G. K. Chesterton, *Autobiography,* 71. Chesterton's cousin, A. K. Chesterton, was active in Sir Oswald Mosley's British Union of Fascists.
30. Coughlin, *Father Coughlin's Radio Discourses, 1931–1932,* 122.
31. John P. Diggins, *Mussolini and Fascism: The View from America.*
32. Coughlin to Mussolini, March 1, 1933, Busta 165, fasciola 23, Central State Archives of Italy (CSA).
33. Ibid.
34. Italian Ministry of Foreign Affairs to Washington Embassy, telegram, April 7, 1933, Coughlin File, CSA.
35. Italian Ambassador in Washington to Ministry of Foreign Affairs, telegram, May 8, 1933, CSA.
36. For a discussion of these dynamics, see Philip V. Cannistraro and Theodore P. Kovaleff, "Father Coughlin and Mussolini: Impossible Allies," 432–445.
37. Coughlin, *Series of Lectures, 1935–36,* 50–51.
38. Italian Ambassador in Washington to Rome, November 16, 1935, CSA.
39. Italian Ambassador in Washington to Ministry of Foreign Affairs, October 22, 1936, CSA.
40. Coughlin to Mussolini, September 6, 1938, Coughlin File, CSA.
41. "The Salvation of Spain," *Tablet,* February 25, 1939, 245–246.
42. *Social Justice,* June 13, 1938.
43. Author interview with Paul Weber, 1984.
44. Coughlin radio address, January 15, 1939.
45. Coughlin, *Social Justice,* January 30, 1939.
46. *Social Justice,* April 10, 1939.
47. Ibid., April 25, 1938.
48. Ibid., August 15, 1938.
49. Report of conversation between Arnold Lunn and Coughlin, December 14, 1940, Coughlin File, Archdiocese Archives of Detroit.
50. Quoted in R. Benewick, *The Fascist Movement in Britain,* 27–28.
51. Quoted in D. S. Lewis, *Illusions of Grandeur: Mosley, Fascism, and British Society, 1931–81,* 12.
52. Ibid., 94–95.
53. Ibid., 94.
54. Ibid., 95.
55. Ibid.
56. Ibid., 81. Also See Nicholas Mosley, *Beyond the Pale,* 294–295.

57. Mosley, *Beyond the Pale,* 334.

58. Ibid., 369. In her book *A Life of Contrasts,* Diana Mosley told how "Unity [her sister] and I, standing at the window of the upstairs room, saw Hitler walking through the trees of the parklike garden that separated the house and the *Reichs-kanzlei*. . . . Behind him came an adjutant carrying a box and some flowers."

59. Sir Oswald Mosley, *My Life,* 29–30.

60. Author interview with Diana Mosley, 1993. When attending a BUF reunion in 1991, Michael Quill, a longtime member, mentioned the "walking stick" instruction given to Mosley.

61. Lewis, *Mosley, Fascism, and British Society,* 139–140. Mosley, *Beyond the Pale,* 399, reprints the letter from Hitler's adjutant to "Mrs. Guinness" [Diana's maiden name], who describes that "aside from technical considerations" the obstacle to the German transmission station was the objections raised by "military authorities."

62. Oswald Mosley to Charles Coughlin, September 8, 1938. Both communications had passed through British intelligence in Bermuda. The letter and Coughlin's reply are contained in the case memorandum written by William Power Maloney in connection with a contemplated prosecution of Coughlin, dated May 8, 1942. I am grateful to William Black for giving me this material.

63. The article appeared in the February 27, 1939, issue of *Social Justice.* Barnes also wrote favorably about Mussolini's anti-Semitic policies in a September 28, 1938, issue of the newspaper.

64. *Social Justice,* February 20, 1939.

65. Ibid.

Chapter 8: Foreign Intrigues

1. FBI report, May 1, 1942, Coughlin File, Freedom of Information Act (FOIA). The quotation is attributed to Stanley Boynton by Morris Steinberg, who did printing for Coughlin's *Social Justice.* In 1942, when the agency was looking into Coughlin's Axis ties, Steinberg went to the FBI about the 1938 incident. Boynton, when questioned about the matter, denied ever making a reference to Coughlin and a trip to Germany. FBI internal report, May 27, 1942, Coughlin File, FOIA.

2. E. David Cronon, *Josephus Daniels in Mexico,* 112.

3. Coughlin radio address, December 23, 1934. In another stirring address on the same subject on March 21, 1937, Coughlin declaimed: "In my hand at this moment, I have a piece of cotton cloth which everyone in this church audience sees that I have. It's dyed red with the blood of one of the first priest martyrs of Mexico. Father Pro! You've not died in vain! Christianity must prevail!"

4. Quoted in Cronon, *Josephus Daniels,* 98–99. Leo V. Kanawada, Jr., *Franklin D. Roosevelt's Diplomacy and American Catholics, Italians and Jews,* 29, indicates that FDR's efforts at informal diplomacy were so controversial within the U.S. Catholic community that when Father John J. Burke, secretary of the National Catholic Welfare Conference, took a role in informal diplomacy between the Mexican and U.S. governments, his efforts were to be strictly secret: he "must not go to the White House or the Department of State, but that some non-public place should be chosen for a meeting."

5. See Cronon, *Josephus Daniels,* 85. Burke told Daniels that "the Vatican frowned not only upon armed rebellion, but also upon Church interference in

politics." Secretary of State Cordell Hull politely warned Daniels to avoid "any utterances or actions in Mexico which were calculated to feed the agitation and violent utterances that were taking place in the United States." Kanawada, *Franklin D. Roosevelt's Diplomacy,* 36.

6. Quoted in Abraham Bernard Magil, *The Real Father Coughlin,* 38.
7. John A. Spivak, *A Man in His Time,* 408.
8. John W. F. Dulles, *Yesterday in Mexico: A Chronicle of the Revolution, 1919–1936,* 648.
9. For a discussion of Allen and Schwinn's links to the Gold Shirts, see Spivak, *Man in His Time,* 406–416 passim. Also see Magil, *The Truth About Father Coughlin.* John Roy Carlson's *Undercover* mentions the Gold Shirts (146, 178, 445) and their links to U.S. backers and sympathizers. They are noted as well in Morris Schonbach, "Native American Fascism During the 1930s and 1940s," 221–222.
10. Butler had developed a reputation for outspoken honesty and even radical activism. His forced retirement in 1930 as marine commandant occurred because he leaked the story of an incident in which Italian dictator Mussolini had run over a child while speeding to a political meeting. In a speech, Butler called Mussolini "a mad dog about to break loose in Europe." Insulted, the Italian government sent a note of protest. Butler was urged to accept early retirement. See *Philadelphia Inquirer,* January 30, 1931.
11. Quoted in Richard Zilg, *Du Pont: Behind the Nylon Curtain,* 292.
12. At first Butler's charges were ridiculed in the press, including the *New York Times.* The alleged plot "of Wall Street interests failed to emerge in any alarming proportion." *New York Times,* August 25, 1934. *Time,* December 3, 1934, called it "a plot without plotters. . . . No military officer has succeeded in publicly floundering in so much hot water as Smedley Darlington Butler."
13. Although McGuire flatly denied that he sought to fund a fascist-style organization, he was vague and inconsistent in his testimony about the financial dealings linked to the alleged organization to be formed under Butler's leadership. See Spivak, *A Man in His Time,* 309–311.
14. Quoted in Gerald Colby, *Du Pont Dynasty,* 324.
15. *New York Times,* May 17, 1935.
16. Agent Dawsey to J. Edgar Hoover, August 8, 1936, Coughlin File, FOIA.
17. Hoover to Attorney General Homer Cummings, memo, August 8, 1936, Coughlin File, FOIA.
18. Ibid.
19. Ibid.
20. General Craig Malin to Hoover, memo, October 16, 1936. Coughlin File, FOIA.
21. Author telephone interview with Hans Schmidt, October 22, 1984. In his 1987 study, *Maverick Marine,* Schmidt cites the fact that Butler "mentioned the Coughlin plot again to an [FBI] agent in 1940 in connection with what [Butler] termed dozens of "screwball" organizations that had invited him to appear as a speaker" (234).
22. Memo to the file, September 24, 1936, Butler File, FOIA.
23. *Social Justice,* September 20, 27, 1937. Coughlin sailed from the United States on August 29, 1937, landing in Hampton five days later. He told the press, "I wanted peace and quiet and decided to come to the most hospitable country in the world." *New York Times,* September 6, 1937.

24. Author interview with Sharon Keyes, niece of Frank Murphy, 1987.
25. Cliveden is the Astor Estate in England. Lady Nancy Astor was the first woman elected to the British Parliament in the twentieth century. Her politics and that of many of her friends focused on avoiding war with Germany. Prominent British leaders and, on occasion, representatives of Germany could be found among the company at the Astors'. In the popular media, those sympathetic to appeasing the Nazis were labeled the "Cliveden Set."
26. Edward Treglown to Frank Murphy, April 14, 1938; reply by Murphy, April 26, 1938. Frank Murphy Papers, Bentley Historical Library, University of Michigan.
27. Sidney Fine and Robert Warner, "Interview with Regent Irene Murphy," July 30, 1964, Michigan Historical Collection, University of Michigan. I was given a copy by Irene shortly before her death.
28. Ibid. Irene Murphy described in detail what Ruth Treglown had told her regarding a visit to a nearby Catholic cathedral (probably Canterbury), where a rare illuminated Bible was on display. According to Treglown, the priest asked her to help him remove the valuable relic by untying the thongs holding it down. When the footsteps of the sexton approached, the project was halted.
29. Ibid.
30. In the course of several interviews with priests and associates who worked with Coughlin over the years, they recounted to me how they might receive a call from a "Mr. Smith" in New York. The FBI files also show that during World War II, Coughlin traveled with one of his staff, under the name of that person as man and wife.
31. Author telephone interview with Betty Treglown, then living in Canada, 1989.
32. Author interview with Joseph P. Wright, 1985.
33. Frank Murphy to Ruth Treglown, May 3, 1938, Bumgartner Papers, Bentley Historical Library, University of Michigan.
34. Author interview with Father Peter Wiethe, 1984.
35. FBI internal report, May 27, 1942, Coughlin File, FOIA.
36. Charles Coughlin passport application form, State Department, May 1, 1941, State Department, Coughlin File, FOIA.

Chapter 9: "Jewish Actions Which Cause Cruel Prosecution"

1. John Higham, "American Anti-Semitism Reconsidered," 243.
2. Ibid., 244–245.
3. Foster Bain to Herbert Hoover, Herbert Hoover Presidential Library.
4. *London Times,* August 30, 1936. See also Morris Janowitz, "Black Legions on the March," in Daniel Aaron, ed., *America in Crisis: Fourteen Crucial Episodes in America,* 304.
5. *London Times,* August 30, 1936.
6. Quoted in Morris Schonbach, "Native American Fascism During the 1930s and 1940s," 305.
7. For a review of the industrialists who supported various pro-fascist and Nazi organizations, see George Seldes, *Facts and Fascism;* Albert E. Kahn, *High Treason: The Plot Against the Peace;* and Gerald Colby, *Du Pont Dynasty.*
8. In 1927, Jung established the American Vigilant Intelligence Federation in Chicago, which made him the first of the "experts" on the menace of domestic communism. His testimony in the Hamilton Fish hearings is noted in Chapter 2.

9. Quoted in the *New Review,* August 27, 1936, Weiner Library, London.
10. Quoted in author interview with Father Peter Wiethe, 1985.
11. Coughlin radio address, "The Enemy Within," February 2, 1930.
12. Coughlin, *Radio Sermons, 1930–1931,* 103.
13. Coughlin radio address, February 19, 1933.
14. Ibid.
15. Ibid., February 26, 1933.
16. Ibid.
17. Quoted in Will H. Hays, *The Memoirs of Will Hays,* 462.
18. Ibid., 464.
19. *Detroit News,* August 11, 1973.
20. Author interview with Myron Steinberg, 1989. Myron and his brother Morris printed Coughlin's *Social Justice* for a period in 1938.
21. Author interview with Father Peter Wiethe, 1986.
22. Quoted in the *Detroit Jewish Chronicle,* November 2, 1934.
23. Quoted in ibid., November 16, 1934.
24. Author interview with Rabbi Leon Fram, 1984.
25. April 12, 1935 address, American Jewish Archives.
26. Coughlin to Isserman, May 28, 1935, American Jewish Archives (AJA).
27. Shrine of the Little Flower, January 22, 1935, quoted in A. B. Magil, *The Real Father Coughlin,* 1939, 33.
28. Quoted from PBS documentary "The Radio Priest" (*American Experience* series), broadcast October 1986. A few days after the speech, on August 31, 1936, Coughlin's *Social Justice* warned, "If certain groups of politically swayed Jews care to organize against Father Coughlin or the National Union they will be entirely responsible for stirring up any repercussions which they will invite."
29. *Social Justice,* April 10, 1939. Isserman was quoted as saying that Jews in America "have an obligation to expose Father Coughlin's plans against democracy."
30. Eric Thuma unpublished interview with Coughlin, 1970.
31. *Congressional Record,* May 5, 1934.
32. Deathridge to Roosevelt, October 18, 1934, Franklin D. Roosevelt Library (FDRL).
33. *Defender* 8, February 1934; Robert E. Hertzstein, *Roosevelt and Hitler, Prelude to War,* 178. Hertzstein notes that Winrod was "one of the first anti-Semites to use the name 'Rosenfeld' for the President."
34. Roosevelt to Philip Slomovitz, March 7, 1935, reprinted in Philip Slomovitz, *Purely Commentary,* 5.
35. Rabbi Stephen Wise to Slomovitz, March 27, 1935, reprinted in ibid., 9.
36. Osborne to Slomovitz, March 21, 1935, reprinted in ibid., 6–7. In a short note, Chase indicated that Slomovitz could publish his letter and facetiously added, "I think I am a better Jew than you are!" (April 2, 1935). Slomovitz replied two days later, "You are a much more interesting man than I originally thought you were, and I got a great thrill out of your letter making claim to better Jewishness than is mine."
37. Ibid., 3.
38. Quoted from Robert Edward Edmonson, "Yom Kippuring America!" *Jacksonville Herald Tribune,* October 6, 1939. The copy was sent by Samuel Kipnis to FDR's secretary, Stephen Early. President's Personal File, FDRL.
39. *Worldwide News Service* (Germany) July 23, 1940, copy in the *Detroit Jewish News* archives.

40. Unpublished interview by Eric Thuma, 1970. Coughlin went on to tell Thuma that FDR "wasn't regarded as one of the first founders of Jewry in this country either. I have a book out there with the pedigree of all the Jews."
41. Lecture pamphlet for Gertrude Coogan, n.d. (1931?), copy given to me by Mary Larkin.
42. Ibid.
43. Quoted from "Talk with Father John Coogan," September 30, 1943. Michigan Civil Rights League Papers, Collections of the Archives of Labor History and Urban Affairs, Walter Reuther Archive, Wayne State University.
44. Author interview with Mary Larkin, 1986.
45. Charles E. Coughlin, *Money! Questions and Answers,* 58, 150.
46. Quoted from "Talk with Father John Coogan," September 30, 1943, Michigan Civil Rights League papers, Walter Reuther Library.
47. Gertrude Coogan to Bishop Michael Gallagher, November 22, 1935, Archdiocese of Detroit Archives (AAD).
48. Coughlin to Gallagher, telegram, September 21, 1936, AAD.
49. Coogan to Gallagher, September 28, 1936, AAD.
50. An article entitled "Author, 81, Braves Snow to Talk" told how "economist Miss Gertrude Coogan battled icy streets and a snow-covered airport so she could reach New Orleans and speak here . . . against internationalism. This fight, which she says is 'waged on behalf of middle class Americans,' is nothing new to her, she's been at it nearly half a century." *New Orleans Times-Picayune,* December 8, 1979.
51. Author interview with Mary Larkin, 1986. Larkin, Coogan's longtime companion, who had been blind most of her life, regained her sight on the day Coogan died in 1984.
52. Quoted in Marcus, *Father Coughlin,* 168. When I interviewed former *Social Justice* writer Joseph Wright in 1985, he recalled Ford's calling the priest "Father Charles."
53. See Robert Lacey, *Ford: The Man and the Machine,* 409. The author states that "Rome featured high in the demonology of Henry Ford Senior" (410).
54. Author interview with Joseph Wright, 1985. Harry Bennett was a key figure in the operations of the Ford Motor Company. His Service Department dealt with a variety of key issues, including labor-management issues. He was notorious for his high-handed and violent approach to restricting union organization at the company.
55. Carol Gelderman, *The Wayward Capitalist,* 222.
56. Gelderman, ibid., 201–202, asserts that Liebold built "a Gestapo of his own within the [Ford] company, keeping elaborate files about every executive."
57. For two years, 1921 and 1922, Ford's newspaper published articles detailing the dominant role Jews played in the cultural, political, and economic life of the United States. Ford aide William J. Cameron was editor of Ford's newspaper. Historian David L. Lewis, *The Public Image of Henry Ford,* chap. 9, offers a detailed review of the series and its origins and impact.
58. According to Gelderman, *The Wayward Capitalist,* 223, when one Jewish employee became upset over the incident, Liebold told her, "You are just one of a lot of Jews who have to go through the same thing. Don't pay any attention to it, and they won't bother you."
59. Liebold was careful to protect Henry Ford by evading a clear answer about direct links: "I think possibly Mr. Ford might have met Father Coughlin person-

ally. But he didn't do so in my presence." "Liebold Reminiscences," 1950, Edison Archive, 1396, Henry Ford Museum.

60. At several points during the 1930s, Coughlin sought to play a major role in labor organizations. For a discussion of his involvement with AIWA, see Alan Brinkley, *Voices of Protest,* 140–141.

61. Gelderman, *The Wayward Capitalist,* 330.

62. Robert Montieth had a notorious past, since he was one of the participants in the famous German-funded coup attempt of 1916 by Sir Roger Casement, a failed effort to overthrow the British government and establish an Irish republic. Casement was hanged; Montieth escaped and found his way to the United States in the 1920s.

63. John A. Spivak, *The Shrine of the Silver Dollar,* 211.

64. Ibid., 211–212.

65. Ibid., 213.

66. Harold L. Ickes, *The Secret Diary of Harold L. Ickes,* 1936–39, entry of August 26, 1939, 706.

67. Author telephone interview with James Roosevelt, 1984. In May 1942, following Coughlin's "silencing," a memorandum circulated within the FBI stating that "Harry Bennett of the Ford Motor Company" was on a list of individuals who contributed [to Coughlin and Gerald L. K. Smith] more than $1,000 in the years 1937, 1938, and 1939." FBI memorandum, Louis Nichols to Tolson, May 30, 1942, Coughlin File, FOIA. The memorandum noted that the confidential list had been sent to FDR by his son Franklin.

68. Ford was the first American to receive the award, created by Hitler himself in 1937; it was the highest honor bestowed on foreigners by the Third Reich. Fifteen hundred prominent Detroiters attended the event at which Hitler's personal congratulations were extended. Liebold received a somewhat lesser award, the Order of Merit of the German Eagle, six weeks later.

69. *Detroit Free Press,* August 1, 1938.

70. Remark made to John Dykema, quoted in Lacey, *Ford,* 387.

71. Clement XII called for the excommunication of Catholics who joined Masonic organizations. This mandate was rescinded only with Vatican II in 1962. For the most contemporary thesis of Jewish-Masonic links, see E. Cahill, *Freemasonry and the Anti-Christian Movement.*

72. Ford is the only American mentioned in Hitler's personal manifesto of political philosophy. Although he did not receive any direct funds from Ford (a widely circulated rumor in the 1920s and later), Hitler acknowledged his debt to the American industrialist: "The struggle of international Jewish finance against Ford . . . has only strengthened the sympathies of the National Socialist Party for Ford and has given the broadest circulation to his book." Quoted in Lewis, *Public Image of Henry Ford,* 143.

73. By the time of Hitler's accession to power in 1933, the German edition had passed through twenty-nine separate printings. See Lewis, *Public Image of Henry Ford,* 148. Despite efforts by the Ford family and officials at the Ford Motor Company, copies of the *International Jew* continue to circulate and are still reprinted today.

74. Coughlin frequently sent form letters warning of the "invisible control Oriental Free Masonry is exercising in public affairs." When I interviewed Father Peter Wiethe in 1985, he gave me a copy of Cahill's *Freemasonry and the Anti-Christian Movement.* The edition he gave me, published in 1959, has quotations from Ford's *The International Jew* and the *Protocols.*

75. *Social Justice,* July 18, 1938.
76. See Lacey, *Ford,* 208.
77. Ibid.
78. Casimir Palmer to Coughlin, July 20, 1938, American Jewish Archives (AJA). Coughlin declared in response, "I am not in opposition to the Jews. I am trying to analyze the thing [Protocols] and help the Jews." Coughlin to Palmer, July 26, 1938, AJA.
79. *Detroit Jewish News,* July 19, 1938.
80. Author interview with Philip Slomovitz, 1985.
81. *Detroit Jewish News,* July 22, 1938.
82. *Social Justice,* September 26, 1938.
83. Marcus, *Father Coughlin,* 254, indicates that E. Perrin Schwartz and Joseph Wright wrote the "Marcin" reply to Slomovitz and that "various staff members" wrote other articles using this pseudonym. My own view is that Coughlin himself wrote the reply to Slomovitz. Five decades later, when interviewed, Slomovitz expressed great surprise at the fact of there being no person named Ben Marcin. Bernice Marciniewicz served Coughlin until his death and helped launch a final effort to have a positive biography written about him. She refused to be interviewed by me.
84. *Social Justice,* November 21, 1938.
85. Ibid., December 12, 1938. Interviewed in 1972 by Robert Gallagher, ("The Radio Priest," 102), Coughlin said he did not know how "I came in touch with these . . . [protocols]. I must have had two hundred copies. . . . I had them in every language. . . . I think I've read everything about the Protocols. . . . I don't know the certain truth about them. . . . I couldn't prove they're false, I couldn't prove they're genuine."
86. Arthur Morse, *While Six Million Died,* 221.
87. Ibid., 223.
88. Ibid., 225.
89. Quoted in Deborah Lipstadt, *Beyond Belief: The American Press and the Coming of the Holocaust, 1933–1945,* 104. Lipstadt notes that "practically no American newspaper, irrespective of size, circulation, location, or political inclination failed to condemn Germany" (99).
90. Transcript, Coughlin radio address, November 20, 1938.
91. Ibid.
92. Ibid.
93. Author interview with Donald Flamm, 1986.
94. Ibid., 1986.
95. Ibid., 1985.
96. Ibid., 1986.
97. Ibid., 1985.
98. *New York Times,* November 23, 1938.
99. *Detroit Free Press,* November 22, 1938.
100. Station WMCA to Coughlin, November 23, 1938, copy given to me by Donald Flamm.
101. *Detroit News,* November 24, 1938.
102. *Berlin Zeitung,* November 22, 1938 (translation); *New York Times,* November 24, 1938.

Chapter 10: Charity Begins at Home

1. Coughlin radio broadcast, November 27, 1938. As late as 1973, Coughlin was praising Fahey, referring to him in a talk at St. Mary's Church in Detroit as "one of the most brilliant priests in all the world since the days of Cardinal Newman" (June 13, 1973 address). Although Fahey died in 1954, the last of his books, *The Mystical Body of Christ and the Reorganization of Society,* continues to be reprinted. For a detailed analysis of Fahey's influence on Coughlin and vice versa, see Sister Mary Athans, *The Coughlin-Fahey Connection.*

2. The concept of modernism that Fahey and Coughlin used is synonymous with the term *naturalism.* Both saw this development in Europe as the major challenge to traditional Catholic thought. In a philosophical sense, the terms mean relying on scientific knowledge to define and explain the world and its reality. In a theological sense, they mean that religious doctrine need not depend on supernatural or divine revelation; rather, all religious truth may be derived from the natural world.

3. At one point, long after his national prominence had faded, Coughlin offered to donate his extensive library of books dealing with Jews to the Detroit Archdiocese. The retired chancellor, Edward J. Hickey, told me he refused it.

4. Cole did make several broadcasts critical of Coughlin, but the fact that they were privately sponsored by Jewish organizations undermined their credibility and fueled a "Judas priest" charge by Coughlin's followers. I was told by Father Wiethe that another example of such a tactic involved a group of Detroit Jewish leaders who allegedly offered to buy Coughlin another church in some other locale so that he would not be so much of a threat. There is no evidence that such an offer was ever made by any group.

5. Coughlin broadcast, December 25, 1938

6. Ibid., March 26, 1939

7. Ibid., November 27, 1938.

8. Ibid., December 11, 1938.

9. Ibid.

10. Ibid., December 18, 1938.

11. Ibid.

12. Quoted in Michael Beschloss, *Kennedy and Roosevelt: The Uneasy Alliance,* 180.

13. Flamm to McNinch, December 21, 1938, copy given to me by Donald Flamm.

14. "Report of Street Demonstrations," private report to Flamm, February 1939, copy given to me by Donald Flamm.

15. *Social Justice,* December 26, 1938.

16. "Report of Street Demonstrations."

17. *Nation,* July 22, 1939.

18. Ibid.

19. "Report of Street Demonstrations."

20. *Nation,* July 22, 1939.

21. "Notarized statement of Milton A. Sadolsky," May 5, 1939, copy provided to me by Donald Flamm.

22. "Notarized statement of J. Edward Silver," May 1939, copy provided to me by Donald Flamm.

23. *Nation,* July 22, 1939.

24. *Social Justice,* May 23, 1938.

25. Letter to editor by "Celia Black," *Social Justice,* July 3, 1939.
26. Monty Noan Penkower, *The Jews Were Expendable,* 95; David S. Wyman, *Paper Walls: America and the Refugee Crisis, 1938–1941,* x. Lack of unity within the Jewish community has been focused on in several studies as a reason that FDR failed to take decisive action. See particularly Rafael Medoff, *The Deafening Silence: American Jewish Leaders and the Holocaust,* and Haskell Lookstein, *Were We Our Brother's Keeper? The Public Response of American Jews to the Holocaust, 1938–1944.*
27. Leo V. Kanawada, *Franklin D. Roosevelt's Diplomacy and American Catholics, Italians and Jews,* 93.
28. Several historians focus on Coughlin's key role in fomenting an anti-Semitic climate: Wyman, *Paper Walls,* 13, 14, 17–19; Lookstein, *Were We Our Brother's Keeper?,* 31, 62, 91; Deborah Lipstadt, *Beyond Belief,* 127; and Medoff, *Deafening Silence,* 19, 20.
29. Arnold Forster, retired general counsel for the Anti-Defamation League, observes in his autobiography, *Square One,* 77–78, "Regrettably, most of us did not spend a major effort on European Jewish questions because . . . during the period of Jewish organizational development the primary concern was not anti-Jewish events in Europe but domestic anti-Semitism."
30. Quoted in Medoff, *Deafening Silence,* 45.
31. Wise to Murphy, April 12, 1938, Frank Murphy Papers, Bentley Historical Library, University of Michigan. Murphy told his secretary to reply with a "noncommittal and brief letter expressing sympathy with the plan to help those in trouble." May 5, 1938, Murphy Papers.
32. Speech of Adolph Hitler to the Reichstag, January 30, 1939, quoted in Raoul de Roussey de Sales, *Adolph Hitler, My New Order,* 594.
33. *Social Justice,* January 30, 1939.
34. Gallup Poll, November 28, 1938.
35. *Social Justice,* March 26, 1939.
36. Ibid., February 27, 1939.
37. Ibid.
38. Ibid., April 3, 1939.
39. "Admission of German Refugee Children," *Joint Hearings before a Subcommittee of the Committee on Immigration, United States Senate, and a Subcommittee of the Committee on Immigration and Naturalization, House of Representatives,* 76th Cong. 1st sess., April 22, 1939, 254–255.
40. Quoted in Wyman, *Paper Walls,* 97. Surprisingly Eleanor Roosevelt did not publicly support the Wagner-Rogers bill.
41. Hitler's initial solution to the "Jewish problem" had been resettlement in Madagascar. See Medoff, *Deafening Silence,* 52. Harold Ickes had suggested that idea as well as Alaska and the Virgin Islands. Even settlement in the Japanese Empire was discussed. Ibid., 65–70.
42. *Social Justice,* August 28, 1939.
43. See Arthur Morse, *While Six Million Died,* 255.
44. *Social Justice,* June 17, 1940.
45. Carlson (alias of Arthur Derounian), *Undercover,* 27.
46. *Life Magazine,* March 6, 1939.
47. Carlson, *Undercover,* 27.
48. *Social Justice,* March 6, 1939.
49. Coughlin radio address, February 26, 1939.

50.   *Chicago Daily News,* August 18, 1940.
51.   John A. Spivak, *Shrine of the Silver Dollar,* 156–157.
52.   Eugene Rachlis, *They Came to Kill,* 122–123.
53.   Author interview with Joseph Wright, 1985.
54.   Goebbels was particularly concerned with reducing the influence of the church and engaged in several propaganda campaigns against it just prior to World War II. Persecution of Catholic clergy opposed to the regime in any manner was stepped up. By 1941, all Catholic publications were totally regimented under Goebbels control. For Nazi-Catholic relations, see Guenter Lewy, *The Catholic Church and Nazi Germany;* for an examination of religion under the Nazis, see Richard Grunberger, *The 12-Year Reich: A Social History of Nazi Germany, 1933–1945.*
55.   Author interview with Joseph P. Wright, 1985. Word of Reardon's visit did not become public until after World War II. See especially O. John Rogge, *The Official German Report,* 303–304.
56.   Translation from the official Nazi party organ, *Volkischer Beobachter,* January 4, 1939.
57.   Quoted in Rogge, *Official German Report,* 304.
58.   Quoted in *Volkischer Beobachter,* January 21, 1939. See Robert Davies, "The 'Volkischer Beobachter' View of the United States During the Third Reich."
59.   Quoted in Fred Taylor, ed., *The Goebbels Diaries: 1939–1941,* 6, entry for January 19, 1939. On February 3, 1939, Goebbels spoke of meeting with Leni Riefenstahl after her trip to the United States. He concluded, "We shall go nowhere there. The Jews rule by terror and bribery. But for how much longer?" (9).
60.   Davies, "'Volkischer Beobachter' View of the United States," 84, notes Hitler's repudiation of "any American intervention in German affairs" and that "irresponsible statesmen [meaning FDR]" should "confine their attentions to their own problems." Hitler speech to the Reichstag, January 30, 1939. Davies suggests these remarks were "possibly" based on the visit from Reardon.
61.   Translation from an article appearing in the *Frankfurter Tagesblut,* February 18, 1939.
62.   *Social Justice,* February 6, 1939.
63.   Ibid., February 13, 1939.
64.   Memorandum of August 11, 1939, from Ernst Woermann, secretary to Foreign Minister Joachim von Ribbentrop, n.d. An extensive foreign policy review by the German foreign office on the "Jewish question" in the United States in 1938 mentioned that "audiences of well-known anti-Jewish priest, Coughlin, have grown to over 20 million." Documents of German Foreign Policy (DGFP), Volume V, Series D, January 25, 1939, 932.
65.   Ibid.
66.   Ibid.
67.   Coughlin radio address, March 26, 1939.
68.   *Social Justice,* October 3, 1938.
69.   Ibid., October 17, 1938.
70.   Ibid., April 24, 1939.
71.   *Social Justice,* September 18, 1939.
72.   Ibid.
73.   Drew Pearson, "Merry-Go-Round" column, October 2, 1939.

Chapter 11: The Trial of the "Brooklyn Boys"

1. Richard Davis, "The Radio Priest," 411.
2. *Social Justice,* June 28, 1938.
3. Unsigned report on the Christian Front meeting at the Paulist Church on July 14, 1938, report of September 16, 1938, Archdiocese of Detroit (AAD).
4. Unsigned report on the Christian Front meeting at the Paulist Church, August 4, 1938, report of October 8, 1938, AAD.
5. *Social Justice,* October 31, 1938.
6. Quoted in the *New York Times,* August 21, 1939.
7. Coughlin editorial, *Social Justice,* July 31, 1939.
8. *Social Justice,* August 14, 1939. Davis, "The Radio Priest," 448, suggests that Coughlin made this disclaimer because of pressure from his archbishop, Edward Mooney.
9. "Fr. Coughlin as a Symbol," undated confidential report to Archbishop Mooney (Summer 1939?), AAD.
10. "Nationalism and the Movement," undated report (Summer 1939?), AAD.
11. Report on "Meeting of the Christian Front," Prospect Hall, Brooklyn, July 28, 1939, AAD.
12. "Nationalism and the Movement."
13. *New York Times,* January 15, 1940.
14. *Detroit Times,* January 15, 1940.
15. The remarks were contained in a speech delivered via an amplified telephone call to a Philadelphia gathering. See *New York Times,* January 17, 1940. Coughlin was also in secret communication with other Christian Front leaders, including Francis Moran of Boston: "The outside world does not need to know what goes on in our communications because they are letters from friends to friends, not meant for publication." Coughlin to Moran, December 19, 1939, copy given to me by former *PM* reporter Luther Conant.
16. Coughlin radio address, "I Take My Stand," January 21, 1940.
17. From deleted portions of the January 21, 1940, radio manuscript, AAD. On February 4, 1940, no Coughlin talk was broadcast because the archbishop had forbidden the delivery of the address entitled "On Trial." The manuscript contains an elaborate discussion of the Christian Front trial as a response to Jewish leftist influence over the Justice Department.
18. Charles Higham, *American Swastika,* 89.
19. *Social Justice,* June 24, 1940.
20. Davis, "The Radio Priest," 429.
21. Ibid., 431.
22. Originally, eighteen individuals were arrested; one was released for lack of evidence, so seventeen went to trial. On April 12, 1940, the day he was to appear at the trial, Claus Gunther Ernecke was found hanged in his apartment.
23. A file sent to me by the Department of the Army under the Freedom of Information Act in the Christian Front Justice Department/FBI file contains an abstract of a report filed September 1, 1939, indicating that a Harold Albert Morton of Toronto, Canada, was linked to a negotiation for the sale of a large number of Lee Enfield rifles and ammunition for what he "believes them to represent [a] Coughlinite or Nazi group." File 2724-507. I was subsequently told, in requesting the full report, that it could not be found in the files.
24. *Social Justice,* June 24, 1940.

25. Ibid., July 8, 1940.
26. The FBI learned of this linkage a few weeks after the Christian Front trial had ended. See "Memorandum for Mr. Tolson," Nichols to Tolson, July 5, 1940, Coughlin FOIA File.
27. Mooney to Apostolic Delegate Amleto Cicognani, February 13, 1940, AAD. On March 4, 1939, Archbishop Mooney had been sent a telegram, signed by six members of the Brooklyn Christian Front (three of whom became defendants in the 1940 trial), which stated in part: "The undersigned section leaders of the Christian Front wish to thank your excellency in behalf of their respective groups for the great guidance you are giving the American people through the mouth-piece of Father Coughlin" (AAD).

Chapter 12: Just a Soldier in the Pope's Army

1. Author interview with Father James Dwyer, 1987.
2. Quoted in Sheldon Marcus, *Father Coughlin,* 21.
3. Ruth Mugglebee, *Father Coughlin,* 155.
4. *New York Times,* April 19, 1932.
5. Cicognani to Gallagher, October 1, 1932, Archives of the Archdiocese of Detroit (AAD).
6. Ibid.
7. I was given access to the log on Father Coughlin in the Vatican's Sacred Congregation of Clergy archives but was not given permission to examine their content. Ten entries appear between 1929 and 1941.
8. John Cooney, *The American Pope,* 37, calls her "Spellman's patron." A decade later, Gallagher was described by Archbishop Edward Mooney, in a letter to Spellman, as "my lovable and overly generous predecessor." Mooney to Spellman, March 27, 1942, AAD.
9. Countess Brady to Edgar Rickard, October 6, 1932, Herbert Hoover Presidential Library.
10. Quoted in the *Detroit News,* December 10, 1934.
11. The proposed statement read in part, "Such attacks [by Coughlin on O'Connell . . . do no good, but rather beget rancor and bitterness and misunderstanding." December 14, 1934, National Catholic Welfare Conference Archives (NCWCA).
12. Coughlin radio address, April 21, 1935
13. Dougherty to Bernardini, May 7, 1935, quoted in Gerald P. Fogarty, *The Vatican and the American Hierarchy from 1870–1965,* 243.
14. Author interview with Father James Dwyer, 1987.
15. Fogarty, *The Vatican and the American Hierarchy,* 245.
16. *New York Times,* July 27, 1936.
17. Ibid., July 31, 1936.
18. Hall to Burke, July 14, 1936, NCWCA.
19. Cable text, National Catholic Welfare Conference News Service, September 2, 1936, NCWCA.
20. *New York Times,* September 3, 1936.
21. Ibid., September 4, 1936.
22. *Washington Star,* September 26, 1936.
23. *New York Times,* September 27, 1936.
24. Apostolic Delegate Cicognani to Gallagher, September 29, 1936, AAD.

25. Quoted in Robert Gallagher, "Radio Priest," 104.
26. Ibid.
27. Letter dated November 5, 1954, quoted in Paul I. Murphy, *La Popessa,* 136.
28. Coughlin radio address, November 7, 1936. Coughlin's mentor, Bishop Gallagher, wired him the same month telling the priest, "I consider you a national institution, invaluable to the safeguarding of genuine Americanism and true Christianity." Quoted in *Social Justice,* November 9, 1936.
29. Coughlin radio address, February 1, 1937. According to historian Leslie Tentler, *Seasons of Grace,* 328, "Why Gallagher persisted in his support for Coughlin is one of the many enigmas to which the now deleted Gallagher papers [of the Archdiocese of Detroit] may once have held the key."
30. Tentler, ibid., 327, notes that Coughlin's activities "had clearly raised anxieties at the Vatican." Bishop Gallagher was told directly that the priest's attacks on FDR were embarrassing the church. See Cicognani to Gallagher, September 29, 1936, AAD.
31. Mooney, as president of the Administrative Board of the NCWC in 1936, was a key figure in responding to a Vatican request that the board rebuke Coughlin for his political activities. No statement was ever issued. Mooney felt it was an exercise in futility since only Coughlin's bishop and Rome itself had the authority to act. See Tentler, *Seasons of Grace,* 326–327.
32. *Central Press,* June 30, 1937.
33. Ibid.
34. *Social Justice,* October 4, 1937.
35. *Michigan Catholic,* October 7, 1937.
36. *Detroit News,* October 8, 1937.
37. Pruitt Semmes letter published ibid., October 9, 1937.
38. Excerpts from pamphlet entitled, "Can Christians Support the CIA?" Copy in AAD.
39. Father Michael A. Grupa, Censor Librorum, September 24, 1937, to Mooney, AAD.
40. *Social Justice,* October 18, 1937.
41. Mooney to Cicognani, October 29, 1937, AAD. Mooney also explained his decision on the basis of Coughlin's articles containing "inaccurate quotations from the Encyclicals of Our Holy Father."
42. *Social Justice,* November 15, 1937.
43. Ibid., November 22, 1937.
44. Ibid., November 29, 1937.
45. Description of Coughlin's visit to the apostolic delegate on November 26, 1937, in Cicognani to Mooney, November 27, 1937, AAD.
46. Ibid.
47. National Catholic Welfare Conference News Service, December 7, 1937.
48. *Social Justice,* December 13, 1937.
49. *Michigan Catholic,* December 9, 1937.
50. Mooney to Cicognani, December 4, 1937, AAD.
51. John R. Robinson, "Behind the Microphone with Father Coughlin," *Real America* (March 1934).
52. Author interview with Philip Johnson, 1984. When I asked Catholic labor activist Paul Weber about Johnson's comment in an interview later in 1984, he expressed doubt that Coughlin ever considered leaving the church.
53. Mrs. John Negil to Mooney, October 7, 1937, AAD.

54. Quoted in James P. Shenton, "The Coughlin Movement and the New Deal," 363.
55. Mooney to Cicognani, October 29, 1937, AAD.
56. Mooney to Cardinal Pacelli, January 17, 1939, AAD.
57. Murial Benziner to Msgr. Michael Ready, December 14, 1941, NCWC Archives.
58. Andrew M. Greeley, *An Ugly Little Secret: Anti-Catholicism in North America.*
59. P. A. Triot to Gallagher, February 18, 1936, NCWC Archives.
60. Ellen McKee to Gallagher, 1936 (n.d.), AAD.
61. *Michigan Catholic,* December 12, 1938.
62. Ibid.
63. Meeting notes between Coughlin and Mooney, December 13, 1938, AAD.
64. Mooney to Cicognani, March 22, 1939, AAD.
65. Mooney to Cardinal Pacelli, January 17, 1939, AAD.
66. This telegram was not found in AAD. It is alluded to in the letter that Mooney sent to Cicognani (February 20, 1939) in response to the delegate's having sent it while Mooney was on vacation.
67. Mooney to Pacelli, January 17, 1939, AAD.
68. Cicognani told Mooney that the Coughlin matter had been referred "to the Holy Father" who "deemed it fitting that I, as Apostolic Delegate, and in the name of the Holy See, should counsel this priest." Cicognani to Mooney, February 13, 1939, AAD.
69. Coughlin to Cicognani, March 7, 1939, AAD. In this same note, the priest denied he had ever encouraged "either directly or indirectly in the past" that letters be written to the Vatican, and he attributed these missives to "this addiction of Americans . . . expressing their approval or disapproval of the acts of public persons."
70. Radio address of Cardinal Mundelein, December 11, 1938.
71. Press release, National Catholic Welfare Conference Press Service, April 12, 1939.
72. *Social Justice,* May 29, 1939. Throughout the spring and summer of 1939, a number of articles about Jews appeared under the pseudonym of Ben Marcin.
73. Mooney to Coughlin, June 10, 1939, AAD.
74. Coughlin to Mooney, June 13, 1939, AAD.
75. Mooney to Coughlin, June 17, 1939, AAD. One week later, Mooney wrote to Coughlin expressing concern over the series of *Social Justice* articles with the byline of Ben Marcin. Criticizing these pieces for their anti-Semitic content, the archbishop asked if "you could use your good offices with Mr. Marcin" not to quote Mooney in a forthcoming book mentioned as an outgrowth of his several articles.
76. Quoted in Robert Gallagher, "The Radio Priest," 104.
77. In *The Fine Art of Propaganda,* Alfred Lee and Elizabeth Lee analyzed Coughlin's speeches in terms of seven "tricks of the trade," verbal strategies of attitude influence.
78. Birkhead was a tireless activist writer whose bulletin was a powerful tool in exposing the machinations of far-right and anti-Semitic organizations. In February 1939 he described Coughlin as "a world troublemaker," in the same category as Hitler and Mussolini, "and typical of the anti-democratic radio propagandist." *Detroit News,* February 26, 1939.
79. Birkhead's memorandum is quoted in Sheldon Marcus, *Father Coughlin,* 175.
80. Drew Pearson column, October 4, 1939.

81. Quoted in the *Detroit News,* February 5, 1940.
82. Excerpts from the rejected radio broadcast manuscript of February 4, 1940, AAD.
83. Pearson and Allan "Merry Go Round" column, September 15, 1940.
84. Mooney to Cicognani, September 15, 1940, AAD.
85. *New York Times,* September 21, 1940.
86. Ibid.
87. Mooney to Cicognani, September 20, 1940, AAD.
88. *Social Justice,* January 13, 1941.
89. According to Tentler, *Seasons of Grace,* 335, "Coughlin had simply outmaneuvered Mooney." The task of censoring *Social Justice* was a task posing a far greater burden on the chancery "than policing a weekly radio address."
90. *Social Justice,* April 10, 1939.
91. Mooney to Coughlin, February 19, 1940, AAD.
92. Coughlin to Mooney, March 9, 1940, AAD.
93. Ibid., April 17, 1939, AAD.
94. "Social Justice Report on April 1 Issue," March 14, 28, 1940, AAD.
95. Deleted portion of April 29, 1940, issue of *Social Justice,* AAD.
96. Coughlin to Mooney, May 16, 1940, AAD.
97. Mooney to Cicognani, June 5, 1940, AAD.
98. "Some Observations of Fr. S. S. Murphy on the Occasion of the visit with Arnold Lunn to Father Coughlin," report, December 14, 1940, AAD.
99. *Social Justice,* June 30, 1941.
100. Mooney to Cicognani, February 13, 1940, AAD.

Chapter 13: "Sentenced to the Silence of a Sealed Sepulcher"

1. *Social Justice,* October 13, 1940.
2. Ibid., June 30, 1941.
3. Ibid., January 6, 1941.
4. Ibid., March 31, 1941.
5. Ibid., May 26, July 7, September 15, October 20, 1941.
6. Ibid., October 20, 1941.
7. Ibid., December 8, 1941.
8. Ibid.
9. John A. Spivak, *The Shrine of the Silver Dollar,* 166–167.
10. Wallace Stegner, "The Radio Priest and His Flock," 245.
11. Sheehy quoted in Harold L. Ickes, *The Secret Diary of Harold L. Ickes,* December 1, 1940, 382. Also see April 17, 1938, 371.
12. See O. John Rogge, *The Official German Report,* 152–172.
13. Viereck's name appears in 1938 and 1939 as a contributor of articles in *Social Justice.*
14. Arnold Forster told me in a 1986 interview that he thought a pro-Nazi academic, Austin App, was the conduit for Coughlin funds. He said he was told this information by David Niles.
15. Samuel Sheiner to Richard Gutstadt, May 31, 1940, Jewish Anti-Defamation Council of Minnesota, Anti-Defamation League Archives.
16. *Detroit Free Press,* July 23, 1943.
17. Braun explained to me in a 1987 interview that "it would not be a good idea to bring up the German funding of Coughlin," since this would be used against

those still sympathetic to National Socialism. He explained that my letter to Schmidt asking about Coughlin funding had not been answered for this reason.

18. See Rogge, *Official German Report,* 304. In a telephone conversation in 1995, Schmidt confirmed the financial link to Coughlin but said he could not recall any details about it.

19. John J. Stephan *The Russian Fascists: Tragedy and Farce in Exile, 1925–1945,* 269.

20. Author interview with Igor Pelypenko, 1986.

21. Ibid.

22. Author interview with Myron Kuropas, 1985.

23. Alexis Pelypenko affidavit, September 28, 1942, quoted in *In Fact,* February 11, 1946.

24. Ibid.

25. Ibid.

26. Ibid.

27. Ibid.

28. Ibid.

29. FBI internal report, August 8, 1941, Pelypenko File, Freedom of Information Act (FOIA).

30. Pelypenko affidavit.

31. Ibid.

32. FBI internal report, July 8, 1942, Pelypenko File. The FBI had found Pelypenko to be unreliable in that he had told the Immigration and Naturalization Service about some aspects of the Coughlin visits that he had held back from the FBI. Pelypenko File, FOIA.

33. Hans Thomsen to Foreign Ministry, telegram, top secret, 1362, July 5, 1940, Documents of German Foreign Policy (DGFP), D, XI, 125.

34. Rogge, *Official German Report,* 304.

35. Thomsen to Foreign Ministry, June 19, 1940, 493, D, XI, 625–626.

36. Ibid., 626.

37. Hans Thomsen to Foreign Ministry, telegram, January 28, 1941, 721, DGFP, D, XI, 1213–1214.

38. J. Edgar Hoover to Adolph A. Berle, May 14, 1940, August Gausebeck File, Record Group (RG) 800.20211, National Archives.

39. J. Edgar Hoover to Watson, May 14, 1940, Franklin D. Roosevelt Library.

40. Fletcher Warren to Hoover, May 17, 1940, State Department, FOIA.

41. FBI report, September 21, 1940, RG 800.20211. Gausebeck File, FOIA. The German banker had reputedly told a friend that he had no intention of registering as an agent of a foreign power and that "the United States government could go to hell."

42. Ibid.

43. Ibid.

44. Westrick's "tour," while aimed at soothing U.S.-German relations, only inflamed them when a secret agenda of anti-FDR lobbying was detected.

45. Rogge, *Official German Report,* 37–38. FBI report, May 5, 1941, RG 800.20211. Also see Curt Riess, *Total Espionage,* 51–55, 292–293, passim.

46. George A. Gordon, State Department to Hoover, August 20, 1941, State Department, Gausebeck File, FOIA.

47. U.S. Congress, House, Special Committee on Un-American Activities, Hearings, *Investigation of Nazi and Other Propaganda,* "Testimony of Walter H. Schallenberg [*sic*]," July 9, 1934, 145–151.

48. FBI field report, P. E. Foxworth to file, March 4, 1942. Gausebeck File, FBI, FOIA.
49. FBI field report, October 28, 1941, Gausebeck File, FOIA.
50. Ibid.
51. FBI field report, Bolivian Foreign Minister to Fletcher Warren, December 23, 1941, RG 800.20211. As late as 1947, Beatrice Alberdi Gausebeck was attempting to recover her seized property in the United States. Her request was denied on the basis that her husband had been "an obnoxious German and an enemy of the United States." Joseph Amshey to J. Edgar Hoover, August 27, 1947, State Department, FOIA.
52. Philip W. Bonsal to Laurence Duggan, January 2, 1942, Department of State, Gausebeck File, FOIA. A February 6, 1944, FBI report also noted that Gausebeck had not indicated his Nazi party membership in his Alien Registration report for 1940.
53. Dorothy Thompson, "On the Record Column," *New York Post,* July 24, 1940.
54. J. Edgar Hoover to John Bugas, internal memo, March 2, 1942, Coughlin File, FBI, FOIA.
55. *Social Justice,* May 26, 1941.
56. Letter to J. Edgar Hoover [name blanked out], December 15, 1941, Coughlin File, FBI, FOIA.
57. *Social Justice,* February 19, 1942.
58. Ibid., March 16, 1942.
59. *Florida Catholic,* March 20, 1942.
60. *PM,* March 30, 1942.
61. Ibid.
62. Citizen letter to the FBI (name blanked out), January 10, 1942, Coughlin File, FBI, FOIA.
63. J. Edgar Hoover to Francis Biddle, January 29, 1942, Coughlin File, FBI, FOIA.
64. J. Edgar Hoover to John Bugas, February 7, 1942, Coughlin File, FBI, FOIA.
65. E. M. Watson to FDR, "Memo," March 30, 1942, Official File 306, Franklin D. Roosevelt Library (FDRL).
66. FDR to Attorney General Biddle, April 3, 1942, Official File 306, FDRL.
67. Francis Biddle, *In Brief Authority,* 238.
68. In a 1986 interview, retired Anti-Defamation League counsel Arnold Forster told me that Maloney worked closely with groups seeking the strongest efforts to prosecute pro-Nazi individuals and organizations. Among these reporters was *Washington Post* journalist John C. Metcalfe, who received the Heywood Broun Award for his investigation of Nazi propaganda being circulated to the public with the congressional franking privilege. See Henry Hoke, *It's a Secret.*
69. Hoover frequently sought to rein Maloney in, especially when Maloney, as a special prosecutor, would use military intelligence agents rather than FBI personnel for his investigations of Coughlin and other individuals. Thus, when Maloney was approached by people suggesting he have Alexi Pelypenko testify or use him in any other way, Hoover immediately perceived this as a challenge to the FBI's integrity. Hoover was eventually successful in getting Maloney kicked upstairs in the Justice Department and out of the role of special investigator.
70. J. Edgar Hoover to John McCormack, February 5, 1942, National Catholic Welfare Conference Archives (NCWCA).

71. Nichols to Tolson, April 6, 1942, Coughlin File, FOIA.
72. Biddle, *In Brief Authority,* 238.
73. FBI file report, 100–4716, March 17, 1942, Coughlin File, FOIA.
74. Ibid.
75. Maloney copy of memo to Wendell Berge, May 11, 1942, author's copy.
76. Ibid.
77. Summarized in Maloney memorandum to Biddle, May 8, 1942, author's copy.
78. Maloney copy of memo to Berge.
79. Ibid.
80. Memo for Tolson, Tamm, and Ladd from Hoover, April 14, 1942, Coughlin File, FBI, FOIA.
81. Ibid.
82. Ibid.
83. Coughlin interview with Richard Gallagher, "The Radio Priest," 103.
84. Agent Thurston to Tamm, internal FBI report, July 23, 1940, Ward FBI File, FOIA.
85. Memorandum for Tamm, from Office of Naval Intelligence (ONI), December 6, 1940, FOIA.
86. ONI report, January 10, 1941, FOIA File. Ward, according to a January 9, 1941, report, was to serve the Japanese by way of "intelligence propaganda and investigate [*sic*] work in San Francisco" (FOIA).
87. Ibid.
88. Ibid.
89. Trayner to Kramer, FBI memo, October 31, 1941, Ward File, FOIA. When no report was sent from the Detroit FBI Office, Hoover complained to his agent in charge, John Bugas, "that [Wendell] Berge [assistant attorney general] was now 'on his back' about the case."
90. Ward statement made to FBI agents, internal report of December 15, 1941, Ward File, FOIA.
91. *Detroit Free Press,* April 21, 1942. An internal FBI memo records a potential embarrassment to the agency in Ward's death: "There was no indication that a subpoena had been served by anyone." Ward had been treated at a local hospital; one of the Syracuse police "had talked to Ward, but had noticed nothing out of the ordinary nor had he seen any indication of a subpoena being served." Ladd to Tamm, FBI internal memo, April 21, 1942, Ward File, FOIA.
92. Asher Schwartz to Attorney General Biddle, April 20, 1942, Coughlin File, FOIA.
93. Christian Front Leaders continued to be investigated during World War II, with "Brooklyn boy" indictee "Jack" Cassidy denied military service. The New York Bar Association also turned down his application for admission to the bar.
94. Quoted in the *New York Times,* April 14, 1942.
95. *Washington Star,* April 17, 1942. Biddle explained to the press that the case would be handled by William Power Maloney and Lieutenant Edward J. Hickey, on loan from naval intelligence.
96. *Washington Post,* April 15, 1942. Coughlin told author Sheldon Marcus, *Father Coughlin,* 215, that he had met Biddle in a face-to-face meeting in Washington and allegedly told him, "You are nothing but a God Damn Coward!" There is no evidence that such a confrontation ever occurred.

97. *New York Times,* April 20, 1942. In the interim, Coughlin's earlier, and rather ludicrous, claim was interpreted by the priest's lawyer not to mean that Coughlin "would dodge complete responsibility for the editorial content of the magazine." Ibid., April 17, 1942.

98. *Detroit Free Press,* April 22, 1942.

99. The grand jury sessions lasted for several weeks and included the calling of Coughlin's office staff. When I interviewed one of them, she told me that when they went to lunch, the government had stationed lip-readers in the dining room to pick up any conversations.

100. Author interview with Edward J. Hickey, 1986. No record of any meeting of Hickey with NCWC officials was found in the archives opened to me, although Hickey suggests that the meeting "was probably off the record."

101. *New York Times,* April 21, 1942.

102. Mumford to Ladd, memorandum, April 22, 1942, Coughlin File, FBI, FOIA.

103. Ibid.

104. Maloney to Coughlin, April 28, 1942, author's copy of letter. Coughlin was never called to testify.

105. See Marcus, *Father Coughlin,* 217.

106. Author interview with Edward J. Hickey, 1985.

107. Author telephone interview with William Power Maloney's son, 1985.

108. Coughlin interview, Robert Gallagher, "The Radio Priest," 105.

109. Coughlin to Postmaster Frank Walker, telegram, Post Office Department Order 17558, May 4, 1942.

110. When Mooney received a letter from the bishop of Brooklyn in October 1941 asking whether it was true that Coughlin was being permitted to give "purely religious discourses" outside of the Archdiocese of Detroit, Mooney responded by saying that it was like "a lawyer asking 'Have you stopped beating your wife?' " He then suggested he would like to meet "informally and confidentially with you" to discuss the matter. Bishop Molloy to Mooney, October 24, 1941; Mooney to Molloy, n.d., AAD.

111. Mooney to Coughlin, April 23, 1942, AAD.

112. Ibid.

113. Ibid.

114. Mooney to Amleto Cicognani, April 24, 1942, AAD.

115. "Coughlin Memorandum," April 28, 1942. Coughlin read the draft out loud. Notes of a meeting between Mooney and Coughlin, AAD.

116. Notes on meeting between Mooney and Coughlin, April 28, 1942, AAD.

117. Ibid.

118. Notes of meeting between Semmes and Mooney, April 30, 1942, AAD.

119. Quoted from individual statements signed by Archbishop Mooney and Coughlin, May 1, 1942, AAD.

120. Mooney to Coughlin, May 2, 1942, AAD.

121. Notes of meeting between Mooney and Coughlin, April 28, 1942, AAD.

122. "Broadcast Memorandum," Drew Pearson, May 16, 1942, Drew Pearson Papers, Lyndon B. Johnson Presidential Library.

123. Coughlin frequently told his associates, "Pacelli was no friend of mine." His close associate, Father Peter Wiethe, told me that "Charlie was shut up" as part of the deal by FDR to have a U.S. representative at the Vatican. The same thesis is asserted in Paul I. Murphy, *La Popessa,* 115–116, 136. Full diplomatic relations were not established until the Reagan Administration.

124. Grace Tully to FDR, October 9, 1941, President's Personal File 425, FDRL.
125. Tully to "Pa" Watson, October 19, 1941, President's Personal File 425, FDRL. FDR's personal file shows a note for October 23, 1941, saying: "OFF THE RECORD, very confidential, and not to be mentioned. Thursday morning, 10:30, the President will receive Myron Taylor and Archbishop Mooney." In the presidential log, there is a blanked-out space for the 10:30 time slot.
126. McIntyre to Mooney, March 5, 1942, AAD.
127. Spellman to Mooney, March 25, 1942, AAD.
128. Mooney to Spellman, March 27, 1942, AAD.
129. Cicognani to Mooney, April 30, 1942, AAD. In his letter, the Vatican official acknowledged that Coughlin's deceit practiced on Mooney would lead to a trial unless the priest agreed to the proposed "silencing" terms.
130. Ibid.
131. Chancellor Edward J. Hickey, Memo, n.d. [April 30?], AAD.
132. *Detroit Free Press,* May 5, 1942.
133. Mooney to Roosevelt, May 9, 1942, AAD.
134. Roosevelt to Mooney, May 11, 1942, AAD.
135. Mooney to Cicognani, May 12, 1942, AAD.
136. Author interview with Father Louis Rohr, 1986.

Chapter 14: "And the Truth Shall Be Known"

1. Letter dated April 17, 1942, Coughlin FBI File, Freedom of Information Act (FOIA).
2. Hoover to Wendell Berge, August 19, 1942, Coughlin FBI File, FOIA.
3. Mooney to Cicognani, October 3, 1942, Archives of the Archdiocese of Detroit (AAD).
4. Internal FBI report, January 9, 1943, Coughlin FBI File, FOIA.
5. John Spivak draft article, sent to Hickey, December 29, 1943, AAD.
6. Notes by observer, "Coughlin Family Activities," September 19, 1943, Michigan Civil Rights League Papers, Walter Reuther Library, Wayne State University.
7. Ibid.
8. Spivak to Hickey, December 29, 1943, AAD.
9. Hickey to Spivak, January 3, 1944, AAD.
10. Letter to Hoover, no name, December 5, 1941, Coughlin FBI File.
11. *People's World,* July 1, 1942. In his 1940 book, *The Shrine of the Silver Dollar,* Spivak had alluded to the "Gold Shirt" ties.
12. Coughlin letter, June 5, 1942, AAD.
13. Ready to Prendergast, June 25, 1942, National Catholic Welfare Conference Archives (NCWCA).
14. John Bugas to Hoover, FBI report, October 21, 1942, Coughlin File, FBI, FOIA.
15. *X-Ray,* April 10, 1944.
16. The source is an article published in Albert Kahn's *The Hour,* February 16, 1944.
17. Agent report of Lenten sermon, March 2, 1944, Coughlin File, FBI, FOIA.
18. *New York Post*, March 2, 1944.
19. *PM,* March 17, 1944.

20. *Chicago Sun,* March 24, 1944.
21. Drew Pearson column, March 26, 1942.
22. Ladd to E. A. Tamm, March 31, 1944, Coughlin File, FBI, FOIA.
23. Ibid. FBI agent Guerin report to Hoover, April 1, 1944, Coughlin File, FBI, FOIA. Agent Guerin's report took on an almost comic tone as he attempted to summarize for Hoover abstract theological themes—for example, "Subject delivered three sermons . . . his talks dealt with the Resurrection and thc fact that this event proved the divinity of Christ." Guerin to Hoover, April 10, 1944, Coughlin File, FBI, FOIA.
24. Mooney to Michael Ready, April 10, 1944. AAD.
25. Hostile attitudes toward Jews seemed to peak in 1944. See Charles Herbert Stember et al., eds., *Jews in the Mind of America,* 110–134 passim.
26. Letter to the Editor, John Francis Farrell, August 18, 1944.
27. *PM,* October 22, 1944.
28. Ibid.
29. Ibid.
30. Coughlin to Moran, December 19, 1939, photostatic copy given to me by Luther Conant.
31. Manuscript draft of Luther Conant's autobiography, "The Gathering Storm," copy given to me by Conant. In Coughlin's letter he told Moran, "I am under the impression that more than 5,000 . . . Christian Front groups can be encouraged through New England by next August [of 1940] at the latest." Coughlin to Moran, December 19, 1939.
32. Ready Memorandum, July 8, 1944, NCWCA.
33. Ready to Mooney, July 8, 1944, AAD.
34. Ibid., July 14, 1944, AAD.
35. The FBI learned that Pelypenko's September 1942 deposition had been arranged by an individual named Stepankowsky, who was at various times paid as an informant for the Anti-Defamation League. When questioned by FBI agents, Stepankowsky indicated he and Pelypenko had divided the $300 fee for the notorious Pelypenko affidavit.
36. Hoover to Caudle, memo, January 28, 1946, Pelypenko File, FBI, FOIA. The FBI was never able to recover the copy given to *PM,* and this may have eventually allowed it to become known to Albert Kahn, who in turn provided it to George Seldes. When I interviewed him in 1985 about the matter, Seldes did not recall what Kahn had told him about the origin of the document he published in 1946.
37. Mumford to Ladd, FBI internal memo, February 6, 1946, Pelypenko File. In 1942, Hoover had described Pelypenko as "an unscrupulous schemer" who should be interned "because he undoubtedly will traffic in intelligence information for anyone who will pay him." Hoover to SAC agent, New York, October 9, 1942, Pelypenko File.
38. *In Fact,* February 11, 1946.
39. "Coughlin Family Activities," Michigan Civil Liberties League, report of Father John Cooney, September 30, 1943, Labor History and Urban Affairs Collection, Reuther Library, Wayne State University.
40. Ray Bellack to Joseph Luther, October 2, 1945, AAD.
41. Coughlin to Hickey, September 17, 1945, AAD.
42. Author interview with Tyler Abell, 1987.

43.   Ibid.
44.   Pearson radio broadcast, February 1, 1949.
45.   *Detroit Free Press,* February 1, 1949; *Detroit News,* February 1, 1949.
46.   Coughlin press release, January 31, 1949. According to a staff member of
      Drew Pearson, Coughlin had heard about the broadcast the day before and
      "was in a state of near collapse. He knew you had the goods on him." Memo
      from "FB" [n.d. 1949?], Pearson Papers, Lyndon Johnson Presidential Library.
47.   Press release, Detroit Archdiocese, February 3, 1949, AAD.
48.   Pearson diary entry, April 30, 1954, quoted in Tyler Abell, *Drew Pearson Di-
      aries, 1949–1959,* 310.
49.   Sheehy to Lee, February 7, 1949, Pearson Papers.
50.   Pearson to his office, telegram, February 2, 1949, Pearson Papers.
51.   *Detroit Free Press,* February 1, 1949.
52.   Pearson radio broadcast, February 8, 1949.
53.   Abell, *Diaries,* 57. Kane was pressured by his superior, T. Lamar Caudel, to
      retract this denial of Coughlin involvement. He did so a month later.
54.   Beltaire to Pearson, May 9, 1949, Pearson Papers.
55.   Abel, *Diaries,* 56. Two days after Pearson's original broadcast, Coughlin had
      telephoned the wife of Pearson's sponsor, Mrs. Frank Lee, demanding that the
      broadcaster be taken off the air (21).
56.   *Detroit Free Press,* October 29, 1949.
57.   *Royal Oak Tribune,* December 15, 1949.
58.   Donahue to Pearson, memo, Pearson Papers.
59.   Pearson diary entry for October 21, 1954 in Abell, *Diaries,* 334.
60.   Author interview with the former Mary Gariepy, 1987. When I spoke with one
      of the librarians handling the Pearson Papers at the Johnson Presidential Li-
      brary, I inquired about further documents connected to the Gariepy case. I was
      told these could not be released, but that they did contain references to alleged
      relationships Coughlin had with several women, apparently including Mrs.
      Gariepy.

Chapter 15: The Ghost of Royal Oak

1.   Author interview with Grant Howell, 1985.
2.   Author interview with Murray Cotter, 1985. On the Barclay's investment, see
     Agent [not named] to J. Edgar Hoover, May 23, 1942, Coughlin, Freedom of
     Information Act file (FOIA).
3.   *Detroit Free Press,* February 10, 1935.
4.   When Coughlin's will was probated in Oakland County in February 1980, it
     showed a total of $30,000 bequeathed to the archdiocese of Detroit, with resid-
     ual earnings from properties granted to nine other charitable organizations.
     The total value of the estate was $150,000. Given the religious artifacts and
     property investments the priest had made, the sum seemed surprisingly small
     to many who were associated with the Shrine of the Little Flower. In 1985 I in-
     terviewed Richard O'Hare, an attorney who had helped Coughlin with finan-
     cial matters. He told me that most of Coughlin's property had been transferred
     out of his estate before his death. O'Hare gave me a copy of a 1977 agreement
     in which Coughlin turned over to his longtime secretary, Eugenia Burke, "in
     consideration of many years of dutiful service . . . all my right, title and inter-

est in and to all my articles of personal and household use and ornament of
very kind and description and wherever located."

5. Author interview with Richard O'Hare, 1985.
6. Author interview with T. Franco, 1987.
7. Ibid.
8. Ibid.
9. Author interview with F. Kluitowski, 1986.
10. Author interview with Father James Hayes, 1984.
11. Author interview with F. Kluitowski, 1986.
12. *MacLean's Magazine,* October 1, 1952.
13. Chancellor John Donovan, memorandum, December 4, 1953, Archives of the
    Archdiocese of Detroit (AAD).
14. *Detroit Free Press,* December 5, 1953.
15. Text of address dated December 4, 1953, copy in AAD.
16. *New York Post,* September 19, 1955.
17. Ibid.
18. *Life Magazine,* November 14, 1955.
19. Author interview with Father Louis Rohr, 1985.
20. Author interview with Paul Weber, 1984.
21. Ibid.
22. *New York Times,* May 26, 1966. One Shrine parishioner told me that Coughlin
    would sit back in the pews of the church and count the number of blacks com-
    ing in for services. She used the term *hide* in the rear pews. Author interview
    with M. McCormack, 1985.
23. *Detroit Free Press,* May 27, 1966.
24. Coughlin's acceptance of the move by his bishop was a matter that deeply con-
    cerned his successor, Father James Hayes. When I interviewed Hayes in 1984,
    he told of his trepidation in "filling such big shoes." The mild-mannered cleric
    recalled that Coughlin had acted cordially toward him.
25. *Detroit News,* May 24, 1967.
26. Quoted in *Detroit Free Press,* December 11, 1968; also see *Newsweek,* De-
    cember 23, 1968.
27. Coughlin, *Bishops Versus Pope,* 47–48.
28. Coughlin attacked Hesburgh for "remaining silent for many, many months
    when atrocious assaults against the Catholic faith and our Holy Father have
    been expressed in theologic circles at Notre Dame University under the guise
    of progress and academic freedom." Ibid., 53.
29. Ibid., 192.
30. Ibid., 38.
31. Coughlin, *Twelve Timely Essays on Antichrist,* 33.
32. Ibid., 72–73.
33. Address at Old St. Mary's Church, Detroit, June 10, 1973, author's copy of
    transcribed remarks.
34. Quoted in *Detroit Free Press,* June 26, 1976.
35. *Wanderer,* November 9, 1979.
36. *Detroit Free Press,* November 1, 1979.
37. Ibid. *Detroit Jewish News* editor Philip Slomovitz summed up his view in the
    November 9, 1979, issue: "Every modern history book, all the works about
    anti-Semitism, by Jews and Non-Jews, contain the name of Charles E. Cough-

lin as one of the leaders in the movement fostering hatred of Jews. That's what Coughlin chose, that's how it remains in all the history books."

38. *The Truth At Last,* no. 347 (1991).
39. "Bitter Memories of Bigotry Live on in Father Coughlin's Parish," *New York Times,* May 25, 1992.
40. Ibid.

References

Primary Interviews and Correspondence

ABELL, TYLER. March 28, 1985.
ANDERSON, JACK. June 27, 1986.
ATHANS, SISTER CHRISTINE. March 17, 1985 (telephone).
BAERTSCHI, CHARLES. September 17, 1985.
BELCZAK, FATHER EDWARD A. October 9, 1984.
BLAIR, FATHER LEONARD P. May 28, 1985.
BRAUN, KARL OTTO. October 10, 1987.
BREITENBECK, MONSIGNOR. April 10, 1986.
BRODERICK, FATHER BRUNNETT. May 10, 1985
BROWN, MRS. J. CAMPBELL. July 18, 1985.
BUCHTA, BERNICE MARCINIEWICZ. November 2, 1985 (telephone).
BUGAS, JOAN. October 18, 1986.
BURKE, EUGENIA. June 14, 1985 (telephone).
BYKOWITZ, REVEREND ALEXANDER. October 28, 1985.
CANFIELD, MONSIGNOR FRANCIS X. May 4, 1984, April 22, 1986.
CLINTON, FARLEY. April 18, 1986.
CONANT, LUTHER. March 14, 1986.
CONWAY, JACK. June 28, 1984, October 28, 1985 (telephone).
CONWAY, MARILYN. June 28, 1984.
COOKE, ALISTAIR. Personal communication, October 12, 1986.
COTTER, MURRAY. March 7, 1985.
CUNEO, ERNEST. June 18, 1986
DEARDON, CARDINAL JOHN. April 24, 1985.
DEROUNIAN, ARTHUR. March 27, November 12, 1986.
DONAHUE, JEAN SCHWARTZ. November 18, 1986.
DONALDSON, MARY. April 26, 1985.
DONOVAN, BISHOP JOHN A. August 27, 1984.
DWYER, FATHER MICHAEL. February 18, 1987.
ELLERMAN, MILTON. February 9, 1987 (telephone).
FINE, SIDNEY. January 23, 1988.
FISHER, EUGENE. March 1, 1985.
FLAMM, DONALD. April 10, 1985, March 28, May 2, 1986.
FLEISCHAKER, MRS. STANLEY. November 29, 1984, February 7, 1985.
FLOOD, MARGARET. June 9, 1987.
FLOOD, THOMAS. June 9, 1987.
FORSTER, ARNOLD. February 20, March 14, November 11, 1986, May 18, 1987.
FRAM, RABBI LEON. May 30, 1984.
FRANCO, ANTONIO. June 18, 1987.
GARIEPY, MARY. December 16, 1986.
GENTNER, FATHER CARL. March 16, 1984.

349

GRAHAM, MONSIGNOR ROBERT, S.J. April 12, 1984.

GRIX, CLARENCE. June 12, 1984.

HABER, WILLIAM. December 12, 1984.

HAILER, FREDERICK C. May 15, 1986.

HAYDEN, MARTIN. May 31, 1984.

HAYDEN, TOM. October 8, 1987.

HAYES, FATHER JAMES L. October 10, 1984.

HERTZ, RABBI RICHARD M. December 4, 1986.

HICKEY, EDWARD J. March 31, 1984, March 2, 1985, April 19, 1986.

HICKEY, MONSIGNOR EDWARD J. April 4, 1984, May 19, 1986.

HIGHAM, CHARLES. April 28, 1985 (telephone).

HOWELL, GRANT. June 8, 1985.

JOHNSON, PHILIP. April 9, 1984.

KAHN, RIETE (MRS. ALBERT E.). June 22, 1985.

KAMP, JOSEPH. June 12, 1986.

KANIA, KASIMIR J. March 4, 1985.

KEATING, FATHER CYRIL. June 8, 1984.

KEELON, JOANNA. October 16, 1985 (telephone), November 10, 1985 (personal interview).

KERNES, MONSIGNOR BERNARD. March 13, 1984.

KEYES, SHARON. April 1, 1987.

KIRKMAN, REVEREND JAMES. May 12, 1986.

KLAPPROTT, AUGUST. October 9, 1987.

KLUITOWSKI, FREDERICK. September 25, 1986.

KOENIG, FATHER ROBERT. December 6, 1984.

KREIG, FATHER JEROME L. June 12, 1985.

KUROPAS, MYRON, SR. October 21, 1985.

LARKIN, MARY. September 24, 1986.

LEWIS, PROFESSOR JAMES. February 3, 1984.

LINDBERGH, ANNE MORROW. Personal communication, November 9, 1984.

LOBENTHAL, RICHARD. March 12, 1985.

LUCE, CLARE BOOTH. Personal communication, June 20, 1984.

MALLON, MONSIGNOR VINCENT. April 14, 1984.

MALONEY, WILLIAM POWER, JR. Personal communication, March 27, June 20, 1984.

MARCUS, SHELDON. June 7, 1984.

MEININGER, HAROLD. June 12, 1985.

MERRITT, MAURICE. November 11, 1985.

MILLS, JACQUELINE. April 24, 1984, April 9, 1986.

MONTIETH, ERNEST. May 17, 1985 (telephone).

MONTIETH, JOSEPH. Personal communication, May 19, 1985.

MOSLEY, LADY DIANA. November, 12, 1991; May 20, 1993.

MULLIN, JANUARIUS. May 14, 1984.

MURPHY, IRENE. December 29, 1986.

MURPHY, FATHER WILLIAM. August 11, 1987.

NADER, FATHER WILLIAM. November 29, 1984.

NEWMAN, HARRY. May 12, 1986.

O'HARE, RICHARD F. April 11, 1985.

PALEY, WILLIAM. May 9, 1984.

PARK, CHARLIE. April 27, 1985.

PEARSON, LUVIE. November 25, 1986.

PELYPENKO, IGOR. February 22–26, 1986.
PEPPER, CLAUDE. April 18, 1985.
QUELLO, JAMES. May 12, 1984.
REARDON, GLADYS. November 27, 1984.
REARDON, PATRICK. August 15, 1987 (telephone).
REDDAN, JOHN. April 24, 1984 (telephone).
REUTHER, VICTOR. November 25, 1986.
RHODES, DOROTHY. March 4, 1985 (telephone).
RICHARDS, ROZENE. May 5, 1984.
ROHR, FATHER LOUIS. November 29, 1985 (telephone).
ROOSEVELT, JAMES. June 4, 1985 (telephone).
ROTH, BETTE. February 9, 1984.
RUSKOWSKI, FATHER CLIFFORD. May 20, 1985.
SAYERS, MICHAEL. April 6, 1985.
SCHERSER, FATHER JAMES. October 30, 1984.
SCHMID, HANS. Personal communication, October 22, 1984.
SCOLLARD, FATHER ROBERT. May 11, 1987.
SELDES, GEORGE. October 15, 1984 (telephone).
SEMMES, RICHARD. June 7, 1985 (telephone).
SHAPIRO, MARY. October 17, 1984.
SHINE, NEIL. October 23, 1984.
SIMONS, LEONARD. April 17, 1986.
SLOMOVITZ, PHILIP. March 8, 1984.
STANTON, FRANK. May 17, 1984.
STEGNER, WALLACE. January 4, 1986 (telephone).
STEINBERG, MYRON S. March 21, 1984, April 23, 1986.
STEINBERG, MRS. NORMAN. April 18, 1989.
STEPHAN, JOHN J. January 30, 1985 (telephone).
STOKES, JANE. January 24, 1984.
SULLIVAN, JAMES. June 23, 1986.
TAYLOR, TELFORD. Personal communication, March 5, 1985.
THOMPSON, MRS. HELEN SCHWARTZ. November 18, 1986.
THUMA, ERIC. Recorded interview with Father Coughlin, September 11, 1970.
UHNAVY, ARLENE. December 27, 1986.
VIERICK, PETER. February 3, 1986 (telephone).
WALROD, MARIE. April 12, 1985.
WARD, HILEY. August 8, 1986 (telephone).
WARNER, ROBERT. February 5, 1988.
WEBER, PAUL. December 7, 1984.
WEDGRIN, TED. March 7, 1985.
WHITE, NORMAN. April 16, 1984.
WHITFIELD, MRS. ROBERT. March 27, 1987.
WIETHE, FATHER PETER. June 6, October 26, 1984, May 30, 1985.
WILLIAMS, G. MENNEN. February 12, 1987.
WRIGHT, MRS. FRANK BUMGARTNER. May 17, 1987.
WRIGHT, JOSEPH. May 9, 1985.

Primary Documents and Archival Sources Consulted

Albert E. Kahn Papers, State Historical Society of Wisconsin, Madison. Courtesy of Reite Kahn.

"An Interview with Regent Irene Murphy and Sharon Murphy Keyes, July 30, 1964" by Sidney Fine and Robert Warner, Michigan Historical Collections, The University of Michigan, transcript copy provided to the author by Irene Murphy.

American Jewish Archives, Cincinnati, Ohio.

Archdiocese of Detroit Archives, Father Coughlin Papers, Detroit, Michigan, U.S.A.

August C. Gausebeck file, National Archives, Washington, D.C.

Bentley Historical Library, University of Michigan, Ann Arbor, Michigan.

Berkshire Evening Eagle, Archives, Great Barrington, Massachusetts.

Blaustein Library, American Jewish Committee Archives, New York.

Burton Historical Collection. Detroit Public Library, Detroit, Michigan.

Central Civil Archives of Italy. "Father Coughlin File." Rome, Italy.

Charles Higham Collection, Archives of the Performing Arts, University of Southern California, University Library, Los Angeles, California.

Detroit Free Press Archives, Detroit, Michigan.

Detroit *Jewish News* Archives, courtesy of Philip Slomovitz, Southfield, Michigan.

Detroit News Archives, Detroit, Michigan. Drew Pearson Papers, University of Texas, Lyndon B. Johnson Presidential Library, Austin, Texas.

Drew Pearson Newspaper Columns, courtesy of Jack Anderson.

Eleanor Baumgartner Papers, Bentley Historical Library, University of Michigan, Ann Arbor, Michigan.

Ezra Pound Papers, Beinecke Rare Book Library, Yale University, New Haven, Connecticut.

Farley Clinton correspondence and unpublished manuscript draft provided to the author by Father Peter Wiethe.

Father Coughlin Papers, Northwestern University, Evanston, Illinois. Courtesy of Sheldon Marcus.

Ford Industrial Library, Redford, Michigan.

Franklin D. Roosevelt Library, Hyde Park, New York.

Freedom of Information Act, U.S. Department of Justice, Federal Bureau of Investigation, Files.

Frank Murphy Papers, Bentley Historical Library, University of Michigan.

Gallup Organization, Survey Reports, Princeton, New Jersey.

George Murphy Papers, Bentley Library, University of Michigan.

Gerald L.K. Smith Collection, Bentley Historical Library, The University of Michigan, Ann Arbor, Michigan.

German Military Archives, Freiberg, Federal Republic of Germany.

Harry S. Truman Presidential Library, Independence, Missouri.

Herbert Hoover Presidential Library, West Branch, Iowa.

Jewish Cultural Museum, Boston, Massachusetts.

Labodie Collection, Harlan Hatcher Library, University of Michigan, Ann Arbor, Michigan.

Liebold Reminiscences, Edison Archives, Henry Ford Greenfield Village Museum, Dearborn, Michigan.

Michigan Civil Rights League, Wayne State University Labor and Union Affairs Collection, Walter P. Reuther Library, Detroit, Michigan.

Michigan Anti-Defamation League Files, Detroit, Michigan.

National Catholic Welfare Conference Archives, U.S. Conference of Catholic Bishops, Washington, D.C. Father Coughlin file.
New York Public Library, New York.
Oakland County Probate Court Records, Pontiac, Michigan.
Private Papers of Donald Flamm, courtesy of Mr. Flamm.
Public Records Office, London, England.
Roper Center, The University of Connecticut, Storrs, Connecticut.
Sacred Heart Fathers and Brothers Archives and Museum, Hobs Corner, Wisconsin.
St. John's Seminary Library, Plymouth, Michigan.
St. Michael's College Archives, The University of Toronto, Toronto, Ontario, Canada.
The University of Notre Dame Archives, Notre Dame, Indiana.
Thomas Corcoran Papers. Library of Congress.
Vatican Archives, Sacred Congregation for the Clergy, Vatican City.
Walter Reuther Library, Labor History and Urban Affairs Archives, Wayne State University, Detroit, Michigan.
Weiner Library, London, England.
William Power Maloney. Selected Papers donated to the author by William Black.
Wisconsin Center for Film and Theatre Research, University of Wisconsin, Madison.
YIVO Institute, New York.

Published Government Documents

U.S. Congress. House of Representatives. Louis T. McFadden's Anti-Semitic Speech and Response. 73d Congress, 1st session, May 29, 1933. *Congressional Record* 77, p. 5, 4538–4540, 4547, 4552–4553.
———— "Admission of German Refugee Children," *Joint Hearings before a Subcommittee of the Senate Committee on Immigration and a Subcommittee of the House Committee on Immigration and Naturalization.* 76th Congress, 1st session, 1939.
U.S. Congress. House of Representatives. Special Committee to Investigate Communist Activities in the United States. *Investigation of Communist Propaganda.* 71st Congress, 2d session, July 25, 1930. (Hamilton Fish Committee).
U.S. Congress. Senate. Elmer Thomas's praise of Coughlin. 72d Congress, 2d session, January 23, 1933. *Congressional Record* 76, pt. 2, 2283–2286.
U.S. Department of Justice. Division of Records. File 38-37-237. Eleven items of correspondence related to Department of Justice's responses to inquiries concerning Father Coughlin, 1935–1939. National Archives.
U.S. Department of State. *Documents on German Foreign Policy,* ser. D, vols. 2–11. 1945, 1959.

Books and Published Articles

AARON, DANIEL, and ROBERT BENDINER. *The Strenuous Decade: A Social and Intellectual Record of the 1930's.* Garden City, NY: Anchor Books, 1970.
ABELL, TYLER. *Drew Pearson Diaries, 1949–1959.* New York: Holt, Rinehart and Winston, 1974.
ADLER, SELIG. *The Isolationist Impulse.* New York: Free Press, 1966.
ADVISE, RONALD D. "The Volkischer Beobachter View of the United States during the Third Reich." Ph.D. dissertation, American University, 1983.

ALLEN, FREDERICK LEWIS. *Since Yesterday: The 1930s in America.* New York: Harper & Row, 1972

"American Institute of Public Opinion Surveys, 1938–1939." *Public Opinion Quarterly,* no. 3 (October 1939): 581–607.

ANDERSON, DOUGLAS. *A "Washington Merry-Go-Round" on Libel Actions.* Chicago: Nelson-Hall, 1980.

APP, AUSTIN J. *German-American Voice for Truth and Justice.* Tacoma Park, Md.: Boniface Press, 1977.

ARROW, ROBERT M. "Catholic Political Power: A Study of the Activities of the American Catholic Church on Behalf of Franco during the Spanish Civil War, 1936–1939." Ph.D. dissertation, Columbia University, 1953.

ATHANS, SISTER MARY. "A New Perspective on Father Charles E. Coughlin." *Church History* (1987): 224–235.

BARNOUW, ERIK. *The Golden Web.* New York: Oxford University Press, 1968.

BAUER, YEHUDI. *American Jews and the Holocaust.* Detroit: Wayne State University Press, 1981.

BAYOR, RONALD H. *Neighbors in Conflict: The Irish, Germans, Jews, and Italians in New York City, 1929–1941.* Baltimore: Johns Hopkins University Press, 1978.

BELL, LELAND V. "The Failure of Nazism in America: The German-American Bund, 1936–1941." *Political Science Quarterly* 85 (December 1970): 585–599.

BELTH, NATHAN C. *A Promise to Keep: A Narrative of the American Encounter with Anti-Semitism.* New York: Times Books, 1973.

BENDINER, ROBERT. *Just Around the Corner.* New York: E. P. Dutton, 1967.

BENEWICK, ROBERT. *The Fascist Movement in Britain,* London: Allen & Unwin, 1972.

BENNETT, DAVID HARRY. *Demagogues in the Depression: American Radicals and the Union Party, 1932–1936.* New Brunswick: Rutgers University Press, 1969.

BENNETT, HARRY, as told to PAUL MARCUS. *We Never Called Him Henry.* New York: Fawcett, 1951.

BESCHLOSS, MICHAEL R. *Kennedy and Roosevelt: The Uneasy Alliance.* New York: Harper & Row, 1987.

BIDDLE, FRANCIS B. *In Brief Authority.* Garden City: Doubleday, 1962.

BINGAY, MALCOLM. *Detroit Is My Home Town.* New York: Bobbs-Merrill, 1946.

BIRD, CAROLINE. *The Invisible Scar.* New York: Pocket Books, 1967.

BLACK, EDWIN. *The Transfer Agreement.* New York: Macmillan, 1984.

BLACKORBY, EDWARD C. *Prairie Rebel: The Public Life of William Lemke.* Lincoln: University of Nebraska Press, 1963.

BOARDMAN, FON W., JR. *The Thirties: America and the Great Depression.* New York: Henry Z. Walck, 1978.

BOORSTIN, DANIEL. *The American Experience.* New York: Random House, 1973.

BRINKLEY, ALAN. *Voices of Protest: Father Coughlin and Huey Long.* Paperback edition. New York: Vintage Books, 1982.

BROWN, ALDEN V. "Friends for a While: Patrick V. Scanlan of the Brooklyn *Tablet* and John A. Ryan on America's Challenge to Catholicism." Paper delivered at the Cushwa Center for the Study of American Catholicism, University of Notre Dame, October 5, 1985.

BROWN, FRANCIS. "Three 'Pied Pipers' of the Depression." *New York Times Magazine,* March 17, 1935.

BUELL, RAYMOND. *Isolated America.* New York: Alfred A. Knopf, 1940.

BUNZEL, JOHN H. *Anti-Politics in America: Reflections on the Anti-Political Temper and Its Distortions of the Democratic Process.* New York: 1965.

BURNER, DAVID. *Herbert Hoover: A Public Life.* New York: Alfred A. Knopf, 1979.

CAHILL, REV. E. *Freemasonry and the Anti-Christian Movement.* Dublin: M. H. Gill and Son Limited, 1959.

CANFIELD, MONSIGNOR FRANCIS X. *A Condensed History of the Archdiocese of Detroit.* Detroit: Archdiocese of Detroit (n.d.) (1983?).

CANNISTRARO, PHILIP V., and THEODORE P. KOVALEFF. "Father Coughlin and Mussolini: Impossible Allies." *Journal of Church and State* 13 (Autumn 1971): 432–445.

CARLSON, JOHN ROY. *Undercover.* New York: E. P. Dutton, 1943.

CARPENTER, HUMPHREY, *A Serious Character:* The Life of Ezra Pound. Boston: Faber, 1988.

CARTER, JOHN FRANKLIN. *American Messiahs.* New York: Simon & Schuster, 1935.

CARTO, WILLIS A. (ED.). *Profiles in Populism.* Old Greenwich, Conn.: Flag Press, 1983.

CHADWIN, MARK L. *The Hawks of World War II.* Chapel Hill, N.C.: University of North Carolina Press, 1968.

CHESTERTON, G. K. *The Autobiography of G. K. Chesterton.* New York: Sheed & Ward, 1936.

———. *The New Jerusalem.* London: Thomas Nelson, 1920.

CHILDS, MARQUIS, "Father Coughlin: A Success Story of the Depression." *New Republic,* May 2, 1934.

COLBY, GERALD. *Du Pont Dynasty.* Secaucus, N.J.: Lyle Stuart, 1984.

COMPTON, JAMES V. *The Swastika and the Eagle: Hitler, the United States, and the Origins of World War II.* Boston: Little, Brown, 1967.

CONOT, ROBERT. *American Odyssey.* New York: Bantam Books, 1974.

COONEY, JOHN. *The American Pope: The Life and Times of Francis Cardinal Spellman.* New York: Times Books, 1984.

COUGHLIN, CHARLES EDWARD. *"Am I an Anti-Semite?" 9 Addresses on Various 'Isms' Answering the Question.* Detroit: Condon Printing Company, 1939.

———. *A Jubilee Memorial.* Royal Oak, Mich.: Private printing, Church Committee, 1966.

———. *Bishops Versus Pope.* Bloomfield Hills, Mich.: Helmet and Sword, 1969.

———. *Father Coughlin, Selected Discourses.* Philadelphia: Educational Guild, 1932.

———. *Father Coughlin's Radio Discourses, 1931–1932.* Royal Oak, Mich.: Radio League of the Little Flower, 1932.

———. *Father Coughlin's Radio Sermons, October 1930–April, 1931 Complete.* Baltimore: Knox and O'Leary, 1931.

———. *Helmet and Sword.* Bloomfield Hills, Mich.: Helmet and Sword, 1968.

———. *Money: Questions and Answers.* Royal Oak, Mich.: National Union for Social Justice, 1936.

———. *A Series of Lectures Broadcast on Social Justice by the Rev. Chas. E. Coughlin of the Shrine of the Little Flower, Royal Oak, Michigan, and Broadcast over a National Network.* Royal Oak, Mich.: Radio League of the Little Flower, 1935.

———. *A Series of Lectures on Social Justice, 1935–1936; Broadcast by Rev. Chas. E. Coughlin over a National Network.* Royal Oak, Mich.: 1936.

———. *Sixteen Radio Lectures, 1938 Series.* Royal Oak, Mich.: Charles E. Coughlin, 1938.

————. *Twelve Timely Essays on Antichrist.* Bloomfield Hills, Mich.: Charles E. Coughlin, 1972.

————. *Who Is Dead—God or Democracy?* Bloomfield Hills, Mich.: Charles E. Coughlin, 1970.

————. *Why Leave Our Own? 13 Addresses on Christianity and Americanism, January 8–April 2, 1939.* Detroit: Inland Press, 1939.

CRANE, MILTON, ED. *The Roosevelt Era.* New York: Boni & Gaer, 1947.

CRONON, E. DAVID. "American Catholics and Mexican Anti-Clericalism, 1933–1936." *Mississippi Valley Historical Review* 45 (September 1958): 201–230.

————. *Josephus Daniels in Mexico.* Madison: The University of Wisconsin Press, 1960.

CURRY, RICHARD O., and THOMAS M. BROWN (EDS.). *Conspiracy: The Fear of Subversion in American History.* Ithaca, N.Y.: Cornell University Press, 1972.

CUSHING, RICHARD, CARDINAL. *Address of Richard Cardinal Cushing at the Golden Jubilee Anniversary of the Ordination of Rev. Charles E. Coughlin at the Shrine of the Little Flower.* Royal Oak, Mich.: N.p., June 1966.

DALLEK, ROBERT. *Franklin D. Roosevelt and American Foreign Policy, 1932–1945.* New York: Oxford University Press, 1979.

DANIELS, JONATHAN. *White House Witness.* Garden City, N.Y.: Doubleday, 1975.

DAVIS, RICHARD A. "Radio Priest: The Public Career of Father Charles Edward Coughlin." Ph.D. dissertation, University of North Carolina, 1974.

DENNIS, LAWRENCE. *The Coming American Fascism.* New York: Harper & Brothers.

DIAMOND, SANDER. *The Nazi Movement in the United States: 1924–1941.* Ithaca: Cornell University Press, 1974.

DIGGINS, JOHN P. *Mussolini and Fascism: The View from America.* Princeton, N.J.: Princeton University Press, 1972.

DIVINE, ROBERT A. *The Illusion of Neutrality.* Chicago: University of Chicago Press, 1962.

DONALDSON, FRANCES. *The Marconi Scandal.* London: Rupert Hart-Davis, 1962.

DORWART, JEFFREY M. *Conflict of Duty: The U.S. Navy's Intelligence Dilemma.* New Brunswick: Rutgers University Press, 1981.

DULLES, JOHN W. F. *Yesterday in Mexico: A Chronicle of the Revolution, 1919–1936.* Austin: University of Texas Press, 1961.

EISMAN, BERNARD. "Reflections of a Radio Priest." *Focus-Midwest* (February 1963): 4–10.

ENZLER, CLARENCE J. *A Catholic Looks at Father Coughlin.* N.p., n.d. (1936?).

ETTINGER, SHMUEL. "Anti-Semitism in Our Time." *Jerusalem Quarterly* 23 (Spring 1982): 95–113.

FAHEY, FATHER DENNIS. *The Mystical Body of Christ in the Modern World.* 3d ed. Waterford, Ireland: Browne and Nolan, 1939.

————. *The Mystical Body of Christ and the Reorganization of Society.* Dublin, Ireland: Regina Publications, 1984 (reprint of the edition published by the Forum Press, Cork, Ireland, 1945).

————. *The Rulers of Russia.* 3d ed. Royal Oak, Mich.: Social Justice Printing Company, 1940.

FARLEY, JIM. *Jim Farley's Story.* New York: McGraw Hill Book Company, 1948.

FARRELL, JAMES T. "Tommy Gallagher's Crusade." *The Roosevelt Era,* 195–224. Edited by Milton Crane. New York: Boni and Guer, 1947.

FECHER, CHARLES A. *The Diaries of H. L. Mencken.* New York: Alfred A. Knopf, 1989.

FEINGOLD, HENRY L. *The Politics of Rescue: The Roosevelt Administration and the Holocaust, 1938–1945.* New Brunswick: Rutgers University Press, 1970.

FERKISS, VICTOR C. "Populism: Myth, Reality, Current Danger." *Western Political Quarterly* 14 (September 1961): 737–740.

———. "Populist Influences on American Fascism." *Western Political Quarterly* 10 (June 1957): 350–373.

FINE, SIDNEY. *Frank Murphy: The Detroit Years.* Ann Arbor: University of Michigan Press, 1975.

FORSTER, ARNOLD. *Square One.* New York: Donald I. Fine, 1988.

———. *Frank Murphy: The Washington Years.* Detroit: Wayne State University Press, 1983.

FINKEL, ALVIN. The Social Credit Phenomenon in Alberta. Toronto: University of Toronto Press, 1989.

FINLAY, JOHN. *Social Credit: The English Origins.*

FLORY, WENDY S. *The American Ezra Pound.* New Haven: Yale University Press, 1989.

FLYNN, GEORGE Q. *American Catholics and the Roosevelt Presidency, 1932–1936.* Lexington: University of Kentucky Press, 1968.

FOGARTY, GERALD P. *The Vatican and the American Hierarchy from 1870–1965.* Stuttgart: Anton Hiersemann, 1982.

FOSTER, ARNOLD AND BENJAMIN J. EPSTEIN. *Danger on the Right.* New York: Random House, 1964.

FRASER, STEVE, AND GARY GERSTLE (EDS.). *The Rise and Fall of the New Deal Order.* Princeton, N.J.: Princeton University Press, 1989.

FRIEDLANDER, SAUL. *Prelude to Downfall: Hitler and the United States, 1939–1941.* New York: Alfred A. Knopf, 1967.

FRIEDMAN, SAUL. *No Haven for the Oppressed: United States Policy towards Jewish Refugees, 1938–1945.* Detroit: Wayne State University Press, 1973.

FRYE, ALTON. *Nazi Germany and the American Hemisphere, 1933–1941.* New Haven: Yale University Press, 1967.

GALLAGHER, ROBERT S. "The Radio Priest" *American Heritage,* (October 1972): 38–41, 100–109.

GELDERMAN, CAROL U. *The Wayward Capitalist.* New York: Dial Press, 1981.

"GENTILE SILVER." *Nation,* May 9, 1934.

GERBER DAVID A. (ED.). *Anti-Semitism in American History.* Urbana: University of Illinois Press, 1987.

GERTZ, ELMER. *Odyssey of a Barbarian: The Biography of George Sylvester Viereck.* Buffalo, N.Y.: Prometheus Books, 1978.

GLOCK, CHARLES Y., AND RODNEY STARK. *Christian Beliefs and Anti-Semitism.* New York: Harper & Row, 1966.

GOEBBELS, JOSEPH. *The Goebbels Diaries, 1939–1941.* Translated and edited by Fred Taylor. Harmondsworth, Middlesex, England: Penguin Books, 1984.

GRAJES, JESUS VELASCO. "El Reverendo Charles E. Coughlin Y El Ascenso Del Fascismo Norteamericano Durante La Decada De Los Treinta." *Estados Unidos,* September 2, 1983, 245–283.

GRANT, DONALD. "Coughlin's New Capital." *Nation,* March 21, 1942, 334–336.

GREELEY, ANDREW M. *An Ugly Little Secret: Anti-Catholicism in North America.* Kansas City: Andras Sheed & McMeel, 1977.

GRUNBERGER, RICHARD. *The 12-Year Reich: A Social History of Nazi Germany, 1933–1945.* New York: Holt, Rinehart and Winston, 1971.

GUTTMAN, ALLEN. *The Wound in the Heart: American and Spanish Civil War.* Glencoe, Ill.: Free Press, 1972.

HACKNEY, SHELDON. *Populism: The Critical Issues.* Boston: Little, Brown, 1971.

HART-DAVIS, RUPERT. *Hugh Walpole, a Biography.* New York: MacMillan, 1952.

HAYS, WILL H. *The Memoirs of Will Hays.* Garden City, N.Y.: Doubleday, 1955.

HERTZSTEIN, ROBERT E. *Roosevelt & Hitler: Prelude to War.* New York: Paragon House, 1989.

HERWIG, HOLGER H. *Politics of Frustration: The United States in German Naval Planning, 1889–1941.* Boston: Little, Brown, 1976.

HIGHAM, CHARLES. *American Swastika.* Garden City, N.Y.: Doubleday, 1985.

HOEHLING, ADOLPH A. *America's Road to War: 1939–1941.* New York: Abelard-Schuman, 1970.

HOKE, HENRY. *It's a Secret.* New York: Reynal & Hitchcock, 1946.

HOLLAND, JOHN J. "The Detroit Banking Collapse of 1933." Dissertation, Graduate School of Business Administration, New York University, 1972.

HOLMES, COLIN. *Anti-Semitism in British Society.* New York: Holmes & Meier, 1981.

HOYT, EDWIN P. *The Tempering Years.* New York: Charles Scribner's Sons, 1963.

ICKES, HAROLD LE CLAIR. *The Secret Diary of Harold L. Ickes.* 3 vols. New York: Simon & Schuster, 1953–1954.

IRVING, JOHN A. *The Social Credit Movement in Alberta.* Toronto: University of Toronto Press, 1959.

ISRAEL, FRED L. *Nevada's Key Pittman.* Lincoln: University of Nebraska Press, 1963.

JACKSON, KENNETH. *The Ku Klux Klan in the City, 1915–1930.* Chicago: Elephant Paperbacks, 1992.

JEANSONNE, GLEN. *Gerald L. K. Smith: Minister of Hate.* New Haven: Yale University Press, 1988.

JOHNSON, NEIL. *George Sylvester Viereck: German–American Propagandist.* Urbana: University of Illinois Press, 1978.

JONAS, MANFRED. *Isolationism in America, 1935–1941.* Ithaca, N.Y.: Cornell University Press, 1966.

JOSEPHSON, MATTHEW. *Infidel in the Temple: A Memoir of the 1930's.* New York: Knopf, 1967.

KAHN, ALBERT E. *High Treason: The Plot against the Peace.* New York: Lear Publishers, 1950.

KANAWADA, LEO V., JR. *Franklin D. Roosevelt's Diplomacy and American Catholics, Italians, and Jews.* Ann Arbor, Mich. UMI Research Press, 1982.

KEE, ROBERT. *1939: In the Shadow of War.* Boston: Little, Brown, 1984.

KESSLER, SIDNEY H. "Fascism Under the Cross: the Case of Father Coughlin." *Library Bulletin* V 33, series 51/52 (1980): 8–12.

KILPATRICK, CARROLL. *Roosevelt and Daniels: A Friendship in Politics.* Chapel Hill, N.C.: University of North Carolina Press, 1952.

KIPPHAN, KLAUS. *Deutsche Propaganda in den Vereinigten Staaten, 1933–1941.* Heidelberg, 1971.

KITSON, ARTHUR, *Cause and Remedy.* London: Cecil Palmer, 1921.

KOLODNY, RALPH L. "Father Coughlin and the Jews: A Reminiscense for Younger Colleagues." *Jewish Digest* (March 1978): 67–72.

KRAMER, DALE. "The American Fascists." *Harper's* (September 1940): 380–393.

KRUEGER, PAMELA. "Father Coughlin." *Detroit News Pictorial Magazine,* June 5, 1966, 17–22.

LACEY, ROBERT. *Ford: The Men and the Machine.* Boston: Little, Brown, 1986.

LASH, JOSEPH P. *Roosevelt and Churchill, 1939–1941.* New York: W. W. Norton, 1976.

LAUFER, PETER. *Inside Talk Radio.* New York: Carol Publishing Group, 1995.

LAVINE, HAROLD. *Fifth Column in America.* New York: Doubleday, Doran, 1940.

LEE, ALBERT. *Henry Ford and the Jews.* New York: Stein & Day, 1980.

LEE, ALFRED MCCLUNG, AND ELIZABETH BRIANT LEE, EDS. *The Fine Art of Propaganda: A Study of Father Coughlin's Speeches.* New York: Harcourt Brace, 1939.

LEVERING, RALPH B. *The Public and American Foreign Policy, 1918–1978.* New York: William Morrow, 1978.

LEVIN, MURRAY B. *Talk Radio and the American Dream.* Lexington, MA: Lexington Books, 1987.

LEWIS, DAVID L. *The Public Image of Henry Ford: An American Folk Hero and His Company.* Detroit: Wayne State University Press, 1976.

LEWIS, DAVID S. *Illusions of Grandeur: Mosley, Fascism, and British Society, 1931–1981.* Manchester: Manchester University Press.

LEWIS, SINCLAIR. *It Can't Happen Here.* New York: Sun Dial, 1936.

LEWY, GUENTER. *The Catholic Church and Nazi Germany.* New York: McGraw Hill, 1965.

LIPSET, SEYMOUR MARTIN. "Three Decades of the Radical Right: Coughlinites, McCarthyites, and Birchers." In Daniel Bell (ed.), *The Radical Right.* New York: Doubleday, Anchor Books, 1964.

————. *The Politics of Unreason.* Chicago: University of Chicago Press, 1970.

LIPSTADT, DEBORAH E. *Beyond Belief: The American Press and the Coming of the Holocaust, 1933–1945.* New York: Free Press, 1986.

Literary Digest, December 23, 1933.

LOOKSTEIN, HASKEL. *Were We Our Brother's Keepers?* New York: Vintage Books, 1985.

LOUCHHEIM, KATIE. *The Making of the New Deal: The Insiders Speak.* Cambridge, Mass.: Harvard University Press, 1983.

LUNT, RICHARD D. "Frank Murphy's Decision to Enter the 1936 Gubernatorial Race." *Journal of Michigan History* (December 1963): 327–334.

LYNCH, FLORENCE MONTEITH. *The Mystery Man of Banana Strand: The Life and Times of Captain Robert Monteith.* New York: Vantage Press, 1959.

MCCARTHY, JOHN P. "Hilaire Belloc in the Late 1930s: Prophet Against Revolution," *The Intercollegiate Review.* Spring 1992, 19–25.

MCCARTNEY, EDWARD C. "The Christian Front Movement in New York City, 1938–1940." Master's thesis, Columbia University, 1965.

MCELVAINE, ROBERT S. *The Great Depression, America, 1929–1941.* New York: Times Books, 1984.

McLean's Magazine, October 1, 1952.

MAGIL, ABRAHAM BERNARD. *The Truth about Father Coughlin.* New York: Workers Library Publishers, 1935.

————. *The Real Father Coughlin.* New York: Workers Library Publishers, 1939.

MANCHESTER, WILLIAM. *American Caesar.* New York: Dell Publishing, 1978.

MANHATTAN, AVRO. *The Vatican in World Politics.* New York: Gaer Associates, 1949.

MARCUS, SHELDON B. *Father Coughlin: The Tumultuous Life of the Priest of the Little Flower.* Boston: Little, Brown, 1973.

MARX, GARY T. *The Social Basis of the Support of a Depression Era Extremist: Father Coughlin.* Monograph 7. Berkeley, Calif.: Survey Research Center, University of California, 1962.

MASON, BRUCE BONNER. "American Political Protest, 1932–1936." Ph.D. dissertation, University of Texas, 1953.

MASTERS, NICK A. "Father Coughlin and Social Justice: A Case Study of a Social Movement." Ph.D. dissertation, University of Wisconsin, 1955.

MEDOFF, RAFAEL. *The Deafening Silence: American Jewish Leaders and the Holocaust.* New York: Shapolsky Publishers, 1987.

MILLER, ARTHUR. *Focus.* New York: Arbor House, 1945, 1984.

MOLEY, RAYMOND. *The First New Deal.* New York: Harcourt, Brace, 1936.

———. *After Seven Years.* New York: Harper, 1939.

MORSE, ARTHUR. *While Six Million Died.* New York: Hart Publishing, 1967.

MOSLEY, NICHOLAS. *Rules of the Game, Beyond the Pale: Memoirs of Sir Oswald Mosley and Family.* Elmwood Park, IL: Dalkey Archive Press, 1991.

MOSLEY, OSWALD. *My Life.* London: Nelson Press, 1968.

MUGGLEBEE, RUTH. *Father Coughlin, the Radio Priest of the Shrine of the Little Flower: An Account of the Life, Work, and Message of Reverend Charles E. Coughlin.* Garden City, N.Y.: Garden City Publishing Company, 1933.

MURPHY, PAUL I. *La Popessa.* New York: Warner Books, 1983.

MYERS, GUSTAVUS. *History of Bigotry in America.* New York: Henry Christman, 1960.

NEURINGER, SHELDON M. *American Jewry and United States Immigration Policy, 1881–1953.* New York: Arno Press, 1980.

NEWELL, LARRY. "Right-Wing Extremism during the Nineteen Thirties." Masters thesis, University of Texas, 1962.

NEWTON, CRAIG. "Father Coughlin and His National Union for Social Justice." *Southwestern Social Science Quarterly* 41 (December 1960): 341–350.

O'BRIEN, DAVID J. "American Catholic Social Thought in the 1930's." Ph.D. dissertation, University of Rochester, 1965.

———. *The Renewal of American Catholicism.* New York: Oxford University Press, 1972.

O'CONNER, RICHARD. *The German-Americans, An Informal History.* Boston: Little, Brown, 1977.

O'REILLY, KENNETH. *Hoover and the Un-Americans.* Philadelphia: Temple University Press, 1983.

PALEY, WILLIAM. *As It Happened: A Memoir.* Garden City, N.Y.: Doubleday, 1979.

PAPERNO, ELEANOR. "Father Coughlin: A Study in Domination." Masters thesis, Wayne State University, Detroit, 1939.

PATTERSON, JAMES T. *Congressional Conservatism and the New Deal: The Growth of the Conservative Coalition in Congress, 1933–1939.* Lexington: University of Kentucky Press, 1967.

PEARSON, DREW, AND JACK ANDERSON. *The Case against Congress.* New York: Simon and Schuster, 1968.

PECORA, FERDINAND. *Wall Street Under Oath,* New York: Simon and Schuster, 1939.

PENKOWER, MONTY NOAM. *The Jews Were Expendable.* Urbana: University of Illinois Press, 1983.

PERLMUTTER, NATHAN AND RUTH A. PERLMUTTER. *The Real Anti-Semitism in America.* New York: Arbor House, 1982.

PLATT, MYLES. "Father Coughlin and the National Union for Social Justice: A Bid for Political Power." Master's thesis, Wayne State University, 1951.

POLENBERG, RICHARD. *Reorganizing Roosevelt's Government: The Controversy over Executive Reorganization, 1936–1939.* Cambridge: Harvard University Press, 1966.

————. *One Nation Divisible: Class, Race, and Ethnicity in the United States since 1938.* New York: Penguin, 1980.

POUND, EZRA. *Jefferson and/or Mussolini.* New York: Liveright, 1935.

QUINLEY, HAROLD E., AND CHARLES Y. GLOCK. *Anti-Semitism in America.* New York: Free Press, 1979.

RACHLIS, EUGENE. *They Came to Kill.* New York: Random House, 1961.

REMAK, JOACHIM. *Germany and the United States.* Stanford: University of California Press, 1959.

RICKENBACKER, EDDIE. *Rickenbacker.* Englewood Cliffs, N.J.: Prentice–Hall, 1967.

RIESS, CURT. *Total Espionage.* New York: G. P. Putnam's Sons, 1941.

RIPPLEY, LA VERN J. *The German-Americans.* Boston: Twayne Publishers, 1976.

ROBINSON, JOHN R. "Behind the Microphone with Father Coughlin, Crusader of Contradictions," *Real America* (March 1934): 29–30.

ROGGE, OETGE JOHN. *The Official German Report.* New York: Thomas Yoseloff, 1961.

ROLLINS, RICHARD. *I Find Treason: The Story of an American Anti-Nazi Agent.* New York: 1941.

ROUSSEY DE SALES, RAOUL. *Adolph Hitler: My New Order.* New York: Reynal and Hitchcock, 1941.

SAYERS, MICHAEL, AND ALBERT E. KAHN. *The Plot against the Peace.* New York: Dial Press, 1945.

SCHLESINGER, ARTHUR M. *The Coming of the New Deal.* Boston: Houghton Mifflin, 1959.

————. *The Politics of Upheaval.* Boston: Houghton Mifflin, 1960.

SCHONBACH, MORRIS. "Native Fascism during the 1930's and 1940's: A Study of Its Roots, Its Growth, and Its Decline." Ph.D. dissertation, University of Southern California, 1958.

SELDES, GEORGE. "Facts and Fascism." *In Fact* (1943).

SHANNON, WILLIAM V. *The American Irish.* New York: Macmillan, 1963.

SHENTON, JAMES P. "The Coughlin Movement and the New Deal." *Political Science Quarterly* 73 (September 1958): 360–366.

SHIRER, WILLIAM L. *Berlin Diary.* New York: Bonanza Press, 1984.

SCHMID, HANS. *Maverick Marine.* Lexington, KY: University of Kentucky Press, 1987.

SIMS, ADAM. "A Battle in the Air: Detroit's Jews Answer Father Coughlin." *Michigan Jewish History* 18 (June 1978): 7–13.

SLOMOVITZ, PHILIP. *Purely Commentary.* Detroit: Wayne State University Press, 1981.

SMITH, GEOFFREY S. *To Save a Nation: American Countersubversives, the New Deal, and the Coming of World War II.* Paperback edition. Chicago: Ivan R. Dee, 1992.

SMITH, SALLY B. *In All His Glory: The Life of William. Paley* Simon and Schuster, 1990.

SODERBERGH, PETER A. "The Rise of Father Coughlin, 1891–1930," *Social Science* 42 (1967): 10–20.

SPITZ, DAVID. *Patterns of Anti-Democratic Thought.* New York: Macmillan, 1965.

SPIVAK, JOHN LOUIS. *The Shrine of the Silver Dollar.* New York: Modern Age Books, 1940.

————. *A Man in His Time.* New York: Horizon Press, 1967.

STEEL, RONALD. *Walter Lippmann and the American Century.* New York: Vintage Books, 1981.

STEGNER, WALLACE EARLE. "The Radio Priest and His Flock." *The Aspirin Age: 1919–1941.* Edited by Isabel Leighton. New York: Simon and Schuster, 1949.

STEIN, MICHAEL. *The Dynamics of Right-Wing Protest: A Political Analysis of Social Credit in Quebec.* Toronto: University of Toronto Press, 1973.

STEMBER, CHARLES HERBERT. *Jews in the Mind of America.* New York: Basic Books, 1966.

STEPHAN, JOHN J. *The Russian Fascists.* New York: Harper & Row, 1978.

STERNHELL, ZEEV. *Neither Right Nor Left: Fascist Ideology in France.* Translated by David Maisel. Berkeley: University of California Press, 1985.

STONE, I. F. *The War Years, 1939–1945.* Boston: Little, Brown, 1988.

STRAUSS, LEWIS L. *Men and Decisions.* New York: Doubleday, 1964.

SWANBERG, W. A. *Citizen Hearst.* New York: Charles Scribner's Sons, 1961.

SWARD, KEITH. *The Legend of Henry Ford.* New York: Rinehart & Company, 1948.

SWING, RAYMOND GRAM. *Forerunners of America Fascism.* New York: Julian Messner, 1935.

SYKES, JOHN. *Nancy: The Life of Lady Astor.* New York: Harper & Row, 1972.

TENTLER, LESLIE. *Seasons of Grace: A History of the Catholic Archdiocese of Detroit.* Detroit, MI: Wayne State University Press, 1990.

Time Incorporated. *Time Capsule/1933.* New York: Time Incorporated, 1967.

TORREY, E. FULLER. *The Roots of Treason: Ezra Pound and the Secrets of St. Elizabeths.* New York: McGraw-Hill, 1984.

TRAINA, RICHARD PAUL. *American Diplomacy and the Spanish Civil War.* Bloomington: Indiana University Press, 1968.

TREFOUSSE, HANS L. (ED.). *Germany and America: Essays in Problems of International Politics and Immigration.* New York: Brooklyn College Press, 1980.

TUGWELL, REXFORD B. *The Brains Trust.* New York: Viking Press, 1968.

TULL, CHARLES JOSEPH. *Father Coughlin and the New Deal.* Syracuse: Syracuse University Press, 1965.

TUMIN, MELVIN. *An Inventory and Appraisal of Research on American Anti-Semitism.* New York: Freedom House, 1961.

VALAIK, J. DAVID. "In the Days before Ecumenism: American Catholics, Anti-Semitism, and the Spanish Civil War." *Church and Society* 13 (1971): 467–477.

VETERANS OF FOREIGN WARS. *Fifth Column Facts.* Kansas City, MO.: National Headquarters, Veterans of Foreign Wars of the U.S., n.d. (1940).

WARD, LOUIS B. *Father Charles E. Coughlin: An Authorized Biography.* Detroit: Tower Publications, Inc., 1933.

WARREN, DONALD I. *The Radical Center: Middle Americans and the Politics of Alienation.* Notre Dame, Ind.: University of Notre Dame Press, 1976.

WASHBURN, PATRICK S. *A Question of Sedition.* New York: Oxford University Press, 1986.

WECHSLER, JAMES. "The Coughlin Terror." *Nation,* July 22, 1939, 92–97.

Whalen, Richard J. *The Founding Father: The Story of Joseph P. Kennedy.* New York: New World Library, 1964.

WILLIAMS, HARRY T. *Huey Long.* New York: Knopf, 1980, 1969.

WILSON, A. N. *Hilaire Belloc.* London: H. Hamilton, 1984.

WOODWARD, COMER VANN. "The Ghost of Populism Walks Again." *New York Times Magazine,* June 4, 1972.

WYMAN, DAVIS S. *Paper Walls: America and the Refugee Crisis, 1939–1941.* New York: Pantheon Books, 1968, 1985.

————. *The Abandonment of the Jews: America and the Holocaust, 1941–1945.* New York: Pantheon Books, 1984.

ZILG, RICHARD. *Du Pont: Behind the Nylon Curtain.* Englewood Cliffs, N.J.: Prentice-Hall, 1974.

Acknowledgments

I N ANY ENTERPRISE that at first appears to be a product of one individual, the reality in fact suggests a virtual network of persons who contribute in numerous significant ways. The author in this case wishes to express his deep appreciation to several of these persons whose help with archival sources was particularly significant. Here I wish to thank Dr. Eugene Fisher of the U.S. Catholic Conference, whose early encouragement and specific authorization to draw on his organizations' archives were of great value to me. Next I wish to thank the Archdiocese of Detroit and its archivist, Roman Godzak, without whose permission and help this book could not have been completed. A special debt of gratitude is owed to Phil Slomovitz, the later editor of the *Detroit Jewish News*, whose conversations and documentary help over a period of several years were invaluable. Let me thank as well Don Wilhelm for his efforts in expediting the release of Federal Bureau of Investigation documents.

Additionally, I wish to thank the staffs of the Franklin D. Roosevelt Library, the Herbert Hoover Presidential Library, the Lyndon B. Johnson Library, the Burton Historical Library, the Bentley Historical Library, the American Jewish Archives, the American Jewish Committee, the Anti-Defamation League, the Archives of the Sacred Congregation of the Clergy of the Vatican, the University of Michigan Labadie Collection, the National Archives, the State Archives of the Italian Government, the Weiner Library of London, the Harry S. Truman Library, the State Historical Society of Wisconsin, the University of California Archives of Performing Arts, and the Beinecke Rare Book and Manuscript Library of Yale University.

I also wish to personally thank the individuals who helped in critical ways with the research for this book. Included here is Mrs. Ruth Dennis in connection with the Herbert Hoover Library materials and Ms. Giulia Barrera for her assistance with the Italian State Archives. To Kristine Woloszynski I owe a special debt of gratitude for her research in the National Archives, Archdiocese of Detroit Archives, President Johnson and Roosevelt Libraries, Library of Congress and the American Jewish Committee archives. She also helped in the conducting of a number of personal interviews. In this regard, I wish to express my thanks to those several dozen individuals who extended to me the courtesy of offering personal interviews, including especially Father Peter Wiethe, Arnold Forster, Donald Flamm, Frank Stanton, William Power Maloney II, Philip Johnson, Sheldon Marcus, Charles Tull, Tyler Abell, the late James Roosevelt, Claude Pepper, Clare Boothe Luce, and G. Mennen Williams.

Special assistance was extended to me by the Roper Institute of the University of Connecticut and the Gallup Institute of Princeton with regard to public opinion data. Here I should give thanks to George Gallup, Jr., and especially to Alec Gallup for his valuable help and encouragement. I wish to thank also historians Leslie Tentler, Sidney Fine, Sidney Bolkowsky, and David Lewis for offering specific advice and support for a project somewhat outside of my academic domain and within their areas of expertise.

Finally, I wish to offer my special gratitude to various members of the publishing staff of The Free Press, especially my editors, Norah Vincent and Bruce Nichols. Particular thanks are owed as well to Beverly Miller, the copyeditor, Michael Mendelssohn, the interior designer, and Loretta Denner, the production editor.

Index